Casual Work Arrangements and Platform-Based Work

Bulletin of Comparative Labour Relations

VOLUME 115

Founding Editor

The series started in 1970 under the dynamic editorship of Professor Roger Blanpain (Belgium), former President of the International Industrial Relations Association. Professor Blanpain, Professor Emeritus of Labour Law, Universities of Leuven and Tilburg, was also General Editor of the International Encyclopedia of Laws (with more than 1,600 collaborators worldwide) and President of the Association of Educative and Scientific Authors Authors. He passed away in October 2016.

General Editor

In 2015 Frank Hendrickx, Professor of labour law at the Faculty of Law of the University of Leuven (Belgium) joined as a co-Editor. Frank Hendrickx has published numerous articles and books and regularly advises governments, international institutions and private organisations in the area of labour law as well as in sports law. He is the Editor-in-Chief of the European Labour Law Journal and General Editor of the International Encyclopaedia of Laws.

Introduction

The Bulletins constitute a unique source of information and thought-provoking discussion, laying the groundwork for studies of employment relations in the 21st century, involving among much else the effects of globalization, new technologies, migration, and the greying of the population.

Contents/Subjects

Amongst other subjects the Bulletins frequently include the proceedings of international or regional conferences; reports from comparative projects devoted to salient issues in industrial relations, human resources management, and/or labour law; and specific issues underlying the multicultural aspects of our industrial societies.

Objective

The Bulletins offer a platform of expression and discussion on labour relations to scholars and practitioners worldwide, often featuring special guest editors.

The titles published in this series are listed at the end of this volume.

Casual Work Arrangements and Platform-Based Work

The Casual Work Agenda as a Way to Enhance the Labour Protection of Platform Workers

Ilda Durri

General Editor
Frank Hendrickx

Founding Editor
Roger Blanpain

Wolters Kluwer

Published by:
Kluwer Law International B.V.
PO Box 316
2400 AH Alphen aan den Rijn
The Netherlands
E-mail: lrs-sales@wolterskluwer.com
Website: www.wolterskluwer.com/en/solutions/kluwerlawinternational

Sold and distributed by:
Wolters Kluwer Legal & Regulatory U.S.
920 Links Avenue
Landisville, PA 17538
United States of America
E-mail: customer.service@wolterskluwer.com

Printed on acid-free paper.

ISBN 978-94-035-3107-6

e-Book: ISBN 978-94-035-3117-5
web-PDF: ISBN 978-94-035-3127-4

Printed in the Netherlands.

Notes on Author

Ilda Durri was born in Albania on 13 May 1990. She is a postdoctoral researcher at the Institute for Labour Law, University of KU Leuven, Belgium, where she also obtained the degree of Doctor of Laws (PhD). Ilda holds a master in European and International Labour (LLM) from the University of Amsterdam, Netherlands, and a master in Civil Law (MSc) from the University of Tirana, Albania. She has held positions such as: project manager and legal assistant in a Brussels-based non-profit organization; blue book trainee at DG Employment of the European Commission; and assistant professor at the Faculty of Law in Tirana. Her main publications include a book on *Gig Economy* published by Edward Elgar, which she has co-edited and authored, two working papers for the International Labour Organization, and a book chapter in the Oxford handbook of the Law of Work.

Funder Acknowledgement

This is the manuscript that I have submitted for obtaining the degree of Doctor of Laws (PhD) at KU Leuven, which was defended on 2 March 2023. This work has been made possible thanks to the funding provided by the Research Foundation Flanders (FWO) under the Odysseus project (Ref. 179461/G0H8118N) on employment rights and labour protection in the on-demand economy, coordinated by Professor Frank Hendrickx and Professor Valerio De Stefano.

Table of Contents

Preface

In the last years, the advent of platform work, i.e., work activities channelled through web platforms or apps, has been at the centre of discussions for being 'an opportunity-generating machine', and especially for a more notorious aspect, that is the poor quality of working conditions associated with it. Work patterns inherent in platform work, such as unpredictable work schedules, an insecurity of work for the future (even for the next minute or hour), the lack of a stable income, and exclusion from even basic protections, have actually been detected since long time ago. They can be traced back to the daily work of dock workers in the late nineteenth century, but also to more contemporary forms of casual work, such as on-call work, or zero-hours work. Accordingly, history seems to repeat itself and to even go to extremes with platform work. Against this background, this book focuses on the intersection that exists between casual work and platform work and explains that, as a result of it, platform work can actually fall into broader regulatory strategies applicable to casual work, hereinafter the casual work agenda. The regulatory challenges deriving from the insecure nature of the work have already been dealt with by national and supranational regulators in the context of casual work. Therefore, this book engages in evaluating an already available blueprint – the casual work agenda – in light of reducing a set of insecurities, such as that of working hours, jobs (work), income, and employment status, associated with platform work. To this end, it first looks into the national legal landscape on casual work in four countries, namely the United Kingdom, Italy, the Netherlands, and Belgium. Afterwards, it expands to the EU level, where the Transparent and Predictable Working Conditions Directive, the Fixed-Term Work Directive, and the Working Time Directive, constitute insightful legal tools. At the same time, the EU proposed directive on Platform Work has been scrutinized, and recommendations to redefine this legal initiative, in light of the best regulatory practices offered by the casual work agenda, have been advanced to EU policymakers.

Acknowledgements

I would not have been able to complete this manuscript without the support of a wonderful group of people.

First of all, I would like to single out two outstanding individuals who have unconditionally supported me throughout the process, my promoters – Prof. Frank Hendrickx and Prof. Valerio De Stefano.

Prof. Hendrickx – the editor of this book and the 'father' of the Institute for Labour Law of KU Leuven – has been a huge support with his numerous advice. We worked together, tirelessly, to improve the manuscript, and he has been a great source of inspiration, always having a smile on his face.

My deepest gratitude extends also to my other promoter Prof De Stefano, who always believed in me and was always there for me, to respond quickly to every question I had. It is because of him (and his *cacio e pepe*) that myself, Mathias, and Harry can count many important professional outcomes, such as books, ILO working papers, but have also established life-long interpersonal relationships.

In particular, I am greatly thankful to my promoters for putting together an excellent jury, without the support and encouragement of whom, my journey to writing this book would not have been so smooth. From the start, they motivated me with their kindness and brilliant suggestions, which significantly enhanced the manuscript. For these reasons, I want to sincerely thank Prof. Nicola Countouris, Prof. Elise Muir, Prof. Paul Schoukens, and Prof. Jacque Herbots. It was a true honour to have been able to collaborate with such an estimated group of professors.

Going back to the time when I took the decision to become a labour lawyer (around eight years ago), there was a special person who motivated me to take the first steps in this right direction. This was my uncle and the Emeritus professor of labour law in Albania – Prof. Kudret Çela. Now that my book is published, I can say that I have never regretted this decision, and I truly hope to have made him somehow proud, as his labour lawyer successor within our family.

My colleagues at the Institute for Labour Law, in addition to being amazing colleagues, have provided important feedback and encouragement for this book. These people are Mathias, Silvia, Stan, Simon, Sara, Frea, Christina, Bettina, Margot,

Josephine, Miet, and Pieter. I would like to say 'thank you', in particular, to Harry, my amazing office companion, with whom I exchanged not only many professional thoughts but also lots of laughter.

And last but not least, I would not have been able to complete this milestone, if I did not have the back of my family - Alma (mother), Ilir (father), and Dalina (sister) - whose extreme dedication, and unconditional love, gave me the force I needed to move forward. Thanks to my small family, I was blessed with the presence and love of my big family. My grandparents, uncles, aunts, and cousins, have continuously fed me with love, which I truly believe is the most powerful engine for inspiration and progress.

Finally, special thanks go to my partner (soon-to-be husband) Nikola who has been quite exceptional in his support to my writing process, and my career goals more broadly. Most importantly, Nikola taught me that true love is not selfish, but on the contrary, it is generous and pushes you to become a better version of yourself.

This bunch of people gave me plenty of sunshine, even when there was not enough in the Belgian sky.

Introduction

This is the manuscript that I have submitted for obtaining the degree of Doctor of Laws (PhD) at KU Leuven, which was defended on 2 March 2023. This work has been made possible thanks to the funding provided by the Research Foundation Flanders (FWO) under the Odysseus project (Ref. 179461/G0H8118N) on employment rights and labour protection in the on-demand economy, coordinated by Professor Frank Hendrickx and Professor Valerio De Stefano.

1 THE SUBJECT

Work arrangements that are alternative to the standard of open-ended and full-time employment represent an important work reality.[1] Within the vast group of non-standard work, *casual work* arrangements, such as zero-hour contracts, on-call, or on-demand work, are growing in numbers and importance.[2] Casual work dates back as early as the late nineteenth century when it was common practice for employers to recourse to daily work, especially in the dock and construction sectors.[3] It is, however, challenging to define casual work, as such work arrangements do not represent a unitary phenomenon. Instead, they are perceived as comprising a broad spectrum of work arrangements, ranging from work of very short duration to long-lasting work arrangements that may be highly unstable.[4] Due to this diversity, the various categories

1. Standard employment remains the predominant form of work in the EU, where 58% of persons in employment work under the standard full-time permanent employment contract, as cited in P. Schoukens & A. Barrio, 'The Changing Concept of Work: When Does Typical Work Become Atypical?', *European Labour Law Journal*, Vol. 8 Issue 4, 2017, pp. 306-332, p. 308.
2. Eurofound, *New forms of employment*, Publications Office of the European Union, Luxembourg, 2015, pp. 1 and 142.
3. S. Fredman, 'Labour Law in Flux: The Changing Composition of the Workforce', *Industrial Law Journal*, Vol. 26 Issue 4, 1997, pp. 337-352, p. 340.
4. V. De Stefano, 'Casual Work Beyond Casual Work in the EU: The Underground Casualization of the European Workforce and What to Do About It', *European Labour Law Journal*, Vol. 7 Issue 3, 2016, pp. 421-441, p. 424; M. Freedland and J. Prassl, 'Employees, Workers and the "Sharing Economy", Changing Practices and Changing Concepts in the UK', *Spanish Labour Law and Employment Relations Journal*, Vol. 6 Issue 1-2, 2017, p. 20.

of casual work often overlap something which adds complexity to the attempts of important institutions to classify these forms of work.[5] Notwithstanding these uncertainties, some authoritative definitions of casual work have been produced. For instance, the International Labour Organization defines casual work as 'work that is executed for a very short period, or occasionally and intermittently, often for a specific number of hours, days or weeks'.[6] Furthermore, Eurofound considers it as 'a type of work where the employment is not stable and continuous, and the employer is not obliged to regularly provide the worker with work, but has the flexibility of calling them in on demand'.[7] For the purpose of this dissertation, a definition of casual work will be further explored and construed.

In the last years, work activities channelled through web platforms or apps have been spreading,[8] a phenomenon labelled as *platform work*.[9] This form of work is cutting-edge in the use of Information and Communications Technology (ICT) means to match the demand and supply sides of labour. Platform work is manifested in a variety of business models and is estimated to have considerable potential for growth in the near future.[10] Despite being so varied, a dichotomy of such work activities has been noted, chiefly including work intermediated and executed digitally (or crowdwork) and work intermediated online, but executed in the 'real' world (or work on demand via apps).[11]

Platform work represents a disputed topic in labour law's current discourse. The reason for this is mainly the legal status given to platform workers by business service agreements. These workers are normally engaged as independent contractors under a self-employed status, consequently excluded from the vast bulk of labour law protections. Nevertheless, this legal status has been questioned under labour law on whether it corresponds to the underlying reality of such work arrangements.[12] A vast part of platforms seems to exercise managerial prerogatives that are typically reserved for employers, without excluding the existence of scenarios where platforms merely

5. In the *ILO* classification, casual work is considered as fixed-term work, while on-call work is considered as part-time work. On the other side, *Eurofound* takes the view that casual work has elements of both part-time work and fixed-term work.
6. International Labour Office-Geneva, *Non-standard employment around the world: Understanding challenges, shaping prospects*, 2016, p. 22.
7. Eurofound, *New forms of employment*, p. 46.
8. M. Wouters, *International Labour Standards and Platform Work. An Analysis of Digital Labour Platforms Based on the Instruments on Private Employment Agencies, Home Work and Domestic Work*, Bulletin of Comparative Labour Relations, Vol. 110, 2021.
9. A wide range of terms are used when referring to platform work, such as 'gig-economy', 'sharing economy', 'on-demand economy', 'collaborative economy', etc. These terms are often used interchangeably in academic and policy discourses.
10. Eurofound, *Aspects of non-standard employment in Europe*, Publications Office of the European Union, Luxembourg, 2017, p. 142.
11. V. De Stefano, 'The Rise of the 'Just-in-time Workforce': On-demand Work, Crowdwork and Labour Protection in the Gig-economy', *International Labour Office, Inclusive Labour Markets, Labour Relations and Working Conditions Branch*. Geneva: ILO, (2016), *Conditions of work and employment series*, Issue 71, p. 1.
12. 'Primacy of Fact' Principle, Point 9 of the ILO Employment Relationship Recommendation, 2006 (No. 198).

function as marketplaces. As the situation stands, platform workers seem to experience a major *labour protection problem*.

This exercise of managerial prerogatives by platform operators, which is typical of employment contracts rather than a self-employment status, coupled with the fact that platform work is often not stable or continuous, makes platform work resemble more casual work arrangements rather than self-employed work.[13] Not only in the legal scholarship but also at the institutional level,[14] there is a growing insight that non-standard employment, including casual work and platform work, are strongly connected. Nevertheless, no in-depth research has been conducted on specifically positioning platform work into the context of casual work arrangements. Platform work presents many of the labour law issues related to casual work, both often linked to deteriorating working conditions.[15] In light of these considerations, this doctoral dissertation makes the assumption that platform work at least significantly overlaps with casual work arrangements. The logical consequence of this overlap is that broader regulating strategies aimed at bettering the regulation of casual work, often protection of casual workers, hereinafter the casual work agenda, may be applicable to enhance the regulation of employment relationships and working conditions of platform workers. This dissertation takes on this challenge and attempts to evaluate the extrapolation of the casual work agenda to the benefit of platform workers' labour protection.

2 CONTEXT AND BACKGROUND

2.1 The Overlap Between Casual Work and Platform Work

Casual workers face high levels of insecurity in all aspects of their working conditions.[16] Being called 'on-demand' by employers, or constantly facing working time insecurity,[17] leads to low levels of job and income security for such workers.[18] Workers do not have any guarantee that they will be provided work in the future, and on top of this, 'they are afraid to turn down an offer for a particular shift, fearing that they will not have any work in the future'.[19] The lack of job security poses problems for the income security of such workers, who are usually paid on a 'pay-as-you-go' basis, hence, only during

13. V. De Stefano, 'Labour Is Not a Technology: Reasserting the Declaration of Philadelphia in Times of Platform-work and Gig-economy', *IUSLabor* 2/2017, pp. 1-17, p. 8; M. Freedland & J. Prassl, 'Employees, Workers and the "Sharing Economy", Changing Practices and Changing Concepts in the United Kingdom', p. 19.
14. International Labour Office-Geneva, *Non-standard employment around the world: Understanding challenges, shaping prospects*, 2016, p. 39.
15. Commission Staff Working Document, Analytical Document, Accompanying the Consultation Document on a possible revision of the WSD in the framework of the EPSR, 2017, p. 21.
16. *Ibid.*, p. 226.
17. I. Campbell, 'On-call and Related Forms of Casual Work in New Zealand and Australia', Conditions of Work and Employment Series No. 102, International Labour Organization, (2018), p. 26.
18. Analytical document of the European Commission, p. 23; Survey conducted by FNV (Federatie Nederlandse Vakbeweging), 'Onzeker werk' [Insecure work], FNV Press, Amsterdam, 2011.
19. Analytical document of the European Commission, p. 29.

the moments they actually work. Such adverse consequences are particularly prominent in the case of the so-called zero-hours contracts, where no minimum working hours are guaranteed at all. With respect to the level of pay, casual work is characterized by low pay,[20] where especially zero-hours workers were noted to experience low pay and in-work poverty.[21] These working conditions are further exacerbated due to a marginalization of these workers, concretely a widespread perception that casual and platform workers work mainly to generate additional income, thus not considered as 'work that merits traditional labour protections'.[22]

Platform workers face the same insecurities, which are even more exacerbated attributed to the fact that they are normally classified as self-employed persons, which leads to their legal exclusion from basic form of labour protection, such as minimum wages, working time protection and the rights to associate in trade unions and collective bargaining. They also experience high insecurity of working hours, which is best illustrated by crowdworkers working in different geographical and time zones, who perform night work or work during unsociable hours.[23] In an ILO survey, the crowdworkers of two leading micro-task platforms reported low levels of pay and insufficient work.[24] Income insecurity is also extreme, considering that some platform workers are normally paid by task and only if the clients are satisfied with the results. Further contributing to the income insecurity are the so-called wage theft practices,[25] i.e., the cases when the client retains the work and refuses to pay the worker without giving any reasons for the refusal. The level of pay is highly problematic, as it is allowed to fall below the minimum living wage, which is especially extremely low for crowdworkers from developed countries, who compete on a global basis and end up being paid in the same way as crowdworkers coming from a developing country.

Such strong indicators, stemming from the institutional level, i.e., the authoritative reports of the International Labour Organization, the staff working documents of the European Commission, but also highlighted in the academic discourse, reveal similar labour market hardships experienced by both casual and platform workers. It is, indeed, the shared features of flexibility, insecurity, and marginalization, which form the basis of the underlying assumption of this research, namely that a significant overlap between platform work and casual work arrangements exists.

2.2 The Casual Work Agenda as a Way to Enhance the Labour Protection of Platform Workers

The main legal consequence of the above assumption is that the *casual work agenda* can be extrapolated in a platform work context, with the aim of shaping a more

20. *Ibid.*, p. 226.
21. *Ibid.*, p. 22.
22. J. Berg, 'Income Security in the On-demand Economy: Findings and Policy Lessons from a Survey of Crowdworkers', International Labour Office, (2016), p. 1. This ILO survey found that 40% of such workers generate their main source of income from crowdwork.
23. V. De Stefano, 'The Rise of the "Just-in-time Workforce ..."', p. 10.
24. J. Berg, 'Income Security in the On-demand Economy: Findings and Policy Lessons from a Survey of Crowdworkers', International Labour Office, (2016), p. 13.
25. *Ibid.*, p. 14.

conducive legal landscape for platform workers. To this end, the legal apparatus on casual work has been examined at both the national and European Union (EU) level. Looking into the national agendas has been done in the form of a comparative legal analysis conducted in four industrialized countries, which adopt a diversity of legal approaches to protect casual workers. As concerns the EU level, at the heart of the regulatory framework on casual work stands the Directive on Transparent and Predictable Working Conditions (TPWCD),[26] which constitutes a direct follow-up to the proclamation of the European Pillar of Social Rights (EPSR). Additionally, other pertinent EU labour law instruments are equally scrutinized, notwithstanding that they are not specifically designed for casual workers, e.g., the Part-Time Work Directive, the Fixed-Term Work Directive, and the Working Time Directive.

In contrast to this vast set of legal safeguards available for casual workers, platform workers enjoy more limited protection, which was developed only recently. It is worth noting that they experienced a severe labour protection gap just a few years ago. The turning point in this regard was the legal initiative of the European Commission, which proposed the adoption of a directive to improve working conditions in platform work.[27] As this directive will be adopted by the EU legislators, it will constitute a *platform work agenda* in the EU arena. By keeping in mind these recent legal developments on platform work, the EU casual work agenda will be evaluated with a view to improve the labour protection of platform workers, as stipulated by the EU draft directive. This idea has also been supported by some scholars, who recommend that prior to adopting new legal initiatives on platform work, it is essential to carry out an evaluation of existing protective schemes. For instance, Aloisi contends that 'every new initiative must entail a careful impact assessment of existing schemes and, possibly, their application or revision'.[28] Prassl also suggests that when new mechanisms need to be designed, they need 'to operate in line with, and complementary to, existing norms'.[29]

3 RESEARCH QUESTION(S)

The central question of this research is the following.

Can the Casual Work Agenda Contribute to Enhancing the Labour Protection of Platform Workers?

With a view to providing a comprehensive answer to this research question, it will be unfolded into four sub-questions, which correspond to the four main parts of this dissertation.

26. Directive (EU) 2019/1152 of the European Parliament and of the Council of 20 June 2019 on transparent and predictable working conditions in the European Union.
27. Proposal for a Directive of the European Parliament and of the Council on improving working conditions in platform work, Brussels, 9.12.2021 COM(2021) 762 final 2021/0414 (COD).
28. A. Aloisi, 'Platform Work in Europe: Lessons Learned, Legal Developments and Challenges Ahead', *European Labour Law Journal*, Vol. 13 Issue 1, 2022, pp. 4-29, p. 17.
29. J. Prassl, *Humans as a Service: The Promise and Perils of Work in the Gig Economy*, Oxford University Press, 2018, p. 116.

(1) What is Casual Work and What Are the Main Legal Features of Casual Work in Selected Industrialized Countries? (Part I)

While defined by major policy and research institutions, as indicated above, casual work as a phenomenon remains difficult to grasp. This dissertation, therefore, starts by attempting to shed some light on the 'chameleonic tendencies' of casual work arrangements. This includes an attempt to define casual work and to explore what is captured under the label of casual work. Subsequently, a comparative legal analysis of casual work in four selected countries, namely the United Kingdom, Italy, the Netherlands, and Belgium, will be conducted. This exercise is paramount for providing different perspectives on regulating casual work at the domestic level.

What is more, in this part, an exploration of the overlap between casual work and platform work will be carried out depending on the national context of the selected countries. On top of this, in line with the extraordinary situation which happened while this research was being written – during the COVID-19 pandemic – Part I provides some insights on the exacerbation of the legal situation of casual and platform workers during this crisis period.

(2) What Is So Peculiar About Platform Work? (Part II)

This part puts the spotlight on platform work, and attempts to discover what is truly novel in this work model. The relevance of this analysis is due, not only in relation to the question of how casual work and platform work are interrelated but also to how these phenomena interact or contrast with traditional employment or more standard forms of work. Peculiarities or overlapping characteristics are relevant for setting out and critically examining the casual work and platform work agenda, as well as building up an approach for regulating casual work. In light of this, issues arising from platform work's idiosyncratic traits will also be discussed shortly.

(3) What Are the Chief Legal Safeguards Available for Casual and Platform Workers in the EU? (Part III)

In addition to the national strategies regulating casual work, this doctoral research opens up to the big picture of regulating casual work at the EU level. In this respect, a set of EU directives come into play, such as the directives on Part-Time Work, Fixed-Term Work, Working time, TPWCD, together with the proposal for a Directive on Platform Work. These instruments are selected in relation to the concept of casual work adopted in this dissertation, and the problem issues for labour protection defined by policy actors as well as literature in the overlapping sphere of casual work and platform work. The EU labour law instruments will be screened with a view to finding proper building blocks for labour protection for both casual and platform workers.

(4) Can the Legal Safeguards on Casual Work Advance the Labour Protection of Platform Workers? (Part III)

The protective standards contained in the casual work agenda will be evaluated on whether they can contribute to bettering the labour protection of platform workers. More specifically, based on the elements of labour protection, which will be explained in section 4.2, an evaluation will be carried out as to whether the casual work agenda is responsive to the labour protection needs displayed in a platform work context. Due regard will also be given to the legal protections contained in the EU draft Directive on Platform Work.

4 METHODOLOGY

4.1 The Nature of This Research and the Sources Used

This research is, in the first place, a legal research. This implies that it mainly draws on legal sources, which include legislative acts, case law as well as legal literature. Normative acts, especially at the domestic level of countries such as the UK, Italy, the Netherlands, and Belgium, have been extensively referred to in the comparative part of this dissertation. In the following parts, a broad examination of the EU legal apparatus on non-standard work, with a special focus on a set of EU directives which target casual and platform work, has been carried out. In parallel to these legislative acts, a wide range of case law coming especially from the national courts of the just-mentioned countries, both lower and highest courts, and the Court of Justice of the EU (CJEU), have been analysed. A prominent reliance on the CJEU jurisprudence was noted with regard to the interpretation of specific provisions in the Working Time and Fixed-Term Work Directives (FTWD), while UK courts' rulings were especially relevant for the interpretation of the 'mutuality of obligations' concept.

Furthermore, with a view to gaining additional insight into the legal sources, other authoritative sources, which have a non-binding legal nature, have been incorporated. For instance, this research recourses to various documents at the EU level, such as reports from Eurofound, studies commissioned by the EU institutions, such as the European Commission, the European Parliament, or the European Economic and Social Committee (EESC), staff working documents, and expert reports on the transposition of directives. In expanding to the broader arena, it is worth mentioning reports of the OECD, working papers and reports of the International Labour Organization, with the prominent examples of the World Employment and Social Outlook (WESO) and the report on non-standard employment, the Employment Relationship Recommendation (2006), No. 198, etc. What is more, throughout this dissertation, academic reflections play an important role in bringing different perspectives on crucial issues, for example, on defining casual and platform work, tracking some historical roots of the phenomenona, etc.

This research also occasionally refers to some interdisciplinary studies, chiefly the outcomes of economic and sociological studies, such as the results of various surveys. In this regard, the survey commissioned by KU Leuven and prepared by IPSOS[30] has been especially useful in Part II, in the exploration of the legal dimension of the working conditions of platform workers, with a particular focus on dependency

30. In the framework of the Odysseus project on employment rights and labour protection in the on-demand economy, of which this PhD research proposal forms part.

and control exercised by the platforms. Other pertinent surveys on the working conditions of these workers include, for instance, the ILO Survey on income security in the on-demand economy,[31] the General Survey from the Committee of Experts on the Application of Conventions and Recommendations (CEACR),[32] and the survey of platform workers in Europe, a technical report of the Joint Research Center (JRC) of the European Commission.[33] Finally, reference is also made to some empirical evidence, with a view to shedding some light on the incidence of casual work arrangements and platform work. To this end, statistics from the Office for National Statistics (ONS) in the UK, the Belgian Statistical Office (Statbel), and Eurofound, represent some of the sources used.

4.2 The Normative Framework

This legal research has a normative dimension as an evaluation is being made of the regulation of both casual work and platform work, together with some proposal for redefining these legal instruments. In the first place, as explained above, it relies on various sources of law, such as legislation and case law. The legal normative acts will be used to assess how casual work is addressed by legal systems and how relevant the normative instruments are in relation to the specific characteristics of this phenomenon, as well as in relation to platform work. This, self-evidently, requires a responsive law approach,[34] meaning that attention will be given to the realities of casual work and platform work, as well as to vulnerabilities that are signalled in such work situations, as will be explained further below.

Another normative dimension comes from comparativism in this dissertation. The study of different country perspectives on casual work, though predominantly descriptive, not only helps to clarify the understanding of what constitutes casual work, and of what the specific problems are which arise or are addressed in this area. It also has the potential to provide regulatory strategies, perhaps pathways, for addressing issues connected with casual work and platform work. It will also give input on how an approach to casual work may serve the agenda for regulating platform work.

The main normative dimension in this dissertation, however, is related to labour protection. The challenge to which this dissertation attempts to contribute is the major *labour protection problem* experienced by a large number of platform workers. It will be examined to what extent regulatory strategies can contribute to the labour protection of casual workers and/or platform workers. The concept of labour protection in this

31. J. Berg, 'Income Security in the On-demand Economy: Findings and Policy Lessons from a Survey of Crowdworkers', Conditions of Work and Employment Series No. 74, International Labour Office, 2016.
32. ILC 109/iii(b) – Promoting employment and decent work in a changing landscape, 2020, Available at: https://www.ilo.org/ilc/ILCSessions/109/reports/reports-to-the-conference/WCMS_736873/lang--en/index.htm.
33. A. Pesole et al., 'Platform Workers in Europe', Publications Office of the European Union, Luxembourg, JRC112157, 2018. Accessible at: https://ec.europa.eu/jrc/en/publication/eur-scientific-and-technical-research-reports/platform-workers-europe-evidence-colleem-survey.
34. F. Hendrickx, 'Foundations and Functions of Contemporary Labour Law', *European Labour Law Journal* Vol. 3 Issue 2 (108), 2012, p. 127.

dissertation mainly refers to insecurity and precariousness. Reducing insecurity and precariousness will be considered to be contributing to the labour protection of platform workers. Both aspects are strongly related, certainly in the context of casual work and platform work. Before explaining these concepts, it should be noted that the contribution to the labour protection issue will be approached by having in mind that, keeping a balance between workers' needs for security, and employers (and workers)' needs for flexibility in the labour market, is paramount.[35] Against this background, this dissertation gives consideration to also employers' (and workers') needs for flexibility,[36] and intends to ensure casual and platform workers with at least some minimum labour protection, in order to answer to the insecurities faced by them. The ILO considers precariousness as associated with seven main areas of insecurity. These insecurities include employment insecurity, earnings insecurity, working hours insecurity, health and safety protections insecurity, social security protections insecurity, training insecurity, and representation and other fundamental principles and rights at work insecurity.[37] Based on a definition from Rodgers,[38] precariousness has been perceived in this report as work which is low-paid, insecure, with minimal worker control, and unprotected by law or collective agreements. In addition, this report stresses a crucial dimension of precarious work – the shifting of the risks from the employer to the worker – a process labelled as the 'demutualization of risks'.[39] The transfer of the insecurities to the worker puts the latter into a vulnerable situation. In a similar vein to this ILO report, the labour economist Guy Standing examines seven labour-related insecurities, which overlap with the ones identified by the ILO.[40] According to the author, such insecurities represent a reality for the working life of many people who live 'without an anchor of stability',[41] a category that he refers to as the 'precariat'.

Another – but similar – approach is derived from Nicola Countouris, who refers to five types of 'legal determinants', or indicators, which can make a work relation precarious.[42] First, Countouris introduces the concept of the immigration status precariousness, by indicating that it has often been overlooked that the 'legal capacity to enter into legal relations, including work relations' is determined by the immigration

35. F. Hendrickx, 'Regulating Flexicurity and Responsive Labour Law', in F. Hendrickx (ed.), *Flexicurity and the Lisbon Agenda, A Cross-Disciplinary Reflection*, Intersentia, Social Europe Series; No. 17, 2008, pp. 123-161, p. 123.
36. The EPSR, Principle 5 (b), p. 14; The TPWCD, Preamble para. 6 and Article 1.
37. International Labour Office-Geneva, *Non-standard employment around the world: Understanding challenges, shaping prospects*, pp. 18-20.
38. G. Rodgers, 'Precarious Jobs in Labour Market Regulation: The Growth of Atypical Employment in Western Europe', Brussels, *International Institute for Labour Studies*, Free University of Brussels, ILO, (1989).
39. ILO, *Non-standard employment ...*, p. 18; Eurofound, *Casual work: Characteristics and implications*, 2019, p. 24.
40. G. Standing, *The Precariat: The New Dangerous Class*, Bloomsbury Publishing, 2011, p. 10.
41. *Ibid.*, p. 1.
42. N. Countouris, 'The Legal Determinants of Precariousness in Personal Work Relations: A European Perspective', *Comparative Labor Law & Policy Journal*, Vol. 34 Issue 1, 2012, pp. 21-46, p. 27.

status.[43] Furthermore, the author points out to the employment status precariousness, which he considers as 'the most radical' determinant, and 'one of the most country specific' ones. This type of precariousness deprives workers of basic labour protections, due to their qualification as independent contractors, undeclared, etc.[44] The next determinants identified comprise the temporal and income precariousness, understood as insecurities which are respectively related to the temporal uncertainty of the work relation, and to 'the availability of steady and decent income'.[45] Lastly, the lack of control over the performance of the work, e.g., on the working hours, gives rise to another type of precariousness, concretely the organizational control one.[46] In this regard, Countouris remarks that the lack of control over working hours can also fall within the notion of temporal precariousness.[47] A final observation made with regard to the different types of precariousness is that they are all interlinked and without clear boundaries between them, for example, income precariousness can emerge from temporal or employment status precariousness.

With consideration to such insecurities, which form the axis of precarious work, casual work[48] and platform work[49] (as will be made more clear below) seem to check all the boxes for being inherently precarious.[50] These work arrangements can be affected by more than one legal determinant of precariousness, with some of the most prominent examples being insecurities related to their employment status, working hours, jobs, income, etc.[51] Finally, it must be noted that, while it is true that precarious work arrangements are proliferating in the labour market,[52] with the prominent examples of casual and platform work, such proliferation can be disrupted by means of regulatory responses at different levels. These regulatory responses to casual work (and platform work) will be first introduced as part of the comparative legal analysis of casual work in four selected countries, and subsequently as part of a broader agenda at the EU level.

While it should be noted that precariousness is not exclusively related to specific forms of work, such as casual work and platform work, it constitutes a much broader and complex notion. For instance, even the most secure form of employment, standard

43. *Ibid.*, p. 27.
44. *Ibid.*, p. 28.
45. *Ibid.*, pp. 30-34.
46. *Ibid.*, p. 34.
47. *Ibid.*, p. 32.
48. M. Freedland, 'New Trade Union Strategies for New Forms of Employment: A Brief Analytical and Normative Foreword', *European Labour Law Journal* 2019, Vol. 10 Issue 3, pp. 179-182, p. 181; Eurofound, *Casual work* ..., p. 7.
49. *Ibid.*, M. Freedland, p. 182; J. Prassl, 'Humans as a service ...', p. 93.
50. I. Campbell, 'On-call and Related Forms of Casual Work in New Zealand and Australia', Conditions of Work and Employment Series No. 102, International Labour Organization, (2018), p. 4.
51. I. Campell, 'Casualised Work Arrangements in Developed Societies: Historical Parallels and New Regulatory Challenges', Forthcoming, p. 2.
52. M. Freedland, 'The Contract of Employment and the Paradoxes of Precarity', *University of Oxford Legal Research Paper Series*, No. 37, 2016, p. 4.

employment, can be precarious under certain circumstances.[53] However, being in a non-standard form of employment does not automatically imply that the work is precarious.[54] Moreover, precariousness can affect certain sectors of the economy more than others; however, this does not exclude a broader outreach to other sectors of the labour market.[55] Guy Standing affirms that the precariat has often been depicted as composed of 'cleaners, care workers, refugees, or migrants'.[56] Deriving from these considerations, it can be concluded that precariousness can influence all forms of work, notwithstanding what their contractual form is, or the sector where they are spread. Indeed, as pointed out by the ILO in its report on non-standard employment, precariousness is mainly related to the quality, or attributes, of the work.[57]

Having regard to these considerations, this dissertation will use, as a reference framework, aspects such as the insecurity of employment status, working hours, jobs, and income. By acknowledging that also other insecurities might be present in both casual and platform work settings, e.g., health and safety,[58] or fundamental principles and right at work[59] insecurities, this dissertation is limited to examining and evaluating only four of them. First, the *employment status insecurity* of platform workers is related to the fact that these workers are often falsely engaged as independent contractors by platform companies. As the employment relationship still remains 'an essential gateway to labour protections',[60] such as the right to minimum wage, collective bargaining, paid leave, working time, and social security protections, platform workers become deprived of basic labour protections associated with the employee status. As Prassl stresses, bringing platform work within the scope of labour law constitutes an important first step for the labour protection of such workers.[61] That said, however, even if platform workers fell within the protective realm of labour law, problems would still persist. These issues vary from 'low income to unpredictable shifts, that result from a lack of guaranteed work'.[62] In this way, Prassl summarizes the other insecurities to which this dissertation touches upon, namely that of working hours, jobs, and income. The *insecurity of working hours* is particularly challenging due to the fact that platform

53. N. Countouris, 'The Legal Determinants of Precariousness in Personal Work Relations: A European Perspective', *Comparative Labor Law & Policy Journal*, Vol. 34 Issue 1, 2012, pp. 21-46, p. 25.
54. European Parliament, *Temporary contracts, precarious employment, employees' fundamental rights and EU Employment Law*, Study for the PETI Committee, 2017, p. 26.
55. N. Countouris, 'The Legal Determinants of Precariousness ...', p. 21.
56. G. Standing, *The Precariat: The New Dangerous Class*, Bloomsbury publishing, 2011, p. 3.
57. International Labour Office-Geneva, *Non-standard employment around the world: Understanding challenges, shaping prospects*, p. 18.
58. A. Cefaliello, C. Inversi, 'The Impact of the Gig-economy on Occupational Health & Safety: Just an Occupation Hazard?', in V. De Stefano, I. Durri, C. Stylogiannis, M. Wouters eds, *A Research Agenda for the Gig-economy and Society*, Edward Elgar Publishing, 2022.
59. A. Bogg, R. Buendia Esteban, 'The Law and Worker Voice in the Platform Economy', in V. De Stefano, I. Durri, C. Stylogiannis, M. Wouters eds, *A Research Agenda for the Gig-economy and Society*, Wouters, 2022.
60. V. De Stefano, I. Durri, C. Stylogiannis, M. Wouters, *Platform Work and the Employment Relationship*, ILO (2021), p. 41; N. Countouris, 'Defining and regulating work relations for the future of work', ILO (2019).
61. J. Prassl, *Humans as a service* ..., p. 107.
62. *Ibid.*

workers often experience a low number of working hours, combined with an irregular and unpredictable nature of these hours, over which they usually lack control. What is more, the presence of long working hours, which might have an unsocial nature, e.g., work during evenings, can also be observed in a platform work context. As the boundaries between the identified insecurities are not clear-cut, the insecurity of working hours can be inextricably linked to the uncertainty of the continuity of employment,[63] an insecurity often referred to as *jobs, or work, insecurity*. The latter is also closely related to *income insecurity*, or in other words, the lack of a stable income. In the case of platform workers, income insecurity can be further exacerbated due to low earnings, which in many instances, can fall below the minimum wage level. This selected set of insecurities will be elaborated in more detail, especially in the countries' comparative analysis part of this dissertation.

Considering the just-mentioned vulnerabilities, the Global Commission on the Future of Work has, indeed, called for an 'urgent action [...] to ensure dignity to people who work "on-call"' .[64] In particular, the Global Commission recommends the establishment of a Universal Labour Guarantee, which would allow all workers, notwithstanding their employment status, to enjoy fundamental rights, e.g., the 'adequate living wage'.[65] In the same vein, the EPSR calls for the prevention of precarious work arrangements. More concretely, in its Principle 5, it also aims to ensure to all workers, notwithstanding their 'employment status, modality and duration',[66] 'fair and equal treatment regarding working conditions, access to social protection and training',[67] by also encouraging conversion towards open-ended employment. A more explicit focus on the need to improve the working conditions of platform workers was then made clear in the mission letter sent by the President of the European Commission, Ursula von der Leyen, to the Commissioner for Jobs.[68] By having regard to the importance that the issue of improving working conditions in platform work has gained in the international arena, it is the intention of this doctoral dissertation to look for *regulatory solutions to counter the labour protection problem* faced by platform workers. More specifically, considering the significant overlap between casual and platform work, the legal instruments which form part of the EU casual work agenda will constitute the normative references of this dissertation. In other words, the casual work agenda will be scrutinized on whether it is useful to better the labour protection of platform workers. To this end, both national and supranational (EU) legal responses to the precarious nature inherent in platform work will be scrutinized. The TPWCD, as a direct follow-up to the proclamation of the EPSR, which puts at the spotlight the protection of especially workers who face a lack of predictability in the organization of their working hours, constitutes certainly the main instrument in this respect. Furthermore, other instruments, such as the Working Time

63. ILO, *Non-standard employment around the world* ..., p. 18.
64. Global Commission on the Future of Work, *Work for a brighter future*, ILO (2019), p. 41.
65. *Ibid.*, p. 12.
66. Preamble to the EPSR, para. 15.
67. Principle 5 (a) EPSR.
68. Mission letter to the Commissioner for Jobs, 2019, p. 5, Available at: https://ec.europa.eu/info/sites/info/files/mission-letter-nicolas-schmit_en.pdf.

Directive and the Fixed-Term Work Directive, will also be screened if they are responsive to the identified labour protection needs. Finally, the analysis will be concluded by evaluating the protections offered by the proposal for an EU Directive on improving working conditions in platform work.

The normative framework set out above is not merely theoretical. It is also supported by empirical data. This can be derived from a survey commissioned by KU Leuven in the framework of the Odysseus project, of which this doctoral dissertation forms part, and is executed by Ipsos. This survey focuses on the legal dimensions of the working conditions of platform workers, and particularly on the autonomy of these workers and the control over their working time.[69] It includes seventy-two semi-structured interviews with platform workers, both crowdworkers and workers on demand via apps, in three European countries, namely France, Belgium, and Italy. These interviews are structured around some key themes, such as platform work in general, the scheduling of working hours, organization and monitoring of work, payment and financial dependency, and relations with other workers. The answers of the interviewed platform workers on these topics show that there is indeed a need to address the labour protection problem, due to the insecurities experienced by them. For instance, platform workers in Belgium reported the problem of fluctuations in their workload and earnings.[70] The income insecurity became more prominent considering that they were paid per task, had no say in the level of their income, and experienced a low level of income, especially crowdworkers, due to harsh competition in the online environments. Such income insecurity was pointed out also by platform workers in Italy, who added that the income level generated from platform work was insufficient for living.[71] Furthermore, insecurity of working hours was reported especially by those platform workers working in the creative sector, who faced 'longer and more irregular working hours' compared to a standard job.[72] Finally, platform workers working mainly in the delivery and transport sector in Belgium indicated that their choice of working hours was hampered by the pressure to work a high number of hours, as the assignment of future jobs was dependent on the hours worked by them and the timely responses to offers of work.

4.3 Methodological Steps[73]

Part I (Casual work) starts as descriptive, and then, for the major part, it maintains a comparative approach. It is descriptive in the sense that it attempts to unfold the meaning of the concept of casual work, based mainly on academic contributions and authoritative definitions coming from important institutions, such as the ILO and the EU. Clarifying this matter serves as a stepping stone to the further goal of this research:

69. Survey commissioned by KU Leuven and prepared by Ipsos, *High level summary of key findings*, 2020.
70. *Ibid.*, p. 12.
71. *Ibid.*, p. 16.
72. *Ibid.*, p. 15.
73. Based on L. Kestemont, 'Handbook on Legal Methodology. From objective to Method', Intersentia 2018.

comparing casual work arrangements in different European countries, approaching casual work conceptually in order to critically understand or contribute to a relevant regulation strategy (in light of labour protection), and setting it off against the phenomenon of platform work. As mentioned, the countries subject to this comparative legal analysis were selected based on the spread of casual work arrangements, and the presence of legal strategies conducive to the labour protection of these workers. These countries are representative of both civil law and common law legal families. The elements that will be examined in this comparative analysis include the general and legal situation of casual work per country, with an emphasis on the employment status and working conditions of these workers; country-specific developments on platform work; and the exploration of the overlap between casual and platform work at the national contexts.

Part II (Platform work) also has, at the outset, a descriptive research objective, in order to clarify the other key concept of this research, namely platform work. Furthermore, it also incorporates a historical account of the origins of casual work, something which points out to a similar work reality with platform work. After having set the background, this part becomes more analytical in nature, as it examines issues, such as what is truly novel in platform work, the extent of control exerted by platforms, the labour protection problem, and several issues arising from the deployment of algorithmic management.

Part III (The applicability of the EU casual work agenda to platform work) incorporates at the same time analytical, evaluative, and recommendatory research objectives. By having as building blocks the two previous parts, it expands to a broader regulatory level, concretely to the EU regulatory apparatus. It starts by presenting the pathway to a European regulatory approach to casual work and delineating the approach maintained by EU legislators towards casual work arrangements. Afterwards, it assesses the most pertinent legal instruments of this agenda for the labour protection of casual workers, and consequently of platform workers, especially in light of countering the insecurities underpinning them, e.g., that of employment status, working hours, jobs and income. In this regard, the importance of the Working Time, Fixed-Term Work, TPWCD, and Platform Work directives for the labour protection needs of casual and platform workers, is outlined. During such analysis, a critical view can be observed of the scope or content of these instruments, based on parameters such as the 'worker' definitions adopted, or the lack of protections against the insecurity of employment status, working time, jobs or income. The principal aim, though, is to evaluate whether this set of protections offered by the casual work agenda, can be helpful in advancing the labour protection of platform workers. Finally, recommendations for redefining the platform work agenda, with a special focus on the Platform Work Directive, will be formulated.

4.4 Limitations of This Research

To start with, the comparative legal analysis of casual work conducted in Part I concentrates on developed countries only. The rationale for choosing exclusively this focus has to do with a research gap noted in the literature in this regard.[74] While research studies and legislative developments on casual work are prominent in developing countries, surprisingly, the same was not noticed in developed ones. The latter is characterized by what De Stefano labels as an 'underground casualization', i.e., a lack of awareness of casual work, combined with scarce legal responses to this phenomenon.[75] Furthermore, the industrialized countries subject to this research were chosen as representatives of a diversity of legal approaches to casual work, ranging from almost inexistent to almost complete regulatory answers. The amount chosen was limited to four, as it was considered suitable to conduct a detailed, rather than superficial research.[76]

As has already been indicated, this doctoral research centres around the overlap between casual and platform work, by attempting to govern the 'zero hours dimension' of platform work. At the same time, it recognizes that the deployment of technology in a platform work context can be associated with some peculiar traits and issues, such as the international dimension of platform work. In this regard, this research briefly points out these idiosyncratic matters, nonetheless, it does not engage in addressing them. This broad subject would warrant separate research to deal with it.

On the choice of the legal instruments subject to this dissertation, the selection was made based on those instruments which contain legal protections to counter the insecure nature of the work. To this end, the directives on TPWCD, Working Time, and Fixed-Term Work have been singled out. The Part-Time Work Directive, for instance, was excluded from this set of instruments, as it does not accord protections in the face of the insecurities inherent to casual work. A pertinent instrument, which was not analysed due to time constraints, is the soon-to-be-adopted directive on Adequate Minimum Wages.[77] 'Connecting the dots' between this instrument and the Draft Platform Work Directive (dPWD) might be essential in light of ensuring enhanced protections for platform workers. Overall, the identified limitations of this doctoral project can be useful to open avenues for future research in this domain.

Finally, this set of legal instruments will be evaluated on whether it is beneficial to reduce a number of labour-related insecurities, by contributing in this way to the labour protection of platform workers. The insecurities chosen for this purpose are limited to four, namely that of employment status, working hours, jobs, and income. Countering the first type of insecurity is essential to bring platform work within the scope of labour law. Moreover, also addressing the insecurity of working hours, jobs, and income, becomes paramount, as these vulnerabilities underpin the very nature of casual (and platform) work, characterized by irregular hours and the lack of a promise of work for the future. This implies that this dissertation does not engage with the

74. V. De Stefano, 'Casual Work Beyond Casual Work in the EU: The Underground Casualization of the European Workforce – and What to Do About it', *European Labour Law Journal*, Vol. 7 Issue 3, 2016, pp. 421-441
75. *Ibid.*
76. D. Pieters, 'Comparative research methods', Lecture held at Young Researchers School Research Design and Methodology in Comparative Social Security, Spetses, Greece, 2021.
77. Proposal for a Directive of the European Parliament and of the Council on adequate minimum wages in the European Union, 2020/0310 (COD).

examination of other insecurities, with some prominent examples being health and safety, or fundamental rights at work insecurities.

5 SOCIETAL AND ACADEMIC RELEVANCE

Platform work represents a phenomenon whose rise has been described as meteoric.[78] Due to a lack of official data, some private studies have revealed the dimension of this phenomenon. For instance, the WESO report of the ILO, which refers to various surveys conducted in North America and Europe, indicates that 0.3% to 22% of the adult population has performed platform work for the period 2015-2019.[79] Furthermore, notable studies conducted in the EU show that platform work constitutes 1% to 3% of total employment.[80] Notwithstanding the relatively small size, many research studies highlight the considerable potential for growth that platform work,[81] but also casual work arrangements such as zero-hours contracts, on-call or on-demand work, have in the near future.[82] All these developments have led the International Labour Organization to consider the emergence of online digital labour platforms, as one of the major transformations in the world of work over the past decade.[83]

Casual work and platform work arrangements are associated with both opportunities and challenges.[84] As highlighted in section 4.2, the intention of this doctoral dissertation is to contribute to the labour protection challenge posed by platform work. To this end, this research aims to assist policymakers and social partners in finding viable legal solutions to tackle this regulatory problem. The proposed legal solution, which will be scrutinized in the framework of this dissertation, consists of contextualizing platform work within broader labour market trends such as the spread of casual work in developed societies. The purpose of doing this is to benefit from more general regulatory strategies, which already apply to casual work, and have the potential to counter the insecurities inherent in casual and platform work.

From an academic perspective, this type of analysis of platform work contributes to a solid understanding of the labour market, contrary to its fragmentation and the

78. J. Prassl, *Humans as a Service: The Promise and Perils of Work in the Gig Economy*, Oxford University Press, 2018.
79. ILO, *World Employment and Social Outlook 2021: The Role of Digital Labour Platforms in Transforming the World of Work*, (2021), p. 19.
80. Z. Kilhoffer, W. De Groen, K. Lenaerts, I. Smits, H. Hauben, W. Waeyaert, E. Giacumacatos, J-P. Lhernould, and S. Robin-Olivier, *Study to Gather Evidence on the Working Conditions of Platform Workers*, Publications Office of the European Union, 2020, p. 45.
81. Eurofound, *Aspects of non-standard employment in Europe*, Publications Office of the European Union, Luxembourg, 2017, p. 142; Global Commission on the Future of Work, *Work for a brighter future*, ILO, (2019), p. 44; Eurofound, *Back to the future*, Introduction part.
82. Eurofound, *New forms of employment*, Publications Office of the European Union, Luxembourg, 2015, pp. 1 and 142.
83. J. Berg et al., *Digital Labour Platforms and the Future of Work, Towards Decent Work in the Online World*, ILO Report, (2018): https://www.ilo.org/global/publications/books/WCMS_645337/lang--en/index.htm.
84. European Parliament News, Better working conditions for all: Balancing flexibility and security, 2018, Accessible at: http://www.europarl.europa.eu/news/en/headlines/society/20181018STO16583/better-working-conditions-for-all-balancing-flexibility-and-security.

creation of complicated new categories of work. Indeed, more and more scholars, but also international institutions, are rejecting the idea of pigeonholing platform work as a separate dimension of labour markets. Instead, they are pointing out the similarities between platform work and non-standard employment, especially the shared traits displayed with casual work. In this context, Dukes frames platform work within the broader framework of 'on demand work', and recommends the application of 'an existing legal framework and lines of legal reasoning' to platform work.[85] Notwithstanding this broad acknowledgement of the linkage between casual and platform work, no in-depth legal analysis of enhancing the labour protection of platform workers by looking at the casual work agenda has been conducted so far. It is this type of analysis which grants the ground-breaking character to this doctoral research. Through this study, the aim is not only to enrich the current literature with a different perspective but also to forward some recommendations to EU policymakers for enhancing the level of protection of platform workers. Last but not least, it is worth mentioning that another important analysis, which also adds some more originality to this doctoral research, is the comparative legal analysis of the casualization of work in industrialized countries. Such a comparative analysis has been overlooked by the existing literature,[86] and hence, this dissertation also engages in filling in this research gap.

85. R. Dukes, 'On Demand Work as a Legal Framework to Understand the Gig Economy', in *A Research Agenda for the Gig Economy and Society*, eds V. De Stefano, I. Durri, C. Stylogiannis, M., Wouters, pp. 133-149, p. 133.
86. M. Freedland, J. Prassl, 'Employees, Workers and the "Sharing economy", Changing Practices and Changing Concepts in the United Kingdom'; V. De Stefano, 'The Rise of the "Just-in-time Workforce": On-demand Work, Crowdwork and Labour Protection in the Gig-economy'.

Part I A Comparative Legal Analysis of Casual Work in Four Industrialized Countries

CHAPTER 1
Defining Casual Work

1.1 WHAT IS CAPTURED UNDER THE LABEL OF CASUAL WORK ARRANGEMENTS?

Casual work stands in stark contrast with the standard employment relationship,[87] which constitutes a 'stable, open-ended and direct arrangement between a dependent, full-time employee and their unitary employer'.[88] Nevertheless, there is no widely accepted definition of what is considered casual work.[89] This definitional challenge has been acknowledged by important institutions and the labour law scholarship, which perceive casual work arrangements as comprising a broad spectrum of work arrangements.[90] Moreover, it is very common for national legislations to refer to casual work without explicitly defining it.[91] The lack of a common understanding of casual work creates problems for regulators and policymakers and also contributes to abuses related to this form of work. Against this background, the aim of this introductory part

87. M. O'Sullivan et al., *Zero Hours and On-call Work in Anglo-saxon Countries*, Springer, 2019, p. 6, 2019.
88. P. Schoukens and A. Barrio, 'The Changing Concept of Work: When Does Typical Work Become Atypical?', p. 308, citing Stone, K.V.W. and Arthurs, H. (2013), 'The Transformation of Employment Regimes: A Worldwide Challenge', in Stone, K.V.W. and Arthurs, H. (eds), *Rethinking Workplace Regulation: Beyond the Standard Contract of Employment*, New York: Russell Sage Foundation, pp. 1-20.
89. International Labour Office – Geneva, *Non-standard employment around the world, Understanding challenges, shaping prospects*, 2016, p. 23.
90. For instance in the latest Eurofound report on casual work, 'Casual Work: Characteristics and Implications', New Forms of Employments Series, Publications Office of the European Union, Luxembourg, 2019, p. 3 and 4; ILO, *Non-Standard Employment* Around the World: Understanding Challenges, Shaping Prospects, 2016., p. 23; V. De Stefano, 'Casual Work Beyond Casual Work in the EU: The Underground Casualization of the European Workforce-and What to Do About it' *European Labour Law Journal*, Vol. 7 Issue 3, 2016, p. 424; M. Freedland and J. Prassl, 'Employees, Workers and the "Sharing Economy", Changing Practices and Changing Concepts in the UK', p. 20.
91. International Labour Office-Geneva, *Non-standard employment around the world, Understanding challenges, shaping prospects*, p. 23.

is to shed some light on this issue and highlight some main features of casual work arrangements.

Before delving into this issue, the Cambridge dictionary provides some clarification on the meaning of the word 'casual', which is used, *inter alia*, in the labour law context.[92] In this framework, 'casual' has been identified to mean something which is not regular or fixed, and when used as a noun, it refers to 'workers who are not employed permanently but only when a company needs them'. Additionally, when searching for the word 'casual', a word associated with it is 'casualization', which instead refers to 'the process of work or jobs, becoming less likely to be regular or permanent'.

By having regard to this non-legal clarification, this part's focus will be on how supranational institutions, international ones, and the labour law scholarship deal with defining the issue of casual work arrangements. To this end, also some studies which position casual work arrangements into broader categories of employment will be considered; and multiple overlapping terms, which create further confusion on this matter, will be pointed out. For the purpose of this doctoral dissertation, a working definition will be formulated, based on the definitions provided in the authoritative reports of institutions, such as Eurofound and the International Labour Office, but also in the legal scholarship. Finally, work mediated by technology will be briefly presented in the context of casual work arrangements.

1.1.1 Definitional Attempts at the European Level

Up to now, there is no single European legal definition of casual work.[93] A working definition has been adopted by the *European Parliament*, by referring to 'work which is irregular or intermittent, with no expectation of continuous employment'.[94] In the same vein goes as well the definition of the European Foundation for the Improvement of Living and Working Conditions (*Eurofound*). In a study on new forms of employment, Eurofound considers casual work as a form of work 'where the employment is not stable and continuous, and the employer is not obliged to provide the worker with work, but has the flexibility in calling them in on demand'.[95] According to this study, casual work shares elements with both part-time work and fixed-term work. A prominent aspect of this research is the creation of a dichotomy of casual forms of work, which uses as differentiating criteria, the duration and the intermittence or ad hoc nature of casual work arrangements. 'Intermittent work', or work with a short duration, constitutes the first type of casual work, which is usually used for the completion of a task, a project, or a seasonal job. The second form is labelled as 'on-call work' – a form of work with a longer duration, but more instability of working hours,

92. https://dictionary.cambridge.org/dictionary/english/casual.
93. Commission Staff Working Document, Analytical Document, Accompanying the Consultation Document on a possible revision of the Written Statement Directive in the framework of the EPSR, p. 53.
94. Eurofound, *New forms of employment*, Publications Office of the European Union, 2015, p. 46.
95. *Ibid.*

depending on the business needs. Furthermore, sub-categories of on-call work have been identified the 'min-max' contracts, which provide for an amount of guaranteed working hours, and the 'zero-hours contracts', with no guarantee at all. Consequently, the zero-hours contract appears to be the most insecure or precarious form of casual work. Because of this, some countries have explicitly forbidden this form of work.

This definition provided by Eurofound in its 2015 report has been relied upon by the European Commission when adopting a recent directive on *TPWCD*,[96] which includes in its personal scope, *inter alia*, casual workers.[97] This explicit reference can be found in the preparatory stage to draft this legal instrument, concretely in the analytical document of the European Commission, which accompanied the consultation document on a possible revision of the Written Statement Directive.[98] However, the directive in itself neither defines nor explicitly mentions casual work. Instead, a reference to work with unpredictable schedules has been observed,[99] with a particular acknowledgement of the vulnerable situation of zero-hours workers.[100]

1.1.2 Definitional Attempts at the International Level

The *International Labour Office* has conducted in-depth research on non-standard forms of employment (NSE), which resulted in a report published in 2016.[101] According to this report, casual work is understood as 'work that is executed for a very short period, or occasionally and intermittently, often for a specific number of hours, days or weeks'.[102] Four main categories of NSE have been identified in this report, and casual work has been positioned within the category of temporary work. In addition to, a frequent overlap between casual work and on-call work,[103] which falls into the part-time work's category, has been pointed out.[104] As a result, both the ILO and Eurofound point out the blurred boundaries between casual work on one side, and part-time and fixed-term work on the other. What the International Labour Office does differently, though, is that it positions casual work more towards the borders of temporary work, by considering it as very short fixed-term work.

In February 2020, the ILO Committee on the Application of the Conventions and Recommendations (*CEACR)* published a general survey on employment and decent

96. Directive (EU) 2019/ 1152 of the European Parliament and of the Council of 20 June 2019 on transparent and predictable working conditions in the European Union.
97. B. Bednarowicz, 'Delivering on the European Pillar of Social Rights: The New Directive on Transparent and Predictable Working Conditions in the European Union', *Industrial Law Journal*, Vol 48 Issue 4, 2019, pp. 604-623, p. 608.
98. Analytical document, p. 7.
99. Some informative rights and minimum predictability is provided for these workers, respectively in Articles 4 and 5 of the directive.
100. Recital 12 of the directive.
101. International Labour Office-Geneva, *Non-standard employment around the world, Understanding challenges, shaping prospects*, 2016.
102. *Ibid.*, p. 22.
103. Work which is characterized by variable and unpredictable work schedules, according to ILO, NSE, p. 21 and 28.
104. The reasoning for the inclusion of on-call work in the part-time work category is associated with the fact that a significant number of on-call workers are employed on a part-time basis.

work in a changing landscape.[105] In this survey, which refers extensively to the ILO report on non-standard employment, the most common features of casual work have been highlighted, concretely its 'temporary, intermittent or seasonal [nature]; [the detachment] from the ordinary or permanent business activity of the employer; [payment] on a daily or hourly basis, or a combination of all these characteristics'.[106]

The topicality of new forms of work has also prompted research by the Organisation for Economic Co-operation and Development (*OECD*).[107] A 2019 report on new forms of work analyses casual work arrangements, however, without explicitly defining them. This report differentiates between on-call contracts,[108] which have been considered part-time contracts and may contain a clause on the variability of working hours,[109] and other casual work arrangements, such as daily labour, seasonal work, including also voucher-based work. Notwithstanding this difference, an overlap of casual work with on-call work has been acknowledged in several parts of the report,[110] an approach which is also observed in the OECD Employment Outlook 2019.[111]

On the other side, some international labour standards, such as the *Termination of Employment Convention*, 1982 (No. 158) *and Recommendation*, 1982 (No. 166), define casual work only for the purposes of allowing a total or partial exclusion from it. The convention merely considers casual workers, those workers 'engaged on a casual basis for a short period'.

1.1.3 Definitional Attempts at the Academic Level

Many labour law scholars have analysed the casualization of work arrangements, especially in countries where such work arrangements are widespread. Some try to define casual work, while others explain some of the most prominent features of this form of work. In light of this, *Iain Campbell*, in a study about casual work in developed countries, refers to the notion of casualized work arrangements. This label comprises a variety of forms of casual work, and is defined as 'work arrangements that can be terminated at very short notice and/ or do not guarantee specific working-time schedules'.[112]

Scholars' definitional attempts concentrate on specific forms of casual work, such as zero-hours work. In this framework, *Simon Deakin* and *Gillian Morris* stress a total refusal to commit on the part of the employer to offering 'any quantum of work'.[113] In the same vein, *Mark Freedland* and *Nicola Countouris* point out 'work arrangements in

105. ILC109/III(B) – Promoting employment and decent work in a changing landscape.
106. ILC, p. 126.
107. OECD, *Policy responses to new forms of work*, OECD Publishing, Paris, 2019.
108. On-call work includes min-max contracts with a minimum amount of guaranteed working hours, as well as zero-hours contracts, with no guarantee at all.
109. OECD, *Policy responses to new forms of work*, p. 16.
110. *Ibid.*, p. 89.
111. OECD, *Employment Outlook 2019: The future of work*, s. 2.3.11: Short part-time and on-call labour have risen in many countries.
112. I. Campbell, 'Casualised Work Arrangements in Developed Societies: Historical Parallels and New Regulatory Challenges', Forthcoming.
113. S. Deakin and G. Morris, *Labour Law*, 6th ed., Hart Publishing, 2012, p. 167.

which the worker is in a personal work relation with an employing entity [...] for which there are no fixed or guaranteed hours of remunerated work'.[114] Considering that most of the definitions emphasize the employer's total disengagement towards the worker, some scholars complement by providing the worker's perspective also. In this respect, *Collins, Ewing, and McColgan* confirm that there is a lack of a contractual obligation by the worker to accept offers of work.[115] These definitional attempts advanced by the British scholars will be elaborated in more detail in the dedicated chapter on zero-hours work in the United Kingdom.

A legal comparative study on casual work in developed and emerging countries has been conducted *by Valerio De Stefano.*[116] He employs two main criteria to determine the work arrangements which fall within the scope of this analysis. The first criterion is widely used by a high number of national jurisdictions,[117] and it consists of the short duration of employment. The second has to do with the intermittence of work,[118] which, instead, focuses on the 'quantity and distribution of work'.[119] Such a description of casual work arrangements seems to be compatible with the one provided by the Eurofound report.[120] What is more, in another comparative study of casual work, which was focused on *Anglo-Saxon countries*, the label adopted to refer to 'casual work' is 'on-call work'.[121] In addition to underlining the 'chameleonic tendencies' of casual work, this study points out a description of zero-hours and on-call work, as 'a form of employment where the employer either guarantees no hours or few hours of work, and all or much of the working hours are offered at an employer's discretion'.[122]

1.1.4 A Broader Context and Multiple Overlapping Terms

Prior to exploring the multiple overlapping terms surrounding casual work arrangements, it is worth noting that some studies position casual work within some broad categories of employment and, hence, into a broader discussion. For instance, Eurofound has considered casual work as *'very atypical' non-standard work*, contrary to part-time, fixed-term, and temporary agency work, which represent the typical and regulated spectrum of NSE.[123] The 'very atypical' category mentioned in this study is comprised of part-time work of fewer than 10 hours a week, very short fixed-term

114. M. Freedland and N. Countouris, 'The Legal Construction of Personal Work Relations', *OUP*, 2012, pp. 318-319.
115. H. Collins, K. Ewing and A. McColgan, Labour Law, Cambridge University Press, 2012, p. 243.
116. V. De Stefano, 'Casual Work Beyond Casual Work in the EU: The Underground Casualization of the European Workforce – and What to Do About it', *ELLJ* 2016, Vol. 7 Issue 3, 2016.
117. The maximum duration of employment is noticed to be six months in a significant number of national jurisdiction.
118. *Ibid.*, p. 424.
119. J. Messenger, P. Wallot, 'The Diversity of Marginal Part-time', *INWORK Policy Brief* No. 7, ILO (2015).
120. Eurofound, *New forms of employment*, 2015.
121. M. O'Sullivan et al., 'Zero-hours and On-call Work in Anglo-Saxon Countries,' Springer, 2019, p. 6.
122. *Ibid.*, p. 7.
123. Eurofound, *Flexible forms of work: 'very atypical' contractual arrangements*, Report 2010.

contracts, zero hours work, and non-written contracts. Furthermore, much research dedicated to *precarious work* includes, among others, casual work arrangements, and emphasizes that the risk of precariousness is relatively high for casual workers, especially with regard to working hours and pay.[124] On a similar note, in a book dedicated to the temporary workforce in the United States, or the so-called temps, casual workers were perceived as part of the *contingent workforce* described therein.[125]

Various studies employ multiple overlapping terms to refer to casual work arrangements. In this context, the most common overlapping term with casual work is noticed to be '*on-call work*'.[126] While on-call work arrangements are sometimes treated as a distinct employment category, which have as a main feature insecure working hours and falls under part-time employment;[127] in many cases, an overlap between casual and on-call work has been acknowledged. This is illustrated, for instance, by some studies about casual work in Anglo-Saxon countries, where there is no explicit reference to casual work, but instead, the label used to refer to it is on-call work.[128] A further overlap is observed with the concept of '*work on demand*', which as the terminology suggests, is work requested by the employer pursuant to the business needs.[129] This concept is, however, arguably broader than that of 'on-call work', as it includes not only work with insecure working hours but also work of limited duration, which is beyond casual work, such as temporary work.[130] Another approach adopted by certain studies or legal documents is to exclusively focus on certain forms of casual work, as representatives of the whole big category of casual work. For instance, some studies centre on '*no-minimum hours*',[131] or '*zero-hours*'[132] *work arrangements*. Furthermore, '*intermittent work*' or '*very short-fixed term*' have also been referred to, although to a lesser extent than the just-mentioned forms.

1.1.5 The Working Definition Adopted in This Dissertation

The working definition adopted in this dissertation will be based on labour law scholarship, but also on influential reports of supranational and international institutions. The intention is to provide a description of casual work, rather than a fixed definition, which will underline the core features of it identified in the above-mentioned sources. By having in mind that many studies limit their focus to work

124. European Parliament, *Precarious employment in Europe: Patterns, trends and policy strategies*, 2016, p. 109.
125. L. Hyman, *How American work, American business and the American dream became temporary*, Permatemp section, Penguin Random House, (2018)
126. ILO, *Non-standard employment around the world*, International Labour Office, p. 21 and 28, 2016; OECD, *Employment Outlook 2019: The future of work*, p. 89.
127. This is illustrated again in the ILO (2016) report on non-standard employment, OECD (2019) Employment Outlook.
128. M. O'Sullivan et al., 'Zero-Hours and On-call Work in Anglo-Saxon Countries', p. 6.
129. Eurofound, *Work on demand: Recurrence, effects and challenges*, Research report 2018, p. 3.
130. *Ibid.*, p. 5.
131. A. Adams, M. Freedland and J. Prassl, The 'Zero-Hours Contract': Regulating Casual Work, or Legitimating Precarity?, *Oxford Legal Studies*, Research Paper No. 11/2015, p. 19.
132. A. Adams, J. Prassl, 'Zero-Hours Work in the United Kingdom', *International Labour* Office, Conditions of Work and Employment Series No. 101, 2018.

arrangements with some or severe insecurity of working hours, this working definition aims to capture the whole phenomenon, and hence, to formulate a broad and encompassing understanding of casual work arrangements. In light of this, in the course of this doctoral dissertation, casual work will be considered as a label for capturing:

- work arrangements, which have a very short duration and can be called in by the employer on a regular or irregular basis, such as daily work, seasonal work, etc.;
- work arrangements, which can be long-lasting or continuous, but are characterized by some or severe working hours insecurity, which depends on the business needs of the employer, such as min-max and zero-hour work arrangements.

Schematically, casual work will thus refer to work arrangements fitting within these boxes:

Short duration	Long duration
Regular or irregular hours	Irregular hours

1.2 CASUAL WORK AND PLATFORM WORK

Casual work arrangements have proliferated in industrialized economies, also in the context of 'work mediated through online web platforms'.[133] As noted in the case of casual work arrangements, a variety of terms also surround work mediated by technology, or what has been colloquially known as the 'gig economy'. By acknowledging that 'the list of labels grows day by day',[134] some of these labels are: 'sharing economy', 'on-demand economy',[135] 'crowd employment'.[136] In the course of this dissertation, the concept of 'platform work', which is generally associated with more neutrality,[137] will be used as an umbrella term to capture the heterogeneity that underpins this form of work. A definition of platform work has been advanced by the *OECD*, by referring to 'transactions mediated by an app (i.e. a specific purpose software program, often designed for use on a mobile device) or a website, which matches customers and clients, by means of an algorithm, with workers who provide services

133. International Labour Office-Geneva, *Non-standard employment around the world: Understanding challenges, shaping prospects*, p. 8 and 39.
134. V. De Stefano, A. Aloisi, *European legal framework for digital labour platforms*, European Commission, Luxembourg, 2018, p. 6.
135. M. Freedland, J. Prassl, 'Employees, workers and the sharing economy, Changing practices and changing concepts in the United Kingdom', *Spanish Labour Law and Employment Relations Journal*, Vol. 6 Issue 1-2, (2017), p. 2.
136. Eurofound, *New forms of employment*, p. 107; European Parliament, *Precarious employment in Europe: Patterns, trends and policy strategies*, p. 117.
137. European Parliament, Directorate General for Internal Policies, *The social protection of workers in the platform economy*, 2017, p. 21.

in return for money'.[138] Such a definition points out a two-fold distinction of platform work, which scholars have referred to as crowdwork and work-on-demand via apps.[139] Crowdwork consists of an online platform matching the labour demand and supply on a global basis, with work executed online, with an example being that of Amazon Mechanical Turk. By comparison, work-on-demand via apps connects by means of an app, both sides of labour on a local basis, as work needs to be executed in the local labour market, with prominent examples such as Uber or Deliveroo.

Contrasting approaches can be observed with respect to the relation between platform work and casual work arrangements. The technological innovation inherent in platform work seems to be the main reason to oppose, not only to position this work typology within the context of casual work but also to simply consider it as work.[140] By recognizing that this technological component may, indeed, constitute a peculiar feature of platform work; platform work is, nonetheless, being positioned more and more within the framework of casual work arrangements. In light of this, the International Labour Office, in the non-standard employment report, includes in a shared analysis, both non-standard and platform work, by especially pointing out the similarities platform work has with casual work.[141] Such an approach has been further confirmed by the CEACR general survey, which recognizes that 'digital platform work is on many occasions casual work'.[142] Against this background, many scholars have studied 'the zero-hour contract in platform work',[143] or considered it as 'a set of digitally intermediated zero-hours contracts',[144] or as 'the casual work of the XXI century'.[145] In the same vein, Eurofound considers platform work as 'internet-enabled casual work', by acknowledging that one mode of operation of casual work is through online platforms.[146]

Both casual and platform work rely on an 'on-demand' or 'just-in-time work-force',[147] a pool of workers who are called upon at the employer's discretion. Being called upon only when the business needs arise implies being subject to unpredictable working schedules, which can be associated with high levels of insecurity on the working conditions of such workers, and with flexibility that is mainly unilateral on the

138. OECD, *Policy responses to new forms of work*, p. 14.
139. V. De Stefano, 'The Rise of the Just-in time Workforce ...', p. 4.
140. J. Prassl, *Humans as a Service*. 'The Promise and Perils of Work in the Gig Economy', The innovation paradox, *OUP*, 2018.
141. International Labour Office-Geneva, *Non-standard employment around the world: Understanding challenges, shaping prospects*, p. 39.
142. ILC109/III(B) – *Promoting employment and decent work in a changing landscape*, p. 127.
143. A. Fabrellas, 'The Zero-Hour Contract in Platform Work. Should We Ban It or Embrace It?', IDP: Revista de Internet, Derecho y Politica, Issue 28 2019.
144. M. Freedland, J. Prassl. 'Employees, Workers and the Sharing Economy, Changing Practices and Changing Concepts in the United Kingdom', p. 7.
145. V. De Stefano, 'Labour Is Not a Technology, Reasserting the Declaration of Philadelphia in Times of Platform: Work and Gig-economy', *IUSLabor* 2/2017, p. 9.
146. Eurofound, *New forms of employment*, p. 47.
147. The 'just-in-time workforce' is facilitated by ICT means in the case of platform work. This terminology is used by V. De Stefano in 'The Rise of the "Just-in-time Workforce": On-demand Work, Crowdwork and Labour Protection in the Gig-economy' *Comp. Lab. L. & Pol'y J.* Vol. 37, 2015.

side of the employer.[148] In assessing the implications of new forms of employment for working conditions, Eurofound provides evidence, that both casual work and platform work are often linked to deteriorating working conditions, such as job insecurity, income insecurity, irregularity of working hours, low levels of pay, etc.[149] The existing working conditions faced by casual workers are further exacerbated by platform work, attributed to the fact that platform workers are normally classified as self-employed persons, which leads to their legal exclusion from basic form of labour protection, such as minimum wages, working time protection and the rights to associate in trade unions and collective bargaining.[150]

Such strong indicators, stemming from the institutional level, i.e., the authoritative reports of the International Labour Office, Eurofound, but also highlighted in the academic discourse, reveal similar labour market hardships experienced by both casual and platform workers. Departing from the above-mentioned considerations, focused on the shared features of flexibility and insecurity underpinning casual and platform work, this doctoral dissertation's assumption is that there is at least an overlap between platform work and casual work arrangements. This assumption will be elaborated below, as part of the comparative legal analysis of casual work in some industrialized countries.

1.3 A PRELUDE TO THE COMPARATIVE LEGAL ANALYSIS OF CASUAL WORK

The aim of the first part of this dissertation is to conduct a comparative legal analysis of casual work in selected industrialized countries. Embarking on this comparative research was spurred by a genuine lack in the existing analysis, of a detailed and extensive comparative legal analysis of the casualization of work in industrialized countries. Therefore, this doctoral research aims to contribute towards filling in this research gap. The focus in industrialized countries was chosen based on the proliferation of casual work in these countries, which is combined with a lack of awareness, or even reluctance, by national legislators there, to deal with this phenomenon. This lack of awareness on the spread of casual work has been labelled by De Stefano as 'an underground casualization',[151] and it is associated with a lack of legal responses to casual work in these countries. On the opposite side of the spectrum, casual work in developing countries has constituted the subject of much research and legal developments.

148. This flexibility is considered as 'employer-oriented' by I. Campbell, 'On-call and Related Forms of Casual Work in New Zealand and Australia', *ILO* 2018, p. 4; Eurofound, *New Forms of Employment*, p. 2.
149. Eurofound, *New Forms of Employment*, p. 143.
150. The European Parliament demonstrates that platform workers face a risk of precariousness due to the lack of access to labour rights, lack of social security coverage and involuntary self-employment, in *Precarious employment in Europe: Patterns, trends and policy strategies*, Study for the EMPL Committee, 2016, p. 171.
151. V. De Stefano, 'Casual work beyond casual work in the EU: the underground casualization of the European workforce – and what to do about it' *European Labour Law Journal*, Vol. 7 Issue 3, 2016.

In addition to contributing to this research gap, this comparative analysis will also be insightful in providing an answer to the main research question of this dissertation. Exploring the legal features of casual work in some industrialized countries, with a focus on their casual work agenda, can serve as a preliminary step in answering the question[152]: can the casual work agenda contribute to enhancing the labour protection of platform workers? What is more, the assumption of this dissertation, namely that casual work and platform work overlap to a certain extent, will be further elaborated in this comparative part.

As subjects of this comparative analysis have been chosen four industrialized countries: the United Kingdom, Italy, the Netherlands and Belgium. As it can be observed, the UK is the only non-EU country. The only implication that this fact brings for the study is that the UK does not have to transpose anymore into its legal system the EU labour laws, which will constitute the crux of the upcoming chapters.[153] Regarding the amount of countries chosen, the selection of four countries was thought as suitable to conduct a detailed, rather than a superficial research. They were chosen based on the spread of casual work arrangements within their national boundaries, combined with the presence of national legal strategies, as a potential source of labour protection for casual workers. The diversity of these legal strategies is beneficial for this comparative legal analysis, as different regulatory solutions entail that different lessons can be learned with respect to casual work.

Concerning the structure of these country chapters, they provide insights on the general situation of casual work per country (e.g., definitions, incidence, etc.); the legal framework governing it, with a focus on the employment status and working conditions of these workers; country-specific developments on platform work; and the exploration of the overlap between casual and platform work at the national contexts. In line with the major changes brought by the COVID-19 pandemic, some considerations were also included on the impact of the pandemic on the working conditions of casual and platform workers.

The comparative analysis starts with the study of casual work in the *United Kingdom*, where a high incidence of especially zero hours work – a form of casual work which can have a long-lasting duration but is characterized by insecure working hours – has been noted. Notwithstanding the prominent spread of this extreme form of casual work, a loose regulation has been adopted at the national level, which risks leaving these workers exposed to many work-related insecurities. The employment status of zero-hours workers, which very often fall within a third employment category, constitutes a further peculiarity of the UK legal system, which distinguishes it from the other countries analysed in the context of this dissertation.

The subsequent chapter delves into the Italian regulatory approach to forms of casual work, such as on-call and zero-hours contracts. Contrary to the UK, *Italy* opts for tight regulation of casual work, with a wide range of legal limitations applicable to on-call work, e.g., on the duration of the contract, workers' age, etc. Furthermore, a

152. D. Pieters, 'Comparative research methods', Lecture held at Young Researchers School Research Design and Methodology in Comparative Social Security, Spetses, Greece, 2021.
153. EU legislation and UK law https://www.legislation.gov.uk/eu-legislation-and-uk-law.

potential overlap, *inter alia*, between casual and vouched-based work will also be scrutinized, due to some ambiguous boundaries observed in this regard.

Along the same lines as Italy, *the Netherlands* also tightly regulates forms of casual work, an issue which will be explored in the third country chapter. The purpose of the Dutch legislator is to encourage the spread of flexible work arrangements, including casual ones, however, by paying due attention to the labour protection of these workers. To this end, casual workers in the Netherlands can benefit from both specific legal measures targeting their peculiar needs, but also from some more general ones, which are applicable to all workers.

At the heart of the last country chapter stands *Belgium*, as a notable example of a country which promotes standard employment, and limits the flexible one. This will be illustrated by the limitations imposed on intermittent work and the complex legal situation faced by zero-hours workers in Belgium. What is more, in the Belgian context, overlaps of casual work also with some more secure forms of work, such as flexi-jobs and voucher-based work, will be examined. Subsequent to the individual country chapters, the final chapter of this part will provide a digest of regulatory approaches to casual work, by evaluating their potential to contribute to the labour protection of casual workers.

CHAPTER 2

Zero-Hours Contracts in the United Kingdom

2.1 ZERO-HOURS CONTRACTS IN THE UK IN A NUTSHELL

Zero-hours contracts represent a widespread, and the most extreme form of casual work in the United Kingdom (UK),[154] with no guarantee of working hours at all. Under UK domestic law,[155] these contracts are lawful,[156] however, they have been provided with a legal response solely concerning the prohibition of the so-called exclusivity clauses, according to which workers promise to work exclusively for one employer.[157] Recent statistics show that around one million workers are involved in these work arrangements[158] and an 'explosive growth'[159] is noticed in the usage of such contracts by employers. Notwithstanding that the major developments of zero-hours contracts in the country have been observed in the last years,[160] they do not constitute a recent

154. Z. Adams and S. Deakin, Work is intermittent but capital is not: what to do about zero hours contracts, Institute of Employment Rights, 2014, Available at: https://www.ier.org.uk/comments/work-intermittent-capital-not-what-do-about-zero-hours-contracts/.
155. The Employment Rights Act (ERA) 1996, section 2A.
156. In other countries, such Austria, France, Belgium, these contracts are not generally allowed according to A. Adams and J. Prassl, 'Zero-Hours Work in the United Kingdom', *International Labour Office*, Conditions of Work and Employment Series No. 101, 2018, Table 1, p. 6.
157. Part 27 (A) (3) of the ERA stipulates that 'any provision of a zero hours contract which (a) prohibits the workers from doing work or performing services under another contract or under any other agreement or (b) prohibits the worker on doing so without the employer's consent is unenforceable against the worker'.
158. ONS, *Contracts that do not guarantee a minimum number of hours: April 2018*, p. 2. Available at: https://www.ons.gov.uk/releases/contractsthatdonotguaranteeaminimumnumberofhoursapril2018. More details on the size of this phenomenon will be provided later on in this chapter (section 2.b.iv).
159. A. Adams, M. Freedland and J. Prassl, 'The "Zero-Hours Contract": Regulating Casual Work or Legitimating Precarity?', *Legal Research Paper Series* 2015, University of Oxford, p. 1.
160. *Ibid.*, p. 2.

labour market phenomenon.[161] As Barnard contends, precariousness has long been present in the UK labour market, although 'the political debate has coalesced around those employed on zero-hours contracts'.[162]

Since 2015, the only regulation on zero-hours contracts concerns the prohibition of exclusivity clauses. This legal situation can arguably alter, after the Government's response to the report commissioned by it to forward recommendations on modern working practices,[163] also known as Taylor's review. The Queen has also promised in one of her speeches 'to improve the fairness of zero hours contracts for low paid workers'.[164] Employers, on their side, seem happy to reap the benefits associated with zero-hours work,[165] while British trade unions require an outlaw of zero-hours practices.[166]

Overall, the UK has been labelled as a notorious user of these types of contracts. Indeed, as Eurofound points out, 'zero-hours contracts [in the UK] are characterized by less clearly defined employment rights, less income security, and worse work-life balance'.[167] This situation stands in stark contrast with countries such as Italy and the Netherlands, where zero-hours contracts are subject to specific minimum standards to protect workers, and the extreme flexibility associated with zero-hours contracts has not been recognized.[168]

2.2 TWO SIDES OF THE SAME COIN: THE GOOD AND DARK SIDE OF ZERO-HOURS CONTRACTS IN THE UK CONTEXT

2.2.1 The Good Side: The Flexible Employer and Worker

Starting with the *business side*, employers use zero-hours contracts to deal with the fluctuating demands or peaks and troughs of their business.[169] In this way, they can actually save costs by avoiding paying workers when work is not needed. Therefore, these contracts appear to be very convenient for employers, with some of them placing

161. A. Adams and J. Prassl, 'Zero-Hours Work in the United Kingdom', *International Labour Office*, Conditions of Work and Employment Series No. 101, 2018, p. 4; M. Freedland, 'The Employment Contract and the Paradoxes of Precarity', University of Oxford, Legal Research Paper Series, Paper No. 37/2016, 2016, p. 17.
162. C. Barnard, 'New Forms of Employment in the United Kingdom', *Bulletin of Comparative Labour Relations*, New Forms of Employment in Europe, Chapter 35, p. 365.
163. Good work: the Taylor review of modern working practices, Available at: https://www.gov.uk/government/publications/government-response-to-the-taylor-review-of-modern-working-practices.
164. HM Government, The Queen's Speech 2014 – Lobby Briefing, London, June 2014, 18.
165. A. Adams and J. Prassl, 'Zero-Hours Work in the United Kingdom', *International Labour Office*, Conditions of Work and Employment Series No. 101, 2018, p. 35.
166. TUC blog, A ban on zero-hours contracts – a victory for Irish trade unions, Available at: https://www.tuc.org.uk/blogs/ban-zero-hours-contracts-victory-irish-unions. *See also*: https://www.tuc.org.uk/take-action-unions-are-fighting-stamp-out-zero-hours-contracts.
167. Eurofound, *New Forms of Employment*, 2015, p. 68.
168. S. Deakin, 'New Forms of Employment: Implications for EU Law: The Law as It Stands', *Bulletin of Comparative Labour Relations*, New Forms of Employment in Europe, (2016), Chapter 3, p. 51.
169. CIPD, *Zero-hours contracts: Myth and reality*, Research Report, 2013, p. 37.

such contracts at the heart of their business model.[170] This has been confirmed by a survey conducted by the Chartered Institute of Personnel and Development (CIPD), a human resources company, which found out that '45 per cent of employers reported using zero-hours contracts as part of a long-term strategy'.[171] On the *labour side*, a part of zero-hours workers claims that they prefer such contracts to fixed and regular working hours.[172] Working on such contracts seems to suit their needs for flexibility,[173] contributing to a better combination of work with other study, family, or personal duties. Eurofound confirms this, by emphasizing the benefits for some workers, such as students, or those willing to combine work and private life.[174] The director of Seasoned Events, an event caterer in London, contends that zero-hours contracts suit the flexibility needs of both employers and employees. According to him, the company offered to many zero-hours workers, who worked for it for many years, the opportunity to convert to full-time employment, but apparently workers opted 'to stay on variable contracts because it means they can do what they want, when they want'.[175] On the *government side*, the Secretary of State emphasized the positive aspects associated with zero-hours work, by primarily mentioning the flexibility that it brings for both employers and workers, but also the role of this type of work as a pathway to employment for young people.[176] In the same vein as the consultation document of the UK government, being offered an employment opportunity was preferred over being unemployed.[177] The business community also maintains that unemployment rates would be higher, if zero-hours contracts were not available for workers.[178] Furthermore, Eurofound points out that such contracts can also be a mean to generate additional income, or they can lead to the improvement of workers' skills.[179] The latter aspect can, nonetheless, be questionable in the case of low-skilled jobs.

Flexibility for both parties, employment over unemployment, skills enhancement, and a potential pathway to stable employment, compose the good part of the emergence of zero-hours contracts. However, as both sides of the coin should be

170. J. Kenner, 'Inverting the Flexicurity Paradigm: The United Kingdom and Zero Hours Contracts', in *Core and Contingent Work in the European Union: A Comparative Analysis*, eds Ales, E., Derinert, O., and Kenner, J., Oxford: Hart Publishing, 153-184, Bloomsbury Collections, 2017, p. 157.
171. *Ibid.*, CIPD, p. 13.
172. J. Kenner, 'Inverting the Flexicurity Paradigm: The United Kingdom and Zero Hours Contracts', In *Core and Contingent Work in the European Union: A Comparative Analysis*, eds Ales, E., Deinert, O., and Kenner, J., Oxford: Hart Publishing, 153-184, Bloomsbury Collections, (2017), p. 157.
173. *Ibid.*
174. Eurofound, *New Forms of Employment*, p. 65, referring to ILO 2004.
175. E. Earls, Zero or hero, Blog 2014.
176. A. Adams, M. Freedland and J. Prassl, 'The Zero-Hours Contract: Regulating Casual Work, or Legitimating Precarity?', Legal Research Paper Series 2015, University of Oxford, p. 17 based on BIS, 'Consultation: Zero hours employment contracts', 2013, p. 4.
177. *Ibid.*, p. 21.
178. Public Sector Executive, Vital role for zero hours contracts-CBI, 2013, Available at: http://www.publicsectorexecutive.com/Public-Sector-News/vital-role-for-zero-hours-contracts-cbi-.
179. Eurofound, *New Forms of Employment*, p. 65.

watched equally, the below section demonstrates that many zero-hours workers might experience extreme flexibility and insecurity in their working conditions.[180]

2.2.2 The Dark Side: The Insecure Worker

Working Conditions' Insecurity

On the other side of the coin, many zero-hours workers were observed to work in poor-quality jobs, with insecurity characterizing all aspects of their employment.[181] First off, zero-hours contracts are characterized by the insecurity of working hours, an insecurity that goes hand in hand with the insecurity of income and employment for the future. With respect to the level of pay, the European Commission reveals that casual work is characterized by low pay,[182] where especially zero-hours workers experience low pay and in-work poverty.[183] Such implications for working conditions are illustrated in the UK context, where some anecdotal evidence points out to a group of lecturers working on zero-hours contracts in Bradford, who reported that the working hours and income insecurity associated with this type of work, was causing them to be into serious debts.[184] According to such evidence, 'lots of people on these contracts wouldn't be able to survive without family support'.[185]

Additionally, other important workplace rights, which require a certain continuity of employment, such as sick pay, maternity pay, redundancy pay, and protection against unfair dismissal,[186] can also be difficult to attain for many zero-hours workers.[187] In this regard, a driver for some employers to use zero-hours contracts was observed to be the avoidance of employment obligations, among other things, maternity leave and redundancy pay.[188] Freedland, refers to such an evasion of employment rights through the use of zero-hours contracts by employers, as the 'paradox of

180. J. Kenner, 'Inverting the Flexicurity Paradigm: The United Kingdom and Zero Hours Contracts', In *Core and Contingent Work in the European Union: A Comparative Analysis*, eds Ales, E., Deinert, O., and Kenner, J., Oxford: Hart Publishing, 153-184, Bloomsbury Collections, (2017).
181. Eurofound, *New Forms of Employment*, p. 143.
182. Commission staff working document, Analytical document accompanying the consultation document on a possible revision of the Written Statement Directive in the framework of the EPSR, p. 23. This finding is based on Eurofound research.
183. *Ibid.*, p. 22.
184. A. Adams, J. Prassl, 'Zero hours work in the UK', p. 24. Also a survey found that 57% of zero hours workers find it difficult to budget from month to month (UKCES, 2014).
185. *Ibid.*, Adams and Prassl.
186. For example, according to ERA 1996 s. 108, to bring a claim against unfair dismissal, two years of continuous employment are required.
187. Eurofound, *New Forms of Employment*, p. 59; Z. Adams and S. Deakin, Work is intermittent, but capital is not: what to do about zero-hours contracts, Blog, 2014.
188. J. Kenner, p. 158, based on the findings of the Resolution Foundation research, 'A matter of time: the rise of zero hours contracts', 2013, Available at: https://www.resolutionfoundation.org/publications/matter-time-rise-zero-hours-contracts/. The British trade union, Unite, seems to agree to the just-mentioned reasoning, *see* Economics Online, Zero hours contracts, Available at: https://www.economicsonline.co.uk/Labour_markets/Zero-hours-contracts.html.

precarity'.[189] According to him, casual work arrangements are 'so essentially casual and precarious that it is they who are in the greatest need of that regulatory protection'.[190]

Deterioration of Work-life Balance

The International Labour Office acknowledges that the flexibility associated with non-standard forms of employment should work for both labour and demand sides.[191] On the labour side, the purpose is to enhance the work-life balance of the workers. Nevertheless, 25% of zero-hours workers in the UK have reported experiencing extreme flexibility, and underemployment.[192] Not only insufficient working hours but also unpredictable ones, constitute an issue for the work-life balance of these workers. While, in theory, zero-hours workers can reject unpredictable working hours incompatible with their personal schedule,[193] in practice, these workers were noticed to be afraid to turn down an offer for a particular shift, fearing the sanction of having no work for the future, or the 'zeroing-down' of their contract.[194] De Stefano labels this as the 'implicit threat' mechanism[195] and highlights its prominence in the case of zero-hours work, where the employer has no obligation to offer working hours.[196] In order to keep their employer satisfied, zero-hours workers are bound to accept any offer of employment, instead of choosing convenient working hours for themselves. In a study by the UK Commission for Employment and Skills, it was found that nearly two-thirds of zero-hours workers cannot say no to offers of work from their employer.[197] This is far from a two-sided flexibility but implies instead for what has been considered an employer-led flexibility.[198] Also research conducted at a large retail

189. M. Freedland, 'The Contract of Employment and the Paradoxes of Precarity', University of Oxford, Legal Research Paper Series, Paper No. 37/2016, (2016), p. 16.
190. M. Freedland, 'New Trade Union Strategies for New Forms of Employment: A brief Analytical and Normative Foreword', *European Labour Law Journal*, Vol. 10 Issue 3, 179-182, (2019), p. 4.
191. International Labour Office-Geneva, *Non-standard employment around the world: Understanding challenges, shaping prospects*, 2016, p. 2.
192. A. Adams and J.Prassl, 'Zero hours work in the United Kingdom', p. 15.
193. M. Freedland and J. Prassl in 'Employees, Workers and the 'sharing economy', explain that in zero hours contract '... at least in theory, workers are not obliged to accept any offers of work which might have been made by their employer', p. 19.
194. The Resolution Foundation Research, 'A matter of time: the rise of zero hours contracts', 2013, p. 18.
195. De Stefano labels this as the 'implicit threat' mechanism in 'Smuggling flexibility: Temporary working contracts and the 'implicit threat' mechanism', *Bocconi Legal Studies Research Paper* No. 1433350, 2009. This mechanism consists in the workers' fear and reluctance to exercise their contractual and labour rights afraid that their temporary contract may not be renewed or prolonged, should they do so.
196. V. De Stefano and A. Aloisi, 'Fundamental Labour Rights, platform work and human-rights protection of non-standard workers', *Bocconi Legal Studies Research Paper* Series, 2018, p. 10.
197. N. Pickavance report, 'Zeroed out: The place of zero hours contracts in a fair and productive economy', p. 9, based on UKCES 2014, 'Flexible contracts: behind the headlines', Available at: https://assets.publishing.service.gov.uk/government/uploads/system/uploads/attachment_data/file/302989/flexible-contracts-final.pdf. The data are based on a survey of 2,000 individuals across the UK from their online panel, for the period from 6 to 18 December 2013.
198. I. Campbell uses this terminology in 'On-call work and related forms of casual work in New Zealand and Australia', ILO (2018), p. 4.

company in the UK provides evidence that zero-hours contracts could adversely impact these workers 'family life, caring responsibilities and personal relationships'.[199] A similar result has been confirmed by a report published by the Department of Sociology of the University of Cambridge.[200]

Health Implications

In addition to the above-mentioned consequences, the insecurity characterizing zero-hours contracts may adversely affect also the workers' physical and mental health. The University College London has carried out research on zero-hours contracts, and the results show that young people working in such contracts are 'at higher risk of poor mental health than people on stable contracts'.[201] Research from the University of Cambridge also confirms the link between unpredictable working schedules, especially when there is a last-minute change, with psychological well-being.[202] In the social care industry in the UK, where zero-hours contracts are quite widespread,[203] these workers have indicated that they feel 'stressed out and burned out'.[204] Furthermore, a link between zero-hours contracts and tiredness at work was established following the investigation by the Rail Accident Investigation Branch, on the death of a railway zero-hours worker hit by a train.[205] The fatigue leading to fatal consequences was found to be caused by having only three and a half hours of sleep between night shifts. Further evidence shows that cardiovascular diseases are directly linked to workplace insecurity,[206] an inherent feature of zero-hours contracts. On top of this, low job control was also associated with other diseases such as cancer, strokes, and gastrointestinal disorders.[207]

2.3 THE CONSEQUENCES OF THE HETEROGENEITY OF ZERO-HOURS CONTRACTS

The above section on the good and dark side of zero-hours contracts implies that such contracts are displayed in various forms. In this regard, Adams, Freedland, and Prassl note that they can range from secure, preferred choice and well-paid employment, to

199. A. Adams and J. Prassl, 'Zero-Hours Work in the United Kingdom', p. 31.
200. A. Wood and B. Burchell, 'Zero hours contracts as a source of job insecurity amongst low paid hourly workers', *University of Cambridge*, Individual in the Labour Market Research Group, p. 19.
201. Centre for Longitudinal Studies, UCL, Being on a zero hours contract is bad for your health, new study reveals, Available at: https://cls.ucl.ac.uk/being-on-a-zero-hours-contract-is-bad-for-your-health-new-study-reveals/. The researchers analysed the data of more than 7,700 people living in England, who were born in 1989-1990.
202. A. Wood and B. Burchell, 'Zero Hours Contracts as a Source of Job Insecurity …', p. 8.
203. Adams and Prassl, 'Zero Hours Work in the UK', p. 20.
204. Financial Times, Zero hours take huge physical and mental toll, Available at: https://www.ft.com/content/d8d82ebe-9cbc-11e8-88de-49c908b1f264.
205. The Guardian, Rail worker killed by train in South London was on a zero hours contract, Available at: https://www.theguardian.com/business/2019/jul/12/rail-worker-killed-by-train-in-south-london-was-covering-for-brother.
206. Adams and Prassl, 'Zero Hours Work in the UK', p. 31.
207. Marmot, Fair society, Heathy lives: The Marmot Review, 2010.

insecure, necessity-driven and low-paid jobs.[208] Other authors refer to this heterogeneity as 'the chameleonic tendencies' of casual work.[209] Such a prominent variety, confirmed not only at the academic level but also at the governmental one,[210] can be associated with complexities and lack of clarity on essential aspects of zero-hours contracts. For instance, there is no universal definition of zero-hours contracts, notwithstanding several definitional attempts by scholars to shed light on this phenomenon. Not having a unified definition complicates the issue as well for official statistical bodies in providing an accurate measurement on the incidence of these work arrangements. Complications extend, as well, to labour law, with zero-hours workers, wandering between three different employment statutes in the UK, namely that of employee, limb (b) worker, and self-employed. The working conditions of zero-hours workers can also differ, with some experiencing more security and higher pay, and many of them placed on the other side of the spectrum, with no security and without the possibility of making ends meet.[211] The just-mentioned consequences of the heterogeneity of zero-hours contracts will be elaborated on in the following sections.

2.3.1 The Lack of a Unified Employment Status for Zero-Hours Workers

It comes as no surprise that the wide variety of zero-hours contracts represents a challenge in correctly determining the employment status of these workers. The importance of the employment status, which is determined by the court on a case-by-case basis, lies in defining the scope of labour protection for zero-hours workers. While each employment status is associated with diverse labour rights, falling within the self-employed status poses the risk for workers to be excluded from almost all labour protections. Prior to digging into this issue, it is crucial to provide a clarification on the British system of employment, which is different from most of those adopted in Continental Europe.

2.3.1.1 An Introduction to the British Tri-partite Regime of Employment

Determining the employment status is a prerogative of the national judiciary system, which has to review the facts of each individual case, or as described by Deakin, 'paint a picture in each individual case'.[212] This picture is painted by having as guidance the principle of the primacy of facts, which instructs the national judiciary to give weight to the facts relating to the performance of work, instead of the formal agreement

208. A. Adams, M. Freedland and J. Prassl, 'The Zero-Hours Contract: Regulating Casual Work, or Legitimating Precarity?', p. 5.
209. M. O'Sullivan, 'Zero Hours and On-call Work in Anglo-Saxon Countries', p. 6.
210. House of Commons, Oral answers to questions, 2013, Available at: https://publications.parliament.uk/pa/cm201314/cmhansrd/cm131016/debtext/131016-0001.htm.
211. TUC blog, Zero-hours contracts, what you need to know and why they should be banned, 2019, Available at: https://www.tuc.org.uk/blogs/zero-hours-contracts-what-you-need-know-and-why-they-should-be-banned.
212. S. Deakin and G. Morris, *Labour Law*, p. 169.

entered by the parties.[213] The UK courts have extensively referred to this principle in their reasoning,[214] and have also restated it in the specific context of zero-hours contracts.[215]

The outcomes of the British courts have to come within a tri-partite regime of employment, which is composed of (i) employees, (ii) workers, and (iii) self-employed.[216] Section 230 of the Employment Rights Act (ERA) 1996 lays down two statutory employment statuses, namely that of (i) 'employee' and (ii) 'worker'. Pursuant to such provisions, '(i) "*employee*" means an individual who has entered into or works under ... a contract of employment'.[217] However, the notion of (ii) '*worker*' includes (a) an employee working under a contract of employment, and '(b) an individual who has entered into or works under any other contract, whether express or implied and (if it is express) whether oral or in writing, whereby the individual undertakes to do or perform personally any work or services for another party to the contract whose status is not by virtue of the contract that of a client or customer of any profession or business undertaking carried on by the individual; and any reference to a worker's contract shall be construed accordingly'.[218] Moreover, it is not impossible for zero-hours workers to fall outside the scope of employment protection, concretely in the category of (iii) *self-employed* operating under contracts for services and running businesses on their own account. At the outset, the court scrutinizes whether an employment relationship is present, with a view to ensure to the workers a passport to a full set of rights under employment law.[219] When this is not the case, a secondary gateway to basic employment rights is possible, concretely through the employment status of the 'worker', or as it is colloquially known – limb (b) worker. In the *Costwold* case,[220] the Employment Appeal Tribunal (EAT) did not find an 'employee' status for a casual worker, in the absence of the mutuality of obligation. Instead, the court decided to grant basic labour protections to the worker, according to a limb (b) worker's status.

But how do British employment tribunals take their decisions on employment status? Considering that the UK is a country belonging to the common law legal system, the British courts refer to a multi-factor test, which is alleged 'notorious for its complexity',[221] and where no factor is decisive on its own. To start with the '*control*' test, it requires subordination of the employee to the employer in the way work is

213. Employment Relationship Recommendation 2006 (No. 98), para. 9.
214. ILO, *Non-standard employment around the world ...*, p. 262.
215. *Autoclenz Ltd v. Belcher and others* [2011] IRLR 820 (SC).
216. Other examples of countries adopting a three-tiers system of employment in Europe include Spain, Italy and to a certain extent Germany and Austria, according to V. De Stefano and N. Countouris, *New Trade Union Strategies for New Forms of Employment*, ETUC 2019, p. 19.
217. Section 230 (1) of ERA 1996.
218. *Ibid.*, s. 230 (3) (b).
219. J. Kenner, 'Inverting the Flexicurity Paradigm: The United Kingdom and Zero Hours Contracts", In *Core and Contingent Work in the European Union: A Comparative Analysis*, eds Ales, E., Deinert, O., and Kenner, J., Oxford: Hart Publishing, 153-184, Bloomsbury Collections, (2017), p. 161.
220. *Cotswold Developments Construction Ltd v. Williams* [2006] IRLR 181, EAT.
221. S. Deakin, and G. Morris, *Labour Law*, Hart Publishing 6th ed., 2012, p. 131.

performed.[222] To continue with, the '*integration*' test provides that the employees should be subject to the rules and procedures of an organization, rather than to the personal command of the employer.[223] However, the integration test is not that efficient in the case of employers making use of 'outsourcing' and the employment of workers with marginal attachment to the firm.[224] According to Deakin, this is the rationale that modern case law's focus has been shifted to two other tests, concretely that of 'economic reality' and 'mutuality of obligation'. The '*economic reality*' test demands that when a worker works for another person, the employer should take the risk of loss and profit in the business.[225] Following this logic, casual workers who have a high degree of personal autonomy, but are economically dependent on the employer, can be classified as employees. The '*mutuality of obligation*' test is a variant of the control test, demanding the employee to accept work when offered by the employer,[226] or what Freedland defines as 'mutual promises of future performance'.[227] This test has been 'particularly pertinent to cases involving atypical workers,'[228] and it comprises a tricky requirement to be proved in the zero-hours work setting.[229] According to Deakin and Morris, the existence of the mutuality of obligation will be an indicator for either an employment or limb (b) worker's contract.[230] However, Prassl observes that the mutuality of obligation is frequently used by the courts as a criterion for 'employee' status, requiring an 'umbrella' contract linking the individual contracts.[231] Pursuant to him, if mutuality of obligation would also be required for limb (b) worker's contract, this would put at risk 'an increasing number of labour market participants-from zero-hours contracts to those working for digital "gig economy" platforms of being deprived from even basic employment rights associated with limb (b) worker' status'.[232]

2.3.1.2 Where do Zero-Hours Workers Belong in the British Tri-partite Regime of Employment?

Adams, Prassl, and Freedland have argued that, in general, the more unstable and insecure a work arrangement is, 'the higher the chance that it would fail to be classified

222. *Ibid.*, p. 159.
223. *Ibid.*, p. 161.
224. This test is usually problematic for situations with blurred organizational boundaries, according to *Regulating the employment relationship in Europe: a guide to Recommendation No. 198*, International Labour Office, Governance and Tripartism Department. Geneva: ILO, 2013, p. 41.
225. S. Deakin, and G. Morris, *Labour Law*, p. 162.
226. *Ibid.*
227. M. Freedland et al., 'The Contract of Employment and the Paradoxes of Precarity', University of Oxford, Legal Research Paper Series, Paper No. 37/2016, (2016).pp. 21-22.
228. *Regulating the employment relationship in Europe: a guide to Recommendation No. 198*, International Labour Office, Governance and Tripartism Department. Geneva: ILO, 2013, p. 50.
229. S. Deakin and G. Morris, *Labour Law*, pp. 159-169.
230. *Ibid.*, p. 164.
231. J. Prassl, 'Pimlico plumbers, Uber drivers, cycle couriers, and court translators: who is a worker?', *Oxford Legal Studies Research Paper* No. 25/2017, p. 7.
232. *Ibid.*, p. 9.

as a contract of employment'.[233] Against this background, the 2013 Consultation document of the British government[234] has indicated that the most common scenario regarding zero-hours workers is to be classified as either employees or limb (b) workers.[235] However, the final word is reserved to the judiciary, which decides on a case-by-case basis and is triggered by the workers' requests to determine their employment status.

There are noticed two main approaches of British tribunals in interpreting the mutuality of obligation in the context of zero-hours work. The first approach identified can be perceived as a restrictive one, as no mutuality of obligation was found in the case of zero-hours work arrangements.[236] Such an approach was evident in two prominent judgments in the 1980s. Nevertheless, with the passing of time, the British tribunals' approach to the mutuality of obligation seems to have changed towards more inclusiveness.[237] To start with the first approach, representative judgments are Nethermere[238] and O'Kelly.[239] In *Nethermere (1984)*, the court did not find a mutuality of obligation, and highlighted that this requirement is a '*sine qua non* for the existence of a contract of service'. Also, in the *O'Kelly (1984)* case, which was about 'regular casuals', who were offering their services at regular intervals, the court did not find an umbrella contract for employment, or individual engagements to constitute a contract of service. The same approach was followed to a certain extent in a later case – *Carmichael*[240] *(1999)* – where the Court of Appeal considered 'casual as required' tour guides as employees, only for the moment they were performing work. This decision was then changed by the House of Lords, as according to Lord Irvine, the price to pay for flexibility is the denial of employment rights.[241]

The second and more inclusive approach can be observed in recent case law. Consequently, an increasing number of zero-hours workers in the UK are brought within the scope of employment protection. As these rulings show, the employment status of zero-hours workers can be established in one of the two ways:[242] under (i) an 'umbrella' contract linking the individual contracts or (ii) an individual/ 'spot' contract constituting an 'employee' or 'worker' contract, when there is continuing work.[243] The

233. A. Adams et al., 'The Zero-Hours Contract: Regulating Casual Work, or Legitimating Precarity?', European Labour Law Network Studies, p. 12.
234. Department for Business, Innovation and Skills, Consultation on zero hours employment contracts, 2013, Available at: https://assets.publishing.service.gov.uk/government/uploads/system/uploads/attachment_data/file/267634/bis-13-1275-zero-hours-employment-contracts-FINAL.pdf, p. 7.
235. According to Eurofound' s report *New forms of employment* p. 59, it is unlikely for self-employed to be on zero hours contracts.
236. According to J. Kenner, 'Inverting the flexicurity paradigm' p. 163, in the 1980s judgments, the court has made an 'aggressive use' of the mutuality of obligation.
237. A. Adams et al., 'The Zero-Hours Contract: Regulating Casual Work, or Legitimating Precarity?'.
238. *Nethermere (St Neots) Ltd v. Gardiner and Taverna*, [1984] IRLR 240.
239. *O'Kelly and Others v. Trusthouse Forte plc*, [1984] 1QB90.
240. *Carmichael and Another v. National Power plc*, [1999], 1WLR 2042.
241. J. Kenner, 'Inverting the Flexicurity Paradigm', p. 163.
242. S. Deakin, 'New Forms of Employment: Implications for EU Law: The Law as It Stands in New Forms of Employment in Europe', in *Bulletin of Comparative Labour Relations*, 2016, p. 49.
243. S. Deakin and G. Morris, *Labour Law*, p. 169.

establishment of an individual engagement as a contract of service accords workers access to numerous employment rights. However, the establishment of an umbrella contract can give access to even a wider set of employment rights, as it also includes those which depend on the continuity of service.[244] However, it can be quite rare for courts to find the existence of such a contract. In the *St Ives (2008)* case,[245] the court determined that, in a long and well-established regular work pattern, there was mutuality, even when the employee was not engaged on any particular shift, or when he was entitled to refuse any particular shift. This approach of the judiciary raised employers' concerns, who decided to respond to it by inserting no mutuality of obligation clauses in zero-hours work arrangements. In the *Autoclenz (2011)* case,[246] the court stated that notwithstanding the insertion of these clauses, courts should look at the parties' actual legal obligations. *Pulse Healthcare (2012)*[247] was the following case, that confirmed the court's decision in *Autoclenz* and presented some positive outcomes for zero-hours workers. The judgment concluded that individual wage-work bargains could be regarded as miniature contracts of employment, provided that there is control, economic reality, and the employer pays the employee for the agreed shift.[248] The court went even further by identifying a global contract of employment for care workers in the *Pulse Healthcare* case.

To sum up, the answer to the question of the employment status of zero-hours workers in the UK cannot be a crystal clear one. As previously explained, this is because the determination of the employment status is very fact-specific and needs to be triggered by workers in each individual case. This may result in the most vulnerable workers not bringing their cases to the court and, therefore, being excluded from important employment rights. However, as demonstrated above, the good news is that when cases are brought before British tribunals, they increasingly bring these workers within the protective scope of employment law. This judicial approach can actually open the green light to other zero-hours workers and serve as a driver for them to demand their missing employment rights.

2.3.1.3 *Entitlements Associated with the Employment Status*

Determining the employment status is crucial, as it establishes the employment rights to which zero-hours workers are entitled to. This can be a full, a half, or even no package of employment rights, respectively associated with the status of employee, limb (b) worker, and self-employed. The full package of employment rights is attained when an 'employee' status is granted.[249] This package comprises access from basic employment rights, e.g., minimum wage and working time, to rights requiring continuity of service and other important employment rights. The half package of

244. *Ibid.*, p. 165.
245. *St Ives Plymouth Ltd v. Mrs D Haggerty* [2008] UKEAT/0107/08.
246. *Autoclenz Ltd v. Belcher* [2011] UKSC 41, [2011] 4 All ER 745 [32].
247. *Pulse Healthcare Ltd v. Carewatch Care Services Ltd* [2012] UKEAT 0123/12/BA.
248. J. Kenner, 'Inverting the Flexicurity Paradigm', p. 165.
249. C. Barnard, 'New Forms of Employment in the United Kingdom', in *Bulletin of Comparative Labour Relations*, New Forms of Employment in Europe, 2016, p. 365.

employment rights cuts on these rights and ensures solely basic employment rights for zero-hours workers, who fall under the limb (b) status of worker. On the extreme side of the spectrum, self-employed find themselves almost with no package of employment rights.[250]

At the outset, it would be interesting to clarify the content of the 'half package' of employment rights, as this legal feature is quite peculiar to the UK compared with most European labour law systems.[251] Zero-hours workers classified as limb (b) workers enjoy a limited set of employment rights. First of all, they enjoy the basic right to the national minimum wage, which is paid to them while they are actually working, based on an hourly rate.[252] Therefore, these workers are not paid when 'they turn up for work in the hope of being hired'.[253] Furthermore, they are protected against arbitrary deductions from pay.[254] With respect to working time rights, zero-hours workers are entitled to rest periods, a limit on their maximum weekly working hours, and paid annual leave on a pro-rata basis.[255] Other rights comprise collective labour rights[256] and protection against discrimination in employment.[257] Notwithstanding that this set of employment rights constitutes a promising one, it is not complete, and hence, zero-hours workers miss out on important employment rights.[258]

The set of employment rights expands and becomes complete when zero-hours workers are classified as 'employees' by the judiciary. Not only the above-mentioned entitlements are included but also significant employment rights, which require some continuity of service from the worker, such as the right to sick pay, maternity and paternity leave and pay, protection against unfair dismissal, and redundancy pay. According to the ERA 1996, employees must have two years of continuous service to be protected against unfair dismissal.[259] To the widest set of employment rights are attached as well some important employment rights, such as the right to request flexible working, the right to request time to train, and minimum advance notice.[260] Having statutory rights is paramount, however, the practical exercise of these rights is equally important. With respect to this, difficulties are noticed for zero-hours workers trying to exercise their right to be protected against unfair dismissal, as such a right requires a long and continuous period of service. According to Kenner, there is

250. Self-employed enjoy the protection from discrimination in employment according to the Consultation document 2013, p. 8.
251. As previously said, only European countries such as the UK, Spain, Italy and Germany and Austria to a certain extent have introduced a third category of employment, namely the 'worker' category.
252. Section 3, National Minimum Wage Regulations 1999.
253. J. Kenner, 'Inverting the Flexicurity Paradigm', p. 171.
254. Consultation document on zero hours employment contracts 2013, p. 8.
255. Working Time Regulations 1998, SI 1998/1833.
256. V. De Stefano and N. Countouris, 'New Trade Union Strategies for New Forms of Employment' *ETUC*, Brussels, (2019), p. 27.
257. Consultation document on zero hours employment contracts, 2013, p. 8.
258. Eurofound emphasizes that many employment rights in the UK depend on continuity of employment. Such continuity is considered as archaic by Deakin in his blog *Work is intermittent but capital is not: what to do about zero hours contracts*, and M. Taylor in his report on modern working practices.
259. ERA 1996, s. 108 (1).
260. Consultation document on zero hours employment contracts, 2013, p. 8.

'uncertainty whether a temporary cessation with no further work being offered, amounts to "dismissal" in law'.[261] In light of this, Deakin considers the right not to be unfairly dismissed as an 'impossible prospect' for zero-hours workers.[262]

Against this backdrop, Eurofound points out that zero-hours workers in the UK have 'less clearly defined employment rights', compared to other countries where casual work has been spread.[263] This can arguably be attributed to the extrapolation of the intermediate category of employment to many zero-hours workers at the domestic level. In contrast, many European countries adopt a binary system of employment,[264] something which might increase the chances for many zero-hours workers to enjoy the full set of labour rights. Therefore, zero-hours workers in the UK are deprived of key rights, which they seem to enjoy, at least in theory, in other European countries. To this end, a normative proposition, which Nicola Countouris and Valerio De Stefano have put forward, can be conducive to the legal situation of zero-hours workers in the UK.[265] At the heart of this proposal stands the creation of a new and universal employment status – the 'worker' – who should have access to all employment rights.[266] This universal status would extend to workers mainly providing personal labour, and who do not genuinely operate a business on their own account.[267] In compliance with this definition, zero-hours workers, who currently fall into the limb (b) workers' category, can become entitled to the full package of employment rights.

2.3.2 A Lack of Consistency in the Definition of Zero-Hours Work

Legal Scholarship Definitions

Notwithstanding the existence of a heterogeneous group of zero-hours contracts, several British scholars have attempted to shed some light on this issue. According to Simon Deakin and Gillian Morris, 'zero-hours contracts encompass all cases where the employer unequivocally refuses to commit itself in advance to make any given quantum of work available'.[268] Furthermore, Mark Freedland and Nicola Countouris point out 'work arrangements in which the worker is in a personal work relation with an employing entity [...] for which there are no fixed or guaranteed hours of remunerated work'.[269] As it can be observed, the 'common thread' between these

261. J. Kenner, 'Inverting the Flexicurity Paradigm', p. 170.
262. Z. Adams and S. Deakin, *Work Is Intermittent but Capital Is Not: What to Do About Zero Hours Contracts*, Centre for Business Research, University of Cambridge, (2014).
263. Eurofound, *New Forms of Employment*, p. 68.
264. For instance the Netherlands, France, Sweden, Belgium. The binary system is still the backbone of labour protection systems, *see* N. Countouris and V. De Stefano, *New Trade Unions Strategies for New Forms of Employment*, p. 23 and 64.
265. V. De Stefano and N. Countouris, *New Trade Unions Strategies for New Forms of Employment, ETUC*, Brussels, (2019).
266. *Ibid.*; The Institute of Employment Rights, Rolling Out the Manifesto for Labour Law, 2018, para. 10.
267. *Ibid.*, p. 65.
268. S. Deakin and G. Morris, *Labour Law*, p. 167.
269. M. Freedland and N. Countouris, The Legal Construction of Personal Work Relations, Oxford University Press, 2012, pp. 318-319.

definitions is the lack of guaranteed hours of work from the employer. In also adding the workers' perspective to the definitions, two scenarios can be noticed, depending on the worker's approach to offers of work made to him by the employer. The definition advanced by Hugh Collins, Keith Ewing, and Aileen McColgan can illustrate this. These scholars draw a distinction between 'zero-hours contracts where the employee promises to be ready and available for work, but the employer merely promises to pay for time actually worked', and 'arrangements where again the employer does not promise to offer any work, but equally in this case the employee does not promise to be available when required'.[270] Mark Freedland and Jeremias Prassl, on their side, define the zero-hours contract as including, 'a wide range of arrangements in which workers are not guaranteed a fixed (or indeed any) number of hours in a particular period and, at least in theory, in which they are not obliged to accept any offers of work which might have been made by their employer'.[271] In a nutshell, two scenarios can be noticed with regard to zero-hours contracts, where employers do not guarantee any working hours. On the one hand, workers promise to be available for work; on the other hand, they do not make such a promise. In reality, nonetheless, the fear of not being renewed, labelled as the 'implicit threat mechanism' compels zero-hours workers to accept offers of work, even if they have not promised that beforehand.

A Normative Definition?

In search for a legal definition of zero-hours contracts, the most appropriate domestic law to refer to is the ERA 1996. Since 2015, this act has dedicated Part 2A to the partial regulation of zero-hours contracts.[272] The statutory definition of zero-hours contracts provided in this section is restricted only for the purposes of the section, which is the prohibition of exclusivity clauses in zero-hours contracts. This definition, provided in Part 27 (A), (1) of the ERA, is in line with the academic attempts to define zero-hours work arrangements. Pursuant to this provision, a zero-hours contract is a contract where '(a) the undertaking to do or perform work or services is an undertaking to do so conditionally on the employer making work or services available to the worker', and (b) 'there is no certainty that any such work or services will be made available to the worker'. As noted, this is the only available legal response to zero-hours contracts in the United Kingdom, restricted only to governing a certain aspect of this form of work.

Definition in Policy Documents

In response to the concerns over the potential abuse related to zero-hours contracts, the government launched an official consultation document in 2013,[273] according to

270. H. Collins, K. Ewing and A. McColgan, 'Labour Law', Cambridge University Press, 2012, p. 243.
271. M. Freedland and J. Prassl, *Employees, Workers and the 'Sharing Economy: Changing Practices and Changing Concepts in the United Kingdom'*, Oxford Legal Studies Research Paper (2017), p. 19.
272. Part 2(A) was inserted in 2015 by Small Business, Enterprise and Employment Act.
273. Department for Business, Innovation and Skills, Consultation on zero hours employment contracts, 2013, Available at: https://assets.publishing.service.gov.uk/government/uploads/system/uploads/attachment_data/file/267634/bis-13-1275-zero-hours-employment-contracts-FINAL.pdf.

which, the zero-hours contract is defined as 'an employment contract in which the employer does not guarantee to the individual any work, and the individual is not obliged to accept any work offered'. Several scholars have criticized the enshrinement of a definition of zero hours work in a policy document because it might support the assumption that zero-hours contracts represent a unitary category of employment.[274] On the other side, the most recent consultation document of the government on measures to address one-sided flexibility – the Good Work Plan-[275] does not provide a definition of zero-hours contracts. Instead, it responds to the Taylor Review report of modern working practices[276] and commits to policy and legislative changes with respect to zero-hours contracts.

Definition Adopted for Statistical Purposes[277]

The Labour Force Survey (LFS) and the Business Survey (BS) are considered the most reliable statistical surveys in the UK, both administered by the ONS. While the LFS relies on the self-reporting of individuals, the BS relies, instead, on contracts of employment.[278] With regard to zero-hours contracts, the ONS recognizes that under this label can come diverse work practices, something which leads to definitional complexities, but also to difficulties in accurately measuring this phenomenon in the UK. Nevertheless, the ONS provides a definition of zero-hours contracts, which individuals can get only upon a request for clarification. Such a definition was necessary to ensure an estimate of the number of zero-hours workers and contracts in the UK. In its most recent empirical evidence on zero-hours contracts,[279] the ONS refers to them as 'contracts that do not guarantee a minimum number of hours'.

According to the most recent estimate of the LFS[280] covering the period from October to December 2017, 901,000 individuals, representing 2.8% of the workforce, were in a zero-hours contract as their main job. In November 2017, the BS asked a sample of 5,000 businesses[281] and received responses from 2,737 of them. The estimates coming from the businesses' responses indicate that there are 1.8 million 'contracts that do not guarantee a minimum number of hours', representing 6% of all

274. A. Adams et al., 'The 'Zero-Hours Contract': Regulating Casual Work, or Legitimating Precarity?', p. 6.
275. Department for Business, Energy and Industrial Strategy, 'Good Work Plan, Consultation on measures to address one-sided flexibility', 2019, Available at: https://assets.publishing.service.gov.uk/government/uploads/system/uploads/attachment_data/file/818674/Good_Work_Plan_one_sided_flexibility-consultation_.pdf.
276. M. Taylor, 'Good work: the Taylor review of modern working practices', 2017, Available at: https://www.gov.uk/government/publications/good-work-the-taylor-review-of-modern-working-practices.
277. Information on the incidence of zero hours contracts in the UK will be provided in parallel to the definitions adopted by the statistical bodies.
278. A. Adams, Z. Adams and J. Prassl, 'Legitimizing Precarity: Zero-Hours Contracts in the United Kingdom', in *Zero-Hours and On-call Work in Anglo-Saxon Countries*, eds M. O'Sullivan et al., 2019, pp. 41-65, p. 45.
279. ONS, *Contracts that do not guarantee a minimum number of hours: April 2018*, p. 2, Available at: https://www.ons.gov.uk/releases/contractsthatdonotguaranteeaminimumnumberofhoursapril2018.
280. *Ibid.*
281. *Ibid.*, p. 6.

employment contracts in the UK. The LFS recently repeated the exercise for the period from April to June 2019. The results showed that 896,000 people are now working on zero-hours contracts, amounting to 2.7% of the workforce.[282] Therefore, a slight decrease was noticed in the number of zero-hours workers in the UK, notwithstanding that the picture is incomplete without the BS estimates for the same period.

2.3.3 A Variety of Working Conditions

Working Hours (in) Security

As the very notion 'zero hours' suggests, zero-hours workers are ensured with zero guaranteed hours of work, with 75% of them experiencing unpredictable hours, which vary every week.[283] Adams and Prassl indicate that 25% of zero-hours workers are underemployed,[284] while a poll of the Trade Union Congress (TUC) found that a larger share of these workers, concretely 59%, wanted to work more hours.[285] Therefore, the insecurity of working hours is reflected not solely in the number of hours, but also in the scheduling of these hours. In this context, O'Sullivan highlights that 'regularity, scheduling and control of hours are as important issues of contestation as the number of hours of work'.[286] As already explained in the section about the dark side of zero-hours work, the scheduling of working hours can end up being fixed by the employer, as any objection from the worker's side can lead to the 'zeroing-down' of the working hours. This has been illustrated by a CIPD survey on both businesses and workers, where '20 percent of firms reported penalizing zero hours workers for not accepting work';[287] and 17% of 450 respondents working on zero-hours arrangements reported being sometimes penalized for not accepting work, with 3% of them reported to be always penalized.[288] The above-mentioned sanctions imposed on zero-hours workers were further confirmed by a TUC poll, which pointed out that 35% of zero-hours workers were threatened with no future offers of employment if they turned down offers of work.[289]

This presumed one-sided fixed schedule needs to be communicated in advance to the workers, in order to not further adversely impact them. Eurofound provides

282. EMP17: People in employment on zero-hours contracts, August 2019, Available at: https://www.ons.gov.uk/employmentandlabourmarket/peopleinwork/employmentandemployeetypes/datasets/emp17peopleinemploymentonzerohourscontracts.
283. I. Brinkley, *Flexibility or insecurity? Exploring the rise in zero hours contracts*, The Work Foundation, 2013, p. 21.
284. A. Adams and J. Prassl, 'Zero-Hours Work in the United Kingdom', p. 15.
285. TUC, 'Great jobs with guaranteed hours, what do workers really think about 'flexible' zero-hours contracts?', p. 9.
286. M. O'Sullivan, 'Introduction to Zero Hours and On-call Work in Anglo-Saxon Countries', p. 5.
287. CIPD, *Zero-Hours Contracts: Myth and Reality*, Research Report, 2013, p. 37; S. Deakin, 'New Forms of Employment in Europe', *Bulletin of Comparative Labour Relations* Vol. 94, 2016, p. 47.
288. *Ibid.*
289. TUC, 'Great jobs with guaranteed hours, what do workers really think about 'flexible' zero-hours contracts?', p. 9.

evidence that in the UK, the notice period for zero-hours workers can be very short,[290] with even less than 24 hours in some instances. A poll conducted by the TUC found that 73% of zero-hours workers had less than 24 hours' notice for their next work offer.[291] Moreover, a minimum notice needs to be given not only for offers of work but also in case of cancellation of shifts. In this regard, the standard practice is that employers do not give any advance notice for shifts' cancellation, or even worse, they notify the worker just at the start of the shift that work is no longer available.[292] With respect to the length of working hours, the most common scenario is that of zero-hours workers experiencing very short working hours. Nevertheless, it is not excluded that zero-hours workers find themselves working for very long hours, with an example being some workers providing care services commissioned by a UK local government.[293]

Contrary to the above-mentioned insecurity of working hours, some zero-hours workers were found to experience also some working hours security. For instance, the claimants in the *O'Kelly* case were casual workers with regular work schedules, a category labelled as the 'regular casuals'. *St Ives* case also looked into the situation of casual workers with a long and well-established regular work pattern, something which led to the establishment of the mutuality of obligation.

Job and Income (in) Security

Working hours insecurity goes hand in hand with jobs and income insecurity.[294] This means that zero working hours translate into 'zero' or no job, and hence, zero income is associated with it. Research conducted on a UK retailer demonstrates the frustration of these workers to survive in these types of contracts, as 'nobody can possibly survive on three and a half hours' pay a week'.[295] Moreover, it gets even more challenging in the weeks when there is no work at all, as some other workers reveal that 'irregular shifts mean that some weeks [they] earn nothing'.[296] The fluctuating income associated with zero-hours work brings financial hardships for these workers and impacts the planning of their finances. This is illustrated by a TUC poll, where 54% of participants believed that they could barely manage their household expenses.[297] What is more, workers with family responsibilities might be hit even harder by financial insecurity.[298] Another aspect of the financial hardship that many zero-hours workers face is getting into debt,[299] and difficulty accessing credit due to their unstable financial situation. For

290. Eurofound, *New forms of employment*, p. 68.
291. *Ibid.*
292. S. Deakin, 'New Forms of Employment in Europe', p. 47.
293. Eurofound, *New forms of employment*, p. 67.
294. A. Wood and B. Burchell, 'Zero Hours Contracts as a Source of Job Insecurity Amongst Low Paid Hourly Workers', University of Cambridge, Individual in the Labour Market Research Group, (2014), p. 5; J. Kenner, 'Inverting the Flexicurity Paradigm', p. 156.
295. A. Wood and B. Burchell, p. 11.
296. TUC 'Great jobs with guaranteed hours, What do workers really think about 'flexible' zero hours contracts?'; Scott Gilfillan, 'Zero-hours contracts – what you need to know and why they should be banned', 2019.
297. *Ibid.*, TUC, p. 9.
298. Pickavance report, p. 14.
299. A. Adams and J. Prassl, 'Zero-Hours Work in the United Kingdom', p. 23.

example, some zero-hours workers working for McDonalds provided evidence that they were struggling to get loans, mortgages, and mobile phone contracts.[300]

Nonetheless, some differing evidence comes from the same case study of the UK retailer and shows instances of zero-hours workers not being affected by unpredictable work schedules.[301] These workers did not have caring responsibilities, and unless big changes, they seemed not to be concerned about unpredictable work schedules. What is more, being a regular casual, as mentioned in the previous section, can be associated with more jobs and income security.

Level of Pay

Eurofound research points out the existence of a link between casual work and low levels of pay.[302] This link has been more specifically confirmed in the UK context, where zero-hours workers were found to work mainly in low-paid jobs.[303] The low pay associated with zero-hours work can be attributed to having fewer hours of work in comparison to workers in other types of contracts,[304] but also to the fact that their hourly wage rates appear lower than average.[305] TUC research affirms that four in five zero-hours workers across the UK suffer lower hourly wage rates than permanent workers.[306] In addition, research conducted by the UK Resolution Foundation reveals that 'zero hours contract workers earn lower gross weekly pay than those who are not'.[307]

According to a study by the European Parliament, zero-hours workers working in the sectors of retail and hospitality in the UK are more susceptible to the risk of low pay and in-work poverty, which was identified as medium to high in their case.[308] The situation exacerbates when, in addition to low pay, zero-hours workers appear to face in-work poverty, with more than three-quarters of them earning less than the living wage.[309] A report by Feeding Britain describes the harsh reality of workers going hungry on zero-hours contracts, who are even forced to turn to food banks in order to survive.[310]

300. Taylor Review Report, p. 49.
301. A. Wood and B. Burchell, 'Zero Hours Contracts as a Source of Job Insecurity Amongst Low Paid Hourly Workers', p. 11.
302. Analytical document of the EC, p. 22 based on Eurofound, *New forms of employment*, 2015.
303. *Ibid.*, Eurofound, p. 68.
304. The ONS found that employees on zero hours contracts worked an average of 25 hours a week, according to European Parliament Study, *Precarious employment in Europe: Patterns, Trends and Policy Strategies*, p. 124.
305. A. Adams and J. Prassl, 'Zero-Hours Work in the United Kingdom', p. 12.
306. TUC research, available at: https://www.independent.co.uk/news/uk/politics/most-workers-on-zero-hours-contracts-are-paid-less-than-the-national-average-wage-9246957.html.
307. European Parliament Study, *Precarious employment in Europe: Patterns, Trends and Policy Strategies*, p. 124.
308. *Ibid.*, p. 125.
309. Independent, Most workers on zero-hours contracts are paid less than the national average wage, 2014, Available at: https://www.independent.co.uk/news/uk/politics/most-workers-on-zero-hours-contracts-are-paid-less-than-the-national-average-wage-9246957.html.
310. Feeding Britain, When Work Doesn't Pay, Working paper on zero hours contracts, Accessible at: https://heidiallen.co.uk/newsite/wp-content/uploads/2019/07/Work-doesnt-pay_-002.pdf.

Further confirmation comes from a brewing company in the UK, which indicated that its zero-hours workers were actually experiencing in-work poverty.[311]

While many zero-hours workers appear to suffer from low pay and in-work poverty, there can also be some contrasting instances. In this regard, Adams, Freedland, and Prassl reveal that zero-hours workers can also be involved in well-paid jobs.[312] With regard to these workers, it was observed that they attempt to tackle the low level of their income, by working for long working hours.[313] Nevertheless, these long working hours come with a price to be paid, which is a distorted work-life balance.[314]

2.4 PLATFORM WORK AS ZERO-HOURS WORK

2.4.1 An Overview of Platform Work in the UK

Platform work has become an integral part of the UK labour market, where it is proliferating at a high speed.[315] The most common terminology used in policy circles across the country is 'gig economy', as suggested by the Taylor review report.[316] Notwithstanding the difficulties in capturing the real size of the phenomenon at the national level, which displays a fast-evolving nature, some studies provide some data in this regard. In this respect, a study by the Joint Research Centre of the European Commission (JRC) indicated that workers, who regularly work on a platform (every week), in countries such as the UK and the US, represent about 1% to 2% of the workforce.[317] Another survey carried out by the CIPD, reported that 4% of the 5,019 UK-employed persons who acted as respondents, were involved in platform work, in at least one occasion in the previous twelve months.[318] The sheer diversity of business models surrounding platform work is certainly highlighted in the UK context, where some salient examples of platforms, which operate in the local market, comprise Uber

311. Good Work: The Taylor Review of Modern Working Practices, p. 43.
312. A. Adams, M. Freedland and J. Prassl, 'The "Zero Hours Contract": Regulating Casual Work, or Legitimating Precarity?', Oxford Legal Studies, Research Paper No. 11/2015, (2015), p. 5; M. Freedland and J. Prassl, 'Employees, Workers and the "Sharing Economy, Changing Practices and Changing Concepts in the UK', *Spanish Labour Law and Employment Relations Journal*, Vol. 6 Issue 1-2, (2017), p. 20.
313. Eurofound, *New Forms of Employment*, p. 67.
314. *Ibid.*
315. The Guardian, 'Gig economy in Britain doubles, accounting for 4.7 million workers', (2019), Available at: https://www.theguardian.com/business/2019/jun/28/gig-economy-in-britain-doubles-accounting-for-47-million-workers.
316. Eurofound, *Employment and working conditions of selected types of platform work*, Publications Office of the European Union, Luxembourg, 2018, p. 9.
317. C. Codagnone, F. Abadie, and F. Biagi, 'The Future of Work in the Sharing Economy. Market Efficiency and Equitable Opportunities or Unfair Precarisation', Luxembourg: Publications Office of the European Union, *JRC 101280*, 2016.
318. CIPD, 'To gig or not to gig? Stories from the modern economy', 2017, p. 4.

(transport services), Deliveroo (food delivery), TaskRabbit (domestic services),[319] Pimlico plumbers (maintenance services).[320]

The UK case law has been quite dynamic on the issue of the employment status of platform workers. Legal actions initiated by Uber riders,[321] Citysprint couriers,[322] and Pimlico plumbers,[323] turned into landmark cases for the employment rights of platform workers at the national level. The importance of such legal decisions consisted in the extension of the third employment category, concretely that of limb (b) 'worker', in a platform work context.[324] Accordingly, these platform workers became entitled to national minimum wage and working time rights, whereas in the *Pimlico* case, also to employment equality rights.[325] The outcome of such cases has been remarked as a victory by the media,[326] while the legal scholarship comments with a less enthusiastic tone.[327] In their analysis, scholars point out a still limited set of employment rights for platform workers, compared to the full package of employment rights associated with the 'employee' status. According to them, the limited rights can help platform workers to deal with basic problems, but they would arguably still face long-term ones, such as low pay problems and unpredictable working shifts.[328]

Without going into details, it is worth emphasizing some crucial elements the British courts considered in the determination of the employment status issue. In this regard, reference was made to the 'reality of the relationship between parties',[329] and to the tight control exerted by platform companies through setting the route and fixing the fare, through the rating system, or the deactivation of riders who refuse to accept trips.[330] Furthermore, the UK courts have frequently ruled on the issue of substitution clauses in the context of the platform economy.[331] In the *Citysprint* case, the court did not find a practical exercise of the right to be substituted; hence, it ruled in favour of workers' claim to be considered as limb (b) workers. On the contrary, in the *Deliveroo* case, the Central Arbitration Committee considered the substitution right as a genuine

319. M. Freedland and J. Prassl, 'Employees, Workers and the "Sharing Economy, Changing Practices and Changing Concepts in the UK', *Spanish Labour Law and Employment Relations Journal*, Vol. 6 Issue 1-2, (2017), p. 4.
320. For more information on the registered platform workers in the UK, please have a look at: Eurofound, *Employment and working conditions of selected types of platform work*, p. 12.
321. *Aslam, Farrar and Ors v. Uber*, Case No. 2202550/2015, decision of 28 October 2016.
322. *Dewhurst v. Citysprint UK Ltd* ET/2202512/ 2016.
323. *Pimlico Plumbers Ltd & Anor v. Smith* [2017] EWCA Civ 51.
324. M. Freedland and J. Prassl, 'Employees, Workers and the "Sharing Economy"', p. 15.
325. *Ibid.*, p. 16.
326. The Guardian, 'Uber loses right to classify UK drivers as self-employed', Available at: https://www.theguardian.com/technology/2016/oct/28/uber-uk-tribunal-self-employed-status?CMP=share_btn_tw.
327. For example, M. Freedland and J. Prassl, 'Employees, Workers and the "Sharing Economy"'.
328. *Ibid.*, p. 17.
329. R. Hunter, J. Prassl, 'Worker Status for App-driver: Uber-rated?,' *Oxford Human Rights Hub*, 2016, Available at: http://ohrh.law.ox.ac.uk/worker-status-for-app-drivers-uber-rated/.
330. *Uber* case, paras 89-92.
331. V. De Stefano, I. Durri, C. Stylogiannis, M. Wouters, 'Platform Work and the Employment Relationship', International Labour Office Working Paper 27, 2021.

right, which precluded the couriers from undertaking work personally for the company, and hence, to be 'workers' of that company.[332]

2.4.2 Platform Work Perceived as Zero-Hours Work Intermediated by Technology

Growing insights at the national level point out platform work being part of broader trends toward the casualization of work arrangements. In this spirit stands, for instance, the work of British scholars such as Mark Freedland and Jeremias Prassl. In his book dedicated to the gig economy, Prassl acknowledges that platform work represents 'nothing new under the sun', but it is, instead, an '[extreme] example of labour market practices that have been around for centuries'.[333] Furthermore, in an article co-authored by Freedland and Prassl, they position platform work against the background of casual work arrangements and perceive it as 'a set of digitally intermediated zero hours contracts'.[334]

The reason for such an affinity between both forms of work can be found in their underlying work realities. As the working conditions of zero-hours workers in the UK have already been elaborated, the working conditions of platform workers, which entail an affinity between both forms of work, will be pointed out. At the outset, it should be noted that the work reality of platform work arrangements can arguably be even more precarious than the one faced by casual workers. In this regard, Prassl contends that platform work can be even more precarious than the underpaid zero-hours contracts which were offered by the Sports Direct company.[335]

Unpredictable work demands constitute an integral feature also for platform work, which goes in conjunction with income and job insecurity. For instance, studies carried out on Uber drivers highlight the unpredictable character of their working hours, in many cases, also experience long working hours.[336] What is more, the CIPD study provides evidence of the extreme income insecurity experienced by platform workers, who in case of an unexpected income loss, could arguably afford from less than one month to two months of living.[337] A further similarity, associated with more deterioration on the platform work's side, can be observed with regard to the low pay of these workers. In the case of platform workers, their payment can easily fall below the minimum wage, due to their often exclusion from the scope of employment protection. Studies affirm that Uber drivers faced the risk of receiving even less than a

332. Central Arbitration Committee 14 November 2017, Case No. TUR1/985(2016), *IWGB v. RooFoods Limited T/A Deliveroo*.
333. J. Prassl, 'Humans as a Service: The Promise and Perils of Work in the Gig Economy, Oxford University Press, 2018, p. 73.
334. M. Freedland and J. Prassl, 'Employees, Workers and the 'Sharing Economy', p. 7.
335. J. Prassl, *Humans as a service* ..., p. 41. *See also*, the Guardian's article: https://www.theguardian.com/business/2015/dec/09/how-sports-direct-effectively-pays-below-minimum-wage-pay.
336. F. Field, A. Forsey, 'Sweated Labour: Uber and the 'Gig Economy'', *Business and Human Rights Resource Centre*, 2016, p. 5.
337. CIPD, 'To gig or not to gig, stories from the modern economy', 2017, p. 16.

third of the national living wage, after costs associated with their work, such as gasoline and depreciation, were deducted from their payment.[338]

These working conditions are further exacerbated due to a marginalization of these workers, concretely a widespread perception that both casual and platform workers work mainly to generate additional income, thus not considered as 'work that merits traditional labour protections'.[339] This implies that both types of workers might face a legal or practical exclusion from labour protections, with more severe implications on the platform workers' side. As already explained, zero-hours workers can be legally qualified within one of the three categories of employment in the UK. Even in the event of falling under the best scenario, that of 'employees', zero-hours workers can be practically excluded from important labour rights, which are dependent on a minimum length of service, such as the protection against unfair dismissal. On the other side, platform workers are found to generally lack labour protection. Nevertheless, with consideration of the precedent set by the British courts,[340] platform workers can trigger litigations to become entitled to at least some basic labour rights, which are associated with the limb (b) worker's status.

To conclude, the just-mentioned common features inherent in both casual and platform work clearly point out an affinity, or overlap, between these work arrangements.

2.5 CONCLUSION

Zero-hours contracts in the UK seem to display two contrasting aspects, concretely a positive and a negative one. On the positive side seems to stand the flexibility for employers in managing the peaks and troughs of their businesses, but also the work-life balance for some workers, together with a pathway towards employment, an enhancement of skills and a source of additional income. When turning to the negative side, working conditions in zero-hours work appear to be insecure, starting from working hours insecurity, which goes hand in hand with jobs and income insecurity, and continuing with other missing labour rights. In addition to this, workers' flexibility and the work-life balance brought by zero-hours contracts were called into question, as workers were not free to reject offers of work. On top of this, physical and mental health implications were also associated with zero-hours contracts.

The positive and negative sides of zero-hours contracts reveal the heterogeneous nature of this form of work. The consequences of such diversity are reflected, first, in the absence of an agreed definition on zero-hours contracts. Second, the employment status of these workers, and hence the labour protections extended to them, seem also to be diverse. As the most common scenario is being classified as a limb (b) worker,

338. *Ibid.*, F. Field, A. Forsey, 'Sweated Labour: Uber and the 'Gig Economy'', *Business and Human Rights Resource Centre*, (2016).
339. J. Berg, 'Income Security in the On-Demand Economy: Findings and Policy Lessons from a Survey of Crowdworkers', *ILO*, p. 1. This ILO survey found out that 40% of such workers generate their main source of income from crowdwork.
340. *Uber, Citysprint, Pimlico plumbers* cases.

British zero-hours workers can end up being deprived of several important employment rights. Third, the heterogeneity is further expressed in the variety of working conditions these workers face. In a nutshell, working conditions in this type of employment can range from reasonably secure working hours and employment, which is generally experienced by 'regular casuals', to extremely insecure employment; from well-paid jobs to low-paid jobs leading to in-work poverty; and from flexible employment to extremely flexible and not flexible at all, when the fear of the 'implicit threat' mechanism is pressing.

The just-mentioned working conditions appear to be quite similar to the ones experienced by platform workers, a resemblance which led some British scholars to regard platform work as zero-hours contracts mediated by technology. The insecurity of working hours, jobs, and income, together with low levels of pay, can be even more exacerbated in the situation of platform workers. This vulnerability experienced by casual and platform workers becomes even more concerning in the context of the COVID-19 outbreak.[341] Zero-hours and platform workers in the UK can be partially or fully excluded from labour protection. As it is quite common for them to fall within the intermediate employment category, they will miss out on some labour and social security rights, such as sick pay or unemployment benefits,[342] which become even more essential to cope with the global health crisis. What is more, in many cases these workers do not qualify for protection against dismissal, hence, employers can easily terminate their employment relationship, which becomes very opportune for them in the COVID-19 times. In the UK, a study on the economic impact of the COVID-19 found that 15% of workers 'with variable hours set by their employer [were] unemployed 'definitely' or 'probably' because of the coronavirus, compared to 4% of permanent employees.[343] Furthermore, these vulnerable workers do not even qualify for governmental income replacement schemes, such as short-time schemes,[344] which help workers to retain their job and income,[345] or self-employed income support schemes.[346] Considering the challenges posed to the world of work by the pandemic of COVID-19, the highlighted vulnerability of casual and platform workers will be further mentioned in the other country chapters of this dissertation.

341. N. Countouris, V. De Stefano, K. Ewing, M. Freedland, 'Covid-19 crisis makes clear a new concept of 'worker' is long overdue', Social Europe, April 2020, Available at: https://www.socialeurope.eu/covid-19-crisis-makes-clear-a-new-concept-of-worker-is-overdue.

342. V. De Stefano, 'Labour and social protection in times of Covid-19', Available at: https://www.youtube.com/watch?v=UQPzbdP0kEY&feature=youtu.be.

343. This share is expected to have increased, as the survey data was collected on 25 March 2020. A. Adams-Prassl, T. Boneva, M. Golin, Ch. Rauh, *Inequality in the impact of the coronavirus shock: New survey evidence for the UK*, IZA Discussion Paper No. 13183, 1 April 2020, p. 3.

344. Or temporary unemployment scheme as mentioned in F. Hendrickx, 'The coronavirus and the new world of work: renewed labour law questions', Regulating for Globalization Blog, April 2020, Available at: http://regulatingforglobalization.com/2020/04/01/the-coronavirus-and-the-world-of-work-renewed-labour-law-questions/.

345. V. De Stefano, 'Labour and social protection in times of Covid-19'. Available at: https://www.youtube.com/watch?v=UQPzbdP0kEY&feature=youtu.be.

346. N. Countouris, et al., 'Covid-19 crisis makes clear a new concept of 'worker' is long overdue', Social Europe, April 2020.

CHAPTER 3

Lavoro Intermittente in Italy

3.1 FROM ALMOST NO REGULATION TO SOME REGULATION OF CASUAL WORK

Labour market regulations encountered in Anglo-saxon and continental European countries seem to display a divergent approach to security and flexibility.[347] While the continental European model is characterized by tighter regulation and an extension of labour protection to workers; the focus of the Anglo-saxon model is, instead, in more flexibility, higher employment, which is associated with a degree of in-work poverty.[348] The first chapter of this dissertation focused on a representative country from the Anglo-saxon model - the United Kingdom - which showed to regulate zero-hours contracts loosely. In the second chapter, the focus is shifted to the pattern adopted by a continental European country - Italy - which tightly regulates casual work.

According to a study by the European Parliament on precarious employment in Europe, 'labour market regulation is held to be a key factor affecting risk of precariousness'.[349] Deriving from these considerations, in those labour markets which adopt solid labour regulations, the risk of precariousness is expected to be lower than in labour markets which do not follow the same approach.[350] Accordingly, Italy can be expected to have a lower level of precariousness related to casual work, compared to the United Kingdom, which only loosely regulates this form of work. The findings of the same study by the European Parliament revealed that zero-hours contracts constitute one of the main risks of precariousness in the UK.[351] When turning to Italy, *lavoro intermittente*, a prominent form of casual work at the national level, for which

347. European Parliament, *Precarious employment: Patterns, trends and Policy Strategies in Europe*, p. 28.
348. Denmark constitutes an exemption in this regard, where the high flexibility has not been associated with in-work poverty.
349. *Ibid.*, p. 28.
350. *Ibid.* However, this also depends on the personal circumstances of the worker.
351. European Parliament, *Precarious Employment* ..., p. 46.

a detailed legal framework is provided, does not seem to display a high risk of precariousness in the country.[352]

3.2 DEPICTING THE BIG PICTURE OF *LAVORO INTERMITTENTE* IN ITALY

As noted, Eurofound differentiates between two main types of casual work, concretely intermittent and on-call work.[353] On the one hand, intermittent work, or very short fixed-term work, refers to work for a very short period, where the employer approaches the employee on a regular or irregular basis. It is usually used for the completion of a project or a specific task. In intermittent work, working hours are guaranteed, but for a very limited period. On the other hand, on-call work refers to a continuous relationship between the parties, but the employer calls the employee only when the business needs arise. Within this typology of casual work, a few working hours can be guaranteed, known as the min-max contracts, or no working hours can be guaranteed at all, the so-called zero-hours contracts. In general, in the EU countries is noticed the presence of a single form of casual work, so either intermittent or on-call work. Italy constitutes an exception from this practice, as both forms of casual work are present in the country.[354] Nevertheless, more attention has been paid to on-call work, which in Italy is commonly referred to as *lavoro intermittente*, or *lavoro a chiamata*.[355]

Italy introduced atypical contracts in 1984, with a view to contributing to the decline of unemployment at the national level.[356] Nevertheless, it was only in 2003 that *lavoro intermittente* was introduced. Since 2003, *lavoro intermittente* has been subject to a normative evolution in Italy, which brought various changes to this legal institute. The labour market reforms, which altered the rules applicable to this form of work, became well known under the names of the politicians who proposed them. To start with, the *Biagi labour market reform (2003)*[357] introduced for the first time this type of work, altogether with other non-standard employment contracts, as a legal form of employment.[358] It was only after a few years, concretely in 2007, that the institute of

352. *Ibid.*, p. 44. In order to deal with the precarious situation of its atypical workers, Italy seems to go in the direction of levelling down the protection enjoyed by the insiders of the labour market, instead of levelling up the protection of its outsiders, according to O. Rymkevich, 'The Impact of Atypical Work in Italy and Russia', *European Labour Law Journal* Vol. 7 Issue 1, 2016, pp. 81-108, p. 107.
353. Eurofound, *New Forms of Employment*, p. 46.
354. Eurofound, *Casual work: characteristics and implications*, p. 1.
355. G. Ceneri, P. Rausei, 'Il lavoro intermittente e la forza della contrattazione aziendale', *ADAPT LABOUR STUDIES* e-Book series n. 77, 2019; The Italian Times, Contratto a chiamata 2020, cos'e e comme funziona, requisiti, durata, Available at: https://www.theitaliantimes.it/economia/contratto-a-chiamata-cos-e-come-funziona-requisiti-durata-retribuzione_291119/.
356. European Parliament, *Precarious Employment ...*, p. 28.
357. Law No. 30 of 2003.
358. F. Bano, 'Contratti flessibili: Lavoro a tempo parziale e lavoro intermittente', *Lavoro e diritto*, 2-3/2006, p. 293; M. Freedland, 'Rethinking the Personal Work Contract', *Current Legal Problems*, Vol. 58, Issue 1, 2005 pp. 517-542, OUP, p. 529.

lavoro intermittente was abolished with the welfare law.[359] Nevertheless, it was re-introduced again with another law in 2008,[360] to undergo further changes with the *Fornero labour market reform (2012)*.[361] Currently, *lavoro intermittente* finds a detailed regulation in a dedicated section of the Legislative Decree 15 June 2015, No. 81.[362] Such a legislative decree was introduced as part of the *labour market reform of Renzi (2015)*, known as the *Jobs Act*.[363]

The intention of the Italian lawmakers in presenting *lavoro intermittente* as a legal form of employment, was mainly to offer more employment opportunities, especially helping people entering (young people) and re-entering (displaced persons) the labour market. In addition, another essential aim was to tackle undeclared work or *lavoro grigio*.[364] For this reason, this form of work is widely used in the agriculture and household services. Nevertheless, a prominent spread of *lavoro intermittente* in Italy is noted in hotels and restaurants, where 60% of all employees are employed on a casual basis.[365] The importance of this form of work has been gradually growing, as statistics reveal that more and more people are involved in these types of contracts. Comparing the data from 2015 to 2017 shows that 12% of young people worked in these contracts in 2017, which is two times more than in 2015.[366] According to Eurofound, there were 436,946 on-call workers in 2017.[367] In 2018, there were more than 550.000 people hired in these contracts.[368] This increase seems to be especially attributed to the abrogation of the old vouchers system.[369] Nevertheless, as several legal limitations apply to *lavoro intermittente*, it constitutes a very small percentage of the Italian workforce.[370]

3.3 THE LEGAL FEATURES OF *LAVORO INTERMITTENTE* IN ITALY

Notwithstanding the normative evolution that *lavoro intermittente* has been subject to, this part will focus on the current legislative framework which applies to this form of work. As previously mentioned, Legislative Decree No. 81 of 15 June 2015, hereinafter Legislative Decree 81/2015, contains the main rules to govern this legal institute, including a legal definition, various restrictions, such as the overall duration of employment or the age of workers, formal requirements, and the typology of *lavoro*

359. International Encyclopedia for Labour Law and Industrial Relations, Editor: F. Hendrickx, Kluwer Law Online, p. 56.
360. Law No. 112/2008.
361. Act No. 92/2012.
362. Articles 13-18 of Legislative Decree 15 June 2015, No. 81.
363. The Jobs Act includes, *inter alia*, D. Lgs. 15 giugno 2015, nr.81, 'Disciplina organica dei contratti di lavoro e revisione della normativa in tema di mansioni, a norma dell'articolo 1, comma 7, della legge 10 dicembre 2014, n. 183'.
364. Eurofound, *New forms of employment*, p. 57.
365. ILO, *Non-standard employment around the world* ..., p. 125.
366. Istat, Rapporto 'Il mercato del lavoro 2018. Verso una lettura integrate', p. 7, Available at: https://www.istat.it/it/files/2019/02/Rapporto-mercato-del-lavoro.pdf.
367. Eurofound, *Casual work* ..., p. 11.
368. F. Barbieri, 'Lavoro a chiamata dal turismo alla sanita', 2019, Available at: https://www.ilsole24ore.com/art/-lavoro-chiamata-turismo-sanita-AEcBqTKH.
369. Eurofound, *Casual work* ..., p. 16.
370. *Ibid.*

intermittente. In addition, circulars of the Minister for Employment and Social Policies can be used to provide further clarification in relation to the rules stipulated in the L. Degree 81/2015. According to the Italian lawmakers, *lavoro intermittente* is considered subordinated or dependent work,[371] only for the periods of actual work. During periods of inactivity, no economic or normative treatment is extended to the worker, unless the worker has promised his availability to the employer, in which case the right to availability indemnity is applicable.[372] These features of the Italian system of regulation of *lavoro intermittente* will stand at the heart of the section below.

3.3.1 A Legal Definition

While some countries do not provide either minimum labour protection to forms of casual work or a legal definition,[373] Italy stands on the other side of the spectrum. The section regulating this type of work starts with legally defining the contract of *lavoro intermittente*. According to Article 13(1) of the Legislative Decree 81/2015: 'The contract of *"lavoro intermittente"* is the contract, also fixed-term, by means of which a worker makes himself available to an employer, who can *use the work performance in a discontinuous or intermittent way* according to the needs identified in the collective agreements, *also for predetermined periods during the week, month or year*. In the absence of a collective agreement, the Minister of Labour and Social Policy shall determine the situations where "lavoro intermittente" may be used.'[374]

According to this definition, two scenarios are available for allowing *lavoro intermittente* in Italy.[375] In the first case, the worker or *lavoratore intermittente* has no guarantee of working hours and remains at the disposal of the employer, who calls him 'in a discontinuous or intermittent way', in order to respond to the needs identified in collective agreements, and hence, not to the enterprise's general needs.[376] If these needs are not identified in collective agreements, they have to be identified in a decree of the Minister of Labour and Social Policies.[377] I in the second case, the worker can enjoy some guarantee by knowing that the work can be carried out 'in predetermined periods during the week, month or year'. Ceneri and Rausei refer to these two scenarios, as *lavoro intermittente* for objective requirements, and *lavoro intermittente* for temporal requirements.[378] In the case of a breach of the contractual clauses of the

371. *Ibid.*, p. 8.
372. Article 13(4) of Legislative Decree 81/2015.
373. One notable example is the United Kingdom, as already shown in Chapter 1.
374. This translation is based on the European Court of Justice Case C-143/16, *Abercrombie & Fitch Italia Srl v. Antonino Bordonaro*, 2017, para. 8, Available at: https://eur-lex.europa.eu/legal-content/EN/TXT/HTML/?uri=CELEX:62016CJ0143&from=EN.
375. V. De Stefano, 'Casual Work Beyond Casual Work in the EU ...', *European Labour Law Journal*, Vol. 7 Issue 3, 2016, p. 434.
376. S. Deakin, 'New Forms of Employment in Europe', p. 51.
377. Cliclavoro, Lavoro intermittente o a chiamata, Available at: https://www.cliclavoro.gov.it/NormeContratti/Contratti/Pagine/Contratto-di-lavoro-intermittente-o-a-chiamata.aspx.
378. G. Ceneri, P. Rausei, 'Il lavoro intermittente e la forza della contrattazione aziendale', ADAPT, (2018), p. 2.

collective agreement, which explicitly excludes the use of intermittent work, the consequence is the conversion of the contract into a full-time and permanent one.[379]

3.3.2 Limitations

Age Restriction

Pursuant to Article 13(2) of Legislative Decree No. 81, employers can, in all circumstances, offer *lavoro intermittente* to workers who are less than 24 years old and those who are more than 55 years old. This constitutes what has been labelled as *lavoro intermittente* for subjective reasons.[380] With regard to these subjects, employers can have the freedom to call them in, according to their business needs, without being restricted by the needs specified in collective agreements.[381] Such a provision of the law seems to be compatible with one of the aims for introducing this form of work, concretely sustaining people to enter and re-enter the labour market, as its implications lie mainly on young and displaced persons. The Fornero labour market reform presented this provision in the current form,[382] with the rationale that the flexibility associated with this form of work matches the needs of these two groups.[383] While supporting the entering and re-entering in the labour market of persons under 24 years old and those above 55 years old, this provision constitutes at the same time a limitation for employers to recourse to *lavoro intermittente* for workers belonging to a different age category.

What is more, Article 13(2) explicitly states that this contract can terminate automatically when a worker reaches the age of 25 years. This provision has been interpreted in the *Abercrombie & Fitch* case of the CJEU.[384] In this case, the referring court asked in a preliminary ruling, whether such a national provision is contrary to the principle of non-discrimination based on age, contained in both the Equal Treatment Directive,[385] and Article 21(1) of the Charter of Fundamental Rights of the European Union. The CJEU concluded that such a provision, which allows an employer to dismiss an intermittent worker as soon as the age of 25 has been reached, does not constitute age discrimination in breach of the above-mentioned legal acts. The justification lies in the fact that this 'provision pursues a legitimate aim of employment and labour market policy and the means laid down for the attainment of that objective are appropriate and necessary'.[386]

379. *Ibid.*, p. 3.
380. *Ibid.*
381. Article 13(2) of Legislative Decree No. 81.
382. Beforehand, also persons over 45 years of age could be included in this type of contract, without referring to the needs established in collective agreements.
383. Eurofound, *Casual work: Characteristics and implications*, p. 10.
384. Case C-143/16, *Abercrombie & Fitch Italia Srl v. Antonino Bordonaro*, 19 July 2017.
385. Council Directive 2000/78/EC of 27 November 2000 establishing a general framework for equal treatment in employment and occupation.
386. Case C-143/16, para. 47.

Overall Duration of *Lavoro Intermittente*

The Italian legislator has also decided to put a limit to the overall duration of this type of contract. Pursuant to Article 13(3) of Legislative Decree 81/2015, *lavoro intermittente* is allowed for each worker for up to 400 days of actual work within a period of three calendar years with the same employer. Circular No. 35/2013[387] clarifies the rules for the calculation of this period. If this period is exceeded, the consequence consists of the automatic conversion of *lavoro intermittente* into a standard employment contract of full-time and indefinite duration. However, there is an exception to this rule with regard to three specific sectors,[388] which frequently experience intermittent needs to use this form of work for a longer period. The law explicitly mentions tourism, public service, such as bars, restaurants, hotels, and entertainment sectors.

Further Limitations

To be noted is that *lavoro intermittente* is expressly not allowed in public administration in Italy.[389] In this respect, the Supreme Court of Italy has emphasized in a decision, that it is prohibited for civil servants to be involved in this type of work, even outside working hours.[390] Moreover, Article 14 of the Legislative Decree 81/2015 mentions three cases, when it is forbidden to recourse to *lavoro intermittente*. First, it is forbidden to use this type of work to substitute workers who exercise the right to strike. Second, recourse to *lavoro intermittente* is prohibited 'at production units in which collective redundancies have occurred within the previous six months and which involved workers assigned to the same tasks as those covered by the intermittent employment contract, or at production units in which there is a suspension of work or a reduction in working hours under the redundancy fund, which affect workers assigned to the tasks referred to in the intermittent employment contract'.[391] Third, *lavoro intermittente* cannot be used by employers, who have not carried out the risk assessment, in accordance with the legislation on the protection of workers' health and safety.

The ban on exclusivity clauses has not been explicitly stipulated in the legal framework regulating *lavoro intermittente*. This is contrary to other countries, such as the UK, where this became necessary, due to the widespread practices of employers in including exclusivity clauses in zero-hours contracts. Notwithstanding the lack of a prohibition in Legislative Decree 81/2015, a circular in Italy seems to clarify this situation. Pursuant to Circular No. 4/2005 of the Minister of Labour and Social Policies,[392] the *lavoratori intermittenti* can provide their services to more than one

387. Circolare N. 35/2013, Available at: https://www.cliclavoro.gov.it/Normative/Circolare_29_agosto_2013_n.35.pdf.
388. Ilsole 24 ore, Lavoro a chiamata: nessun limite d'impiego per alberghi, bar e ristoranti, Available at: http://amp.ilsole24ore.com/pagina/AE3bwaFH.
389. Article 13(5) of the Legislative Decree 81/2015.
390. Corte di Cassazione, sez. Lavoro, sentenza 11 luglio – 30 novembre 2017, n. 28797, Available at: https://www.studiocerbone.com/corte-cassazione-sentenza-30-novembre-2017-n-28797-licenziamento-disciplinare-sottoscrizione-ulteriore-contratto-lavoro-chiamata-svolgimento-mera-collaborazione-principio-del/.
391. Translated from Italian using the translation tool Deep L Translator.
392. Circolare No. 4/2005 del Ministero del Lavoro e delle Politiche Sociali, Cumulo con altri contratti di lavoro, p. 5.

employer, provided that the performance of more than one job is feasible and that there is no competition between the two or more employers.[393]

Formal Requirements

The contract of *lavoro intermittente* must be stipulated in writing, for the purpose of proofing some specific elements. These compulsory elements have been specified in Article 15 and comprise: (a) the duration and hypothesis, either objective or subjective, which allow for the conclusion of the contract in accordance with Article 13; (b) the place and modalities of the availability, eventually guaranteed by the worker, and the worker's notice of call, which cannot be less than one working day; (c) the economic and regulatory treatment of the worker for the service performed and the related availability indemnity, where applicable; (d) the form and modalities, by which the employer is entitled to request the performance of the work, as well as modalities for measuring such a performance; (e) the timeframe and modalities of payment of the salary and the availability indemnity; (f) safety measures necessary in relation to the type of activity provided in the contract.

In addition to these formal requirements, the law stipulates as well another obligation for the employer. According to Article 15(2) of the Legislative Decree 81/2015, employers have to inform representatives of trade unions on an annual basis, on their recourse to the contract of *lavoro intermittente*. Furthermore, employers have an obligation to notify prior to starting work: (a) workers at least one working day in advance, and (b) the territorial direction of labour competent by territory, before the performance of a service, the duration of which is not more than thirty days.[394] In the case of breaching this last obligation, a fine from EUR 400-EUR 2,400 will be imposed on the employer for each worker, for whom there was a duty to notify the authorities.

3.3.3 The Typology of *Lavoro Intermittente*

Based on the just-mentioned legal framework, different types of *lavoro intermittente* contracts can be identified. To start with the duration of this type of contract, it can be concluded either for a fixed-term or indefinite period.[395] However, it should be noted that in the case of *lavoro intermittente* concluded for a fixed-term period, the rules which will be applicable, will be those governing intermittent work,[396] instead of those regulating fixed-term work.[397] Another typology of this form of work is created by the promise of the worker to accept offers of work. As the employer calls in the intermittent worker when the business needs arise, the worker can either promise or not promise, to accept offers of work. While in other national systems, this does not entail any

393. The Italian Times, Contratto a chiamata 2020: cos'e e come funziona, requisiti, durata, Available at: https://www.theitaliantimes.it/economia/contratto-a-chiamata-cos-e-come-funziona-requisiti-durata-retribuzione_290120/.
394. Article 15(3) of the Legislative Decree 81/2015.
395. Ceneri and Rausei, 'Il lavoro intermittente e la forza della contrattazione aziendale', p. 2; Eurofound, *Casual work: characteristics and implications*, p. 8.
396. Article 13-18 of the Legislative Decree 81/2015.
397. *Ibid.*, Articles 19-29.

difference,[398] in Italy, it gives rise to a typology of *lavoro intermittente*, concretely with or without availability indemnity or *indennità di disponibilità*. Even in the case of such a promise by the worker, the employer would be under no obligation to offer work, or guarantee some working hours. Instead, the employer has an obligation to pay monthly compensation for the availability of the worker. Article 16 of the Legislative Decree 81/2015 provides some clarification in relation to this compensation accorded to the worker. The amount of the availability indemnity is determined by collective agreements, however, it cannot be below a minimum level established by the decree of the Minister of Labour and Social Policies.[399] The availability indemnity is subject to social security contributions for its actual amount.[400] Special rules apply to availability indemnity in the case of illness or other events, which make the worker temporarily unavailable to work.[401] In such cases, the compensation will be suspended, and the worker has an obligation to inform the employer about it. In breach of this obligation, the worker may lose the availability indemnity for a period of fifteen days. What is more, the unjustified refusal to accept an offer of work may constitute not only dismissal grounds but also lead to the return of the availability indemnity, already granted before the refusal.[402]

3.3.4 The Application of the Legal Rules in Practice

Notwithstanding the enshrinement of the just-mentioned legal rules on *lavoro intermittente*, some misuses have been noted with regard to this work arrangement in practice. For instance, Eurofound reports that Italian employers use these contracts in several cases when standard employment contracts would have been more suitable.[403] This finding has also been confirmed even in a more recent report by Eurofound,[404] according to which, Italian employers continue to circumvent labour regulation and avoid the associated costs, by using casual work contracts, instead of standard ones. Other abuses have also been observed to take place in Italy, for example, employers misreporting the real number of hours performed by intermittent workers.[405] Furthermore, the applicability of the availability indemnity can also be different in practice. In this framework, Eurofound states in a report about work on demand,[406] that the availability indemnity in Italy represents something exceptional. In general, workers fear refusing calls of work, as this might threaten future job opportunities. What is labelled as the 'implicit threat' mechanism by some labour law scholars is again

398. For instance, as already explained, in the United Kingdom.
399. Article 16(1) of Legislative Decree 81/2015.
400. *Ibid.*, para. 3.
401. *Ibid.*, para. 4.
402. *Ibid.*, para. 5.
403. Eurofound, *New Forms of Employment*, p. 70, based on Isfol Report (2006).
404. Eurofound, *Casual Work: Characteristics and Implications*", New forms of employments series, Publications Office of the European Union, Luxembourg, (2019) p. 27.
405. *Ibid.*
406. Eurofound, *Work on Demand: Recurrence, Effects and Challenges*, Research Report 2018, p. 7.

pressing, and workers seem to be willing to accept calls, even if no availability indemnity is guaranteed to them.

One important factor, which could be attributed to the persistence of such abuses, was found to be the reluctance of workers to report them. Intermittent workers fear not only rejecting calls of work but also reporting such abusive conduct, as this can be translated into no shifts for the future, or losing the opportunity for more stable employment. Nevertheless, a recent shift was noticed in this regard, with workers being more prone to report these abuses to trade unions.[407]

3.4 *LAVORO INTERMITTENTE*: OVERLAPS WITH OTHER FORMS OF WORK

3.4.1 An Overlap with Voucher-Based Work for Occasional Working Activities

While it is true that the boundaries between various forms of non-standard employment can be blurred,[408] in the Italian labour market, this becomes prominent in the context of *lavoro intermittente* and voucher-based work for occasional work activities, hereinafter voucher-based work.[409] Voucher-based work has proliferated in a few European countries, *inter alia*, Italy,[410] where it was introduced by Legislative Decree No. 276 of 2003.[411] Initially, it was introduced for certain activities, such as grape harvesting,[412] and it targeted specific groups of workers, such as students, retired persons, and housewives. Therefore, the original aim of presenting voucher-based work consisted in tackling informality and integrating some marginalized groups of workers. Over time, the just-mentioned restrictions on activities and categories of workers to be involved in voucher-based work were abolished. With the liberalization of the legislation on voucher-based work in Italy,[413] a boom in their use was noted, while the effectiveness in tackling informality was put into question.[414]

The voucher-based work scheme for occasional work constitutes a form of work with a peculiar method of payment. Eurofound indicates that the worker is paid in vouchers, which the employer acquires from a third party, that is usually the

407. *Ibid.*, p. 30.
408. ILO, *Non-standard employment around the world ...*, p. 23.
409. Eurofound, *New forms of employment*, p. 82.
410. *Ibid.* Other countries where voucher-based work is prominent include Greece, Belgium, France, etc.
411. Eurofound, *Italy: New voucher-based scheme provokes debate*, 2017, Available at: https://www.eurofound.europa.eu/publications/article/2017/italy-new-voucher-based-work-scheme-provokes-debate.
412. Eurofound, *New forms of employment, Voucher-based work, Italy*, p. 1, Available at: https://www.eurofound.europa.eu/sites/default/files/page/field_ef_documents/45_-_ef1461_-_it-service_vouchers_final.pdf.
413. This liberalization happened for the first time in 2012, as pointed out by V. De Stefano, and A. Aloisi, *European legal frameworks for digital labour platforms*, European Commission, Luxembourg, 2018, p. 32.
414. ILO, *Non-standard employment around the world ...*, p. 26.

government.[415] The voucher comprises a package of hourly pay and social security coverage, where the hourly pay varies around EUR 8-EUR 9, and the remaining part goes for social security and administration costs.[416] The individual income tax does not apply to voucher-based work.[417] However, 'the voucher worker does not benefit from unemployment insurance, maternity leave and so on'.[418]

Another pivotal feature of voucher-based work concerns its use, which is restricted to specific tasks, fixed-term assignments,[419] or, as stated by the law, occasional or sporadic working activities.[420] At this point, an overlap with *lavoro intermittente* occurs, considering that employers can use the latter in a discontinuous or intermittent way, according to the needs generally identified in collective agreements, but also for predetermined periods during the week, month or year. The existence of this intersection and the different legal restrictions applicable to both types of work, imply that whenever there are limitations in place for *lavoro intermittente*, employers tend to recourse to voucher-based work and *vice versa*. By way of example, the abolishment of the vouchers system in 2017 led to an increase in the number of *lavoro intermittente*.[421] As already indicated with respect to *lavoro intermittente*, voucher-based work can also be misused. Therefore, instead of using it on an occasional or discontinued basis, some Italian employers were observed to regularly use this type of work, instead of standard work.[422] Moreover, further abuse was reported by trade unions, which expressed their concern on the issue of employers 'paying only some wages in vouchers and the rest in cash'.[423]

With a view to limit such abuses, voucher-based work was abolished with Legislative Decree Law 17 March 2017 No. 25.[424] Nonetheless, shortly afterwards, it was re-introduced with some modifications in Article 54-*bis* of the *Legislative Decree No. 50 of 24 April 2017*.[425] Further alterations were also brought by Article 2-*bis* of the so-called Dignity Decree.[426] According to the current legal framework applicable to voucher-based work for occasional work activities, two different schemes were detected based on the users of it, namely private individuals, and ' "other clients" such as self-employed workers, professionals, entrepreneurs, associations, NGOs and public

415. Eurofound, *New Forms of Employment*, pp. 84-85.
416. Eurofound, *New forms of employment, Voucher-based work, Italy*, p. 3.
417. Eurofound, *Italy: New voucher-based scheme provokes debate*.
418. Eurofound, *New forms of employment, Voucher-based work, Italy*, p. 3.
419. Eurofound, *New forms of employment*, p. 82.
420. Article 54-*bis*, 13 of Legislative Decree No. 50/2017. *See also*: https://www.inps.it/nuovoportaleinps/default.aspx?itemdir=51100#h3heading1.
421. Eurofound, *Casual work ...*, p. 11.
422. S. Michalopoulos, 'Proper voucher use will move people into labour market, EU official says', Available at: https://www.euractiv.com/section/economy-jobs/news/commission-proper-voucher-use-will-move-more-people-into-labour-market/1141564/.
423. C. Balmer, 'Italy scraps employment voucher system to avoid referendum showdown', Available at: https://uk.reuters.com/article/uk-italy-employment-reform/italy-scraps-employment-voucher-system-to-avoid-referendum-showdown-idUKKBN16O1UV.
424. European Commission, Flash reports on labour law 2017, p. 34.
425. The legislative decree No. 50/2017 laying down urgent financial provisions, initiatives for local and regional authorities, further assistance for areas affected by earthquakes and development measures, came into force with the Law No. 96 of 21 June 2017.
426. D. Legge 12 Luglio 2018, n. 87, known as Decreto Dignita.

administrations'.[427] The first scheme, which is used for family needs, is known as 'libretto famiglia', while the second one is 'PrestO voucher'. Depending on the user of the voucher scheme, some restrictions apply with respect to the activities allowed, workers included, and economic thresholds. Concerning the permitted activities, individual users can use this form of work only for domestic and care services, while public administrations can use it only for activities that have a solidarity nature.[428] However, private sector clients who want to use voucher-based work must also comply with certain conditions. To be able to use the voucher-based scheme, they should only employ up to five permanent employees;[429] be a construction or extractive company; and use it as part of subcontracting agreements. What is more, agricultural firms can employ only specific categories of workers, such as students, retirees, unemployed, and beneficiaries of income support through this type of contract. Additionally, a crucial restriction related to voucher-based work is compliance with economic thresholds. For instance, for each worker, a maximum yearly income of EUR 5,000 should not be exceeded.[430] Furthermore, financial limits also apply to clients who want to use this form of work.[431] A final limitation prohibits workers who have, or had in the previous six months, a subordinated relation, or coordinated and continuous collaboration with employers, to offer voucher-based services to these employers.[432]

As already explained, while both forms of work serve the same needs, they are subject to different restrictions imposed by the Italian legislator. Voucher-based work seems to be subject to wider restrictions extended to its activities, workers involved, and financial thresholds. However, *lavoro intermittente* is more encouraged for specific activities such as tourism, public services, and entertainment, where the maximum duration of 400 days per three years with the same employer can be disregarded. Moreover, certain categories of workers are particularly encouraged to be included in this form of work, concretely young people, who are less than 24 years old, and workers who are more than 55 years old. Contrary to voucher work, *lavoro intermittente* is not allowed in the public administration domain.

3.4.2 An Overlap with Platform Work

3.4.2.1 Platform Work in the Italian Context

Platform work has inevitably emerged also in Italy. The emergence in the Italian context, dates back around ten years ago, with a first prominence of the services

427. Eurofound, *Italy: New voucher-based scheme provokes debate.*
428. For example, projects that target people in need; emergency activities in response to natural and environmental disasters; solidarity activities and social, cultural, sports or charitable events.
429. With the exception of hotels and accommodation companies operating in the tourism sector, which are allowed to have employed up to eight permanent employees, in order to use the services of voucher workers, who need to be exclusively students, retirees, unemployed and beneficiaries of income support, as provided by Article 2-*bis* (c) of D. Legge 12 Luglio 2018, n. 87, known as Decreto Dignita.
430. Article 54-*bis*, 1(a) of Legislative Decree 50/2017.
431. *Ibid.*, Article 54-*bis*, 1.
432. *Ibid.*, Article 54-*bis*, 5.

delivered online. Later on, in 2018, a prevalence of the services delivered in the physical world was noted.[433] Therefore, the two forms of platform work,[434] namely crowdwork and work on demand via apps, which differ based on the place of the execution of work, can be found at the domestic level. This dichotomy, however, is not a rigid one, as a wide variety of business models can be found within these categories. For instance, online platform work can range from micro-tasks, which usually comprise dull and repetitive tasks such as tagging photos, to intellectual tasks, such as the design of a logo.[435] However, some of the offline platforms, which operate in the Italian local market, include, for instance: care services (Le Cicogne), cleaning (Helpling), food delivery (Deliveroo), and manual craft (Tabbid).[436] What is more, a wide array of terms is observed when referring to platform work, among which, 'economia dei lavoretti'[437] has often been used in the Italian context, a term which suggests a distance from the traditional vocabulary of the labour market.[438] Regarding the size of the phenomenon, in the lack of official statistics, some estimates indicate that its incidence can range from 700 to one million workers, corresponding to 2.6% of the Italian workforce.[439] The outcomes of another survey conducted by FEPS, Uni Europa, and the University of Hertfordshire, reveal that 22% of working-age people had provided services through a platform, even though only half of them provided services at least weekly.[440]

The food delivery sector of the platform economy has attained increased attention at the national level.[441] Food delivery couriers have grabbed the attention of the media, the judiciary system, and lawmakers in Italy. The drivers of such a focus were the protests organized by Foodora couriers in Turin, calling for better working conditions, coverage of work-related expenses, and a reclassification of their employment relationship as a subordinate one.[442] Nevertheless, as the protests and strikes did not bring the desired outcomes, the food couriers decided to initiate litigation. The

433. V. De Stefano, A. Aloisi, *Digital age, Employment and working conditions of selected types of platform work, National context analysis Italy*, Eurofound Working Paper, 2018, p. 2.
434. Many international institutions and scholars refer to such a dichotomy, for instance, J. Berg et al., *Digital Labour Platforms and the Future of Work, Towards Decent Work in the Online World*, ILO Report, 2018, p. XV.
435. Eurofound, *Employment and working conditions of selected types of platform work*, p. 14.
436. V. De Stefano, A. Aloisi, *ibid.*, p. 3.
437. Translated into English as gig-economy.
438. For a complete list of terms used in Italy to refer to platform work, *see* Eurofound, *Employment and working conditions of selected types of platform work*, p. 10.
439. V. De Stefano, A. Aloisi, *Digital age, Employment and working conditions of selected types of platform work, National context analysis Italy*, p. 3, based on the online survey of Fondazione Rodolfo DeBenedetti, where 15,000 respondents from the working-age population participated.
440. U. Huws, N.H. Spencer, S.D. Syrdal, and K. Holts, *Work in the European gig economy: Research results from the UK, Sweden, Germany, Austria, The Netherlands, Switzerland and Italy*, FEPS, UNI-Europa and University of Hertfordshire, 2017, p. 16. Platform work was defined in this survey as paid work via an online platform.
441. Eurofound, *Employment and working conditions of selected types of platform work*, p. 41.
442. A. Tassinari, V. Maccarrone, 'The Mobilisation of Gig Economy Couriers in Italy: Some Lessons for the Trade Union Movement', *Transfer: European Review of Labour and Research*, 3/2017, p. 354.

judicial outcomes reached by the Employment Tribunal,[443] and the Appeal Court in Turin,[444] were unfavourable. According to these rulings, the flexibility enjoyed by the couriers in accepting and rejecting offers of work constituted a decisive element for the confirmation of the independent contractor's status.[445] In contrast with these decisions, the Italian Supreme Court ruled that the employment protection legislation is applicable to work organized by another party (the so-called *lavoro etero-organizzato*), *inter alia*, by a platform, unless a collective agreement says otherwise.[446] Notwithstanding that Foodora company does not operate in Italy anymore and the judgments of higher courts are not binding for the lower ones,[447] this ruling has the potential to bring a ray of hope for the labour protection of other platform workers.

At the legislative level, some provisions relevant to platform work have been recently adopted in Italy. The existing legal framework,[448] which is part of the Jobs Act reform package, was amended through a recent legislative decree.[449] The subsequent changes introduced an expansion to the personal scope of application of Article 2 of the Legislative Decree No. 81/2015, where 'workers whose personal performance is organized by the client even by means of digital platforms' are now covered by all employment and labour protections unless a collective agreement stipulates differently.[450] Furthermore, a new chapter was added to this normative framework, to specifically regulate the situation of self-employed delivery couriers, who operate in urban areas, by using bicycles or motor vehicles, in the unlikely event that they do not fall within the scope of application of Article 2.[451] Some of the protections applicable to these delivery couriers comprise, *inter alia*, a written form of contract, mandatory insurance against accidents at work and occupational diseases, and wages to be determined by social partners within one year of the entry into force of the law, otherwise national collective agreements in similar sectors should be referred to.[452] What is more, delivery couriers are also covered by a collective agreement in the logistics sector.[453]

443. Sentenza n. 778/2018, Available at: https://www.bollettinoadapt.it/wp-content/uploads/2018/05/7782018.pdf.
444. Sentenza n. 26/2019.
445. V. De Stefano, 'Platform work and labour protection. Flexibility is not enough', Available at: http://regulatingforglobalization.com/2018/05/23/platform-work-labour-protection-flexibility-not-enough/?doing_wp_cron=1583405629.7317709922790527343750.
446. *La Corte Suprema di Cassazione* 24 gennaio 2020, Case No. 1663/2020.
447. A. Aloisi, V. De Stefano, 'Delivering employment rights to platform workers', 2020, Available at: https://www.rivistailmulino.it/news/newsitem/index/Item/News:NEWS_ITEM:5018.
448. Legislative Decree of 15 June 2015, n. 81 disciplina organica dei contratti di lavoro e revisione della normativa in tema di mansioni, a norma dell'articolo 1, comma 7, della legge 10 dicembre 2014, n. 183.
449. Legislative Decree of 3 September 2019, n. 101 disposizioni urgenti per la tutela del lavoro e per la risoluzione di crisi aziendali.
450. A. Aloisi, V. De Stefano, 'Delivering employment rights to platform workers'.
451. Capo V-bis, Articolo 47-*bis*, comma 1, Legislative Decree no. 81 of 15 June 2015.
452. *Ibid.*, Articolo 47-*ter*.
453. Eurofound, *Employment and working conditions of selected types of platform work*, p. 43.

3.4.2.2 *Platform Work Perceived as Casual Work Intermediated by Technology*

After having a brief overview of platform work in Italy, platform work will be observed in a broader context, where some common threads with casual work arrangements will be explored in the Italian context. Platform work is cutting-edge in the use of Information and Communication Technology (ICT) means to match the demand and supply sides of labour at a very high speed, something which has not been encountered in the past.[454] Nevertheless, in many instances, platforms go beyond this matchmaking function[455] and intervene in the standard-setting of the work performance. This interference can be manifested in elements[456] such as selecting workers and performing check-ups before allowing them to use the service,[457] fixing prices, setting standards, e.g., wearing a uniform,[458] or controlling through the rating system,[459] something which may lead to arbitrary exclusions of workers from the platform in case of poor ratings.[460] Such an intervention resembles the exercise of the managerial prerogatives that are typically reserved for employers, and at this point, the issue becomes pertinent in a labour law context. By acknowledging solely the innovation and entrepreneurship spirit underlying platform work, a denial of workers' rights and exacerbation of their working conditions might occur.[461] What is more, in addition to restoring the scope of labour law,[462] it becomes essential to look for the specific position of platform work within the labour law ambit as a second step.

Against this background, ILO officials have included in a shared analysis, both non-standard and platform work, pointing out the similarities of platform work with forms of non-standard employment, especially with casual work.[463] Such an approach is further confirmed by the research conducted by FEPS, Uni-Europa, and the University of Hertfordshire, on work in the European gig economy.[464] This research includes as a case study, *inter alia*, Italy, and according to the main findings, platform work has been perceived not as a distinctive form of work, but as 'part of a continuum of casual,

454. V. De Stefano, 'The rise of the just-in-time workforce ...', p. 6.
455. J. Prassl, *Humans as a Service: The Promise and Perils of Work in the Gig Economy*, Oxford University Press, 2018, p. 5.
456. The European Court of Justice referred to some of these elements in case C-434/15, *Asociación Profesional Élite Taxi v. Uber Systems Spain SL*, 2017. For a brief overview of this case *see*: I. Durri, *Asociación Profesional Élite Taxi v. Uber Systems Spain SL*, Cambridge University Press, 2019.
457. J. Prassl, *Humans as a service ...*, p. 55.
458. For instance TaskRabbit workers have to wear bright green t-shorts showing the company's logo.
459. J. Prassl, *Humans as a service, the promise and perils of work in the gig economy*, p. 5.
460. H. Doug, ' Fired from Uber: why drivers get deactivated, and how to get reactivated', Ride sharing driver, 2016.
461. J. Berg and V. De Stefano, 'La gig-economy e il "nuovo" lavoro occasionale', Available at: https://archivio.eticaeconomia.it/la-gig-economy-e-il-nuovo-lavoro-occasionale/.
462. J. Prassl, *Humans as a service ...*, p. 105.
463. International Labour Office-Geneva, *Non-standard employment around the world: Understanding challenges, shaping prospects*, p. 39.
464. U. Huws et al., *Work in the European gig economy: Research results from the UK, Sweden, Germany, Austria, The Netherlands, Switzerland and Italy*, p. 201.

on-call, temporary or other forms of contingent work',[465] with blurred boundaries, especially with forms of casual or just-in-time work.[466] In the Italian context, the discussion on platform work has been quite lively, and some labour law scholars have, indeed, suggested framing platform work within broader labour market trends, concretely the casualization and fragmentation of labour relations.[467] De Stefano and Aloisi propose in this regard to extend the current legal framework to platform workers, instead of adopting specific laws for them.[468] In the same vein, the Italian National Institute of Social Security (INPS) considers the most appropriate legal regime to regulate platform work that on *lavoro intermittente o a chiamata*, as a regulatory option which offers both flexibility and security at the same time.[469]

The rationale for suggesting the position of platform work in the context of casual work arrangements seems to be the precariousness underlying the working conditions in both forms of work. In the public debate in Italy, it has been acknowledged that platform work is associated with a degradation of working conditions.[470] In the context of platform work, the lack of guaranteed working hours has been highlighted, as the working hours of platform workers can last for even a few minutes.[471] In observing the working hours of Deliveroo riders operating in Italy, it was noticed that their working times were not set in the contract with the company, and their right to choose them was dependable on the rating and ranking systems.[472] What is more, these workers experienced not only very long hours but also underemployment, whereas online platform workers, who work in different geographical and time zones, were often bound to work at night or during unsocial hours, in order to answer the calls of clients that are based in different zones of the world.[473]

Furthermore, both casual and platform workers face also other similar issues, such as jobs and income insecurity, with more exacerbation on the platform work's side. In the case of platform workers, their income insecurity was attributed to the frequent changes in prices by platform companies and the business models adopted by them.[474] Income insecurity also becomes extreme, considering that platform workers

465. *Ibid.*, p. 10.
466. *Ibid.*, p. 48.
467. V. De Stefano, A. Aloisi, *Employment and working conditions of selected types of platform work, National context analysis, Italy*, p. 4; V. De Stefano, 'The rise of the just-in-time workforce ...', p. 11.
468. *Ibid.*
469. INPS (Istituto nazionale della previdenza sociale) (2018), XVII Rapporto Annuale, L'INPS al servizio del Paese.
470. V. De Stefano, A. Aloisi, *Employment and working conditions of selected types of platform work, National context analysis, Italy*, p. 4.
471. V. De Stefano, A. Aloisi, *Il lavoro che vogliamo, governare le technologie per reinventare il futuro*, Laterza 2020, p. 155.
472. Don't Gig Up! Project, Final Report, eds T. Haipeter, D. Owczarek, M. Faioli, and F. Iudicone, 2020, p. 11.
473. V. De Stefano in 'The Rise of the "Just-in-time Workforce": On-demand Work, Crowdwork and Labour Protection in the Gig-economy', International Labour Office, Inclusive Labour Markets, Labour Relations and Working Conditions Branch-Geneva: ILO, Conditions of work and employment series; No. 71, (2016) p. 10.
474. Kilhoffer et al., *Study to gather evidence on the working conditions of platform workers*, 2020, p. 75.

are normally paid by task, and in case of poor ratings, they can be deprived of getting paid. Further contributing to the income insecurity are the so-called wage theft practices,[475] i.e., the cases when the client retains the work and refuses to pay the platform worker, without giving any reasons for the refusal.

Casual work arrangements are generally associated with low income and in-work poverty.[476] This implies that platform workers, who in many cases work only for a few minutes, have an even lower income.[477] Furthermore, their level of pay is highly problematic, as it is allowed to fall below the minimum living wage, which is especially extremely low for online workers from developed countries. In the Italian context, national experts noted that platform workers did not meet the minimum income requirements for the purposes of mandatory social security.[478] In another study, Italian experts also point out that the costs associated with platform work, such as gas, insurance, etc., are usually paid by platform workers, who are not entitled to a reimbursement in this regard.[479]

On top of this, both forms of work can be excluded from some, or the entirety, of labour protections associated with the employee status.[480] As concerns *lavoratori intermittenti* in Italy, they have the status of 'employees' only for the periods of actual service, and hence, they can end up being excluded from some important labour rights, which require a minimum length of service.[481] On the other side, the majority of platform workers are legally qualified as self-employed by the platforms.[482] Nevertheless, in light of recent rules, platform workers might become entitled to all labour protections, notwithstanding their employment status. This happens in case the court establishes the existence of *lavoro etero-organizzato*, or work organized by another party, *inter alia*, through a platform.[483] In the absence of this establishment, some labour and social security protections can still be ensured, although only to a certain segment of the platform economy, namely that of the self-employed delivery couriers.[484]

To sum up, the above-mentioned shared features of insecurity, extreme flexibility, and marginalization, can pave the way to considerations of platform work as an extreme form of casual work.

3.5 CONCLUSION

As it has been explained, Italy provides the example of a country, that extensively regulates a certain form of casual work, namely on-call work, known as *lavoro*

475. Analytical document of the European Commission, p. 14.
476. *Ibid.*, p. 226.
477. *Ibid.*, p. 60.
478. Eurofound, *Employment and working conditions of selected types of platform work*, p. 47.
479. Kilhoffer et al., *Study to gather evidence on the working conditions of platform workers*, p. 74.
480. For platform workers *see* V. De Stefano, A. Aloisi, *Employment and working conditions of selected types of platform work, National context analysis, Italy*, p. 5.
481. Article 13(4) of the Legislative Decree 81/2015.
482. A notable exemption can constitute YouGenio, an Italian platform which provides domestic services, which offers employment contracts to its workers.
483. Article 2 of the Legislative Decree 81/2015.
484. *Ibid.*, Capo V-bis.

intermittente at the national level. This form of work has been subject to various normative changes, which comprise, *inter alia*, an abolishment in 2007. Currently, *lavoro intermittente* is increasing in numbers and importance, however, it still represents a small share of the Italian workforce, due to the legal restrictions in place. At the outset, the current legal framework provides a detailed legal definition of *lavoro intermittente*. According to it: (a) no working hours can be guaranteed to these workers, who can be called in according to the intermittent or discontinuous needs of the employer, which must be pre-identified in collective agreements; or (b) some guarantee of work can be possible, for predetermined periods during the week, month or year. On the employment status of these workers, the *lavoratore intermittente* is considered as a worker only for the periods of actual work, which implies an exclusion from crucial labour protections, which depend on the length of service. What is more, one purpose of the Italian lawmaker for introducing this form of work, consists in facilitating the entry into the labour market of young workers (less than 24 years old) and the re-entry of potentially displaced workers (over 55 years old). With respect to these categories of workers, they can be called in to respond to the intermittent or discontinuous needs of the enterprise, without these needs being determined in advance in a collective agreement. Furthermore, *lavoro intermittente* is encouraged in the tourism, public service, and entertainment sector, where the general restriction on the overall duration of employment to 400 days per 3 years with the same employer, is not applicable. Another peculiar feature of the Italian regime is the stipulation of the right to a monthly availability indemnity, as a reward for workers who promise to be available for work. Nevertheless, in practice, this on-call allowance might remain exceptional, due to workers' fear of rejecting calls of work.

Lavoro intermittente in Italy does not represent a watertight typology, and as such, frequent overlaps have been observed with other forms of work, which have proliferated in the country. Against this background, an overlap is noticed between *lavoro intermittente* and voucher-based work for occasional work activities, where voucher-based work represents an important feature of the Italian labour market. Both forms of work aim to fight informal work and create employment opportunities, especially for marginalized workers. *Lavoro intermittente* is more predominant in the public service sector; voucher-based work is allowed only for certain activities depending on the user of it. For instance, private individuals can only use it for domestic and care services. Notwithstanding their differences, both forms of work are used to respond to the same needs, concretely to the discontinuous or occasional needs, while divergent legal restrictions apply to them. The above-mentioned overlap implies that when legal restrictions for voucher-based work are in place, employers tend to recourse to *lavoro intermittente*. *Vice versa*, voucher-based work was used instead of casual work arrangements when restrictions on the latter were in place. Current legal restrictions applicable to voucher-based work consist of the type of activities and workers allowed, but also economic thresholds for workers and clients who want to use it. On the other side, the most common legal restrictions applicable to *lavoro intermittente* comprise the predetermination of discontinuous needs in collective agreements, limitation in the overall duration of employment and further prohibitions, e.g., the prohibition for it to be used to replace workers, who exercise the right to strike. A further overlap, which represents the crux of this dissertation, is the one between casual work and platform work. Discussions at the academic and institutional level in Italy have pointed out framing platform work within broader trends of casual work arrangements. The reason for this can be found in the precarious working conditions faced by both categories of workers. This is even more exacerbated in the situation of platform workers, e.g., Deliveroo riders in Italy demonstrate to have a lack of guaranteed working hours, which entails income and job insecurity for this kind of workers. Furthermore, low levels of pay, and a lack of reimbursement of work-related costs, was further observed in the Italian context.

In the exceptional times of the COVID-19 outbreak, the precariousness faced by casual and platform workers has been further highlighted,[485] and the consequences of their exclusion from labour protection are felt more than ever. For instance, many *lavoratori intermittenti* in Italy are excluded from some labour and social security rights depending on the length of service, e.g., sick pay and unemployment benefits, the enjoyment of which can be paramount in this crisis period. However, the majority of platform workers are excluded not only by some but also from the entirety of labour protections. Notwithstanding that the Italian Supreme Court's ruling opened up a promising perspective by recognizing *lavoro etero-organizzato* in the context of platform work – a category that is entitled to full labour protections – platform workers still need to trigger litigations to this end. Furthermore, these workers seem to fall outside the scope of protection of government schemes in response to the pandemic, such as short-time schemes, or even more general measures such as one-off payments, loans, and mortgages relief.[486]

485. N. Countouris, V. De Stefano, K. Ewing, M. Freedland, 'Covid-19 crisis makes clear a new concept of 'worker' is long overdue', Social Europe, April 2020, Available at: https://www.socialeurope.eu/covid-19-crisis-makes-clear-a-new-concept-of-worker-is-overdue.
486. V. De Stefano, 'Labour and social protection in times of Covid-19', Available at: https://www.youtube.com/watch?v=UQPzbdP0kEY&feature=youtu.be.

CHAPTER 4
On-call Work in the Netherlands

4.1 THE WIDE ARRAY OF NON-STANDARD FORMS OF EMPLOYMENT IN THE DUTCH LABOUR MARKET: THE POSITION OF ON-CALL WORK

In the EU, the predominant type of employment remains the standard one.[487] Nevertheless, in 2014, standard employment constituted only 34% of the total employment in the Netherlands.[488] Therefore, the prominence of flexible work arrangements was highlighted more than in any other EU Member State, leading to its label as 'Europe's flexible employment champion'.[489] Some more recent studies based on the statistics provided by the Dutch Central Bureau of Statistics (CBS) have shown that this situation has changed, and the share of the Dutch workforce having permanent contracts has now reached 61%.[490]

Notwithstanding the current dominance of standard employment, the Netherlands represents a country with a great wealth of non-standard forms of employment. To mention only some of the most widespread forms of non-standard employment are part-time work, fixed-term work, temporary agency work, payroll work, and on-call

487. P. Schoukens and A. Barrio, 'The Changing Concept of Work: When Does Typical Work Become Atypical?', *ELLJ*, Vol. 8 Issue 4, 2017, p. 308.
488. European Parliament, *Precarious Employment: Patterns, trends and Policy Strategies in Europe*, Study for the EMPL Committee, 2016, p. 59.
489. M. Kremer, R. Went, A. Knottnerus, *For the Sake of Security, the Future of Flexible Workers and the Modern Organization of Labour*, The Netherlands Scientific Council for Government Policy (WRR), The Hague, 2017, p. 7.
490. ESPN Flash Report 2018/67, *New dutch draft law to reduce the gap between permanent and flexible contracts*, European Social Policy Network, p. 1; S. Burri, S. Heeger-Hertter, S. Rossetti, 'On-call Work in the Netherlands: Trends, Impacts and Policy Solutions', International Labour Office, Conditions of Work and Employment Series No. 103, 2018, p. 4; M. Kremer et al., 'For the Sake of Security, the Future of Flexible Workers and the Modern Organization of Labour', p. 13.

work arrangements.[491] Among these types of work relations, the predominance of part-time employment has been noticed, something which led to the Netherlands being considered the champion of part-time employment in the world, and at the same time, a champion of quality part-time work, as well.[492] Part-time work in the Netherlands constitutes 40 % of employment,[493] or around half of the employees work part-time.[494] Many scholars[495] and international organizations[496] have positioned on-call work arrangements within the context of part-time work, by considering it as very atypical part-time work. But while part-time work does not usually represent a risk of precariousness, on the other hand, zero-hours work arrangements, as a form of on-call work, can be related to a high level of precariousness due to 'low pay, inadequate social security coverage and a lack of access to labour rights'.[497] Additionally, precariousness in the Netherlands is also strongly related to the fast growth of self-employed workers without employees, the so-called ZZP (*zelfstandigen zonder personeel*).[498] In 2018, around 1.1 million people were working as ZZP in the Netherlands, making up around 12 % of the workforce.[499] These self-employed workers are being extended to sectors, such as healthcare or construction, where workers were traditionally qualified as employees. The result of the new qualification as self-employed is a precarious situation, where these workers are often paid less than the minimum wage.[500] Supranational organizations, such as the OECD, but also the European Commission, have urged the Netherlands to stop the growth of these precarious self-employed workers.[501] Nevertheless, as the OECD highlights, the general level of jobs insecurity in the Netherlands is less prominent compared to other OECD countries.[502]

By acknowledging that the Netherlands is embracing a wide variety of non-standard forms of employment, this part will focus on one specific form of it, concretely on-call work arrangements. As previously mentioned, Eurofound identifies a dichotomy of casual work arrangements into intermittent and on-call work. Against this background, on-call work (*oproepkracht*) appears to be more prominent in the

491. OECD, *Input to the Netherlands Independent Commission on the Regulation of Work*, 2019; Eurofound, *New forms of employment in Europe*; International Encyclopedia for Labour Law and Industrial Relations, Editor: F. Hendrickx, Kluwer Law Online.
492. International Labour Office, *Non-standard employment around the world, Understanding challenges, shaping prospects*, p. 126.
493. European Parliament, *Precarious employment …*, p. 77.
494. ILO, *Non-standard employment …*, p. 125.
495. G. H., Van Voss, 'Atypical Employment Relationships: The Position in the Netherlands', in *Restatement of Labour Law in Europe: Atypical Employment Relationships*, eds Bernd Waas and Guus Heerma van VossHendric Stolzenberg, Oxford: Hart Publishing, 2019, pp. 591-622, p. 607.
496. OECD, *Employment Outlook 2019*, The future of work, p. 60.
497. European Parliament, *Precarious employment …*, p. 137.
498. *Ibid.*, p. 48.
499. International Encyclopedia for Labour Law and Industrial Relations, p. 81.
500. R. Blanpain and F. Hendrickx, eds, 'New Forms of Employment in Europe', *Bulletin of Comparative Labour Relations*, Vol. 94 2016, p. 293.
501. International Encyclopedia for Labour Law and Industrial Relations, p. 82.
502. OECD, *Input to the Netherlands Independent Commission on the Regulation of Work*, 2019, p. 3.

Netherlands,[503] in comparison to intermittent work. This is actually a general trend underpinning industrialized countries, where casual work arrangements usually display in the form of on-call work, *inter alia*, zero-hours contracts.[504]

Studies show that on-call work constitutes the fastest-growing type of flexible work arrangement in the Netherlands.[505] The general feeling spread around the country is that it is becoming something normal.[506] In 2004, the Netherlands was identified as the country with the highest incidence of on-call work in Europe, and since then, the incidence of on-call work arrangements has more than doubled. For instance, in 2016, there were around 551,000 on-call workers, who represented 8% of the workforce.[507] According to the National Office of Statistics (CBS), in 2017, there were 546,000 people employed on on-call work.[508] Studies show that the Netherlands still constitutes the country with the highest incidence of this type of work arrangement in Europe.[509]

With regard to the sectors where this form of work is widespread, a high proportion of casual work has been noted mainly in education and healthcare.[510] On-call work arrangements can also be found in other sectors, such as 'commerce, hotels and catering, culture and recreation'.[511] In contrast, the use of zero-hours contracts and on-call contracts by agreement is not allowed in hospitals and nursing homes.[512] On the main reasons for employers to use on-call contracts, the Netherlands' Institute for Social Research survey identified 'fluctuations in the company's workload', and sickness of employees.[513]

4.2 THE TYPOLOGY OF ON-CALL WORK IN THE NETHERLANDS

Prior to exploring the typology of on-call work arrangements in the Netherlands, providing a definition of these work arrangements is essential. In this framework, a legal definition has been introduced by the Balanced Labour Market Act (*Wet arbeidsmarkt in balans* (Wab)),[514] a recently adopted law, which brought important changes

503. Eurofound, *Casual work: characteristics and implications*, p. 1.
504. ILO, *Non-standard employment* ..., p. 21.
505. OECD, *Employment outlook 2019*, p. 60.
506. Eurofound, *Casual work* ..., 2019, p. 18.
507. OECD, *Employment Outlook 2019*: The Future of Work, 2019, p. 60, based on S. Burri et al., On-call Work in the Netherlands: Trends, Impacts and Policy Solutions', ILO 2018.
508. Eurofound, *Casual work* ..., p. 11.
509. OECD, *Input to the Netherlands Independent Commission on the Regulation of Work*, 2019, p. 3.
510. Eurofound, *Casual work* ..., p. 12.
511. Eurofound, *New forms of employment*, p. 62.
512. International Encyclopedia for Labour Law and Industrial Relations, p. 78, based on the Social Agreement of April 2013, para. 195.
513. Eurofound, *Casual work* ..., p. 13.
514. Law of 29 May 2019 amending Book 7 of the Dutch Civil Code, the Allocation of Workforce by Intermediaries Act, the Social Insurance Financing Act and any other laws to improve the balance between permanent and flexible employment contracts (Balanced Labor Market Act), Available at: https://zoek.officielebekendmakingen.nl/stb-2019-219.html.

to the rules on on-call workers[515] stipulated in the Dutch Civil Code (CC).[516] According to Article 628(a)(9), Book 7 of the CC, on-call work agreements are defined as those arrangements in which '(a) the scope of the work is not fixed as a number of hours per unit of time of no more than one month; or no more than one year and the employee's right to remuneration is spread evenly over that unit of time; or (b) the employee is not entitled to the salary determined according to period of time pursuant to Article 628(5) or (7) or Article 691(7), if he has not performed the agreed work'.[517]

The Dutch government has provided a simplified clarification of the above-mentioned legal definition, with the purpose of informing entrepreneurs on these types of work arrangements.[518] According to such a simplified definition, on-call work is explained as referring to situations when '(b) the employee is not paid for hours that are not worked, [or] (a) the number of working hours in the period of a week, month or year at most is not fixed'.

With this in mind, on-call work arrangements in the Netherlands are displayed in three main forms. To start with, *zero-hours contracts*, with no guaranteed hours of work, can also be found in the Netherlands.[519] In comparison to the UK, where these contracts have gained a dominant position in the labour market, in the Netherlands, they can be found alongside other forms of on-call work, which can offer some more security, such as min-max contracts. Nevertheless, while zero-hours workers in the UK are not obliged to accept offers of work, zero-hours workers in the Netherlands are, in principle, excepted to accept these offers if called in by employers.[520] In the second typology of on-call work, that of *min-max contracts*, workers are ensured with some security, as they have a minimum number of guaranteed hours during the week, month or year. An increase in the minimum number of guaranteed hours is possible and can be requested, in case workers work more than that. This request has to be based on the average number of working hours performed in the last three months.[521] Furthermore, these workers are also provided with a maximum number of hours; if this threshold is exceeded, an additional pay rate is applicable. Both min-max and zero-hours contracts can be concluded for a fixed-term, or open-ended period.

The third option to have an on-call contract, which is considered the less popular one in the Netherlands, is through an *on-call contract by agreement*. Even in this third work scenario, the employer calls the worker when needed, and the latter has no

515. L. Mendelson PC, 'New rules regarding on-call workers in the Netherlands are in effect', Lexology, January 2020, Available at: https://www.lexology.com/library/detail.aspx?g=37826b2c-4abb-4b91-9b5e-5691de55246e.
516. Dutch Civil Code, Book 7, Title 10, Article 628a, Available at: https://wetten.overheid.nl/BWBR0005290/2020-07-01.
517. Translated with the translation tool DeeplL translator. Additionally, the definition provided in the International Encyclopedia of Labour Law and Industrial Relations, p. 78, has been consulted.
518. Government information for entrepreneurs, Available at: https://business.gov.nl/regulation/on-call-employees/.
519. OECD, *Employment Outlook*, p. 148.
520. V. De Stefano, 'Casual Work Beyond casual work in the EU: the underground casualization of the European workforce – and what to do about it', *European Labour Law Journal*, Vol. 7 Issue 3, 2016, p. 438.
521. Article 7: 610b CC.

obligation to answer the call.[522] However, at the moment the worker accepts the call, a fixed-term contract comes into effect.[523] Therefore, a fixed-term contract is concluded, every time an agreement is reached between parties. A limitation applies to the conclusion of fixed-term contracts, as only three of these contracts, or a maximum duration of thirty-six months, are permitted with the same employer.[524] The fourth contract, or the contract concluded after thirty-six months, is deemed permanent if such contracts have succeeded each other at intervals not exceeding six months. This is known as the chain rule for fixed-term contracts (*ketenregeling*) in the Netherlands.

4.3 THE LEGAL FRAMEWORK FOR ON-CALL WORK IN THE NETHERLANDS

The main rules governing on-call work contracts can be found in Book 7, Title 10, Article 628a of the Dutch Civil Code (*Burgerlijk Wetboek*). This main legal framework on these types of contracts has been altered by several amendments over time, where three important legislative moments can be highlighted in this regard: the Flexibility and Security Act (1999),[525] the Work and Security Act (2014)[526] and the Labour Market in Balance Act (2020),[527] which was enacted as part of the Cabinet's Coalition agreement 'Trust in the future' 2017-2021. To be noticed is that derogations from these legislative acts are possible by means of collective agreements,[528] which have impacted in making these laws 'semi-mandatory'. Such derogations may diminish the legal protections to which on-call workers are entitled. Nevertheless, exemptions are only permitted from some legal provisions, as it will be demonstrated in the next section.

While the purpose of this chapter is to focus on current labour protection rules for on-call workers, a brief overview of legal acts, which have impacted the legal situation of on-call workers, will be provided. To start with, the *Act on Flexibility and Security (Wet flexibiliteit en zekerheid)*, hereinafter the Flexicurity Act, entered into force in 1999. As the very name of this act shows, it aimed to establish a balance between both the needs of employers and those of workers in on-call work, respectively in harmonizing flexibility and labour protection' needs. Many of the rules introduced by this act, which provide essential safeguards for on-call workers, are still valid nowadays. A crucial aspect of this act consists in setting out two main legal presumptions, one on the employment contract,[529] and the other on the number of guaranteed working hours.[530] The importance of this act also lies in presenting a minimum income for on-call workers, namely a minimum guarantee of three paid working hours, in case the

522. OECD, *Employment Outlook*, p. 87.
523. Eurofound, *Casual work* ..., p. 8.
524. Article 7: 668a (1) CC.
525. Act of 14 May 1998, Available at: https://zoek.officielebekendmakingen.nl/stb-1998-300.html.
526. Act of 14 June 2014, Available at: https://wetten.overheid.nl/BWBR0035254/2020-01-01.
527. Act of 29 May 2019, Stb. 2019, 219, Available at: https://zoek.officielebekendmakingen.nl/stb-2019-219.html.
528. S. Burri et al., 'On-call work in the Netherlands: Trends, impacts and policy solutions', p. 20.
529. Article 7:610a CC.
530. *Ibid.*

employer calls the employee for less than three working hours.[531] According to the second evaluation of this act, the inclusion of such a provision for on-call workers led to employers offering more part-time work and fixed-term work contracts than on-call ones, and even to some employers not offering this minimum pay to their on-call workers in practice.[532] The above-mentioned safeguards will be elaborated on in the next section of this chapter. In addition, the Flexicurity Act presented the previously mentioned chain rule or 3x3 rule, which stipulates the conversion into a permanent contract 'after three consecutive fixed-term contracts or after a maximum duration of 36 months'.[533] To sum up, the Flexicurity Act provided for regulation of on-call contracts by improving the labour protection of on-call workers, but at the same time, it restricted the use of such contracts by employers, which led to a decline in their incidence.[534]

In 2013, the social partners in the Netherlands concluded a social agreement, which would constitute the basis for the Work and Security Act (Wet Werk en Zekerheid).[535] This act aimed to encourage the use of permanent contracts while discouraging the use of flexible work arrangements.[536] It modified, *inter alia*, the chain rule by providing for conversion into an open-ended contract after three successive fixed-term contracts, or after a maximum duration of twenty-four months. Pursuant to this law, interruptions between such contracts were allowed for a period of six months.[537] Moreover, derogations on the legal provisions, which can worsen the situation of workers, appear to be more restricted than before. For instance, the extension of the six-month period, under which an employer can be excluded from the obligation to pay wages when work is unavailable, is not allowed for 'on-call workers who work structurally',[538] but only for those who work incidentally during peak periods.

The rapid growth of casual work arrangements in the Netherlands served as a drive for the Dutch government to sign a coalition agreement between the party leaders in October 2017. This cabinet's coalition agreement for the period 2017-2021 became known as '*Trust in the Future*' (*Vertrouwen in de toekomst*), and it comprised, *inter alia*, measures on labour market issues.[539] This agreement had a double intention: to make permanent employment less permanent and flexible employment less flexible.[540] Concerning zero-hours work arrangements, the agreement pointed out the necessity to 'tackle the permanent availability' of these workers, in order to grant them the

531. S. Burri et al., 'On-call Work in the Netherlands: Trends, Impacts and Policy Solutions', p. 21.
532. *Ibid.*
533. *Ibid.*
534. Eurofound, *New forms of employment*, p. 55.
535. Work and Security Act (Wet Werk en Zekerheid) of 10 June 2014.
536. S. Burri et al., 'On-call Work in the Netherlands ...', ILO 2018, p. 21; Eurofound, *Casual work ...*, 2019, p. 32.
537. *Ibid.*, S. Burri et al., p. 21.
538. *Ibid.*
539. Coalition Agreement 'Trust in the future', Available at: https://www.kabinetsformatie2017.nl/documenten/publicaties/2017/10/10/regeerakkoord-vertrouwen-in-de-toekomst.
540. Coalition Agreement, p. 25.

opportunity to take up other job offers.[541] Moreover, this agreement once again provided a change in the chain rule, which consisted of the extension to three years of the period after which fixed-term contracts would be converted into permanent contracts.

A major legislative development in Dutch labour law, which was accepted as part of the just-mentioned coalition agreement, was the *Balanced Labour Market Act* (WAB).[542] In the same vein as the coalition agreement, the WAB also intended to make flexible employment less flexible[543] and reach a balance between employees in permanent contracts and those on flexible contracts of employment.[544] More specifically, on on-call work, this act brought crucial changes as of 1 January 2020. It provided important safeguards for on-call workers in the Dutch labour market, which complemented the existing ones in the Dutch Civil Code, by further strengthening the legal position of these workers. The recently taken legal measures aimed to grant such workers 'more income security and to combat unnecessary availability'.[545]

4.4 IMPORTANT SAFEGUARDS FOR ON-CALL WORKERS

Over time, the increase in the incidence of on-call work arrangements, which were often associated with precarious working conditions, prompted the Dutch legislator to introduce legal guarantees to this end. Due to such legal measures, the Netherlands was considered a country which heavily regulates zero-hours work,[546] standing in stark contrast with the UK.[547] The legal rules on this form of work, have gone through positive changes, with a very recent update brought by the Balanced Labour Market Act, as a result of which, the legal situation of on-call workers has greatly improved. Many commentators have welcomed the legal protections accorded to on-call workers in the Netherlands, and hence, they have considered 'the Dutch experiment as successful'.[548]

With respect to the legal measures in place for on-call workers, a dichotomy composed of some general and specific measures can be observed. While the general measures can be applicable beyond the on-call work relationship, the specific rules are tailor-made for on-call work arrangements and consider the unstable nature of the job. These specific measures come mainly as an outcome of the Balanced Labour Market

541. *Ibid.*
542. Eurofound, *Living and Working in the Netherlands*, May 2020, Available at: https://www.eurofound.europa.eu/country/netherlands.
543. *Ibid.*
544. Human in Progress Netherlands, 'WAB: Approved bill on Balanced Labour Market Act, Several changes to varying employment laws', Available at: https://hrmnetherlands.com/bill-balanced-labour-market-act/.
545. L. Mendelson PC, 'New rules regarding on-call workers in the Netherlands are in effect', Lexology, January 2020, Available at: https://www.lexology.com/library/detail.aspx?g=37826b2c-4abb-4b91-9b5e-5691de55246e.
546. ILC109/III(B), *Promoting employment and decent work in a changing landscape*, p. 131.
547. V. De Stefano, A. Aloisi, *European Legal Framework for Digital Labour Platforms*, European Commission, Luxembourg (2018), p. 31.
548. *Ibid.*

Act. Both types of measures, equally important for the legal situation of on-call workers, will be elaborated below.

4.4.1 General Legal Measures

4.4.1.1 The Legal Presumption of an Employment Relationship

Legal presumptions on the existence of an employment relationship can be established in various legal systems, however, in different ways.[549] The Netherlands is one of the countries which stipulates a statutory presumption in favour of an employment relationship. Such a legal presumption was presented for the first time in the Flexicurity Act, and it requires the relationship to have a certain duration and continuity in order to be qualified as an employment one. In this way, this presumption can be particularly useful for workers on flexible contracts, especially zero-hours workers. In order to benefit from this presumption and automatically have an employment contract, a person needs to perform work on a weekly basis, or for at least 20 hours per month, over three consecutive months, for the same person.[550] The employee who makes a claim does not need to prove evidence for the existence of an employment relationship, as he/she automatically benefits from this general presumption. On the other side, these presumptions can be rebutted by the party who provides with work, or the presumed employer, who will have the burden of proof in this regard.

4.4.1.2 The Legal Presumption of Minimum Guaranteed Hours

In addition to the employment relationship's presumption, a second presumption, which ensures some working hours, has been provided.[551] According to it, in an employment contract that has lasted at least three months, the contracted number of hours will correspond to the monthly average of the three preceding months.[552] This rule can affect the legal situation of zero-hours workers in the Netherlands, as pursuant to it, zero-hours work can last for only three months. In other words, in the first three months, zero-hours workers have no guaranteed working hours, and hence, they are paid only for the actual working hours.[553] After three months, some stability for these workers is provided by the Dutch legislator, a stability comparable to the one experienced by on-call workers in min-max contracts. In accordance with the above-mentioned presumption,[554] after three months, zero-hours workers are entitled to some guaranteed working hours, which are equal to the average hours worked in the

549. Regulating the employment relationship in Europe: a guide to Recommendation No. 198/International Labour Office, Governance and Tripartism Department. Geneva: ILO, 2013, p. 28.
550. Article 7:610a CC.
551. S. Burri et al., 'On-call Work in the Netherlands ...', p. 23.
552. Article 7:610b of the Dutch Civil Code; V. De Stefano and A. Aloisi, *European legal framework for digital labour platforms*, p. 31.
553. Eurofound, *New forms of employment*, p. 56.
554. Articles 7: 610a and 610b CC.

previous quarter and are paid by the employer even when there is no work available. However, in order to benefit from this entitlement, workers need to have worked for a certain period, concretely 'at least once weekly or for at least twenty hours per month for 3 consecutive months'.[555] This obligation upon the employer to pay for the guaranteed hours is called the continued payment of wages obligation.[556] Finally, this minimum guaranteed hours' safeguard is not an absolute one, as it can be waived by social partners through a collective agreement, by allowing in this way zero-hours contracts to last longer.

4.4.1.3 Equal Labour Protection with Workers in Standard Employment Relationships

On-call workers do not always enjoy equal rights with workers in standard employment. As noted, in the United Kingdom, it is quite rare for zero-hours workers to be classified as employees. As has already been indicated, the majority of zero-hours workers are entitled only to basic labour rights, which are associated with limb (b) worker's status. Furthermore, having a self-employed status is also not excluded for zero-hours workers in the UK. On the other side of the spectrum, on-call workers, who perform work in the Dutch labour market, appear to be in a more favourable position. Generally, these workers are entitled to the full package of employment rights on equal footing with standard employees.[557] The legal presumption of an employment relationship is quite conducive according to the employee status to on-call workers, and hence, a full package of labour rights. To mention only a few of the labour rights to which on-call workers are entitled to are the right to minimum wage, protection against dismissal, entitlement to holiday pay and sick pay, etc. However, the fact that some of these entitlements depend on the actual number of working hours[558] may weaken the legal position of these workers in practice. A further weakness can also be related to the lack of enforcement of these rights by on-call workers, who appear to be 'hesitant to stand up for their rights'.[559] Concerning the right to sick pay, the on-call worker can become entitled, only if sickness happens during the call period.[560] In this case, the

555. V. De Stefano, 'Casual work beyond casual work in the EU ...', *European Labour Law Journal*, Vol. 7 Issue 3, 2016, p. 438; Article 7: 610ba CC.
556. Information provided by the Government of the Netherlands, Available at: https://business.gov.nl/running-your-business/staff/recruiting-and-hiring-staff/hiring-on-call-employees-with-a-zero-hours-contract/.
557. Government information for entrepreneurs, 'Hiring on-call employees with a zero-hours contract', (2020), Available at: https://business.gov.nl/running-your-business/staff/recruiting-and-hiring staff/hiring-on-call-employees-with-a-zero-hours-contract/; G. Van Voss, 'Atypical Employment Relationships: The Position in the Netherlands', In *Restatement of Labour Law in Europe: Atypical Employment Relationships*, eds Waas, B., and Van Vosshendric Stolzenberg, G.H., Assisted by Oxford: Hart Publishing, 591–622, (2019)., p. 608; Eds F. Hendrickx and R. Blanpain, 'New Forms of Employment in Europe', *Bulletin of Comparative Labour Relations*, 2016, p. 293.
558. Eurofound, *Non-standard forms of employment: Recent trends and future prospects*, 2018, p. 56.
559. G. Van Voss, 'Atypical employment relationships ...', p. 608.
560. Government.nl, Available at: https://business.gov.nl/running-your-business/staff/recruiting-and-hiring-staff/hiring-on-call-employees-with-a-zero-hours-contract/.

employer has to pay for the hours of the call. The sick pay amounts to at least 70% of the Dutch minimum wage. Moreover, on-call workers in the Netherlands are fully covered by social security protections, which, unfortunately, does not appear to be the case in many other countries.[561] On the other side, Eurofound's report on casual work in Europe points out that, in several instances, casual workers in the Netherlands were found to have a self-employed status – a status which deprives them of the majority of labour protections.[562]

4.4.2 Specific Legal Measures

4.4.2.1 Minimum Guaranteed Income: Three Hours' Pay for Calls Lasting Less than Three Hours

In addition to the general legal protections available to all workers, on-call workers in the Netherlands also benefit from some specific safeguards, which consider the casual and unstable nature of their job. Against this background, the Flexicurity Act introduced a minimum guaranteed income for on-call workers for the first time. According to the legal provision laid down in the Civil Code, on-call workers are entitled to three hours' pay, in case they are called in to work for less than three hours,[563] i.e., workers who are called in to work for one or two hours may benefit from this minimum income. However, this entitlement is conditional upon the employment contract having an unspecified number of weekly hours, or the employment contract having a number of agreed hours less than fifteen hours per week, but which are still irregular hours.[564] In the last instance, workers in min-max contracts can benefit from this financial guarantee, only if they fulfil this weekly working hours threshold.[565] Moreover, this legal guarantee also applies to zero-hours workers, who are in greater need of this guaranteed income than workers in min-max contracts.[566]

The purpose of this minimum guaranteed income is to counteract, or at least to mitigate, the vulnerability experienced by on-call workers. These workers face income instability due to the variability of their working hours, which, combined with a low level of pay, makes it hard to meet even the basic living needs of on-call workers.[567] What is more, the hourly wage of on-call workers is found to be lower than the hourly wages of standard workers, mainly attributed to the low-skilled nature of their tasks.[568] In addition to soothing the vulnerability and enhancing the protection of on-call workers in the Netherlands, the purpose of this legal safeguard is also related to the

561. Eurofound, *Non-standard forms of employment* ..., p. 60.
562. Eurofound, *Casual work* ..., p. 16.
563. Article 7: 628a (1) CC.
564. *Ibid.*
565. J. Dop (Russell Advocaten), 'On call employees', 2019, Available at: https://www.russell.nl/publication/on-call-employees-netherlands-rights-obligations.
566. Eurofound, *New forms of employment*, p. 56.
567. S. Burri et al., 'On-call Work in the Netherlands ...', p. 43.
568. *Ibid.*, p. 49.

discouragement of employers from calling in workers to work for a very short period.[569] A case presented to the Supreme Court in the Netherlands sheds some light on the application of the three hours pay rule to on-call workers. According to the court's ruling, a taxi driver who performed several separate short trips in one day should have been given three hours' pay for each time the driver worked for less than three hours.[570]

A paramount feature of this three hours pay' financial guarantee is its absolute nature, i.e., no derogations from it are allowed by means of collective agreements. As has already been mentioned and will be further demonstrated below, many legal guarantees available for on-call workers can be deviated by social partners. Therefore, the three hours pay' guarantee constitutes an absolute right for on-call workers, which they should enjoy every time they are called in to work for less than three hours. Nevertheless, the enshrinement of this legal guarantee does not ensure its practical application, as it is up to employers to comply with this legal obligation. In the event employers do not fulfil this legal duty, workers have the option to bring their case to the court.

4.4.2.2 Four Days Advance Notice and Financial Compensation for Cancelled/Changed Shifts (WAB)

The Balanced Labour Market Act brought in a positive change with a view to eliminate the permanent availability of on-call workers. This was done by stipulating the employer's obligation to call the worker in – in writing or electronically – at least four days in advance.[571] In case of no conformity with this advance notice by the employer, the on-call worker has no obligation to respond to the call of work.[572] Furthermore, the legal framework provides for the consequences of a cancellation, or a change, in the call for work by the employer, which occurs within four days prior to the start of work.[573] In this case, the employer has to pay the worker financial compensation, amounting to the wages to which the worker would be entitled if he had performed the work.

The advance notice safeguard available to on-call workers can constitute a subject of derogation by social partners through collective agreements. Under a collective agreement, they can reduce the advance notice up to twenty-four hours, but cannot completely waive it. Accordingly, the permanent availability of on-call workers is no longer possible in the Netherlands. Moreover, the four days advance notice applies not only to a call to work by the employer but also in case of termination of the

569. G. Van Voss, 'Atypical Employment Relationships ...', p. 608.
570. HR 3 May 2013, *NJ* 2015/105, *JAR* 2013/140, *RAR* 2013/100 (*Van der Meulen/Wolters*).
571. Article 7: 628a (2) CC.
572. Government information for entrepreneurs, 'On-call employees', Available at: https://business.gov.nl/regulation/on-call-employees/.
573. Article 7: 628a (3) CC.

employment relationship by the worker.[574] In other words, the worker has the obligation to notify the employer about the termination of the employment relationship four days in advance, if a collective agreement has not provided a shorter notice period.

4.4.2.3 *Offer for a Fixed Number of Working Hours after One Year of On-call Work (WAB)*

The Dutch legislator has provided legal protections to on-call workers during different moments of their employment relationship. As noted, before an on-call work arrangement starts, workers are entitled to a four days advance notice. The legal position of on-call workers keeps strengthening over time, with a view to equipping these workers with some stability. For this reason, the Balanced Labour Market Act has provided an obligation upon employers, to offer a fixed number of working hours to on-call workers after one year of work.[575] More details on the conditions for making such an offer are provided in the Civil Code. To start with, the offer has to be made by the employer in writing, or electronically, within one month. The worker can accept or decline this offer also within one month. Even if the worker declines such an offer, the employer's obligation to offer fixed working hours will still apply after the next twelve months. Regarding the determination of the fixed number of working hours, reference shall be made to the average amount of working hours in the previous twelve months. To be noticed is that, successive contracts between one worker and different employers, must be considered as successive with regard to the work performed, and are thus included in the calculation of the twelve months period.[576]

A failure to comply with this obligation by the employer can entitle the worker to claim the wages not received 'for the hours for which the offer should have been made'.[577] Workers can raise such a claim within five years.[578]

4.4.2.4 *The Chain Rule: A Permanent Contract for On-call Workers in Fixed-Term Contracts*

On-call work arrangements can be concluded either for a definite duration or an indefinite one. It is possible, however, for on-call workers in fixed-term contracts to have a permanent one, after completing a certain number of fixed-term contracts, or after working for a certain period. Therefore, the opportunity to have a permanent contract is considered another form of protection for on-call workers, as the permanent contract is associated with long-term stability. According to the already mentioned chain rule, or 3x3 rule of fixed-term contracts, on-call workers can have a permanent

574. Government information for entrepreneurs, 'Hiring on-call employees with a zero-hours contract', Available at: https://business.gov.nl/running-your-business/staff/recruiting-and-hiring-staff/hiring-on-call-employees-with-a-zero-hours-contract/.
575. Article 7: 628a (5) CC.
576. Article 7: 628a (7) CC; G. Van Voss, 'Atypical Employment Relationships …', p. 609.
577. Article 7: 628a (8) CC.
578. *Ibid.*

contract after three consecutive fixed-term contracts, or after being for three years in fixed-term contracts with the same employer.[579] However, these fixed-term contracts must have succeeded each other, at intervals not exceeding six months. In the past, on-call workers could benefit from a permanent contract after being for two years in fixed-term contracts,[580] but such a provision has been altered, and the current rules require a three-year duration of fixed-term contracts before the conversion into a permanent contract.[581]

4.5 PLATFORM WORK IN THE NETHERLANDS

4.5.1 Platform Work in the Netherlands in a Nutshell

Platform work in the Netherlands has been referred to with a wide variety of terms, such as the gig economy, platform economy, sharing economy, and on-demand economy.[582] In the national language, the notions which are used to refer to platform work were found to be *deeleconomie*, *platform economie* and *klus economie*. The predominant part of platform work in the Netherlands is composed of physical or on-location tasks, mainly in the sectors of transport and household services, such as taxi rides, meal delivery, and household errands.[583] In this regard, data from Eurofound's survey demonstrate that, as of spring 2018, in the Netherlands, Uber calculated around 7,450 drivers; Deliveroo had over 2,000 riders up to January 2018, while Werkspot, a home repairs platform, registered around 8,100 users.[584] In addition to the just-mentioned platforms, some of the most prominent ones, which operate in the Dutch local labour market, include Helpling (cleaning), Thuisbezorgd (food delivery), and Roamler (photo making).[585] Notwithstanding the dominance of on-location tasks in the Dutch labour market, online tasks, which demand a higher level of skills and require specialized training, such as software development, are also quite present.[586] This share of online tasks in the Netherlands appears to be higher, than in other countries with a prevalence of on-location tasks.[587]

Regarding the size of platform work in the Netherlands, no national evidence has been provided yet in this regard.[588] CBS, the National Office of Statistics, has indicated that it is attempting to address this challenge.[589] Nevertheless, despite the lack of

579. Article 7: 668a (1) CC.
580. The Work and Security Act.
581. The Balanced Labour Market Act.
582. Eurofound, *Employment and working conditions of selected types of platform work*, 2018, p. 10.
583. *Ibid.*, p. 9.
584. *Ibid.*, p. 12.
585. Seo economisch onderzoek, *De opkomst en groei van kluseconomie in Nederland*, in opdracht van Ministerie van Sociale Zaken en Werkgelegenheid, Amsterdam 2018, p. 10.
586. *Ibid.*, p. 16
587. *Ibid.*, p. 13.
588. Kilhoffer et al., *Study to gather evidence on the working conditions of platform workers*, 2020, p. 279.
589. CBS mapping online platforms, 2019, Available at: https://www.cbs.nl/en-gb/corporate/2019/12/cbs-mapping-online-platforms.

official data, some studies have attempted to shed some light on this issue. For example, pursuant to a study commissioned by the Dutch Ministry of Social Affairs and Employment, which was conducted by Seo economisch onderzoek, the size of platform economy in the Netherlands is quite small and it constitutes only 0.4% of the number of jobs at the national level, which corresponds to 34,000 active platform workers.[590] On the one hand, other studies have provided some more figures in this respect. For instance, research conducted by FEPS, Uni-Europa, and the University of Hertfordshire in 2017, found that around 9% of the Netherlands' population has performed platform work.[591] On the other hand, the COLLEEM survey indicates a 10.6% of platform workers in the Netherlands.[592] This survey considers the UK as the country with the highest incidence of platform work in Europe, while it observes that the Netherlands has a relatively high incidence of platform work. What is more, future potential for growth of the platform economy is also expected in the Netherlands.[593]

The employment status of platform workers has constituted a subject of controversy between platform operators and workers in the Netherlands, with food delivery platforms being at the centre of the debate.[594] Some main platforms operating in the Dutch market have made their position clear in a public hearing, concretely that they provide a mere intermediation between the supply and demand sides of labour.[595] Some platform operators have even suggested to the government to allow them to buy collective social security benefits, which they would then sell to platform workers at a reasonable price.[596] In contrast to the platforms' stance, many platform workers have claimed to have an employment relationship with platform companies. For this reason, they have organized several marches and strikes in major cities in the Netherlands, which in many cases have been supported by the Federation of Dutch Trade Unions (FNV). Such protests involved mainly food delivery riders, which formed a Riders' Union in the Netherlands. As a response to such actions, Deliveroo proposed to these workers, *inter alia*, insurance against occupational accidents, a proposal considered insufficient by the riders and FNV.

The employment status of platform workers was also brought to the 'doors' of Dutch courts. In this regard, the lawsuits against Deliveroo brought two contradictory decisions by the same court in Amsterdam. These rulings were triggered by a change in the contracts offered by Deliveroo to its riders. For the period from September 2015 until the beginning of 2018, Deliveroo was offering fixed-term contracts to its riders. Afterwards, Deliveroo required the riders to enter into contracts for services, in order to stay registered with the platform. The ruling issued by the court in this case

590. Seo economisch onderzoek, *De opkomst en groei van de kluseconomie in Nederland*, p.i.
591. U. Huws et al., *Work in the European Gig Economy: Research Results from the UK, Sweden, Germany, Austria, the Netherlands, Switzerland and Italy*, 2017.
592. A. Pesole et al., *Platform Workers in Europe*, Publications Office of the European Union, Luxembourg, 2018.
593. *Ibid.*, p. 39.
594. Kilhoffer et al., *Study to gather evidence on the working conditions of platform workers*, p. 279.
595. Eurofound, *Employment and working conditions of selected types of platform work*, p. 39.
596. *Ibid.*

constituted the first one on platform economy in the Netherlands.[597] In this ruling,[598] the Subdistrict Court of Amsterdam denied the existence of an employment relationship between parties and concluded that Deliveroo correctly offered a contract for services to its riders. The court's reasoning was based on the flexibility of working time enjoyed by Deliveroo riders.[599] According to the court, such freedom ruled out the existence of subordination under the Dutch Civil Code. The court attached great importance to the agreement between the parties, where the worker agreed to work on a self-employed basis.[600]

In contrast, in 2019, the same court took a different decision on the same issue, concluding that Deliveroo riders have an employment relationship with the platform.[601] The second lawsuit against Deliveroo was initiated by FNV, which reached a successful outcome not only for Deliveroo riders but also, more broadly, it set a precedent on the issue of the employment status in the platform economy. The court's reasoning was based on the limitations imposed by Deliveroo on riders' flexibility. In this respect, the court considered 'the [worker's] dependence on Deliveroo to be more important than the independence of the delivery man'.[602] This ruling also provided for a retroactive application of the collective bargaining agreement for professional goods transport by road to the relationship between Deliveroo and its riders.[603]

Another interesting case that the Dutch courts dealt with concerned the Helpling platform. In the *Helpling* case, the court established an employment relationship between the Dutch cleaners and the households (users of the services), instead of acknowledging such a relationship with the platform company. Instead, the court qualified the Helpling platform as a private employment agency. As a result, Helpling in the Netherlands permits its workers to be employed, which is not the case in other countries where it operates. Moreover, in the Netherlands, there are cases of platforms that have voluntarily decided to become temporary work agencies, e.g., the platform Ploy, which is owned by Randstad and serves to complete the interim needs for staff of employers in the hospitality sector.[604] On the opposite side of the spectrum stand some platforms which are very fast to change their practices, in order to evade the legal obligations arising from an employment relationship. For instance, some food delivery platforms in the Netherlands used to require their riders to wear uniforms. However, once they learned that this could constitute an indicia towards an employment relationship, they removed such a requirement.[605]

597. A. Arteaga, 'Platform economy in the Netherlands: Deliveroo rider is self-employed', 2018, Available at: https://www.terralex.org/tlglobal/publications/platform-economy-in-the-netherlands-deliveroo-rider-is-self-employed.
598. Rechtbank Amsterdam 23 juli 2018, Case No. ECLI: NL: RBAMS: 2018: 5183.
599. V. De Stefano, I. Durri, C. Stylogiannis, M. Wouters, 'Platform Work and the Employment Relationship', *ILO*, 2021, p. 47.
600. Rechtbank Amsterdam 23 juli 2018, Case No. ECLI: NL: RBAMS: 2018: 518, para. 28.
601. Rechtbank Amsterdam 15 juli 2019, Case No. ECLI: NL: RBAMS: 2019: 198.
602. *Ibid.*
603. Kilhoffer et al., *Study to gather evidence on the working conditions of platform workers*, p. 115.
604. V. De Stefano et al., *Platform work and the Employment Relationship*, p. 21; Also available at: https://www.appfoundry.be/cases/randstad-ploy.
605. From expert interviews, CEPS, EFTHEIA and HIVA-KU Leuven, *Study to gather evidence on the working conditions of platform workers*, p. 122.

4.5.2 Exploring the Overlap Between Platform Work and On-call Work Arrangements in the Netherlands

Research conducted by FEPS, Uni-Europa, and the University of Hertfordshire, which includes as a case study also the Netherlands, underlies that platform work does not constitute a distinctive form of work but is rather a part of casual work arrangements.[606] This has also been affirmed in the Dutch context by a study commissioned by the Ministry of Social Affairs and Employment. This study indicates that in case the relationship between the platform and the worker is characterized as an employment one, the specific contract concluded between parties should be either a zero-hours contract or a min-max one.[607] The main reason for perceiving platform work as having common threads with casual work arrangements, especially with zero-hours work arrangements, was found to be the precariousness faced by workers in both forms of work.[608] As an illustration of the insecurities experienced by platform workers in the Dutch context can serve, the agreement concluded between Deliveroo in the Netherlands and its riders. Such an agreement was disclosed in a court case initiated against Deliveroo in 2018.[609] The provisions of this agreement stipulated the freedom of food delivery riders to work and choose their working hours.[610] Regarding the right to choose these hours, Deliveroo in the Netherlands provides a priority access in specific time slots to riders who have a higher performance than the others, based on several factors.[611] According to Deliveroo, it is entirely up to the worker to choose when to perform work, and there is no obligation to accomplish minimum guaranteed hours. Nevertheless, the 'real' freedom of choosing whether to work is hampered, by the unavailability of work, which is reserved to top performing riders. What is more, Deliveroo has emphasized through this agreement that it is under no obligation to offer work to the workers.[612] The same holds true for the workers' side, as there is no obligation to accept calls of work. However, not responding three times to job calls may lead to a dismissal with immediate effect. Another aspect of the insecurities experienced by platform workers comprises income insecurity. Pursuant to the provisions of this agreement, riders are paid per delivery (also not guaranteed),[613] thus, not entitled to a periodic and stable income in the form of a monthly salary.

The study commissioned by the Dutch Ministry of Employment and Social Affairs has also elaborated on the precarious working conditions faced by platform workers. The focus of this study was the precariousness of workers working via apps, especially in the meal delivery, household, and transport industries. This study provides evidence not only about the income insecurity experienced by these workers but also about their

606. U. Huws et al., *Work in the European Gig Economy* ..., 2017, p. 10.
607. Seo economisch onderzoek, *De opkomst en groei van de kluseconomie in Nederland*, p. 67.
608. *Ibid.*, p. 69.
609. Rechtbank Amsterdam 23 juli 2018, Case No. ECLI: NL: RBAMS: 2018: 518.
610. *Ibid.*, Facts, 1. Services contractor, para 1.1.
611. *Ibid.*, 7. Right to design a replacer, para. 1.12.
612. *Ibid.*, Facts, 1. Services contractor, para. 1.1.
613. *Ibid.*, 3. Reimbursement and invoicing, para. 3.1.

generally low level of income.[614] For these workers, it is difficult to gain a minimum living income, which is further reinforced by the underemployment experienced by them. This means that the minimum income can be reached only if these workers work for many hours (if available). The situation exacerbates for the cab industry, where some necessary expenses need to be made for the car. The job security issue is further pointed out, as the employer has no contractual obligation to offer work to the platform worker.[615] Pursuant to this study, job insecurity is again more highlighted in the cab industry, in contrast to the household services and meal delivery sectors. Finally, this study finds out that the precariousness characterizing platform work is not fundamentally different from the one inherent in other forms of employment.[616]

Against this background, previous research from the European Parliament on precarious employment in Europe shows that zero-hours work contracts in the Netherlands are associated with a high level of precariousness, i.e., 'low pay, inadequate social security coverage and a lack of access to labour rights'.[617] The same issue was also underlined in a report by the Federation of Dutch Trade Unions (FNV), which considered the insecurity of working hours and pay as inherent to zero-hours work in the Netherlands.[618] Nevertheless, this vulnerable nature of zero-hours work can be counteracted through a wide set of legal protections enshrined in the Dutch Civil Code.

Frequently, on-call and platform work are deprived of partial or full labour protection, associated with the employee status. In the Dutch legal context, on-call workers are generally covered by labour protection, with the exception of labour rights depending on seniority. Platform workers, on the other side, experience a lack of labour protection, due to the self-employed status accorded by the platforms. Notwithstanding the importance of some recent Dutch courts' rulings, which determine an employee status, the protections accorded are limited to individual cases only. Once again, the just-mentioned shared insecurities that both zero-hours workers and platform workers have in common, lead to the assumption that there is at least an overlap between both forms of work, also in the Dutch context.

4.6 COVID-19 IN THE NETHERLANDS: THE INCLUSION OF CASUAL AND PLATFORM WORKERS IN THE NATIONAL SCHEMES AGAINST THE PANDEMIC

The coronavirus has caused a 'once-in-a-century health crisis',[619] with adverse consequences in all spheres of the economy, *inter alia*, massive job losses, including workers in standard forms of employment. Considering that workers with stable employment

614. Seo economisch onderzoek, *De opkomst en groei van de kluseconomie in Nederland*, p. 67.
615. *Ibid.*, p. 68.
616. *Ibid.*, p. 70.
617. The European Parliament, *Precarious employment ...*, p. 137.
618. European Public Service Forum, 'Zero hours and the spread of precarious employment', Available at: https://www.epsu.org/article/zero-hours-and-spread-precarious-employment.
619. The Brussels Times, 'Effects of the pandemic will be felt for decades, says WHO', August 2020, Available at: https://www.brusselstimes.com/news/124505/coronavirus-pandemics-effects-will-be-felt-for-decades-says-who/.

are suffering from the effects of the pandemic, the situation is expected to be exacerbated for the most vulnerable workers, who stay at the edge of the labour market. Already with unstable jobs and low income, these workers will be the ones who will be hit even harder by this economic crisis. Against this background, at the heart of this section will be the potential inclusion of some vulnerable workers, such as casual workers and platform workers, in the measures undertaken by the Dutch government against the COVID-19 pandemic.

Shortly after the lockdown of countries happened, the Dutch government responded to this unusual situation, by adopting the Emergency Jobs and Economy Package on 17 March 2020.[620] Such measures have a wide scope of application, including also 'the postponement of taxpaying and the relaxation of credit provisions'.[621] However, the focus of this section will be on one specific pillar of this emergency package, concretely on the measures aimed to preserve the jobs and income of employees and self-employed workers, which are respectively contained in the NOW (Temporary Emergency Bridging Measure for Sustained Employment)[622] and TOZO (Temporary Emergency Bridging Measure for Self-Employed Professionals)[623] schemes.

The NOW program intends to safeguard the salaries and jobs of employees, by compensating their wage costs to employers whose turnover' loss is at least 20% due to the corona crisis.[624] The higher the turnover loss of the employer, the higher the subsidy from the government, e.g., in case of a 100% loss suffered by the employer, the compensation granted was 90% of the salary. The Dutch government has continuously and explicitly called to safeguard the jobs and income of, *inter alia*, workers on flexible contracts, including on-call workers, many of whom became unemployed at the beginning of the pandemic.[625] What is more, it was found that around 80% of on-call workers have either lost their jobs or experienced a substantial reduction in working hours, during the coronavirus situation.[626] Despite the Dutch government's call to promote and safeguard this form of work, the reality has been harsh for these workers,

620. Government of the Netherlands, 'Coronavirus: Dutch government adopts package of new measures designed to save jobs and the economy', 17 March 2020, Available at: https://www.government.nl/latest/news/2020/03/19/coronavirus-dutch-government-adopts-package-of-new-measures-designed-to-save-jobs-and-the-economy.
621. H. Bennaars, 'Covid-19 and Labour Law in the Netherlands', *European Labour Law Journal*, Vol. 11 Issue 3, 2020, pp. 324-331, p. 324.
622. Government information for entrepreneurs, 'Corona crisis: Temporary Emergency Bridging Measure for Sustained Employment NOW', Available at: https://business.gov.nl/subsidy/corona-crisis-temporary-emergency-measure-now/.
623. Government information for entrepreneurs, 'Temporary Bridging Measure for Self-Employed Professionals TOZO', Available at: https://business.gov.nl/subsidy/temporary-bridging-measure-self-employed-professionals-tozo/.
624. The NOW scheme was extended until 1 July 2021 (NOW 3), Available at: https://business.gov.nl/subsidy/corona-crisis-temporary-emergency-measure-now/.
625. H. Bennaars, 'Covid-19 and Labour Law in the Netherlands', *European Labour Law Journal*, Vol. 11 Issue 3, 2020, pp. 326-327; B. ter Haar, 'Covid-19 and Labour Law: The Netherlands', *Italian Labour Law e-Journal*, Special, Vol. 13 Issue 1, 2020, p. 2.
626. J. Pieters, 'Temps and flexible staff facing lost wages, unemployment: Union', 15 July 2020, Available at: https://nltimes.nl/2020/07/15/temps-flexible-staff-facing-lost-wages-unemployment-union.

who could barely ensure work and income even before the pandemic's outbreak. Looking for a solution in social security protection is not easy either.[627] It is very probable that on-call workers do not qualify for unemployment benefits, due to their lack of continuity in employment, as a result of the casual nature of their jobs. Therefore, notwithstanding the good intention of the Dutch government towards these workers, an exacerbation of their vulnerability was highlighted in this unusual health situation.

Another important scheme provided at the national level comprises financial support for self-employed workers, known as the TOZO scheme. In order for the self-employed to benefit from it, they needed to comply with certain conditions. Some of these requirements comprise: a level of income that must fall below the social minimum, a Dutch nationality or an equal nationality (?), a legal residence, and the business to be practised in the Netherlands.[628] The financial compensation applicable to these self-employed workers was set up to EUR 1,500 (net) per month for a maximum period of three months. Self-employed could also apply for a loan with low interest. The TOZO scheme supporting self-employed was, in general, perceived as a successful one.[629]

As constantly repeated throughout this dissertation, platform workers are normally qualified as self-employed by the platforms. Due to this qualification, platform workers who exercise their business in the Netherlands can become eligible for financial compensation, or a loan with low interest, provided by the TOZO scheme. While the condition to have an income falling below the social minimum can be complied with by a vast part of these workers, the scheme appears to exclude those self-employed workers who do not have a Dutch nationality (or an equal nationality?), but also crowdworkers, who perform their jobs online, instead of a physical place. Currently, there are no data available on platform workers who have received this subsidy from the government, however, at least in theory, many Dutch workers working via apps should be eligible for such compensation.

4.7 CONCLUSION

The Netherlands provides an important case study for the exploration of on-call work, as it not only displays the highest incidence and fastest growth of this form of work in Europe but also sets out a detailed legal framework to govern it. At the national level, alongside zero-hours work arrangements, can also be found other forms of on-call

627. H. Bennaars, 'Covid-19 and Labour Law in the Netherlands', *European Labour Law Journal*, Vol. 11 Issue 3, 2020, p. 327 and p. 331.
628. Government information for entrepreneurs, 'Temporary Bridging Measure for Self-Employed Professionals TOZO', Available at: https://business.gov.nl/subsidy/temporary-bridging-measure-self-employed-professionals-tozo/.
629. A. Heerekop, 'Zelfstandingen over TOZO: Gemeente die snel uitkeert, wordt het meest gewaardeerd', Available at: https://www.fnv.nl/nieuwsbericht/algemeen-nieuws/2020/05/zelfstandigen-over-tozo-gemeente-die-snel-uitkeert; H. Bennaars, 'Covid-19 and Labour Law in the Netherlands', *European Labour Law Journal*, Vol. 11 Issue 3, 2020, p. 328.

work, such as min-max and on-call contracts by agreement. In comparison to zero-hours contracts, these two forms of on-call work grant some more security to workers. For instance, minimum and maximum hours are ensured for min-max workers, while workers involved in on-call contracts by agreement have the chance to have a fixed-term contract, at the moment they accept employers' calls. Many important safeguards for on-call workers were introduced quite early, with the Flexibility and Security Act (1999), culminating with the enactment of the Labour Market in Balance Act (2020). A first conducive legal measure for these workers is the presumption of an employment relationship, according to which, workers who have a three months duration of their relationship, associated this with a weekly, or at least twenty hours per month frequency, can benefit from all the entitlements associated with the employee status. This presumption signifies a major step forward, especially for zero-hours workers, who can have some security after three months of work, including some minimum guaranteed hours on the basis of the hours worked in the previous quarter. In addition, the WAB lays down some further protections, with a view to combat the permanent availability and provide some income and job security for on-call workers. For this reason, an advance notice of four days was introduced, altogether with the right to get an offer for fixed working hours after one year of on-call work. These new rights for on-call workers can be considered major achievements, in line with the protections introduced by the TPWCD, while in stark contrast with the almost inexistent protections for zero-hours workers in the UK.

The just-mentioned developments on on-call work in the Netherlands should not be studied in isolation, but rather in interrelation with other developments, such as those on platform work. Many scholars, but also international and national institutions, identify common features between both work typologies, e.g., the insecurity of work and income associated with a low level of pay. However, there is notably more exacerbation on the platform workers' side, due to a total lack of labour protection resulting from an imposed self-employed status. Some Dutch courts have ruled on the employment status of platform workers, with the notable example of the same court delivering contradictory rulings on the very same issue between Deliveroo and its riders. Interestingly, in the *Helpling* case, the Dutch court identified an employment relationship, however, between the workers and the service users.

The outbreak of the COVID-19 pandemic seems to have exacerbated the already existing precarious situation of on-call and platform workers, notwithstanding the Dutch government's efforts to support them during this extraordinary period. Since the start of the pandemic, many on-call workers were not only left without jobs, but they were also unable to qualify for unemployment benefits. The introduction of the NOW scheme, which supports employers in keeping the jobs of flexible workers, was helpful for a number of on-call workers. While only a very limited number of platform workers could fall within the remit of the NOW scheme, a part of these workers was presumably eligible for the TOZO scheme, e.g., Dutch workers who work via apps. Overall, through the introduction of the just-mentioned legal avenues, the Dutch government has arguably shown some support to mitigate the vulnerabilities of on-call and platform workers during this harsh health and financial crisis.

CHAPTER 5

Intermittent Work in Belgium

5.1 THE *STATUS QUO* OF NON-STANDARD FORMS OF EMPLOYMENT IN BELGIUM

Belgium represents a country with a high prominence of the standard employment relationship, which is characterized by full-time, indefinite, and subordinate employment with a single employer. According to a recent study by the National Bank of Belgium, the share of standard employment appears to be higher than the EU average, as concretely, nine out of ten employees work under this type of contract.[630] However, the high prominence of the standard employment relationship in Belgium does not signify that various forms of non-standard employment are absent at the national level. Among these non-standard forms of employment, the so-called typical forms of non-standard employment, such as fixed-term work, part-time work, and temporary agency work,[631] appear to be especially prevalent in the Belgian labour market.

To start with, *part-time work*[632] can be considered quite popular in Belgium, as around one out of four workers are involved in this form of work.[633] What is more, short part-time work, considered less than ten hours per week,[634] is also present in Belgium. This form of work constitutes subject to some legal limitations, e.g., the working time of these workers should not go below one-third of the weekly working time of full-time employees, who are employed in the same employment category

630. M. Nautet, C. Piton, *An Analysis of Non-standard Forms of Employment in Belgium*, NBB Economic Review, 2019, p. 6.
631. G. Van Guys, *Belgium: Flexible forms of work: Very 'atypical' contractual arrangements*, Eurofound report, 2010, Available at: https://www.eurofound.europa.eu/publications/report/2010/belgium-flexible-forms-of-work-very-atypical-contractual-arrangements.
632. Loi sur le travail of 16 March 1971.
633. According to Statbel, the Belgian statistical office, around 28% of the workforce is employed part-time, 2017-2020, Available at: https://statbel.fgov.be/nl/themas/werk-opleiding/arbeidsmarkt/deeltijds-werk#figures.
634. G. Van Gyes, *Belgium: Flexible forms of work: Very 'atypical' contractual arrangements*.

within the company.[635] Exceptions to this rule are provided with regard to some sectors, such as cleaning, public administration, etc.[636] Additionally, each period of work cannot be less than three working hours.[637] An advance notice of five days has also been provided for work with a variable schedule.[638]

Furthermore, much attention has been paid to *temporary work* in Belgium, both at the academic and policy level.[639] Even though temporary work represents a relatively low share in the Belgian labour market, a surge in the number of temporary contracts was noted, as employers preferred offering a temporary contract, instead of a permanent one.[640] A prominent aspect of temporary contracts in Belgium consists of the use of very short fixed-term contracts. In this regard, Belgium has even surpassed the EU average, with one out of four temporary contracts concluded in less than a month.[641] According to a study by the European Parliament on precarious employment in Europe, short-term contracts of less than three months are also widely spread in Belgium.[642]

On the other side of the spectrum stand some 'atypical' or extreme forms of non-standard employment,[643] *inter alia, casual work* arrangements, which will constitute the focus of this chapter. Pursuant to the working definition of casual work adopted in this PhD dissertation, casual work arrangements display chameleonic tendencies, ranging from work of very short duration, which is called in by the employer on a regular or irregular basis; but also work of long duration, which is, however, underlined by working hours insecurity. This description of casual work is in the same line with the dichotomy of casual work identified by Eurofound, consisting respectively of intermittent work and on-call work. While both forms of casual work are present in Belgium to a certain extent, intermittent work appears to be the one that has gained more predominance. The dominant position of intermittent work in Belgium stands in contrast with the previously studied countries of this dissertation, especially the United Kingdom and the Netherlands, where a prevalence of on-call and zero-hours work arrangements was observed. Moreover, the spread of intermittent work in Belgium seems to run counter to the general tendency noted in industrialized countries, characterized by a prominent spread of on-call work arrangements. In the same way as other industrialized countries, the lack of a statutory definition of casual work arrangements has also been noted in Belgium.[644]

---

635. M. Nautet, C. Piton, *An analysis of non-standard forms of employment in Belgium*, NBB Economic Review, 2019, p. 11.
636. G. Van Gyes, *Belgium: Flexible forms of work ....*
637. Article 21, Loi sur le travail, 16 Mars 1971, Available at: http://www.ejustice.just.fgov.be/cgi_loi/change_lg.pl?language=fr&la=F&cn=1971031602&table_name=loi.
638. Eurofound, *Work on demand: Recurrence, effects and challenges*, Publication Office of the European Union, Luxembourg, 2018, p. 6.
639. *Ibid.*, G. Van Gyes.
640. *Ibid.*, M. Nautet, C. Piton, p. 15.
641. *Ibid.*, p. 8.
642. European Parliament, *Precarious Employment: Patterns, trends and Policy Strategies in Europe*, p. 13.
643. *Ibid.*, G. Van Gyes.
644. M. Wouters, P. Pecinovsky, 'Marginal Part-Time in Europe: 2018's Expansion of Flexi-Jobs in Belgium', *Comparative Labour Law and Policy Journal*, 2018, iss. Dispatch No. 9, p. 1.

In addition to the aforementioned forms of casual work, other forms of flexible work have also proliferated in Belgium. To be mentioned in this regard is the expansion of the *flexi-jobs* schemes, *voucher-based work,* and *platform work*. These work arrangements display similar features with casual work, due to their flexible and casual nature, and hence, an overlap can be observed between them. As a result of this potential overlap between flexi-jobs, voucher work, and platform work with casual work, they will be positioned within the casual work arrangements' category, and hence, analysed against this background.

Overall, as it will be shown in the subsequent section, Belgium's approach towards flexible work arrangements consists of the restriction of the very flexible ones by means of heavy regulation.[645] The reason for this seems to be the over flexibility that these forms of work bring, especially on the employers' side, and the little security they bring for workers.

5.2 IN SEARCH FOR CASUAL WORK ARRANGEMENTS IN BELGIUM

5.2.1 Intermittent Work

Both forms of casual work identified by Eurofound, can be found in the Belgian labour market. Nevertheless, they manifest important differences from each other in the Belgian context. On the one hand, intermittent work is quite popular and subject to statutory regulation,[646] and on the other hand, on-call work is spread only to a limited extent, and no regulatory framework is provided in this regard.

The most common form of casual work in Belgium – *intermittent work* – has been subject to legal regulation since 2007, with some legislative changes occurred in 2013.[647] The terms used in the national context to refer to this form of work, both in the French and Dutch languages, comprise '*travail occasionnel*' and '*gelegenheidsarbeid*'. According to Eurofound's report on new forms of employment, intermittent work is considered work of very short duration, for the completion of a task, such as a project or seasonal job, or work for a very specific number of working days.[648] This work scenario is implemented in Belgium, with the aim to deal with peak periods in the tourism sector, and by setting a permitted duration of two consecutive days. Other legal features of intermittent work comprise a limitation on the maximum number of days per year for both employers and workers, with respectively two hundred days at the disposal of employers, while fifty days per year are granted to workers in order to benefit from this system. Employers can employ workers also beyond the 200 days' limitation, however, in this case, workers need to be granted an employee status.

645. Eurofound, *Work on demand: Recurrence, effects and challenges*, p. 6.
646. Arrêté royal relatif à l'occupation des travailleurs occasionnels dans le secteur de l'horeca, 12 Novembre 2013, Available at: https://www.etaamb.be/fr/arrete-royal-du-12-novembre-2013_n2013206324.html.
647. Eurofound, *New forms of employment*, p. 49; V. De Stefano, A. Aloisi, *European legal framework for digital labour platforms*, p. 32.
648. Eurofound, *New forms of employment*, p. 46.

Furthermore, full social security coverage is ensured to intermittent workers, notwithstanding the very short duration of their work. This is done through the provision of a lump sum of EUR 8.22 per hour, and up to a maximum of EUR 49.32 per day, which is paid by the employer for social security contributions.[649] In other national legal systems, casual workers normally lack the social right to full social security coverage.[650] Belgium, therefore, attempted to give an official status to work that would otherwise have been done informally. Additionally, intermittent workers who are employed under the Belgian scheme are entitled to the same labour rights as workers in standard employment relationships.

With regard to the incidence of intermittent work arrangements in Belgium, Eurofound's report on non-standard forms of employment sheds some light on this respect. Around 10.000-13.000 intermittent contracts were identified in the tourism sector in Belgium,[651] with a prominence of these contracts observed mainly in the horeca (hotels, restaurants, catering) sector.

5.2.2 On-call Work Arrangements

On the other side of the spectrum stand *on-call work* arrangements, which could have a long duration, but are characterized by high insecurity of working hours. This typology of casual work displays a low profile in Belgium. The rationale for this can be found in its low incidence, which has been questioned if there is one at all,[652] and the lack of a regulatory framework, which implies a high legal uncertainty surrounding it, with a broad assumption that it would be legally difficult to arrange as an independent contractual format of work. It would rather appear in light of more regular employment, where 'being on-call' would be seen in addition to performing normal working hours, like in on-call or availability services.[653] Furthermore, on-call contracts in Belgium do not even constitute the subject of much research.[654] No current legal definition has been provided for this type of contract, which some have considered a sui generis one.[655] Goldfays, nevertheless, describes the on-call contract, or '*contrat de travail à l'appel*', as 'an umbrella contract which can be concluded either part-time or full-time, for a definite or indefinite period, through which the parties agree that the

649. Instructions administratives ONSS – 2019/1/ Les cotisations de securite sociale, Le travail occasionnel dans le secteur de l'horeca, Available at: https://www.socialsecurity.be/employer/instructions/dmfa/fr/2019-1/instructions/socialsecuritycontributions/calculationbase/occasionals_horeca.html.
650. Eurofound, *Non-standard forms of employment: recent trends and future prospects*, 2018, p. 27.
651. *Ibid.*, p. 28.
652. Commission Staff Working Document, Analytical document accompanying the consultation document, Second phase consultation of Social Partners under Article 154 TFEU on a possible revision of the Written Statement Directive (Directive 91/533/EEC) in the framework of the EPSR, 2017, p. 154.
653. Judgment of the Court of 21 February 2018, *Ville de Nivelles v. Rudy Matzak*, Case C-518/15, ECLI:EU:C:2018:82.
654. W. Rauws, 'New Forms of Employment in Belgium', *Bulletin of Comparative Labour Relations*, New forms of employment in Europe, eds R. Blanpain and F. Hendrickx, 2016, p. 147.
655. M. Goldfays, 'Travailleurs à la demande: zero-hours Contracts', *Kluwer-Orientations* 2014/8, p. 3.

employer can, in an irregular way, call in the worker for the performance of determined tasks or services'.[656]

The most problematic aspect of on-call work arrangements in Belgium is related to the most extreme form of this type of work: *zero-hours work*. Zero-hours contracts are associated with no guarantee of working hours, and accordingly of work and income. This total lack of security may constitute an issue pursuant to the general rules of Belgian contract law, which provide for the invalidity of contracts with an undetermined object.[657] In this regard, Goldfays clarifies that, the object of on-call contracts consists in the work to be performed by the worker, and the remuneration to be paid in return by the employer.[658] Therefore, the contract has a determined, or determinable remuneration, and task to be performed, which rule out its invalidity. According to her, the fact that the working hours are not fixed at the moment of the conclusion of the contract does not threaten the validity of on-call work contracts. Many studies conducted by international organizations and scholars have pointed out the complex legal situation of zero-hours work in Belgium.[659] Belgium does not explicitly allow or forbid these types of work arrangements. Instead, some studies suggest that Belgium does not recognize zero-hours work,[660] or they are not possible at the national level. Compared to countries such as Luxembourg and Bulgaria, which have explicitly forbidden this type of work,[661] the Belgian approach seems to be vague, as it does not explicitly clarify whether zero-hours work arrangements are forbidden or not at the domestic level. However, with consideration of the current rules enshrined in the Belgian Labour Code, zero-hours contracts might hardly be possible in practice, as they appear to collide with working time rules.[662]

5.3 A POTENTIAL OVERLAP WITH OTHER FLEXIBLE WORK SCHEMES

5.3.1 The Flexi-Job Scheme

While on-call work arrangements display a low profile in Belgium, another form of casual work, which resembles to on-call work arrangements,[663] but at the same time, does not 'go as far as allowing on-call work', is the *flexi-job scheme*.[664] In a study on work on demand, Eurofound refers to the flexi-job scheme as a proxy for work on

656. *Ibid.*
657. Articles 1108 and 1126-1130 of the Belgian civil code. Available at: http://www.ejustice.just.fgov.be/cgi_loi/change_lg.pl?language=fr&la=F&cn=1804032133&table_name=loi.
658. M. Goldfays, 'Travailleurs à la demande: zero-hours contracts', p. 4.
659. For instance, the Analytical document of the European Commission, p. 154.
660. European Parliament, *Precarious Employment: Patterns, trends and Policy Strategies in Europe*, p. 122.
661. The Analytical document of the European Commission, p. 54.
662. Loi sur le travail, 16 Mars 1971.
663. OECD, *Policy responses to new forms of work*, Annex A, Questionnaire.
664. *Loi portant des dispositions diverses en matière sociale* of 16 November 2015; Royal Decree of 13 December 2016 brought some changes to the flexi-job scheme.

demand in Belgium.[665] The flexi-job scheme was adopted in 2015, with the purpose of tackling undeclared work and providing workers with supplementary income by means of a secondary job.[666] Nevertheless, to be eligible for this type of work, some prerequisites must be completed. Initially, flexi-jobs are allowed only in certain sectors. When the scheme was adopted, this type of work was allowed only in the hospitality, or horeca sector (hotels, restaurants, bars); as of January 2018, it expanded to the retail industry, e.g., supermarkets, hairdressers, bakeries, etc.[667] In 2018, the Brussels Times, a Belgian news website and magazine in Belgium, provided some data on the incidence of this form of work, which, by then, counted around 50.000 jobs, with their main prominence in the horeca sector.[668]

What is more, while there is no limitation on the amount of working hours or days that a 'flexi-jobber' is permitted to perform work, a limited personal scope is nonetheless noticed. In compliance with the designation of flexi-jobs as complementary jobs, only workers who are employed by another employer than the flexi-employer, for at least four-fifths of the hours of a full-time job in the respective industry, the so-called 4/5th rule, can be eligible for this scheme.[669] Later on, the personal scope of the flexi-jobs scheme got extended to also include another category, that of retired persons. Such an expansion resulted in an increased attractiveness to this scheme by retired persons, as in 2018, there were around 1,200 retired flexi-jobbers. Additionally, 'young teachers who work on a contractual basis (instead of the standard fixed appointment) can do flexi-jobs even during the summer break when they are in factual state of unemployment' are also allowed by law to perform a flexi-job.[670]

One further legal requirement, more of a formal nature, consists of drawing up a framework agreement, composed of some mandatory information about the parties and the work to be performed. This framework agreement serves as a preliminary step prior to the conclusion of an employment contract by the parties. Upon the conclusion of such a contract, the flexi-jobber is obliged to perform the work. This employment contract can be concluded for a definite term or a clearly defined job, however, only a limited number of fixed-term contracts are allowed in Belgium unless a justification is provided in this regard. Once the prerequisites have been accomplished, both flexi-jobbers and employers can benefit from an advantageous financial situation.[671] In this regard, the flexi-jobber is exempt from paying income taxes, and the employer receives a tax benefit as well.[672] Furthermore, the flexi-jobber is fully covered by social security protections and is entitled to an hourly minimum wage of EUR 8.82, together with a flexi holiday pay.

665. Eurofound, *Work on demand*, p. 9.
666. OECD, *Policy responses to new forms of work*, 2019, p. 78.
667. *Loi Programme* of 25 December 2017.
668. O. Schneider, 'Nearly 50.000 flexi-jobs filled in 2018', The Brussels Time, 2019, Available at: https://www.brusselstimes.com/news/belgium-all-news/52949/nearly-50-000-flexi-jobs-filled-in-2018/.
669. M. Wouters, P. Pecinovsky, 'Marginal part-time in Europe: 2018's expansion of flexi-jobs in Belgium', *Comparative Labour Law and Policy Journal*, 2018, iss. Dispatch No. 9, p. 1.
670. *Ibid.*, p. 4.
671. M. Nautet, C. Piton, *An analysis of non-standard forms of employment in Belgium*, p. 7.
672. Eurofound, *Work on demand*, p. 8.

Notwithstanding these restrictions presented by the law to limit the use of flexi-jobs in order to not cause a disruptive effect on the standard employment relationship,[673] trade unions in Belgium have opposed this scheme. These trade unions contend that the flexi-jobs scheme has hampered standard employment contracts, and constitutes precarious work.[674] The issue was even brought to the Belgian Constitutional Court, which ruled that the flexi-job scheme did not threaten the standard employment relationship. According to the Court, the purpose of inserting the four-fifths rule was to employ people who were already in quasi-permanent employment, and not to undermine permanent contracts.[675] In this way, this ruling reveals something important about the limits of flexibility, as only people with existing social protection can do flexi-jobs. After the release of this decision, the government conducted an impact assessment of the flexi-jobs scheme, which indicated that permanent jobs in the hospitality sector were not hampered at all.

To conclude, the very flexible and casual nature of work underlying both the flexi-jobs scheme and on-call work leads to an overlap between flexi-jobs and casual work arrangements. Nevertheless, as was already mentioned, the flexi-jobs scheme is not as extreme as on-call work, due to the applicable legal restrictions to it in Belgium, which intend to keep flexi-jobs as a complementary form of work. Limitations extend especially to the category of workers, but also sectors where flexi-jobs can be used. To be noticed is that, if eventually, the just-mentioned legal limitations get loosened, especially the 4/5th rule, the implication will be that the flexi-jobs scheme will get closer to that of on-call work arrangements.

5.3.2 Voucher-Based Work

The proliferation of *voucher-based work* in Belgium constitutes another work scheme, which presumably overlaps with the typology of casual work arrangements. This scheme, also known as the '*titres-services*' or '*dienstencheque*' in the national context, was launched in Belgium in 2004.[676] The purpose for the promotion of this new form of work consisted in: combatting informality in the labour market, with a special focus on the domestic sector; boosting employment opportunities; reintegrating long-term unemployed workers; and ensuring a better work-life balance for the users of the service.[677] Furthermore, this type of work offered the opportunity for better social security protection, and in some instances, better pay.[678] In this respect, voucher workers enjoy full social security coverage, and their working hours' pay appears to be higher than the minimum hourly wage.[679] Since its adoption in Belgium, this scheme

673. *Ibid.*, p. 6.
674. M. Wouters, P. Pecinovsky, 'Marginal part-time in Europe ...', p. 2.
675. *Ibid.*, p. 3.
676. Loi du 20.07.2001 visant à favoriser le développement de services et d'emplois de proximité et Arrêté royal du 12.12. 2001 concernant les titres-services.
677. European Parliament, *Precarious employment*, p. 176.
678. *Ibid.*, p. 117.
679. *Ibid.*, p. 84.

has become very popular. In 2013, around 130,000 workers and 947,000 users were part of it,[680] an incidence which exceeded the initial expectations for this work scheme.

The peculiar feature of this form of work consists in its method of payment: the service voucher. The voucher comprises a package of both hourly pay and social security coverage. Compared to other national systems where a direct relationship between the voucher worker and the client is observed, in Belgium, a kind of merger between voucher-based work and temporary agency work is noticed, as an intermediary is provided between the voucher worker and the client.[681] Consequently, the Belgian voucher-based work scheme involves several actors. To start with, a recognized service voucher company, which has the role of the employer, serves as an intermediary for the employment of voucher workers. This service voucher company can be a temporary work agency, but also a commercial business, a public institution or a private non-profit organization,[682] and it should be recognized by the federal government.[683] These subjects are heavily subsidized by the state, while the scheme in itself is considered 'the most heavily subsidized scheme of its kind in Europe'.[684] However, another company is assigned to deal with the issuance of service vouchers. As of 2014, Sodexo is assigned to perform this duty in the Belgian context. The users of the service, or the clients, purchase the vouchers from Sodexo, where each voucher amounts to one working hour's pay of the voucher worker. The clients also choose among the recognized service voucher companies, which will assign a voucher worker according to their needs.

Eurofound, in its study on new forms of employment, refers to the overlap between voucher-based work and casual work arrangements.[685] The reason for this overlap can be found in the underlying casual nature of both forms of work, where the workers are called in based on the business needs of the employers. To be noticed is that, however, in this Eurofound study, the voucher-based scheme is evaluated as a positive development,[686] standing in contrast with casual work arrangements, which are, more often than not, associated with poor working conditions.[687] The success of the Belgian model of voucher-based work is further confirmed in the study conducted by the European Parliament on precarious employment, which points to this work typology as a good practice. Notwithstanding that also voucher work can be characterized by jobs and income insecurity, a certain stability is offered to these workers in Belgium, after having worked for three months. After completing three months of work, these workers become entitled to some minimum guaranteed hours, concretely

680. Eurofound, *New forms of employment*, 2015, p. 94.
681. V. De Stefano, A. Aloisi, *European legal framework for digital labour platforms*, European Commission, Luxembourg, (2018), pp. 32-33.
682. *Ibid.*, p. 33.
683. R. Blanpain, 'Belgium', in *International Encyclopedia for Labour Law and Industrial Relations*, ed. F. Hendrickx, *Kluwer Law Online*, 2012, p. 142.
684. The state subsidizes around 70% of this scheme, according to I. Marx, D. Vandelannoote, *Matthew runs amok: The Belgian service voucher scheme*, IZA Working Paper, 2014, Abstract and p. 1.
685. Eurofound, *New forms of employment*, p. 46.
686. W. Rauws, *New forms of employment in Belgium*, p. 157.
687. *Ibid.*, p. 143.

thirteen hours per week, with a unit price of EUR 9, altogether with an offer for a permanent employment contract. While the voucher companies can conclude with voucher workers either a fixed-term contract or a permanent one, the vast majority of the contracts concluded so far were observed to be fixed-term ones.[688] An opportunity to have a permanent contract is, however, envisaged after the third month of the work. Another positive aspect of this type of work in Belgium is related to the hourly wage of voucher workers, which is considered a decent one. Nevertheless, as only a few working hours are guaranteed, the level of income experienced by these workers can still remain low. Full coverage by social security provided for voucher workers also represents a step forward to counter the insecurity, which is inherent in work arrangements with a casual nature.

The Belgian legislator has introduced further legal limitations applicable to this work typology. In comparison to the Italian voucher work model, which is allowed for any type of activity, voucher work in Belgium is permitted only for domestic services. What is more, a maximum number of 500 vouchers per year, which also correspond to working hours, are allowable per client.[689] Nevertheless, exceptions are provided considering the domestic needs of vulnerable persons, such as older ones, single parents, parents of children with disabilities, etc.[690] This category can make use of a 2000 vouchers per year quota. On the other side, no restrictions are provided in Belgium with regard to the category of workers eligible to perform voucher-based work.

5.3.3 Platform-Mediated Work in the Belgian Context

The lack of a universal definition of platform work has also been acknowledged by the National Labour Council (NLC), an important public body in Belgium, which deals, *inter alia*, with labour law issues.[691] This council is composed of representatives from both employers and workers' sides, and delivers opinions on diverse social issues to either the competent minister or the Belgian Parliament, besides their capacity to conclude national collective agreements.[692] In its report on the digitalization of the collaborative economy, the NLC indicates that platforms can exercise both an intermediary function between the demand and supply sides of labour, but they can also go beyond being a mere intermediary.[693] The group of platforms studied by the NLC comprises both general and specialized platforms, where the latter serve to provide specific services, such as computer programming. With regard to general platforms,

688. Eurofound, *New forms of employment*, p. 94.
689. V. De Stefano, A. Aloisi, *European legal framework for digital labour platforms*, pp. 32-33.
690. Eurofound, *New forms of employment*, p. 83.
691. Conseil National du Travail, Conseil Central de l' Economie, Rapport No. 107, *Diagnostic des partenaires sociaux concernant la digitalisation et l'économie collaborative – Execution de l'accord interprofessionnel 2017-2018*, Available at: http://www.cnt-nar.be/RAPPORT/rapport-107-FR.pdf.
692. Eurofound, National Labour Council, Available at: https://www.eurofound.europa.eu/efemiredictionary/national-labour-council; http://www.cnt-nar.be/Qui-sommes-nous.htm.
693. Conseil National du Travail, Conseil Central de l' Economie, Rapport No. 107, pp. 60-61.

NLC points out those which offer virtual work with a global reach, but also non-virtual work, such as babysitting, house cleaning, and gardening, which can be exercised within a certain geographical area. In Belgium, a predominance of on-location tasks has been observed, especially of those requiring a low level of skills.[694] Such tasks are related primarily to the household and transport sectors, however, also professional services provided in a platform are widespread in Belgium.

The National Labour Council, in its report on the digitalization of the collaborative economy, provides a non-exhaustive list of terms surrounding platform work. Nevertheless, the most common terms used in the national context to refer to platform work comprise mainly '*économie collaborative*' and '*économie de plateforme*' in the French language, and '*deeleconomie*' in the Dutch language. Furthermore, some economists of the National Bank of Belgium refer to the concept of the sharing economy.[695] However, to be noticed is that, all these concepts appear to have a broader scope than platform work, as they additionally include activities, such as sharing of goods, assets, or services, with Airbnb constituting a notable example in this regard.[696]

The determination of the size of platform work in Belgium has been associated with several statistical challenges.[697] The lack of a common definition in this regard, together with the rapid evolution of platforms and platform work, seem to be some of the factors contributing to this challenge. Nevertheless, some surveys and studies attempt to give an approximate size of the phenomenon in Belgium. For example, a study conducted by PricewaterhouseCoopers (PwC) in 2016 pointed out the existence of more than 275 collaborative economy platforms operating in nine European countries.[698] Out of 275 platforms, around 25 platforms were identified in Belgium in that period. In 2018, the European Commission Flash barometer also provided some data: around 18% of the Belgian population was involved in the sharing economy, compared to 8% in 2016.[699] This participation rate was noticed to be lower in comparison to Belgium's neighbouring countries, especially France and the United Kingdom, but also lower than the European average, which was 23%.[700] Notwithstanding these outcomes, the potential for growth of platform work has also been highlighted in the Belgian context,[701] where an increase in this phenomenon was already noticed.[702]

Some legislative developments on platform work have put Belgium in the spotlight, as one of the first European countries to introduce dedicated legislation in

694. Eurofound, *Employment and working conditions of selected types of platform work*, 2018, p. 14.
695. R. Basselier, G. Langenus, L. Walravens, 'The Rise of the Sharing Economy', *Economic Review*, September 2018, Available at: https://www.nbb.be/en/articles/rise-sharing-economy.
696. *Ibid.*, p. 58.
697. Summary of the article on 'The rise of the sharing economy', p. 6; CNT Rapport No. 107, p. 2.
698. R. Vaughan, R. Daveio, *Assessing the size and presence of the collaborative economy in Europe*, PwC UK, Impulse paper for the European Commission, 2016.
699. EC Flash Eurobarometer 438 (2016) and 467 (2018) – The use of collaborative platforms.
700. Eurofound, *Employment and working conditions of selected types of platform work*, p. 65.
701. R. Basselier et al., 'The rise of the sharing economy', p. 2; Eurofound, *Employment and working conditions of platform workers*, p. 65.
702. CNT Rapport No. 107, p. 2.

this field, namely the program law of 1 July 2016,[703] or the so-called De Croo act, named after the minister who proposed it. De Croo act had manifold purposes, such as combatting informality in the labour market, promoting entrepreneurship, reducing the administrative burdens to platform work activities, and providing more clarity on the tax and social security status of people working in the sharing economy.[704] Within its legal scope would fall only services between individuals, whereas renting and delivery of goods were excluded.[705]

This legal framework established a favourable tax regime for most of the activities in the sharing economy.[706] This act, however, became subject to changes over time, such as with the 2018 Act, which was built on the 2016 De Croo Act.[707] When the law was introduced in 2016, the applicable tax rate amounted to 10%;[708] as of 2018, no tax rate was applicable to platform work-mediated activities, with a maximum monthly income of EUR 500 and a maximum yearly income of EUR 6,340 (gross).[709] Up to this predefined ceiling, the incomes were considered 'miscellaneous income', instead of professional ones, and a favourable fiscal regime was implemented. A further legal obligation consisted of the registration and recognition of platforms by the competent Belgian authority. These recognized platforms had an obligation to report on a yearly basis on the payments made in favour of the service providers.[710]

Notwithstanding that the major outcome of the 2018 Act was related to the tax regime, its implications were also extended to other areas, such as labour law and social security law. According to this legislative act, the tax-free platform workers, gaining up to the predefined ceiling of EUR 6,340 per year and EUR 500 per month, were excluded from labour and social security law. What is more, these platform workers were also excluded from the social security provisions for self-employed workers,[711] hence, finding themselves in a 'social law free zone'.[712] In contrast, the 2016 Act did not explicitly exclude platform workers from labour protection.[713]

Therefore, the 2018 Act has constituted the subject of several criticism. In their diagnosis on the platform economy, the Belgian social partners pointed out the law as a pathway to more complexity, unfair competition, and associated with adverse

703. Loi-programme du 1 Juillet 2016, Available at: http://www.ejustice.just.fgov.be/cgi_loi/change_lg.pl?language = fr&la = F&table_name = loi&cn = 2016070101.
704. CNT Rapport No. 107, p. 71.
705. *Ibid.*, p. 72.
706. Also travail associative and services occasionnels entre les citoyens were included in its scope of application.
707. Loi relative à la relance économique et au renforcement de la cohésion sociale du 18 Juillet 2018, Available at: https://www.ejustice.just.fgov.be/cgi_loi/change_lg.pl?language = fr&la = F&table_name = loi&cn = 2018071803.
708. https://www.lexgo.be/en/papers/tax-law/individual-tax/collaborative-economy-new-legal-framework-enters-into-full-force-on-1-march-2017,111327.html.
709. V. De Stefano et al., *Platform work and the employment relationship*, p. 24.
710. Kilhoffer et al., *Study to gather evidence on the working conditions of platform workers*, p. 109.
711. Article 30 of Loi relative à la relance économique et au renforcement de la cohésion sociale du 18 Juillet 2018.
712. Y. Stevens, J. Put, 'Het laatste heilige huisje: professionele apartheid in de sociale zekerheid', in R. De Corte, M. De Vos, P. Humblet, F. Kéfer and E. Van Hoorde, eds *De taal is gans het recht. Liber Amicorum Willy van Eeckhoutte*, Mechelen, Kluwer, 2018, p. 147.
713. Sections 35-43 loi-programme du 1 juillet 2016.

consequences in terms of social protection and tax revenues.[714] Additionally, this tax reform was seen as promoting the legal qualification as self-employed,[715] even for instances where the reality of the relationship between the parties points out a different direction. Complaints from both the employers' and workers' sides brought this act to the Belgian Constitutional Court. The outcome was that the Court declared the 2018 Act unconstitutional, with effect as of 1 January 2021.[716] According to the Court, a different tax treatment was noticed, on one side between platform workers who were either self-employed or employees, and on the other side, other workers who earned less than EUR 6,340 per year. As no reasonable justification was provided for this different treatment, the act was considered an infringement of the Belgian constitution. Therefore, as of January 2021, these workers would again fall under the original 2016 Act, which provided them with a favourable tax treatment, and at the same time, it did not explicitly exclude them from labour protection.[717]

Moreover, the 2018 legislation on platform work has been further criticized for worsening the working conditions of delivery workers, as its enactment corresponded to the termination of an agreement between Deliveroo Belgium and SMart. This agreement was considered beneficial for the labour and social security protections of the majority of Deliveroo workers.[718] Deliveroo started operating in Belgium in 2015 and became a pioneering platform in the food delivery sector in the Belgian labour market. SMart was a cooperative, which was initially providing services in the creative industries, and decided to expand into the field of platform work.[719] The outcome of this expansion was a partnership between SMart and Deliveroo, which granted the opportunity to platform workers to have an employment relationship with SMart. As of May 2016, Deliveroo riders had the option to either work as self-employed for Deliveroo or as employees of Smart. The result showed that 90% of Deliveroo riders opted for an employment contract.[720] The reason for adhering to the SMart scheme consisted in reaping benefits such as training, insurance, a minimum pay of three hours, equipment costs, etc.,[721] in exchange for a share of their earnings (6.5%). Even though such benefits were not considered the most ideal for this segment of platform workers, they marked a step forward in extending some protections to these workers.[722]

714. CNT Rapport No. 107, p. 4.
715. J. Drahokoupil, A. Piasna, *Work in the Platform Economy: Deliveroo Riders in Belgium and the SMart Arrangement*, ETUI Working Paper 201901, (2019), p. 39.
716. Cour constitutionnelle du 23 avril 2020, Case No. 53/2020, Available at: https://www.const-court.be/public/f/2020/2020-053f.pdf.
717. Sections 35-43 loi-programme du 1 juillet 2016; V. De Stefano et al., *Platform work and the employment relationship*, p. 24.
718. J. Drahokoupil, A. Piasna, *Work in the Platform Economy: Deliveroo Riders in Belgium and the SMart Arrangement*, ETUI Working Paper 2019.01, (2019).
719. Eurofound, *Employment and working conditions of selected types of platform work*, p. 54.
720. J. Drahokoupil, A. Piasna, *Work in the platform economy: Deliveroo riders in Belgium and the SMart arrangement*, p. 9.
721. Kilhoffer et al., *Study to gather evidence on the working conditions of platform workers*, p. 121.
722. Z. Kilhoffer, K. Lenaerts, *What is happening with platform workers' rights?, Lessons from Belgium*, CEPS Publications, 2017, Available at: https://www.ceps.eu/ceps-publications/what-happening-platform-workers-rights-lessons-belgium/.

The partnership between Deliveroo Belgium and SMart came to an end in 2017,[723] after a reform undertaken unilaterally by Deliveroo in its payment system. Instead of the initial method of payment per working hour, Deliveroo altered this method into a payment per delivery. Many scholars argue that this action undertaken by Deliveroo 'coincided with the tax relief model presented by De Croo'. An obligation was, hence, imposed on Deliveroo riders to switch their status to that of self-employed workers. The majority of Deliveroo riders expressed dissatisfaction in this regard, as they were evaded from the previously ensured income security.[724] This dissatisfaction escalated into protests and strikes on their side.[725] In addition to the protests against the termination of the agreement with SMart, platform workers involved in food delivery in Belgium have also undertaken other organizing initiatives. Against this background, these workers have established the *'Collectif des coursiers'* or the collective of bike couriers in Belgium, composed of food delivery couriers of Deliveroo, Takeaway, and Uber Eats,[726] with the aim to, *inter alia*, improve their collective voice.

5.3.3.1 Exploring the Overlap with Platform Work

The overlap between casual work and platform work has been pointed out and elaborated on in detail in the previous chapters of this dissertation. In addition to what has been already mentioned, the focus of this part will be in the exploration of such an overlap in the Belgian context.

To start with, many platform workers in Belgium were excluded from labour protection by the 2018 Act. The Belgian Constitutional Court, however, decided that platform workers could not be ruled out that easily from labour protection. In the same vein went as well the decision of the Administrative Commission for Employment Relationships in Belgium, which has the competence to regulate labour relations.[727] These public approaches constitute a major step in bringing platform work within the scope of labour law. Once within the labour law ambit, an exploration of the specific position of platform work, either as part of broader labour market trends or as a brand new form of work, becomes essential. In light of this, De Stefano and Aloisi suggest positioning platform work within the typology of casual work. With reference to Belgium, these scholars point out the intermittent work scheme, as a suitable legal framework for enhancing the labour protection of platform workers at the national level.[728]

723. However with effect from January 2018.
724. J. Drahokoupil, A. Piasna, *Work in the platform economy: Deliveroo riders in Belgium and the SMart arrangement*, p. 29.
725. *Ibid.*, p. 10.
726. Eurofound, *Employment and working conditions of selected types of platform work*, p. 55.
727. A. De Becker, M. De Coninck, NEWEFIN Project, New employment forms and challenges to industrial relations, Country report Belgium, p. 32; PwC, *Gig economy employment status*, 2019, p. 9, Available at: https://www.pwclegal.be/en/news/gig-economy-employment-status-belgium.html; K. McCann, 'Contracts could soon change for Deliveroo couriers', Brussels Express, (2018), Available at: https://brussels-express.eu/contracts-could-soon-change-for-deliveroo-couriers/.
728. V. De Stefano, A. Aloisi, *European legal framework for digital labour platforms*, p. 32.

In exploring the overlap between casual and platform work in Belgium, some features of both forms of work will be scrutinized. An insightful source on the working conditions of a segment of the platform economy, concretely Deliveroo riders in Belgium, is provided by a working paper of the European Trade Union Institute (ETUI). The data presented by this study were based on online surveys of Deliveroo riders, which resulted in 500 responses, but also data shared by SMart, the cooperative which used to provide an employment relationship to these workers. The aforementioned data point out a precarious situation faced by Deliveroo riders in Belgium, especially after the termination of the agreement with SMart, which was translated into the loss of the employment status of these workers. More specifically, the work of Deliveroo riders in Belgium was characterized by a very low number of working hours, which also had an unpredictable nature. Concretely, these workers were found to work an average of 23 hours per month, reaching a maximum of 155 hours per year.[729] Compared to full-time workers, who work on average for 160 hours per month, the working hours of these platform workers appear to be significantly lower. In addition to the modest number of hours worked, an exacerbation occurs when considering the unsocial nature of their working hours, e.g., during weekends and evenings, and their unpredictability, which varies on a weekly basis.[730] Such indicia seem to run counter to the flexibility claim for many workers involved in this form of work. Indeed, many platform workers have complained about the lack of the promised flexibility.[731]

The lack of the working hours' guarantee is certainly interlinked with the lack of a guaranteed job and income. Considering that the majority of Deliveroo riders indicated as their main source of income the one deriving from platform work, they seem to be trapped in a very vulnerable situation. It was observed that also those platform workers, who had another job that provided them with additional income, were usually employed in non-standard forms of employment, or even informal work. This unstable situation is further exacerbated when combined with a low level of income. The data provided by both the riders and the cooperative SMart revealed a gross monthly income of EUR 249, which falls far below the minimum wage level in Belgium.[732] In order to increase this amount, workers could work for longer hours (conditional upon the availability of work), but still with no certainty of reaching even the minimum income level. Moreover, even workers who have family obligations, and were engaged in longer working hours, earned only EUR 720 per month on average.[733] On the other hand, students involved in these riding activities were found to have even lower hourly pay and consequently gain less income.[734] In case platform workers have to cover as well work-related materials or equipment, their income level will further level down, exacerbating their already modest incomes.

729. J. Drahokoupil, A. Piasna, *Work in the platform economy: Deliveroo riders in Belgium and the SMart arrangement*, p. 16.
730. *Ibid.*, p. 34.
731. *Ibid.*, p. 28.
732. J. Drahokoupil & A. Piasna, *Work in the platform economy: Deliveroo riders in Belgium and the SMart arrangement*, p. 18.
733. *Ibid.*, p. 15.
734. *Ibid.*, p. 18.

Belgium, in general, displays a low level of in-work poverty.[735] The European Parliament notes that temporary contracts represent one of the main risks of precariousness at the national level, due to their association with in-work poverty and a low level of job security.[736] Stemming from such considerations, workers with contracts of even a shorter duration, such as workers in casual work arrangements, can presumably be more adversely impacted by in-work poverty and job insecurity. Therefore, casual work arrangements, which are present in the Belgian labour market, are expected to display similar features of precariousness. However, different forms of casual work can be associated with different levels of work-related insecurities. To start with, intermittent work is characterized by a very short duration, as intermittent workers can work up to two consecutive days, with a maximum of fifty days per year. This very short duration indicates that the insecurity of work and income is an inherent feature of this form of work. Such insecurity is further exacerbated when it comes to on-call workers, another group of casual workers, whose work relation can be long, but is characterized by high insecurity of working hours. It is not hard to imagine that zero-hours workers, who have no working hours guarantee, suffer the most adverse consequences in this regard. Notwithstanding the low incidence of on-call work in Belgium, these workers seem to be at risk of a particularly vulnerable situation.

Flexi-jobs were also created to fulfil unexpected business needs. What flexi workers share in common with on-call workers is the working hours' insecurity, together with work during unsocial hours and unpredictable work schedules. Nevertheless, the legal obligation to have another job in order to be involved in this work scheme seems to be an indicator that distances this form of work from being related to a precarious situation. Notwithstanding the very flexible nature of the flexi-jobs scheme, the fact that these workers are already employed, cannot arguably leave them exposed to the insecurity of jobs and income, which is frequently experienced by on-call workers.

With regard to voucher workers who perform services in the Belgian labour market, insecurity of working hours, which goes hand in hand with the insecurity of work and income, is observed especially during the first three months of work. According to the relevant Belgian regulation, a certain stability is offered to these workers after three months of work, such as a minimum amount of thirteen hours per week, altogether with the option to have a permanent employment contract. What is more, their hourly wage is noticed to be higher than the Belgian minimum hourly wage. It was due to such reasons that the European Parliament considered voucher-based work in Belgium as a good work practice.[737]

In addition to the aforementioned insecurities inherent in the working conditions of both platform and casual workers, an exclusion from labour protection is quite common for both categories of workers. Such an exclusion is certainly more prominent in platform work arrangements, due to the self-employed qualification that platforms

735. V. Buffel, I. Nicaise, *In-work poverty in Belgium*, European Social Policy Network, 2019, p. 7; European Parliament, *Precarious employment* ..., p. 67.
736. *Ibid.*, European Parliament, p. 13 and p. 42.
737. *Ibid.*, p. 176.

give to platform workers in their terms and conditions. In the Belgian legal landscape, the exclusion of platform workers from labour protection has also been statutorily set out in the 2018 Act, however, this is not the case anymore as of January 2021. Furthermore, public bodies, such as the Administrative Commission, are striving to accord labour protection to platform workers, notwithstanding that platform operators are appealing these decisions. With respect to casual workers, Belgium has opted for strict regulation of their legal situation, contrary to countries whose approach goes in the opposite direction, such as the UK. The Belgian legal framework provides regulation for intermittent work, flexi-jobs and voucher-based work schemes. On the opposite side, extreme forms of casual work, such as on-call work arrangements and zero-hours work, are not accorded with any labour protection by the Belgian legislator, and hence, workers engaged in these work arrangements suffer an exclusion on the same footing as platform workers.

5.4 THE PANDEMIC HIGHLIGHTS THE PRECARITY OF CASUAL AND PLATFORM WORKERS IN BELGIUM

The COVID-19 pandemic does not merely constitute a global health crisis. Its outbreak resembles a Medusa, which spreads its tentacles in every sphere of the economy and reaches up to the personal lives of people. Inevitably, the pandemic has also disrupted the world of work, where some of its adverse consequences include massive unemployment, increased inactivity, income loss, etc. Such outcomes have been quite bitter for many workers worldwide, especially for those whose jobs were already precarious, such as casual and platform workers,[738] who have been referred to as 'the weakest link'.[739] In the wording of the ICT Council in Canada, during the pandemic, an exacerbation is noted of 'pre-existing tensions between the economic opportunity provided by the gig economy and the precarious nature of gig work'.[740] These wordings hold true for many platform workers worldwide, who have experienced unemployment, or income loss during the COVID-19 crisis.[741] Furthermore, many standard workers, who have lost their jobs during the pandemic, have turned to platform work to make a living.[742] This has resulted in increased competition, which has further driven the payment down. On the other side, while many of the services offered through a platform have shrunk, some services have encountered an unexpected

738. T. Novitz, 'The Potential for International Regulation of Gig Economy Issues', *King's Law Journal*, Vol. 31, Issue 2, 2020, pp. 275-286, p. 284; Eurofound, *Back to the future: Policy pointers from platform work scenarios, New forms of employment series*, Publications Office of the European Union, Luxembourg, p. 1.
739. N. Countouris et al., 'Covid-19 crisis makes clear a new concept of "worker" is long overdue'.
740. A. Cutean, C. Herron, T. Quan, *Loading: The Future of Work: Worldwide Remote Work Experimentation and the Evolution of the Platform Economy*, Information and Communications Technology Council (ICTC), Ottawa, Canada, July 2020.
741. Eurofound, *Back to the future ...*, p. 1.
742. The Fairwork project, *The gig-economy and Covid 19: looking ahead*, 2020, p. 12.

expansion.[743] During the pandemic, the delivery of food, groceries, parcels, and medical supplies, the provision of care to people in need, and the recourse to ride-hailing services, instead of using public transport, have spiked.[744] Platform workers who were providing these services had to work on the frontline as essential workers.[745] Basically, these workers were confronted with a hard choice: to stay home and face destitution, or to go to work and risk contracting the virus and transmitting it to their families. Similarly, casual workers in Belgium had to face the same tough choice. The horeca sector, where a great prominence of casual workers has been noticed, was obliged to close for the majority of the time since the outbreak. On the other side, many flexi-jobbers who work for the retail industry, especially for supermarkets, had to go to work as essential workers.

Against this background, it is paramount to observe the response of the Belgian government to this deepened precarity. In order to deal with this crisis, many countries have adopted the short-time work scheme, also known as the temporary unemployment scheme.[746] According to this scheme, the worker can be temporarily suspended from the job, while preserving it and the related income (or a part of it). In this case, an unemployment benefit is usually paid by the social security system, but it can be also paid from the public finances. As the unemployment benefit depends on the wages earned, the employer usually pays a supplement on top of it.[747] This scheme, which was already in place in Belgium, became more highlighted in the context of the coronavirus. At the outset of the pandemic, 25% of the active working population in Belgium was found to have recourse to it.[748] For the period between 31 August 2020 and 1 October 2020, applying for this scheme was not that simple, as the pandemic was not considered a force majeure.[749] However, from 1 October 2020, the temporary unemployment scheme with a simplified application procedure, was envisaged to remain in force until the end of June 2021.[750] Importantly, this mechanism includes

743. For more information, *see* Eurofound, *Platform economy: Developments in the Covid-19 crisis*, Dossier July 2020, Available at: https://www.eurofound.europa.eu/data/platform-economy/dossiers/developments-in-the-covid-19-crisis.
744. *Ibid.*, the Fairwork project, p. 12.
745. A. Cutean et al., *Loading: The Future of Work: Worldwide Remote Work Experimentation and the Evolution of the Platform Economy*, Information and Communications Technology Council (ICTC), Ottawa, Canada, 2020, p. 20.
746. V. De Stefano, 'Labour and social protection in times of Covid-19'. Available at: https://www.youtube.com/watch?v = UQPzbdP0kEY&feature = youtu.be.
747. F. Hendrickx, S. Taes, M. Wouters, 'Covid-19 and Labour Law in Belgium', *European Labour Law Journal*, Vol. 11 Issue 3, 2020, pp. 276-285, p. 280.
748. F. Hendrickx, 'The coronavirus and the world of work: renewed labour law questions', *Global Workplace Law and Policy*, April 2020, Available at: http://global-workplace-law-and-policy.kluwerlawonline.com/2020/04/01/the-coronavirus-and-the-world-of-work-renewed-labour-law-questions/.
749. Arrêté royal du 30 mars 2020 visant à adapter les procédures dans le cadre du chômage temporaire du au virus Covid-19 et à modifier l'article 10 de l'arrêté royal du 6 mai 2019 modifiant les articles 27, 51, 52bis, 58, 58/3 et 63 de l'arrêté royal du 25 novembre 1991 portant réglementation du chômage et insérant les articles 36sexies, 63bis et 124bis dans le même arrêté, publié le 2 mars 2020; Office National de l'Emploi, Available at: https://www.onem.be/fr/documentation/feuille-info/e1-0.
750. *Ibid.*

within its personal scope of application solely employees.[751] Hence, platform workers, who are qualified as self-employed by the platforms' business agreements, are not eligible for the benefits of the temporary unemployment scheme. However, intermittent workers and flexi-jobbers in Belgium, who are qualified as employees, and whose work activities were disrupted due to the coronavirus, such as in the horeca sector, can be eligible for the benefits of the temporary unemployment scheme. However, even in this case, the entitlement to this benefit depends upon the employer's will to preserve the workforce. Given the unstable nature of these work arrangements, many employers simply terminated these arrangements.

What is more, the Belgian government has also introduced an income replacement scheme for self-employed workers, whose work activities have been impacted by the epidemic. Pursuant to this scheme, the self-employed workers can apply for '*le droit passerelle*' or a 'bridging right',[752] in case they fall under one of these scenarios: (a) a total interruption of their work activities, (b) a decrease in their income of at least 40%, in the month prior to the one in which they are asking for relief,[753] and (c) an inability to work due to being in quarantine, or providing care to a child. The amount of the financial compensation varies on whether the self-employed had to fully or partially interrupt work. Self-employed workers who fall under one of these cases can apply for financial compensation until 30 June 2021.[754] Notwithstanding that this scheme does not explicitly mention platform workers, the majority of platform workers can be eligible to make use of this 'bridging right', due to their self-employed status.

In addition to the financial assistance provided by the government, some platforms have, to a certain extent, responded to the new challenges posed by the pandemic. The most common response they provided consisted of adopting preventive measures, such as supplying masks, disinfectants, protective gears, etc., which serve to also reassure the customer.[755] Such measures are useful for many platform and casual workers, especially for those working as essential workers during the pandemic. In light of this, the Belgian Federal Public Service of Employment has also adopted a generic guide about safety at work during the pandemic.[756] Moreover, some platforms, such as Uber, and Lyft,[757] have also been offering sick pay to their workers, however,

751. Office National de l'Emploi, Point 3.2, Available at: https://www.onem.be/fr/documentation/feuille-info/e1-0.
752. Loi modifiant la loi du 22 décembre 2016 instaurant un droit passerelle en faveur des travailleurs indépendants et introduisant les mesures temporaires dans le cadre du COVID-19 en faveur des travailleurs indépendants.
753. The Brussels Times, 'Support measures for the self-employed extended until 30 June', 26 February 2021, Available at: https://www.brusselstimes.com/news/belgium-all-news/157288/support-measures-for-the-self-employed-extended-until-june-30/
754. Rtbf, 'Coronavirus en Belgique: prolongation jusqu'au 30 juin des mesures de soutien aux indépendants', 26 Février 2021, Available at :https://www.rtbf.be/info/belgique/detail_coronavirus-en-belgique-prolongation-jusqu-au-30-juin-des-mesures-de-soutien-aux-independants?id = 10706915.
755. Fairwork project, p. 29.
756. https://employment.belgium.be/en/themes/well-being-workers/safety-work-during-coronavirus-crisis-generic-guide.
757. A. Marshall, 'Covid-19 opens the door for gig workers to win sick pay', July 2020, Available at: https://www.wired.com/story/covid-opens-door-gig-workers-sick-pay/

by carefully referring to them as, for instance, 'support payment', to avoid a potential employment classification of their workers.[758] In Belgium, Deliveroo also offered sick pay to its delivery riders who fall sick, or have to isolate themselves because of the coronavirus.[759]

5.5 CONCLUSION

Belgium is a country with a high prominence of standard forms of employment where, according to the National Bank of Belgium, nine out of ten employees work under this form of employment. Accordingly, non-standard forms of employment, *inter alia*, casual work, display a low incidence in the Belgian labour market. The reason for this can arguably be the heavy regulation adopted by Belgium for very flexible forms of work.

In Belgium, intermittent work is more apparent than on-call work. Intermittent work has been identified as the most popular form of casual work in Belgium, something which stands in contrast with other industrialized countries, which experience a prevalence of on-call work arrangements. The Belgian legislator has regulated intermittent work in a legal framework, which allows its use only in the tourism industry, for up to two consecutive days, and a maximum number of days per year. Importantly, intermittent workers in Belgium are ensured full social security coverage. However, on-call work has slight prevalence in Belgium (as a work format beyond availability services in addition to regular working hours), and it does not constitute the subject of any statutory regulation. When it comes to zero-hours work in Belgium, the situation becomes complex and vague, as this work typology is not recognized at the national level and hence, neither prohibited nor allowed.

What is more, some other forms of work in Belgium display a casual and non-stable nature, therefore implying an overlap with casual work. Against this background, the flexi-job scheme resembles with on-call work, however, it does not go as far as allowing on-call work. The main purpose for the creation of this scheme was the provision of supplementary income by means of a secondary job. As a result, the eligible workers for this scheme are those who have a primary job, or are employed for at least four-fifths of the hours of the full-time job. Additionally, also retired persons were allowed to work under this scheme. The flexi-jobbers are permitted to work only in two sectors, namely the horeca and the retail ones. In addition to the full social security coverage, an advantageous financial situation applies to the flexi-job scheme. A further overlap can be pointed out between casual work and voucher-based work in Belgium. Eurofound and the European Parliament have singled out voucher-based work as a good work practice, due to the stability offered to voucher workers after three months of work. After this period, these workers become entitled to minimum guaranteed hours, and can also be offered a permanent employment contract. Another

758. Fairwork project, p. 30.
759. M. Rasche, *Coronavirus highlights sick pay void for platform workers*, Eurofound publications, March 2020, Available at: https://www.eurofound.europa.eu/publications/article/2020/coronavirus-highlights-sick-pay-void-for-platform-workers.

important overlap, which stands at the heart of this dissertation, is the one between casual work and platform work. With regard to platform work, Belgium became the first European country to introduce dedicated legislation to govern it, namely the so-called De Croo Act. In its original version in 2016, this law did not preclude the application of employment legislation to platform workers. Nevertheless, a 2018 Act statutorily classified platform workers as self-employed. The Belgian Constitutional Court quashed this legal act and decided for an application of the 2016 De Croo Act, which does not exclude an employee status for platform workers. In this spirit, other public bodies, such as the Belgian Administrative Commission, are increasingly bringing platform work within the scope of labour law.

To conclude with, the pandemic highlighted even more the vulnerability experienced by casual and platform workers. These workers had to face either unemployment or work as essential workers. The Belgian government responded to this situation by adapting two principal schemes: the short-time work and the income-replacement for self-employed workers' schemes. While casual workers working in the horeca or retail sectors could qualify for the first scheme, if their employers decided to continue the work relationship; platform workers could fall within the ambit of the second one, due to their imposed self-employed status. In addition, some platforms were observed to take preventive measures for their workers, and in some cases, they have even offered sick pay, with an example being that of Deliveroo in Belgium.

CHAPTER 6

A Comparative Legal Analysis of Casual Work in the United Kingdom, Italy, the Netherlands and Belgium

6.1 THE GOVERNANCE OF CASUAL WORK: FROM LOOSE TO TIGHT REGULATIONS

As already seen, countries can adopt different legal strategies to regulate casual work arrangements. For instance, many countries around the world explicitly forbid casual work arrangements.[760] Some other countries, instead, may allow this work typology, however, without explicitly regulating it.[761] The four countries subject to this research do not belong to any of the just-mentioned country groups. In contrast, they go beyond merely allowing forms of casual work, as they implement a casual work agenda, i.e., a set of legal strategies to respond to casual work. These national casual work agendas have been shaped influenced by the countries' affinities to different socioeconomic models, concretely the Anglo-saxon and the continental European one. According to the European Parliament's study on precarious employment in Europe, these two models imply divergent approaches to flexibility and security. For example, the United Kingdom, which is an Anglo-saxon country, focuses more on flexibility and less on security, something which is reflected in the adoption of a loose response to the legal situation of casual workers. On the other side of the spectrum, Italy, the Netherlands, and Belgium, as Continental European countries, have followed a different approach, by opting for tighter regulation of forms of casual work. While Italy and the Netherlands embrace and encourage flexible forms of work, *inter alia*, casual work; Belgium, instead, focuses on incentivizing standard forms of employment, while restricting, and even not recognizing, very flexible forms of work.

760. Countries, such as Bulgaria, France, Luxembourg, etc. have opted for this approach.
761. Countries, such as Croatia, Greece, Slovenia, etc. have adopted this approach.

Another aspect that further emerged during this comparative exercise concerns the predominant forms of casual work per country. The dichotomy recognized by Eurofound in its report on new forms of employment has served as a guide for identifying the predominant forms of casual work. Therefore, the two main forms of casual work, concretely intermittent work and on-call work, including min-max and zero-hours contracts, have been placed at the heart of this analysis. Based on this dichotomy, either one or both forms of casual work have been observed in the selected countries. For instance, the UK represents a country with a prominent proliferation of zero-hours work. Italy and the Netherlands are also characterized by a spread of zero-hours work, which they regulate together with other forms of casual work. The Netherlands, for instance, also regulates min-max contracts and on-call contracts by agreement; Italy governs on-call contracts, or *lavoro intermittente,* in general. On the other end of the spectrum stands Belgium, which maintains a more reserved approach towards on-call work arrangements, and adopts a vague response to zero-hours contracts. In Belgium, heavy regulation is applied to another form of casual work, namely intermittent work, or *travail occasionnel.*

6.2 CONTRASTING LEGAL RESPONSES TO FORMS OF CASUAL WORK

6.2.1 Legal Responses to Zero-Hours Work

In the *United Kingdom,* around one million workers, which constitute around 3% of the workforce, are working under zero-hours work contracts. Until 2015, employers enjoyed full freedom in using this form of work, whenever it was convenient for their business needs. Since 2015, the UK legislator decided to provide a limitation to the unrestricted use of zero-hours contracts. In this regard, a ban on exclusivity clauses was enshrined in the ERA, according to which, zero-hours workers were free to work for more than one employer. This very partial regulation of zero hours work raised many debates at the national level, as a result of which, the UK government promised to legally address this situation in its response to the Taylor review report on modern working practices.

Contrary to the UK, *the Netherlands* has set out a more comprehensive legal framework for on-call work, which also includes zero-hours work. As of January 2020, the legal guarantees applicable to on-call and zero-hours workers were further strengthened by the Balanced Labour Market Act, which introduced changes to the Dutch Civil Code. To start with, zero-hours workers in the Netherlands can benefit from an important safeguard: the legal presumption of an employment relationship. This legal presumption restricts the use of zero-hours contracts with no guarantee of working hours, for up to three months. After three months, some minimum guaranteed hours should be ensured to zero-hours workers, based on the hours worked in the previous three months. However, this legal restriction can be waived by social partners, who can agree for these contracts to last longer than three months. Furthermore, specific legal protections, which consider the unstable nature of zero-hours work, have also been provided for these workers. These protections include a minimum guaranteed income of three working hours for those workers, who have contracts with unspecified working hours and work for less than three hours. Another legal guarantee in favour of zero-hours workers includes a four days advance notice, prior to starting the work. Social partners can agree to reduce this advance notice period, however, only for up to twenty-four hours. Furthermore, such an advance notice must also be complied with by the employer, in case of a shift cancellation or change, which happens within four days before the start of the job. Financial compensation needs to be paid if the employer does not respect such an advance notice. The Dutch legislator goes as far as paving the way to stable employment for on-call and zero-hours workers. After working one-year on-call, the employer is obliged to make an offer of fixed working hours to the worker, based on the number of hours worked in the previous twelve months.

In the same line with the Netherlands, *Italy* regulates on-call work, *inter alia*, zero hours work, through a dedicated section in the Legislative Decree No. 81/2015. The legal definition of on-call work indicates a limitation in the use of zero-hours contracts in Italy. Pursuant to it, workers can work in contracts with no guaranteed working hours, only for a pre-identified reason in a collective agreement, hence, for objective requirements. Consequently, the employer cannot summon the worker, whenever the business needs arise. However, an exception has been provided in this regard for those workers, who are less than twenty-four years old and more than fifty-five years old. Furthermore, pursuant to the Italian legal framework, a monthly payment is ensured to those workers who promise to be available for work. An advance notice of one day prior to the start of the work is also enshrined.

On the other end of the spectrum stands *Belgium*, considering the country's approach to not recognizing zero-hours work. The Belgian response has been identified as vague, as it does not explicitly forbid, or allow, this extreme form of casual work, leading to a complex legal situation. Furthermore, zero-hours contracts in Belgium can hardly be found in practice, as they presumably collide with the working time rules.

6.2.2 Legal Responses to On-call Work

The legal approaches to on-call work will be explained by referring exclusively to two national legal systems, concretely the Italian and the Dutch one. The UK and Belgium have not elaborated a legal response which targets specifically this form of work. In the UK, only zero-hours contracts are provided with a scarce response. As concerns Belgium, a low incidence, the lack of a legal response, and a research gap, have been observed with regard to on-call work, or *contrat de travail à l'appel*.

On the other side of the spectrum, Italy and the Netherlands have constructed a detailed legal framework to regulate on-call work. According to the legal definition enshrined in the Italian Legislative Decree No. 85/ 2015, on-call work can be carried out in predetermined periods during the week, month, or year (for temporal requirements); or even more irregularly, with no guarantee of working hours, but according to the needs pre-identified in collective agreements (for objective requirements). In order to respond to irregular business needs, on-call workers need to belong to a specific age category: under 24 years old and above 55 years old. What is more, a limitation on the overall duration of the on-call contract is provided, with a limit of four hundred days per three years. Nevertheless, this limitation does not apply to the tourism, public service, and entertainment sectors. As it can be observed, on-call work in Italy is particularly encouraged for specific sectors of the economy, but also for specific workers, i.e., young and displaced workers. In addition, on-call work is forbidden in specific cases or domains, such as in public administration. Furthermore, formal requirements and a one day advance notice are also envisaged in the Italian legislation. The reward for the worker's availability, or the so-called availability indemnity, can apply to both zero hours and on-call work in Italy.

The Netherlands recognizes three types of on-call work. In addition to zero hours work, min-max contracts, and on-call contracts by agreement, are part of this casual work's typology. On-call contracts by agreement represent a peculiar form of casual work, as from the moment the worker accepts the call, a fixed-term contract comes into effect. These workers can benefit from the chain rule applicable to the Dutch fixed-term contracts, hence, a permanent contract can be concluded after three consecutive fixed-term contracts, or after three years of fixed-term contracts with the same employer. Furthermore, on-call workers in the Netherlands can benefit from the legal presumption of an employment relationship, but also specific legal measures addressing their unstable situation. These specific legal safeguards are the ones applicable to zero-hours contracts, such as a minimum guaranteed income for work of less than three hours; an advance notice of four days before the start of the work; financial compensation in case the advance notice has not been respected in case of a change or cancellation of shifts; and an offer for a fixed number of hours after working on-call for one year (even with different employers).

6.2.3 The Belgian Legal Response to Intermittent Work

Contrary to the just-mentioned countries, Belgium has opted for the regulation of a less flexible form of casual work, that is intermittent work or *travail occasionnel*. Intermittent work is permitted in Belgium only in the tourism sector, accompanied by a restriction on the duration of intermittent work. Intermittent work can be allowed for up to two consecutive days, and an overall duration of two hundred days per year for the employer, while fifty days per year for the worker to make use of such a contract. Notwithstanding the tight regulation of very flexible forms of work by the Belgian legislator, a positive feature underlying the Belgian legal regime on casual work comprises the full social security coverage for intermittent workers in Belgium. Having full social security rights is not very common for casual workers, who are frequently found to lack such a legal right. The social security coverage of these workers is realized through a daily or monthly statutory lump sum, which is paid by the employer for social security contributions.

6.3 DIVERGENT APPROACHES TO THE EMPLOYMENT STATUS INSECURITY OF CASUAL WORKERS

Casual workers are not always ensured with a passport to the full set of employment rights, which is given by an employee status. The countries studied in this dissertation do not adopt a uniform approach with regard to the employment status of casual workers. Their outcomes will differ especially depending on the application of a bi-partite, or a three-partite regime of employment. For instance, Italy, the Netherlands, and Belgium apply a two-tier system of employment. Therefore, casual workers in these countries will fall either within the employee or the self-employed worker' categories. On the other hand, a three-tier system of employment has been adopted in the UK, where the third employment category, that of the limb (b) worker, has been created. This additional legal category has also been extended to casual workers.

As the final word for the determination of the employment status belongs to the judiciary, the outcomes of the British judiciary show that the most common scenario for zero-hours workers in the *UK* is to be either an employee or a limb (b) worker. These two scenarios imply the application of respectively a full package of labour rights, or just half of this package, which is composed of basic rights, such as the national minimum wage, working time rights, collective labour rights, and protection against discrimination in employment. Nevertheless, even in the best case scenario, i.e., the employee status, these workers are deprived of rights depending on the length of service, such as protection against unfair dismissal. Scholars have considered the protection against dismissal as 'an impossible prospect for zero-hours workers' in the UK, as this entitlement requires two years of continuous employment. The more zero-hours workers perform work on a regular basis, the so-called regular casuals, the higher the chances for their legal qualification as employees. On the other side, the classification of zero-hour workers as self-employed, who have a genuine business activity, has rarely been observed in the UK.

On-call workers in *Italy* are considered employees, only for the periods of actual work. According to the Italian legislation, in periods of inactivity, workers do not enjoy any economic or normative treatment, except for the availability indemnity. As a result of this regulatory approach, many on-call workers risk missing out on important rights, which depend on the length of service, e.g., as the right to sick pay, unemployment benefits, and protection against unfair dismissal.

The vast majority of Dutch on-call workers are classified as employees. The enshrinement of the legal presumption of an employment relationship might have arguably been conducive in this regard. In the event an employment relationship is established, the Dutch government points out that on-call workers enjoy equal labour rights with workers in standard employment. Once again, as some of the labour entitlements depend on the actual number of working hours, the legal position of on-call workers in the *Netherlands* can be weakened in practice. On top of this, it is not excluded for Dutch on-call workers to be legally classified as self-employed workers, as well.

In the same line with the Dutch legal approach, intermittent workers who are employed under the *Belgian* scheme, are considered as employees and entitled to the same labour rights as workers in standard employment relationships. With regard to on-call work in Belgium, some studies point out a sui generis nature of this type of contract. Nevertheless, this nature does not exclude the establishment of an employment contract, once the subordination element has been detected.

6.4 LESSONS LEARNED FROM THIS COMPARATIVE ANALYSIS: HOW DO COUNTRIES RESPOND TO THE INSECURITIES INHERENT IN CASUAL WORK

Conducting a comparative legal analysis of casual work in different countries allows us to explore a diversity of national approaches to casual work and learn some lessons from them. This diversity is quite prominent, as these legal approaches sit between two extreme sides of the spectrum, from loose regulations which grant partial labour protection to casual workers, to detailed regulations which accord broad labour protection to them. As a result, commentators have pointed out some of these countries as notorious users of casual work arrangements, while others as more successful in the governance of this work typology.

As it has been widely elaborated in the previous chapters, casual workers find themselves in a precarious working environment, with insecurity underlying their working conditions, such as working hours, jobs, and income. Furthermore, the level of income of these workers has been observed to be quite low. An exacerbation of these insecurities is experienced by on-call workers, especially zero-hours workers, whose working relations can last for a long period, but remains highly unstable. By having this picture in mind, the inherent insecurities of casual work arrangements need to be counteracted, in view of contributing to the labour protection of these vulnerable workers.

Against this background, a natural question that arises is whether the selected countries have responded to the labour protection needs of casual workers by means of their national regulatory strategies. Starting with the United Kingdom, the response to this question is negative. While it is true that zero-hours workers have the freedom to work for more than one employer in the UK, the British legislator has been hesitant to according even basic labour protection to these workers, unless a court decides otherwise. Future developments in the British casual work agenda might be in their way, however, judging by the existing legal standards, the UK can be considered a notorious user of zero-hours contracts. A legal response to zero-hours contracts in the UK is not only essential to balance both the flexibility and security needs of the parties but is also urgent, considering the explosive growth of this form of work in the UK. The judgments of the courts alone, which can be triggered by individual workers, are not sufficient to grant the deserved labour protection to the large group of zero-hours workers in the UK.

Milder critics extend to the Belgian casual work agenda. Belgium has formulated a vague response to zero-hours contracts, i.e., these types of contracts are not recognized, but at the same time, they are not prohibited. In contrast, Belgian legislation, not only allows but also regulates casual work in the tourism sector. These casual workers are considered as employees and enjoy full social security coverage. Furthermore, restrictions are applicable on the total duration, but also on the permitted number of consecutive days for this form of work. Against this backdrop, Belgium should not only provide with some more clarity on the legal situation of zero-hours work but also regulate the use of casual work beyond the tourism sector, as many workers beyond this sector might be excluded from labour protection. In a nutshell, the regulatory approach chosen by Belgium focuses on restricting the use and duration of casual work, instead of enhancing the labour protection of these workers.

In contrast to the British and Belgian approaches to casual work, the Dutch legal framework seems to pay due attention to the labour protection needs of casual workers, but also to consider the flexibility needs of both parties. Many commentators have positively evaluated the Dutch experiment, especially since the recent adoption of the Balanced Labour Market Act. In the Netherlands, casual workers are covered by a double layer of protection. In addition to the specific legal guarantees which are tailor-made for their needs, general legal safeguards add a further layer of protection to them. In this framework, the legal presumption of an employment relationship and the legal presumption of minimum guaranteed hours represent quite conducive rules for casual workers operating in the Dutch labour market. Pursuant to these legal presumptions, zero-hours workers are permitted to work without having any guarantee of working hours, for only up to three months. After three months, employers are obliged to offer them some guaranteed working hours, equal to the average hours worked in the previous three months. This general legal measure seems to be conducive to the employment status insecurity often experienced by casual workers. Following this measure, other legal safeguards conducive to the working hours security of casual workers can be found in the Dutch agenda. In principle, a four days' advance notice needs to be respected, and a shift cannot be cancelled less than four days prior to starting the job. Financial penalties follow the infringement of the latter obligation for shift cancellation or change. What is more, more income security has been provided for these workers as a minimum income is ensured in case work lasts for less than three hours. The Dutch legislator has also thought of some jobs stability to these workers. In this regard, 'regular casuals', who work on-call for one year become entitled to fixed working hours. A further pathway to more stability for casual workers is ensured by the chain rule, which is applicable to fixed-term contracts. According to it, casual workers are entitled to a permanent contract after three consecutive fixed-term contracts, or after three years of fixed-term contracts with the same employer. To sum up, the legal safeguards introduced in the Netherlands have a protective nature for casual workers, but at the same time, the burden imposed on the employer appears to be a reasonable one, which does not seem to deprive them of the flexibility associated with such contracts.

In the same vein, the Italian approach has a dedicated legal framework for casual forms of work. Nevertheless, the safeguards applicable to casual workers in Italy appear to be different from the Dutch ones. The Italian legislator's main focus consists in the implementation of restrictions on the use of casual work. Based on this restrictive nature, some comparisons can be drawn with the Belgian approach, which is, nevertheless, far more restrictive than the Italian one. According to the Italian legislation, the use of zero-hours work is limited to pre-identified needs in collective agreements, unless young and displaced workers want to work in this type of contract. On the other side, the recourse to casual work, for work that is scheduled in predetermined periods during the week, month, or year, does not need to observe these pre-established needs in collective agreements. Second, a further restriction concerns the duration of these types of contracts, except for the tourism, public service, and entertainment sectors. Notwithstanding the restrictive nature of the Italian scheme, the availability indemnity constitutes a peculiar element of it. This monthly payment seems to ensure some income stability to those casual workers, who promise to be available for work.

To sum up, the Dutch and the Italian responses can be singled out as the most protective casual work schemes. Both frameworks underlie the importance of, first, an advance notice, which is in line with a two-sided flexibility, rather than a one-sided employers' flexibility. Second, both systems provide for a certain income security, either in the form of an availability indemnity or three hours pay for work less than three hours. In addition, some security of working hours and jobs are enshrined for casual workers in the Dutch legal system. In this respect, after working for three months on zero-hours contracts, workers are ensured some guaranteed hours; and after one year of on-call work, they become entitled to fixed working hours. This working hours security goes hand in hand with jobs security, which is further reinforced by the Dutch chain rule. Casual workers in the Netherlands can convert their contract into a permanent ones, following the conclusion of fixed-term contracts.

The Dutch approach has shown to be quite welcoming to casual work arrangements, as the Netherlands has the highest incidence of this form of work in Europe. Furthermore, the security that casual workers avail in the Netherlands counteracts the main vulnerabilities inherent to this form of work. On the other side, the protective, but also restrictive, Italian approach has lowered the number of casual workers in Italy, especially zero-hours workers. The main profile of the Italian casual worker is a young (less than 24 years old), or displaced worker (more than 55 years old), who works in the tourism, public service, or entertainment sectors. Beyond this profile, the use of casual work is quite restricted for either a subjective or a temporal reason. Therefore, the main purpose of introducing casual work in Italy is to integrate these specific categories of workers and serve the needs of certain business sectors.

Finally, an important aspect in ensuring adequate labour protection for casual workers, in addition to the stipulation of a protective legal framework, is the enforcement of this framework. Studies show that employers are especially hesitant to contribute to the income security of casual workers, e.g., to pay for the availability indemnity in Italy, and for three hours for work that lasts less than three hours in the Netherlands. Nevertheless, as demonstrated throughout this first part of the dissertation, the vulnerable nature underpinning casual work should spur employers to be more empathetic and responsible in fulfilling their legal obligations towards casual workers.

Part II Welcome to the World of Platform Work

Chapter 7

Singling Out the Idiosyncratic Features of Platform Work

In the first part of this doctoral dissertation, platform work was merely introduced, by way of analyzing its potential overlap with casual work in the four selected countries. This second part of the dissertation will, instead, put platform work under the spotlight, by highlighting its cutting-edge features, which make it distinct from other forms of non-standard employment, including casual work.

7.1 SETTING THE SCENE

A person is busy behind a screen filling a questionnaire, or creating a logo, as requested by the client of a certain web-based platform. A rider is rushing to bring food to a hungry customer's doorstep, as demanded in a specific location-based application (app). A driver is on her way to pick up the next passenger, just a few minutes after being hailed through an app. These daily life examples serve to display the fascinating world of platform work, which empowered by technology, brings opportunities unheard of in the past.

In trying to shed some light on this 'new' form of work, the first question which naturally comes up is: what is platform work? To provide an answer to this question is challenging, considering the 'near limitless variation'[762] of business models, which also differ per country and operator. In his book dedicated to platform work, Jeremias Adams-Prassl rightly points out that providing an exhaustive list of platforms would 'be outdated before it could be printed'.[763] Nevertheless, attempts have been made to provide some clarity on the phenomenon of platform work. In light of this, Eurofound provides a straightforward definition of platform work as 'the matching of the supply

762. J. Prassl, *Humans as a Service: The Promise and Perils of Work in the Gig Economy*, Oxford University Press, 2018, p. 12.
763. *Ibid.*

of and demand for paid labour through an online platform'.[764] On the other side, the International Labour Organization defines platform work, through the clarification of the notion of digital labour platforms. In its 2021 flagship report entitled 'the World Employment and Social Outlook', hereinafter the WESO report, the ILO refers to platform work as work performed in digital labour platforms, which 'intermediate' work 'between individual suppliers (platform workers and other businesses), and clients, or directly engage workers to provide labour services'.[765] Moreover, this report points out a differentiation between diverse types of digital platforms. Platforms which mediate work are distinguished from platforms that offer services to individual users, with an example being that of social media; and from those that 'facilitate the exchange of goods or services, such as e-commerce or business-to-business platforms'.[766] In the endless 'ocean' of platforms, the focus of this dissertation will be on a small subset of digital platforms: the digital labour platforms.

Despite the heterogeneity of digital labour platforms, a dichotomy of platform work has been proposed by De Stefano, based on the place of execution of work. Accordingly, work performed in the 'online world' has been labelled as crowdwork, while work provided in the 'offline' or 'physical world' is referred to as work on demand via apps.[767] The terminology used by the WESO report to refer to these two types of platforms is, respectively, online web-based platforms and location-based platforms.[768] The common denominator between crowdwork and work on demand via apps consists in the use of a digital tool to 'match' the demand and supply sides of labour at a very high speed, thus providing with a 'just-in-time workforce'. The nature of the tasks performed in the web-based platform, or location-based app, varies from low-skilled and monotonous work (micro-tasks) to intellectual work (macro-tasks). Typically, in crowdwork, tasks such as completing surveys, tagging pictures, creating a logo, translating, or rendering legal services are the most common ones. By comparison, delivery, transport, maintenance, and housekeeping services appear to be the most common tasks encountered in work on demand via apps. Furthermore, depending on the place of the execution of work, the two forms of organizing platform work display different features. Workers performing work in the 'physical world' have gained more visibility and public attention, whereas crowdworkers have been considered invisible or faceless workers, as they execute work in the 'online world' and in complete detachment from their clients or other workers. Crowdwork and work on demand via apps also have a different reach of the workforce. While in work on demand via apps, work can be allocated to the workforce of a 'specific geographical

764. Eurofound, *Employment and working conditions of selected types of platform work*, 2018, Introduction, p. 3.
765. ILO, *World Employment and Social Outlook 2021: The role of digital labour platforms in transforming the world of work*, 2021, Box 1.1, p. 33.
766. *Ibid.*, Introduction, p. 31.
767. V. De Stefano, 'The rise of the 'just-in-time workforce': on-demand work, crowd work and labour protection in the gig-economy', p. 4.
768. *See also* the other report coauthored by J. Berg, M. Furrer, E. Harmon, U. Rani and M. Six Silberman, *Digital Labour Platforms and the Future of Work: Towards Decent Work in the Online World*, Geneva, ILO, 2018.

area';[769] crowdwork can 'outsource' work to a near limitless workforce at a global scale, without limitations to geographical locations. The access to a global workforce grants a cross-border dimension to platform work.

Platform work dates back to the past decade, with a particular surge noticed during the 2008 global financial crisis when individuals were looking for alternative sources of income.[770] Since then, the rise of platform work has been described as meteoric.[771] The advent of this form of work under the technological vest has thrived to the extent that commentators consider it not only as one of the most major transformations in the world of work but also as a true revolution in the workplace.[772] The accurate measurement of this phenomenon represents a further challenge. The fast-evolving nature of platform work and the non-disclosure of data by the platforms are only some barriers to capturing the real size of the phenomenon. In the lack of official data, the reliance has been, instead, in private studies on the incidence of platform work. Some recent evidence is provided by the WESO report, which refers to various surveys conducted in North America and Europe. The estimates of these studies show that 0.3% to 22% of the adult population has performed platform work for the period 2015-2019.[773] Furthermore, 777 digital labour platforms were found to be active until January 2021. Notwithstanding the relatively small size of platform work, many European and international institutions highlight the tendency of platform work to rise in the future.[774] On the other hand, there are also some contrasting opinions, which oppose the idea of platform work constituting the future of work.[775] For example, according to Kalman, the imposition of 'hidden coordination and transaction costs on traditional businesses', will impede the potential growth of platform work in the future.

Platform-based work has been considered 'an opportunity-generating machine'.[776] This work typology brings about many opportunities, starting from a greater number of jobs available. Not only more job opportunities but also access to the labour market is observed to be enhanced for home-bound workers,[777] such as disabled workers. What is more, many workers view platform work as an additional source of income.[778] Platform work also comes with the promise of greater flexibility and a better

769. J. Berg et al., 2018, p. xv.
770. A. Cutean et al., *Loading: The Future of Work: Worldwide Remote Work Experimentation and the Evolution of the Platform Economy*, Information and Communications Technology Council (ICTC), Ottawa, Canada, 2020, p. 11.
771. J. Prassl, *Humans as a Service: The Promise and Perils of Work in the Gig Economy*, Oxford University Press, 2018.
772. R. Dukes, 'Regulating Gigs', *Modern Law Review*, Vol. 83 Issue 1, 2019, pp. 217-228, p. 221.
773. ILO WESO Report, p. 19.
774. Global Commission on the Future of Work, *Work for a brighter future*, 2019, p. 44; Eurofound, *Back to the future*, Introduction part.
775. F. Kalman, 'Yes, the gig economy is great – but it isn't the future of work', Talent Economy, 2016, Available at: https://www.linkedin.com/pulse/yes-gig-economy-great-isnt-future-work-frank-kalman/.
776. A. Cutean et al., *Loading: The Future of Work: Worldwide Remote Work Experimentation and the Evolution of the Platform Economy*, Information and Communications Technology Council (ICTC), Ottawa, Canada, (2020), p. 11.
777. J. Berg et al., 2018, p. 40.
778. Eurofound, *Back to the future*, p. 2.

work-life balance.[779] Workers are not bound by a 9 to 5 time schedule, while clients and platforms can rely on 'a just-in-time workforce'.[780] A survey commissioned by KU Leuven and carried out by Ipsos on the working conditions of platform workers, with a particular focus on the autonomy of these workers, and the control over their working time, confirmed that a great number of respondents valued the flexibility associated with platform work, as 'they could 'connect' and 'disconnect' from the system' when desired by them.[781] This survey was based on interviews with 72 platform workers in three European countries (Belgium, France, and Italy). It will be particularly informative in the third section of this part, where the working conditions of platform workers, and the amount of control exercised by the platforms will be scrutinized. To conclude with another exciting feature of the emergence of platform work, the deployment of technology now ensures access to services and products that were previously inaccessible.[782]

The opportunities associated with platform work, however, constitute only the bright side of the phenomenon. If not properly regulated, this work arrangement can also display a not-so-bright side. Therefore, as Prassl points out, both 'promise and perils'[783] can be associated with platform work. A large segment of platform workers are normally engaged as independent contractors under a self-employed status, consequently excluded from basic form of labour protection, such as minimum wages, working time protection, and the rights to associate in trade unions and collective bargaining. However, this legal status has been questioned by labour lawyers on whether it corresponds to the underlying reality of such work arrangements. The decent work deficit encountered by platform workers has grabbed considerable attention at both the European and international level. Against this backdrop, the Global Commission on the Future of Work recognizes the labour protection challenge brought by technology and calls for the use of technology to support decent work.[784] In the European arena, one of the priorities of the European Commission consists in improving the working conditions of platform workers.[785] This objective has been explicitly mentioned by the president of the European Commission, Ursula von der Leyen, in the mission letter to the Commissioner for Jobs, Nicolas Schmit.[786]

Prior to elaborating on the decent work challenges associated with platform work, the following section considers a historical account of these challenges. Have these challenges already existed in the past, or do they derive exclusively from the innovative nature of platform work?

779. OECD, *Employment Outlook 2019*, The Future of Work, p. 15.
780. V. De Stefano, 'The rise of the 'just-in-time workforce': on-demand work, crowd work and labour protection in the gig-economy'.
781. Survey commissioned by KU Leuven and prepared by Ipsos, *High level summary of key findings*, 2020, p. 5.
782. J. Prassl, *Humans as a Service: The Promise and Perils of Work in the Gig Economy*, Oxford University Press, 2018, p. 25.
783. *Ibid*.
784. Global Commission on the Future of Work, *Work for a brighter future*, pp. 43-44.
785. Eurofound, *Back to the future*, Introduction.
786. Mission letter to the Commissioner for Jobs, 2019, p. 5, Available at: https://ec.europa.eu/info/sites/info/files/mission-letter-nicolas-schmit_en.pdf.

7.2 A REVOLUTION TO THE FUTURE OR A RETURN TO THE PAST?

In the before Christ era (BC), the Chinese philosopher Confucius wisely advised studying the past in order to define the future.[787] Many centuries later, when technological advancements have fundamentally impacted our lives, this quote remains still pertinent. Against this background, in order to better understand the nature of platform work, which constitutes, *inter alia*, the future of work, it is worth taking a step back into past working practices.

In the late nineteenth century, it was common practice for many employees to be 'dependent on employers on a recurrent day-to-day basis for offers of work and pay'.[788] These daily labour practices[789] became prominent, especially among dock and construction male workers.[790] Going back in time, one can imagine a large pool of men workers standing in front of a port, competing against each other, in the hope of getting a few hours of low-paid work. Colonel Brid, the manager of Millwall Docks, revealed the destitution situation of London dockers, who came to work 'without having a bit of food in their stomachs, perhaps since the previous day', a situation which, eventually, impeded them from working for many hours.[791] For the work organization of dock workers, a middleman was appointed to deal with important aspects, such as their selection and termination, the setting of the prices, and the exercise of a tight control.[792] The hiring of dock workers was mainly based on the workers' reputation, which was composed of 'regular attendance, hard work, and obedience'.[793]

By acknowledging these historical roots of casual work, this work typology encountered a surge in the 1980s.[794] Campbell provides evidence for the spread of zero-hours work arrangements, during this time, in a variety of sectors in New Zealand, such as hospitality, cleaning, home care, etc.[795] Within the same period, in the United States, using temporary work as a buffer workforce became the norm. In 1988, the well-known company HP created two additional job categories, namely 'on-call' and 'on-contract'. 'These employees would be like temporary workers, working for shorter periods and filing independent contractor forms for their taxes.'[796] Throughout the twentieth century, the proliferation of casual work arrangements was accompanied

787. https://www.forbes.com/quotes/1930/.
788. I. Campbell, 'On-call and Related Forms of Casual Work in New Zealand and Australia', ILO, 2018, p. 7.
789. Oftentimes, work was not guaranteed even for a full day.
790. S. Fredman, 'Labour Law in Flux: The Changing Composition of the Workforce', *Industrial Law Journal*, Vol. 26 Issue 4, 1997, p. 340.
791. London dock strike 1889, Available at: https://en.wikipedia.org/wiki/London_dock_strike,_1889.
792. J. Prassl, *Humans as a Service: The Promise and Perils of Work in the Gig Economy*, Oxford University Press, 2018, p. 79.
793. V. Jensen, 'Hiring of Dock workers and employment practices in the ports of New York, Liverpool, London, Rotterdam, and Marseilles', *Harvard University Press*, 1964.
794. S. Fredman, 'Labour Law in Flux: The changing Composition of the Workforce', p. 339.
795. I. Campbell, 'Zero-hours Work Arrangements in New Zealand: Union Action, Public Controversy and Two Regulatory Initiatives,' in *Zero-Hours and On-call Work in Anglo-Saxon Countries*, eds M. O'Sullivan et al., Springer, 2019, p. 99.
796. L. Hyman, *TEMP: How American Work, American business and the American Dream Became Temporary*, Penguin Random House, New York 2018, p. 227.

by some regulatory responses in developed societies, which managed to 'partially de-commodify labour power'.[797]

Over the years, casual work arrangements have flourished in both developing and developed economies, however, 'an underground casualization', or lack of awareness about their proliferation, has been observed in several developed societies.[798] Notwithstanding this expansion, history seems to repeat itself, as the same work patterns also underpin contemporary forms of casual work. The current debate on casual work focuses, *inter alia*, on platform work, which arguably constitutes its 'newest' typology.[799] The casual and unstable nature of platform work has raised the question of whether this form of work is truly novel, or simply represents a regress to past casual work practices.[800] At first glance, the technological component of platform work creates the impression that a brand new form of work has emerged. However, as Advocate General Szpunar has warned in the *Elite taxi v. Uber* case, 'one should not be fooled by appearances'.[801] Indeed, many international institutions and scholars have decided to look underneath the platform work' technological vest and focus, instead, on the labour performed in digital platforms. In this spirit, Prassl while acknowledging the innovation brought by technology, points out an 'innovation paradox'. The paradox seems to be related to the work organization in platform work, which according to him, resembles 'long-existing trends in non-standard employment'.[802] In his book section entitled 'The Unicorn's New Clothes', Prassl notes that large pools of workers, together with intermediaries and poor working conditions, have constituted features of the labour markets since many centuries ago.[803] Other defining features of platform work, which do not display anything novel, comprise the provision of tools by the workers and the piece-based mode of compensation.[804] This view on the historical roots of platform work has also been embraced by De Stefano, who refers to platform work as 'a combination and rebranding of long-established models'.[805] Furthermore, the Global Commission on the Future of Work, in its report 'Work for a brighter future',

797. I. Campbell, p. 2, reference to G. Bosch, 'Towards a New Standard Employment Relationship in Western Europe', *British Journal of Industrial Relations*, Vol. 42 Issue 4, 2004, pp. 617-636; Esping-Andersen, *The Three Worlds of Welfare State Capitalism, Cambridge University Press*, 1990.
798. V. De Stefano, 'Casual Work Beyond Casual Work in the EU: The Underground Casualization of the European Workforce and What to Do About It'. *European Labour Law Journal*, Vol. 7 Issue 3, 2016.
799. I. Campbell, 'Casualised Work Arrangements in Developed Societies: Historical Parallels and New Regulatory Challenges', Forthcoming.
800. *Ibid.*
801. Case C-434/15, *Asociación Profesional Elite Taxi v. Uber Systems Spain SL*, Opinion of Advocate General Szpunar, para. 52, 2017, Available at: https://eur-lex.europa.eu/legal-content/EN/TXT/HTML/?uri=CELEX:62015CC0434&from=EN.
802. J. Prassl, 'What if your boss is an algorithm: Economic Incentives, Legal Challenges and the Rise of Artificial Intelligence at Work', *Comparative Labour Law and Policy Journal*, Vol. 41 Issue 1, 2019, pp. 123-146, p. 125.
803. J. Prassl, *Humans as a service*, p. 90; A. Cutean et al., *Loading: The Future of Work: Worldwide Remote Work Experimentation and the Evolution of the Platform Economy*, Introduction.
804. J. Stanford, 'The Resurgence of Gig Work: Historical and Theoretical Perspectives', *The Economic and Labour Relations Review*, Vol. 28 Issue 3, 2017, p. 383.
805. V. De Stefano, 'The Rise of the "Just-in-time Workforce": On-demand Work, Crowd Work and Labour Protection in the Gig-economy', p. 471.

has indicated that platform work is creating 'future generations of digital day labourers'.[806] Departing from these considerations, at the heart of which stand the precarious work reality of many platform workers, some historical parallels can be drawn between casual work and platform work. With more exacerbation of previous challenges incurred in the digital age,[807] platform work can be arguably considered a 'bad' successor of the casualization of work originating in the nineteenth century.

7.3 EXPLORING THE PECULIARITIES OF PLATFORM WORK

7.3.1 The Algorithmic Management: A Cutting-Edge Feature of Platform Work

The Cambridge Dictionary provides some explanation of the meaning of the word 'algorithm'. According to it, an algorithm refers to a set of instructions, which if given to a computer, can help to solve a problem.[808] Furthermore, the WESO report explains algorithmic management as a system which assigns tasks and makes decisions in an automated way, hence, with limited human control.[809] This system is improved 'through self-learning algorithms based on data'. While algorithmic management can be found beyond platform work, it has been pointed out as the main feature of digital labour platforms.[810] This 'clever' algorithm displays numerous functions when deployed in the platform work context.

At the outset, the algorithmic system screens the service providers, who will be allowed to open an account in the platforms, by performing thus, its first function: the *recruitment* one. The entry into the platform can vary from being simple, such as requiring mere internet access, e.g., in microtask platforms, to being more demanding. In the last instance, platforms can make entry conditional upon the provision of previous work samples, or a good performance in different tests.[811] In work on demand via apps, it is noticed that registration can be easily done, however, the actual performance of the work can be subject to additional requirements, such as the provision of the work equipment.[812] A background check, which might comprise the provision of criminal records, alongside financial information, can also be requested by some platforms.[813]

Once the first step has been successfully completed, the algorithm can realize one of its key functions: *matching* the supply (workers) and demand (clients) sides of labour. However, many platforms are increasingly engaging workers to work for them directly. The labour-demand matching, or the intermediation through technological

806. Global Commission on the Future of Work, *Work for a brighter future*, p. 12.
807. I. Durri, 'Regulating the Platform Economy: International Perspectives on New Forms of Work', Book Review, *Comparative Labour Law and Policy Journal* Vol. 42, Issue 237, 2021, p. 2.
808. https://dictionary.cambridge.org/dictionary/english/algorithm.
809. ILO WESO Report, p. 33.
810. J. Berg et al., 2018, p. 8.
811. Eurofound, *New forms of employment*, p. 110.
812. ILO WESO Report, p. 93.
813. Surveys commissioned by KU Leuven and prepared by Ipsos, p. 5.

means, represents a cutting-edge characteristic of platform work, which has not been encountered in other work forms.[814] What is more, such a matching is so fast, that it has been compared with 'lightning speed'. Due to this quick matching, the algorithmic management is able to supply with a 'just-in-time-workforce',[815] a pool of workers who are called upon at the employer's discretion. This workforce enables an immediate satisfaction of employers' business needs. Platforms consider several factors when assigning a certain task to workers. In addition to the worker's availability, previous work experiences, current ratings, or hourly rates; in work on demand via apps, the proximity of the worker constitutes a crucial factor. The ratings and client reviews were found to be the top indicators for task assignment. All these factors, however, can be set aside in certain platforms, where workers pay a fee in order to gain more visibility in the matching process. The matching of both sides can be performed either in an automated way or with some human involvement.[816]

The matching function of algorithms stands at the heart of platforms' claims that they merely function as marketplaces where labour and demand simply meet.[817] Therefore, the majority of business service agreements, underline a self-employed, or independent contractor, status for the persons supplying work in a platform.[818] On the other side, certain indicators point out a different direction: algorithmic management might go beyond this mere match-making function.[819] It has been observed that in a vast part of platforms, the algorithmic system can show an amount of *control*, comparable to the managerial prerogatives that are typically reserved for employers. Indeed, an employee classification of platform workers has been increasingly embraced at the legislative and judicial level.[820] What is more, some platforms have also voluntarily classified their workers as employees, or have allowed their clients to do that.[821] In the academic community, many scholars enthusiastically support an employment relationship within the platform work domain. For instance, Jeremias Prassl explicitly entitles one of its articles: 'Your boss is an algorithm'. To be noted is that the control exerted by the algorithmic 'boss' is even more magnified than the control in traditional 9-to-5 jobs. The reason for such an exacerbation of control can be found in the interference in the worker's private life, such as tracking the workers' location through the global positioning system (GPS),[822] capturing random screenshots of the screen, recording the keystrokes, detecting the drivers' speed,[823] etc. Against this background, an essential question that arises is: how has this tight control been manifested?

814. Kilhoffer et al., *Study to gather evidence on the working conditions of platform workers*, p. 42.
815. V. De Stefano, 'The rise of the 'just-in-time workforce': on-demand work, crowdwork and labour protection in the gig economy'.
816. ILO WESO Report, p. 93.
817. J. Prassl, *Humans as a service ...*, p. 53.
818. V. De Stefano et al., *Platform work and the employment relationship*, p. 15.
819. J. Prassl, *Humans as a service, The promise and perils of work in the gig economy*, p. 5.
820. V. De Stefano et al., *Platform work and the employment relationship*.
821. *Ibid.*, p. 19.
822. Survey commissioned by KU Leuven and prepared by Ipsos, p. 15.
823. H. Mayhew, 'The Morning Chronicle Survey of Labour and the Poor', Vol. 2, *Routledge* 2016, p. 95.

Without excluding the existence of scenarios where platform workers are genuinely self-employed, the algorithmic control is able to monitor crucial aspects of the work performed. In order to trigger an employee status, control does not need to 'extend to every possible detail of the work'.[824] From the beginning, in addition to the selection of workers, an indicator of control exerted by the platforms comprises the *provision of explicit instructions, inter alia,* on how workers should behave with the clients. For instance, the Uber platform requires its drivers to be polite and greet the client with a smile, keep the car clean, open the door, or help with the luggage.[825] Once the worker has accepted the ride, the algorithm also determines the route to be followed by the drivers. In case the drivers do not follow such a route, and the passenger complains, the driver has to bear the responsibility. Furthermore, the flexibility promise associated with platform work remains a mirage in many cases. Workers' freedom to choose working hours can be reduced, as workers might have to log in during certain working hours, especially peak hours when the demand for labour is high. Contrary to high demands for labour, underemployment situations are also very common in platform work. In an ILO survey, 90% of the crowdworkers working for two leading micro-task platforms reported insufficient work. Consequently, these workers do not have much choice in choosing their work and working hours: they accept whatever is available and whenever it is.[826] What is more, crowdworkers working in different geographical and time zones, are often obliged to work at night or during unsocial hours to answer the calls of clients that are based in different zones of the world.[827]

The platforms also exercise a significant degree of control over the work tools. The platforms' business models consist of an asset-light model,[828] where workers own work equipment, such as a smartphone, a laptop, a car, or a bicycle. Notwithstanding that this model might point out a self-employed status for platform workers,[829] platforms can still exert a decisive influence on this aspect. The UK Supreme Court has recently ruled that the Uber company can scrutinize the type of car, which the driver can use.[830] What is more, the Court has highlighted that the real investment in the context of platform work is the technological investment. Such an investment, which is provided by platforms, is a *sine qua non* for the performance of service. Additionally, some platforms have also arranged loans for their workers, in order for them to be equipped with the necessary work tools.[831]

Furthermore, the algorithmic system interferes with another crucial aspect of the relationship between the worker and the client: *price-setting*. In many instances,

824. *Cotter* et al. *v. Lyft Inc.*, Order Denying Cross-Motion for Summary Judgment (n. 16), p. 7.
825. J. Prassl, *Humans as a service* ..., p. 56.
826. J. Berg, 'Income security in the on-demand economy: Findings and policy lessons from a survey of crowdworkers', International Labour Office, Conditions of Work and Employment Series No. 74, (2016), p. 13.
827. V. De Stefano, 'The rise of the "just-in-time workforce" ...', p. 10.
828. ILO WESO Report, p. 89.
829. The Employment Relationship Recommendation (2006), No. 198, para. 13.
830. UK Supreme Court 19 February 2021, Case No. [2021] UKSC 5, *Uber BV and others v. Aslam and others*, §98.
831. J. Prassl, *Humans as a service* ..., p. 68.

platforms unilaterally determine the prices,[832] however, clients and workers can also agree on the pay rate.[833] Platforms can also determine how and when platform workers are paid. The price is usually calculated by algorithms in a dynamic way, by taking into consideration different parameters. For instance, in the taxi sector, consideration is given to the destination of the passenger, the type of vehicle, etc. In cases of increased demand, a surge pricing algorithm can be activated to adopt a surge in the price.[834] Platforms also adopt a digital payment system, where a commission fee is deducted for the service, with the amount determinable by each platform.[835] The fees generally amount to 15% to 30% of the workers' payment.[836] In the case of delivery services, a delivery fee can also be charged. The workers are paid on a 'pay-as-you-go' basis, hence, only for the actual work performed.[837] In addition to this 'standard' payment, platforms can also make use of financial rewards, by displaying, thus, another feature for managing the workforce. These bonuses serve to incentivize workers to stay connected, especially to remain available during peak periods, or unsocial hours. On the other side of the spectrum, these bonus practices contrast with platform work's payment level, which has been observed to be as low, as not reaching even the minimum wage.[838] Especially in crowdwork, the fierce global competition between workers from developing and developed countries contributes to driving the payment further down.[839] This financial situation of platform workers is even more exacerbated when 'wage theft' practices occur, i.e., clients retain the work and refuse to pay platform workers, without giving any reasons for this refusal.[840]

7.3.2 The Peak of Algorithmic Management: The Rating System

In a nutshell, algorithmic management extends to many important aspects of the work, such as selecting workers, matching labour and demand, setting the transactions' price, providing explicit guidelines on how to perform work, etc. The algorithmic management, furthermore, impacts another important aspect of the work: the *evaluation of the work performance*, by means of a rating and/ or review algorithm. The rating system comprises an evaluation of the service received on a scale, which is usually from one to five stars, or other status' symbols. The review system represents a more

832. UK Supreme Court 19 February 2021, Case No. [2021] UKSC 5, *Uber BV and others v. Aslam and others*, §94.
833. Eurofound, *New forms of employment*, p. 110; According to Ipsos survey commissioned by KU Leuven, pp. 7 and 16, crowdworkers were observed to have some more freedom in setting their rates.
834. ILO WESO Report, p. 85.
835. Survey commissioned by KU Leuven and prepared by Ipsos, p. 15.
836. J. Prassl, *Humans as a service …*, p. 60.
837. V. De Stefano, 'The rise of the "just-in-time workforce" …', p. 7.
838. Eurofound, *New forms of employment*, Table 17: Overview of implications of new forms of employment for selected working conditions, p. 139; J. Berg, 'Income security in the on-demand economy …', p. 13.
839. Survey commissioned by KU Leuven and prepared by Ipsos, pp. 12-13.
840. V. De Stefano, 'Introduction: Crowdsourcing, the Gig Economy and the Law', *Comparative Labor Law and Policy Journal*, Vol. 37 Issue 3, p. 5; Analytical document of the European Commission, p. 14.

elaborated evaluation, as it provides the service providers with not merely an evaluation on a given scale, but a comment on the quality of the service. The given reviews and/ or ratings represent the digital reputation of the worker, which constitutes *a sine qua non*, for the provision of work on platforms. In addition to being an essential feature of platform work, the rating and review system, hereinafter the rating system, has also been employed beyond digital labour platforms, with an example being that of the service industry.[841]

This system was designed to aid clients in choosing the best service providers, based on the experiences of other customers.[842] Considering that the workforce providing services in platforms is very large and heterogeneous, a high reliance on the rating system has been observed.[843] The rating system, hence, helps clients choose one worker from the vast pool of workers available on a certain platform. Furthermore, as pointed out in the previous section, the importance of ratings extends as well to the matching process, as a crucial indicator for, *inter alia*, matching labour and demand sides.[844]

In addition to assisting clients, the rating mechanism also serves as a powerful management tool for platform companies.[845] Rather than merely assessing workers' performance, the rating system is instrumental to the platform in exerting control over the workforce.[846] Based on the ratings accumulated per worker, the algorithm makes important decisions impacting workers' future work prospects. For example, a worker who has a high rating will be given a sort of 'elite' status, as access to better and well-paid jobs can be provided.[847] On the other hand, workers whose ratings fall below a pre-defined level can suffer adverse consequences and become subject to disciplinary actions. Such consequences range from the prohibition of access to better-paid and attractive jobs to a temporary or definite deactivation of their profile. In view of these considerations, Prassl refers to the rating algorithm as 'the boss from hell: [an] 'erratic, bad-tempered, unaccountable manager'.[848] 'The boss from hell' can fire the worker with a poor rating, with immediate effect and without giving neither explanation nor warning.[849] In this regard, workers have reported that their relationship with the platform has ended by simply receiving an error message the moment they attempt to

841. ILO WESO Report, p. 97; J. Prassl, 'What If Your Boss Is an Algorithm', p. 10.
842. J. Prassl, 'What if your boss is an algorithm: Economic Incentives, Legal Challenges and the Rise of Artificial Intelligence at Work', *Comparative Labor Law and Policy Journal* Vol. 41, Issue 1, 123-146, (2019). p. 12.
843. M. Wouters, *International Labour Standards and Platform Work. An Analysis of Digital Labour Platforms Based on the Instruments on Private Employment Agencies, Home Work and Domestic Work*, Bulletin of Comparative Labour Relations, 2021, p. 31.
844. ILO WESO Report, p. 24.
845. R. Dukes, 'Regulating gigs', p. 223.
846. Eurofound, *Platform work: maximizing the potential while safeguarding standards?*, p. 13; United States District Court, Northern District of California, *Douglas O'Connor* et al *v. Uber Technologies Inc* et al, No. C-13-3826 EMC, 'Order denying Uber Technologies Inc.' motion for summary judgment, Available at: https://www.uberlawsuit.com/OrderDenying.pdf.
847. J. Prassl, *Humans as a service ...*, p. 62.
848. J. Prassl, 'What if your boss is an algorithm', p. 12; J. Prassl, *Humans as a service ...*, p. 54.
849. M. Six Silberman & H. Johnston, *Using GDPR to Improve Legal Clarity and Working Conditions on Digital Labour Platforms*, ETUI Working Paper 2020, No. 5, pp. 6-7.

log in to the platform. This disciplinary power exercised by platforms, when predefined performance levels are not met, can arguably amount to the exertion of the employers' managerial prerogatives. The employers' prerogatives, as highlighted by Casale, 'to give orders, supervise compliance with orders and penalize employees in situations where the work is not performed according to the prescribed orders', can arguably correspond to platforms' disciplinary power.[850]

But how are the ratings being determined? The clients' evaluation of the service provided by a specific worker is paramount in the ratings' determination. In order for the worker's rating to be created, a summary of all the ratings and reviews from different clients is being considered. Nevertheless, the worker's rating is not fully dependent on the client's feedback, as platforms can also interfere in this respect,[851] by considering the acceptance or rejection of work by the workers.[852] Consequently, workers with a high acceptance rate of tasks are given a higher rating, while workers who have frequently rejected tasks are adversely impacted on their ratings, which is especially the case for workers of micro-task platforms.[853] Amazon Mechanical Turk, for instance, grants a master qualification title to its workers, who have a high approval rate and have performed at least one thousand tasks. Additionally, also other indicators are scrutinized by platforms for the determination of ratings, e.g., the speed of completing a task, especially for workers of delivery platforms; but also if work is performed during peak periods. In some instances, even the lack of feedback from customers can adversely impact the worker's ratings.[854] Finally, the difference between high-quality and low-quality tasks seems to not be taken into account in a reputation system.[855] When all of these just-mentioned indicators are aggregated, it can be said that the worker's reputation in a certain platform has been created.

7.3.3 Peculiar Issues Underpinning the Algorithmic System

As noted above, the deployment of technology in a work context can bring great benefits for all actors involved in platform work, i.e., platforms, workers, and service users. However, in order to maximize the benefits of technological advancements, peculiar issues arising from the use of algorithmic management at work need to be identified and addressed accordingly.

Algorithms and the Unrealized Promise of Neutrality

According to the WESO report, ratings are noted to be especially important for taxi and delivery services.[856] A difference was, nonetheless, noticed in this regard, as Uber drivers generally experienced better ratings than Deliveroo riders. The negative

850. G. Casale, *The Employment Relationship: A Comparative Overview*, Oxford Hart Publishing, ILO, Geneva, 2011.
851. ILO WESO Report, p. 97.
852. V. De Stefano, A. Aloisi, *European legal framework for digital labour platforms*, p. 21.
853. ILO WESO Report, p. 98.
854. *Ibid.*, p. 180.
855. J. Prassl, *Humans as a service ...*, p. 53.
856. WESO, p. 181.

implication on the riders' ratings was related, *inter alia*, to reasons not dependent on them, such as delays caused by restaurants, or traffic congestion.[857] Poor ratings given for subjective reasons were sometimes also observed in the case of Uber drivers, especially when passengers were forbidden to bring beers into the car, or when they were biased about the drivers' race, gender, etc.[858] These cases unfold an important issue underpinning platform companies' rating system: its transparency. This lack of transparency was observed not only in the determination of ratings by the clients but also on how algorithms operate. In the last case, the problem can be detected in the data registered in the source code of algorithms. As humans have inserted this data, the risk is that they may have incorporated their personal biases into the heart of algorithms, and hence, designed an algorithm which is far from neutral. Several studies have pointed out the rating algorithm as 'a black box for workers'.[859] On this subject, Prassl points to reputation algorithms, and clients' behaviours, as opening the door to discrimination practices.[860] Furthermore, under the headline 'the sharing economy is not as open as you might think', the Guardian highlights how older drivers are given a poor rate by college students, while female drivers are down-rated by male passengers in case they do not flirt along with them.[861] The WESO report further affirms the existence of discriminatory practices, by highlighting that 'algorithms are only as good as the data that is fed into them'; hence, the incorporation of biased data will lead to discriminatory algorithms.[862] A difficulty underlies, however, the verification of discriminatory practices: the source code of algorithms is almost impossible to access.[863] The trade secrecy and intellectual property rules stand as a barrier to platform workers in understanding the reasons behind platforms' decisions impacting them. This barrier does not, however, constitute an unbreakable one. Algorithms have been subject to judicial reviews, such as in an Italian court's decision.[864] The Bologna court ruled that the algorithmic system of Deliveroo, which ranked riders and assigned them rides without taking into account the workers' reasons for shift cancellation, was indirectly discriminatory and ordered the platform company to pay financial compensation to the plaintiffs. Furthermore, initiatives were also undertaken at the legislative level in the direction of algorithmic transparency. The Spanish Riders' Law represents a notable

857. H. J. Parkinson, Thumbs down to the fake reviewers ruining the internet for all of us, 2019, Available at: https://www.theguardian.com/commentisfree/2019/aug/07/fake-reviews-internet-ratings.
858. J. Dieza, The rating game. How Uber and its peers turned us into horrible bosses, 2015, Available at: https://www.theverge.com/2015/10/28/9625968/rating-system-on-demand-economy-uber-olive-garden.
859. Eurofound, *Platform work: maximizing the potential while safeguarding standards?*, p. 13.
860. Prassl, *Humans as a Service: The Promise and Perils of Work in the Gig Economy*, Oxford University Press, 2018, p. 62.
861. The Guardian, 'The sharing economy is not as open as you might think', Available at: https://www.theguardian.com/sustainable-business/2014/nov/12/algorithms-race-discrimination-uber-lyft-airbnb-peer.
862. ILO WESO, p. 61; *See also* Financial times, https://www.ft.com/content/eb8b7c0e-ce71-11e9-99a4-b5ded7a7fe3f.
863. Nevertheless, a US District Court for the Northern District of California has granted permission to access such source codes, in a 2018 case of *Waymo v. Uber*.
864. Tribunale Ordinario di Bologna 31 dicembre 2020, Case No. 2949/2019. Available at: http://www. bollettinoadapt.it/wp-content/uploads/2021/01/Ordinanza-Bologna.pdf.

development in this regard.[865] In addition to establishing the presumption of an employment relationship for food delivery riders, this law made it mandatory for platform companies to display to all platform workers the decision-making process of algorithms, which affects their working conditions, access to, and termination of their relationship with the platform. Finally, the lack of transparency does not represent an exclusive concern for rating algorithms, as recruitment,[866] shift assigning, and pricing'[867] algorithms are also arguably covered by this secrecy veil.

On the other side, a counterargument in this regard has also been put forward, concretely, that algorithms can actually contribute to combatting discriminatory practices. In this regard, Travieso refers to algorithms as being 'colour – and gender-blind'.[868] Furthermore, Schor indicates that platforms can actually deploy creative ways to combat discrimination. This can be done, according to her, through punishing passengers, who continuously turn down drivers of colour. What she suggests in this regard is that the next time these biased passengers demand a ride, they should be exclusively served by this group of drivers.[869]

Ratings and Reviews as an Exclusive Property of Platform Companies

Workers' ratings in a certain platform, which have been carefully built over a long period, are usually treated by platform companies as their exclusive property. Platforms justify this approach with, *inter alia,* the use of different metrics to calculate ratings across platforms.[870] In this way, another contentious issue underpinning the rating system unfolds: the lack of the ratings' portability. While it is true that platform workers have the freedom to choose the platform for which to provide their services, the inability to take their ratings with them creates a barrier in their transition across platforms. This mobility bears the risk of losing their good ratings and having to build their digital reputation from scratch, which requires time and financial resources to be accomplished. The higher the ratings are, the more stuck the workers will be in a specific platform's ecosystem. The laçk of ratings' portability impacts not only platform workers' job mobility, but deprives them of retaining their reputation data' benefits, also in case of a change in the platform's business model, or if they get affected by a sudden deactivation. What is more, the negative implications of this 'lock-in effect' can extend beyond platform work. By not possessing a proof of their previous professional

865. Real Decreto-ley 9/2021 de 11 de mayo, para garantizar los derechos laborales de las personas dedicadas al reparto en el ambito de las plataformas digitales, Articulo unico, Uno, Available at: https://www.boe.es/buscar/doc.php?id = BOE-A-2021-7840.
866. https://www.independent.co.uk/life-style/gadgets-and-tech/amazon-ai-sexist-recruitment-tool-algorithm-a8579161.html.
867. ILO WESO Report, p. 88.
868. M. Marta Travieso, 'Regulating Technology at Work', in *Regulating the Platform Economy: International Perspectives on New Forms of Work*, ed. L. Mella Mendez, Routledge, 2020, p. 71; Eurofound, 'Platform work: maximizing the potential while safeguarding standards?', p. 18.
869. G. Harman, The gig economy is not as open as you might think, 2014, Available at:https://www.theguardian.com/sustainable-business/2014/nov/12/algorithms-race-discrimination-uber-lyft-airbnb-peer.
870. ILO WESO Report, p. 97 and 206.

experiences, platform workers risk facing difficulties finding a job in the traditional sectors.[871]

As this workers' portfolio[872] is locked into a single platform,[873] a parallel can be drawn here with the provision of exclusivity clauses by employers, according to which, workers have to work solely for one employer. The obligation to work exclusively for one single employer, which de facto also applies to platform workers, can be an indicator of an employee status rather than a self-employed one, as proclaimed by a vast part of platform operators. However, to be noticed is that, even in case platforms would have to remove this 'lock-in effect', the prohibition of exclusivity clauses alone cannot preclude the employee status, as several indicators need to be considered when determining an employment status.

Many actors at both the European and international level have already acknowledged the importance of the portability of ratings in the context of platform work. Against this background, the Global Commission on the Future of Work, in its report 'Work for a brighter future' underlines the necessity for portable rights and benefits for platform workers.[874] In the same vein, at the European level, the General Data Protection Regulation (GDPR) enshrines the right of data subjects, which can include, *inter alia*, platform workers, to data portability.[875] As a result, platform workers should be entitled to receive and transmit their data to another controller, without any limitation from the former controller of this data. Furthermore, in a resolution adopted by the European Parliament in 2017 – a European Agenda for the collaborative economy – the importance of the portability of ratings and reviews has been highlighted, together with facilitating their transferability and accumulation when transitioning across platforms.[876]

Overlooking the Human Aspect of Platform Work

The deployment of technology in enabling platform work risks making service users exclusively focused on obtaining the best service at the lowest price. This focus implies that they disregard a crucial aspect of work in the platforms, namely that the provider of the service is a human. This customers' approach affects both crowdworkers and workers on demand via apps, with crowdworkers expected to be more adversely affected. This is due to the fact that crowdworkers perform work behind a screen, which might give the perception that the service provider is an IT device, instead of a

871. S. P. Choudary, *The Architecture of Digital Labour Platforms: Policy Recommendations on Platform Design for Worker Wellbeing*, ILO Future of Work Research Paper Series, 2018, p. 27.
872. A. Aloisi, V. De Stefano, S. Silberman, 'A manifesto to reform the gig economy', 2019, Available at: http://regulatingforglobalization.com/2019/05/01/a-manifesto-to-reform-the-gig-economy/.
873. ILO WESO Report, p. 97.
874. Global Commission on the Future of Work, *Work for a brighter future*, p. 36.
875. Regulation (EU) 2016/679 of the European Parliament and of the Council of 27 April 2016 on the protection of natural persons on the processing of personal data and on the free movement of such data, and repealing Directive 95/46/EC (General Data Protection Regulation).
876. European Parliament resolution of 15 June 2017 on a European Agenda for the collaborative economy (2017/2003(INI)).

human being.[877] This commodification of labour is not excluded also in work on demand via apps, even though it is characterized by physical contact between workers and customers. In light of these considerations, the recognition of the human character of work in a platform work context, which runs counter to the perception of labour as 'an extension of an IT device or online platform',[878] becomes essential.[879] Accordingly, the relevance of the fundamental principle 'labour is not a commodity', enshrined in the 1944 Declaration of Philadelphia, is reasserted in the contemporary world of work.[880] Pursuant to this principle, labour cannot be treated as a commodity, or as a separate entity from the human performing it, and hence, human dignity must be protected.[881]

At first sight, the customers' tendency to dehumanize labour in platforms may seem of little importance. Nevertheless, this approach might adversely impact the workers' ratings, which have the power to impede or limit access to the best jobs available on platforms. Therefore, the dehumanization of labour can severely impact platform workers' professional lives, going as far as leaving workers without a basic income, and adversely impacting their future job opportunities. And the strange thing is that, in many cases, customers 'don't know they wield' all this amount of power over platform workers' lives.[882]

Turning to the workers' side, the prospect of harsh ratings has accordingly led to an adaptation in their behaviours. In this regard, with a view to maintaining good ratings, workers on demand via apps were observed to perform 'emotional labour'.[883] Some examples in this respect include: greeting customers with a smile, opening the door of the car for the passengers, giving passengers control of the music in the car, etc.[884] Several drivers have expressed their dissatisfaction in this regard and compared the 'emotional labour' conducted by them with the work of servants.[885] The performance of 'emotional labour' was mainly observed among low-skilled workers, who could not be otherwise differentiated from other workers.[886] What is more, other sacrifices were also observed, by especially crowdworkers, in building and maintaining their good reputation. Their efforts range from lowering the pay rate to performing unpaid work,[887] accepting unattractive and/ or additional jobs,[888] and going as far as tolerating unfair behaviours from clients, such as 'wage theft' practices.

877. V. De Stefano, 'The rise of the just-in-time workforce ...', p. 8.
878. *Ibid.*, p. 8 and p. 33.
879. Eurofound, *Platform work: Maximising the potential while safeguarding standards?*, p. 19.
880. V. De Stefano, 'Labour is not a technology: reasserting the Declaration of Philadelphia in times of platform work and gig-economy', pp. 11-14.
881. ILO Declaration of Philadelphia, I (a).
882. https://www.theverge.com/2015/10/28/9625968/rating-system-on-demand-economy-uber-olive-garden.
883. V. De Stefano, 'The rise of the just-in-time workforce ...', p. 8.
884. https://www.theverge.com/2015/10/28/9625968/rating-system-on-demand-economy-uber-olive-garden.
885. *Ibid.*
886. S. P. Choudary, *The architecture of digital labour platforms...*, 2018, p. 16.
887. J. Prassl, *Humans as a service: The Promise and Perils of Work in the Gig Economy*, Oxford University Press, 2018, p. 32.
888. R. Dukes, 'Regulating gigs', p. 223.

Hearing One Side of the Story: The Asymmetry of the Rating System

The crux of the rating system underpinning work in digital labour platforms is composed of the customers' feedback on their experiences with the workers. More often than not, customers were observed to be the only party who could rate their experiences, while workers, on the other side, have no say in this regard.[889] In this way, another problematic aspect of work in the platforms is displayed: the asymmetric, or one-sided, nature of the feedback system. In the event of reciprocal customer-worker feedback, workers would not only be empowered to tell their side of the story, but they would also be able to help each other, by exchanging information on avoiding scams, bad clients, and search only for the fair ones.[890] Additionally, two-sided feedback would equally benefit both workers and clients, as they would be inclined to handle the accordance of ratings with more care, by arguably fearing a retaliatory action from the other party. In particular, customers would be more distanced from the so-called wage theft practices. In other words, workplace democracy would be boosted when the voices of both parties active in a platform were equally heard.[891]

For the above reasons, some platforms have decided to allow also feedback from the workers' side, with an example being that of Uber. Since 2017, this platform operator has given the opportunity to its drivers, to rate the passengers in turn.[892] The latter do not seem to be particularly aware of their ratings, which they can easily find below their name when logging into the app. Similarly to customers' ratings, workers' ratings can also amount to unfair practices, including discriminatory ones. For example, as pointed out by Langlois, a principal reason for Uber drivers to accord low ratings was noticed to be the lack of tips.[893] What is more, clients can also be deactivated when their ratings fall below a pre-defined ceiling. In this regard, Uber was considering that those customers with a rating 'significantly below average' should be first warned,[894] and then prohibited from accessing the app.

Setting a workers' rating system has also been observed in crowdwork platforms. For instance, with the purpose of making the rating system more symmetric within Amazon Mechanical Turk (AMT), Silberman and Irani decided to create a forum inside it: the Turkopticon.[895] Since 2008, workers working for the AMT can review their 'requesters', based on several criteria, where the main ones include the evaluation of their work, payment, the speed to deliver pay and communication.[896] The establishment of a reciprocal rating system does not preclude the presence of diverse problems within it, such as disagreements on the evaluation criteria of clients, or this forum

889. S. P. Choudary, *The architecture of digital labour platforms* ..., p. 16.
890. https://turkopticon.net/
891. V. De Stefano, 'Introduction: Crowdsourcing, the Gig Economy and the Law', p. 5.
892. The Guardian 2019, https://www.theguardian.com/technology/2019/may/31/uber-to-ban-riders-with-low-ratings.
893. S. Langlois, 'Don't tip your Uber driver? It could cost you a 5-star rating', 2015, Available at: https://www.marketwatch.com/story/dont-tip-your-uber-driver-it-could-cost-you-a-5-star-rating-2015-08-12.
894. https://www.theguardian.com/technology/2019/may/31/uber-to-ban-riders-with-low-ratings.
895. https://turkopticon.ucsd.edu.
896. V. De Stefano, 'Introduction: Crowdsourcing, the Gig Economy and the Law', p. 5.

being converted into a venue for harassment, racism, and insults.[897] On top of these problems, it has also been observed that putting in place a two-sided feedback system does not automatically accord equal power to both clients and workers. In practice, the power of clients' ratings was noticed to precede those of the workers.[898] Clients cannot be easily banned from the platforms in case of negative feedback from workers, except when their rating falls significantly below the predetermined threshold. On the other hand, clients' ratings have a higher impact on workers' access to the platform, as workers are allowed to provide their services on a platform, only if they display high ratings. In other words, a low rating can more adversely affect the workers' access to a certain platform than the clients' access. Deriving from these considerations, the symmetry of the rating system, even when ensured, can remain problematic in practice.

The Obstruction of the Right to Challenge Perceived Unfair Situations

When considering the significant amount of power concentrated in the customers' hands, it becomes essential for platform workers to enjoy the basic right to challenge perceived unfair treatments, such as temporary suspensions, automatic deactivations, poor ratings, or even 'wage theft practices'. More often than not, platform workers are deprived of access to easy, quick, impartial, and affordable dispute resolution mechanisms.[899] Eurofound highlights this issue as an important challenge associated with algorithmic control and the rating system.[900]

The availability of dispute resolution mechanisms in a certain platform can be checked in terms and conditions, which should be easily readable by platform workers. In general, platforms were observed not to provide access to such mechanisms.[901] Aloisi and De Stefano point out the specific situation of crowdworkers, who miss out on their right to appeal, in case their work gets retained by customers without paying for it.[902] These workers are also discouraged from entering into litigation with the platform, as the object of the contestation would be a very small amount of pay.[903] What is more, a great number of platform workers appear to be in the dark about the existence of these grievance mechanisms. According to the ILO Global Survey of workers on freelance platforms, approximately half of the respondents had knowledge about the possibility of filing a complaint against a decision they thought was unfair; however, only 30 % of these workers exercised such a right.[904] The awareness about such grievance mechanisms was observed to be lower for platform workers working in the taxi and delivery sectors, who, in certain cases, reported being sanctioned for their

897. S. Silberman, L. Irani, 'Operating an Employer Reputation System: Lessons from Turkopticon, 2008-2015', *Comparative Labour Law and Policy*, Vol. 37, Issue 3, 2016, p. 21.
898. S. P. Choudary, *The architecture of digital labour platforms*, p. 16.
899. *Ibid.*, p. 26; H. Hauben, K. Lenaerts, W. Wayert, *The platform economy and precarious work*, Study for the EMPL Committee, 2020, p. 53; *See also* Survey commissioned by KU Leuven and prepared by Ipsos, p. 6.
900. Eurofound, *Maximising profits ...*, p. 18.
901. ILO WESO Report, p. 251.
902. V. De Stefano, A. Aloisi, *A European Legal framework ...*, p. 21.
903. ILO WESO Report, p. 100.
904. *Ibid.*, p. 181.

decisions to go forward with their complaints, in the form of deactivation of their accounts.

Against this background, the founders of six platform operators, *inter alia*, Deliveroo, Uber, and Cabify, have come together to sign a charter of principles for good platform work.[905] Among the principles enshrined in this chapter is also the provision of 'transparent and accountable mechanisms' by platforms to find a solution to workers' disputes with clients, but also with other workers.[906]

Going beyond unilateral solutions provided (or not) by platform operators, some potential legal solutions to aid platform workers in seeking redress have also been designed at the EU level. An initiative that goes in this direction is the so-called Platform to Business (P2B) Regulation, whose principal aim is to ensure more fairness and transparency toward business users of online intermediation services.[907] In addition to the transparency measures, this instrument establishes the mandatory creation of a mechanism for handling quickly, internally, and free of charge complaints for business users who seek redress.[908] The providers of online intermediation services have to explain in their terms and conditions the detailed rules for the functioning of this system.[909] Notwithstanding the redress solution offered by this legal instrument, its personal scope of application appears to be narrow, as it is limited to only a certain number of self-employed platform workers.[910] It does not apply, hence, to those platform workers who have an employment contract, or those who provide services for businesses.[911] Many platforms are equally excluded from the Regulation's scope of application, with examples being Uber and Deliveroo, which do not simply provide online intermediation services.[912] In the EU arena, also another instrument can be very pertinent for empowering certain platform workers to challenge the perceived unfair decisions, namely the Proposal for a Platform Work Directive. According to this draft legislation, platform workers are entitled to an explanation from the platform operators for automated decisions which impact their working conditions. In case this explanation is considered unsatisfactory by platform workers, they can request the platforms to review it.[913]

905. https://www.eurofound.europa.eu/data/platform-economy/records/the-charter-of-principles-for-good-platform-work.
906. Principle 7 (2) of the Charter.
907. Regulation (EU) 2019/1150 of the European Parliament and of the Council of 20 June 2019 on promoting fairness and transparency for business users of online intermediation services, Available at: https://eur-lex.europa.eu/legal-content/EN/TXT/?uri=celex%3A32019R1150.
908. Eurofound, *Maximizing profits* ..., p. 13.
909. Article 11(3) of the Regulation.
910. According to Article 2 of the Regulation, business users will include solely those 'private individuals acting in a commercial or professional capacity..., or legal persons, who offer goods or services to consumers ...'.
911. H. Hauben et al., *The platform economy and precarious employment*, p. 53.
912. *Ibid.*
913. Article 8, para. 2 of the directive.

Part III

The EU Agenda on Casual Work and Platform Work: 'Connecting the Dots' Between Past, Present, and Future Legal Developments

> 'Wise leaders connect the past, the present, and the future'
> William Wordsworth

In the same spirit as this quote by the British poet Wordsworth, this doctoral dissertation attempts to 'connect the dots' between past, present, and future legal developments, with the final aim to improve the labour protection of platform workers. As it will be indicated, this part maintains that *sui generis* regulatory responses to platform work alone, with the prominent example of the dPWD, cannot 'constitute a happy-ending to the story of gig workers and employment law'.[914] Instead, opening up to the bigger picture, and looking at the set of existing protective standards applicable to casual work, might be conducive in light of enhancing the labour protection of platform workers.

914. R. Dukes, 'On demand work as a legal framework to understand the gig economy', p. 144.

Chapter 8

The Past: The Pathway to a European Regulatory Approach to Casual Work

8.1 A BROAD CONCEPTION OF THE CASUAL WORK AGENDA

The landscape of the world of work has fundamentally changed.[915] These changes are brought about by globalization, technological advancements, demographic developments,[916] etc., and they have led to the creation of new forms of work, together with the proliferation of existing non-standard forms of employment,[917] especially the very flexible ones. For example, 'work of very short duration, micro work and the deployment of algorithms in the allocation and evaluation of work' represents an important work reality nowadays. Notable examples in this regard are casual work and platform work arrangements.

Non-standard work, which has also been broadly referred to as atypical work,[918] has always been associated with difficulties in being captured within regulatory frameworks. This is because, traditionally, the focus of labour law has been on standard employment.[919] In contrast to standard employment, the non-standard one displays atypical features, such as work performed outside the employer's workplace, irregular working hours, the involvement of multiple parties, payment by task, etc.[920]

915. F. Hendrickx, 'The European Social Pillar: A First Evaluation', *European Labour Law Journal* 2018, Vol. 9 Issue I, pp. 3-6; EPSR, para. 9 of the preamble, p. 7.
916. I. Durri, Review of the book *Regulating the platform economy: International perspectives on new forms of work*, p. 1.
917. K. Riesenhuber, 'European Employment Law', *Intersentia*, 2012, p. 413.
918. C. Barnard, *EU Employment Law*, Oxford University Press, 4th ed., 2012, p. 426; K. Riesenhuber, *European Employment Law*, Intersentia, 2012, Chapter 4.
919. A. Davies, 'Regulating atypical work: Beyond equality', in *Resocialising Europe in a Time of Crisis*, eds N. Countouris and M. Freedland, Cambridge University Press, 2013, p. 13.
920. V. De Stefano, I. Durri, C. Stylogiannis, M. Wouters,' Exclusion by Default: Platform Workers' Quest for Labour Protections', in *A Research Agenda for the Gig Economy and Society*, eds V. De Stefano, I. Durri, C. Stylogiannis, M. Wouters, Edward Elgar Publishing, 2022, pp. 2-4.

Platform work and casual work combine several of these atypical features at the same time, and hence, they further exacerbate existing regulatory challenges. As varied as the vast group of non-standard work arrangements is,[921] so are the legal responses provided to them. While some work typologies have constituted the subject of regulatory activity, some others, such as casual work arrangements, have been overlooked by EU regulators, or at least until recently.

Against this background, the purpose of this part is to explore how a European regulatory approach to casual work has been shaped at the EU level. In order to do this, what Confucius advised many centuries ago, remains still pertinent – we need to 'study the past', in order to understand the future. Therefore, the analysis which will be carried out in this part starts by digging into the historical roots of this European approach. In the quest for the historical origins, broader and interrelated discussions unfold, such as that on flexibility, atypical work,[922] fragmentation of work,[923] or precarious work,[924] which highlight the importance of looking into the big picture of regulating casual work. In light of this, in addition to targeted legal instruments which govern casual work specifically, also more general instruments and discussions on non-standard work might be considered. It is the combination of both broader and more targeted regulatory frameworks, which have jointly contributed to shaping a regulatory setting for casual work at the EU level, which will be referred to in this dissertation as the EU casual work agenda.

Efforts to develop a regulatory matrix for casual work can be traced back to the EU's response to what can be considered the 'first wave of flexibility', which consisted mainly of a set of directives adopted in the 1990s. At the heart of these 1990s instruments stood, *inter alia*, three specific forms of atypical work, namely part-time, fixed-term, and temporary agency work.[925] This triad of work arrangements has been labelled as the 'typical', or 'traditional', part of non-standard employment.[926] This segment contrasts with the very atypical, or very flexible, part of non-standard employment, with an example being casual work. In addition to, as will be demonstrated below, efforts to create a casual work agenda can also be observed in several authoritative documents of the EU institutions, such as social partners' consultations documents, European Parliament's reports, etc.

It was only recently that the EU decided to follow up on these past discussions and bring very flexible forms of work, such as casual work, at the spotlight. This was done by means of a directive on TPWCD, but also by advancing a proposal for a directive on the Working Conditions of Platform Workers, which can arguably constitute the final steps in a longer-standing agenda on casual work at the EU level.

921. European Parliament Working Paper, *Atypical work in the EU*, 2000, p. 29.
922. Eurofound, *Flexible Forms of Work: 'Very Atypical' Contractual Arrangements*, Report (2010).
923. E. Albin and J. Prassl, 'Fragmenting Work, Fragmented Regulation: The Contract of Employment as a Driver of Social Exclusion', *Hebrew University of Jerusalem Legal Studies Research Paper* Series No. 17-39, 2015, pp. 7 and 15.
924. European Parliament, *Precarious employment in Europe: Patterns, trends and policy strategies*, 2016, p. 109.
925. F. Hendrickx, *Handbook on European Labour Law*, 2011, pp. 137-138.
926. G. Van Guys, *Belgium: Flexible Forms of Work: 'Very Atypical' Contractual Arrangements*, Eurofound Report (2010).

Prior to looking into these two legislative instruments, it is necessary to take a step back and scrutinize a series of events that led to their adoption.

8.2 A CASUAL WORK AGENDA IN THE MAKING: A HISTORICAL ACCOUNT OF EVENTS

The early attempts to regulate atypical work can arguably be detected in the 1980s,[927] when some proposals to adopt directives on part-time, fixed-term, and temporary agency work were advanced, however, without being successfully implemented.[928] Nevertheless, it would take a decade later, concretely in the 1990s, for the main legislative events connected to atypical work to happen. These series of events had as a major source of inspiration the 1989 Community Charter of the Fundamental Social Rights of Workers, hereinafter the Community Charter.[929] This Community Charter put the emphasis on the need to improve the living and working conditions of non-standard workers, by mentioning explicitly fixed-term, part-time, temporary and seasonal workers.[930] This spirit set out in the Community Charter was first reflected in the proposals to regulate atypical work in the 1990s,[931] which were part of the Action Plan to implement the Charter.[932] As an outcome of these legislative proposals was the adoption of a directive on the Health and Safety for workers with a fixed-duration employment relationship or a temporary employment relationship.[933] Following a chronological order of events, it was only some months after the adoption of this *Health and Safety Directive*, that the so-called *Written Statement Directive*, again inspired by the Community Charter,[934] got adopted.[935] This directive can be considered as particularly pertinent for non-standard workers, as 'it specifically serves the purpose of providing transparency' for the working conditions of these workers.[936] This purpose has been reflected in some of its legal provisions, according to which, employers needed to provide information to workers also about the expected duration of a temporary contract, and the duration of the daily or weekly working hours, where the latter provision can be especially relevant for part-time and casual workers.[937] As it will

927. K. Riesenhuber, *European employment law*, Intersentia, 2012, p. 415.
928. *Ibid.*
929. M. Bell, E. Ales, Deinert, O. and S. Robin-Olivier, *International and European Labour Law, Article-by-Article Commentary*, Bloomsbury Publishing, 2018, p. 3.
930. Point 7 of the Community Charter of the Fundamental Social Rights of Workers, 1989.
931. COM (90) 228 final, 29.6.1990; OJ C 224, 8.9.1990, p. 8.
932. European Commission, Background paper for first-stage consultations with social partners, Flexibility in working time and security for workers, 1995, p. 4.
933. Council Directive 91/383/EEC of 25 June 1991 supplementing the measures to encourage improvements in the safety and health at work of workers with a fixed - duration employment relationship or a temporary employment relationship.
934. Point 9 of the Community Charter, as pointed out by F. Hendrickx in *Handbook on European labour law*, 2011, p. 157.
935. Council Directive 91/533/ EEC of 14 October 1991 on an employer's obligation to inform employees of the conditions applicable to the contract or employment relationship. This directive is now abolished, and it has been replaced by the TPWCD.
936. K. Riesenhuber, *European employment law*, p. 421.
937. Article 2(2) (e) and (i).

be shown in detail in Chapter 11, casual workers were also subject to ample exclusions from the personal scope of this directive.[938] The Written Statement directive (WSD) was, nonetheless, considered merely informative, and as such, it did not regulate the working conditions of atypical workers.[939] The 1989 Community Charter, furthermore, explicitly stated that an improvement of working conditions was necessary also for the 'duration and organization of working time'.[940] It was in light of these considerations that[941] a *Directive on the organization of the working time*[942] was enacted in 1993.[943] This legal instrument deals with a crucial aspect for especially part-time and casual work arrangements, which is the working time. For this reason, it is paramount to consider this directive alongside other legal instruments on non-standard work.[944] Due to its relevance for casual work, this legal instrument will be explored more in-depth in the following chapter of this dissertation.

The adoption of the Written Statement and the Working Time directives was apparently not considered enough by European lawmakers to govern, *inter alia*, atypical work. They decided to bring again the regulation of specific forms of atypical work at the centre of the discussions. In this vein, the European Commission issued in 1994, a White Paper on the future of European Social Policy, which had a clear priority: the adoption of the proposals on atypical work.[945] Furthermore, in 1995, the background document of the Commission for first-stage consultations with the social partners on the flexibility in working time and security for workers constituted a further step taken in this direction. In this paper, the European Commission recognized a growth of part-time and fixed-term work and acknowledged the Member States' response to them by means of national regulations.[946] Pursuant to this document, these flexible workers, namely part-time, fixed-term, and temporary agency workers, ought to be provided with equal working conditions with their standard counterparts at the EU level.[947] As no agreement was reached at the Council level on a European response to this issue, the Commission decided to initiate the first round of social partners' consultation in this regard.[948]

The outcome of the two-stage consultations of the European social partners was the conclusion of a *Framework Agreement to regulate part-time work* in 1997. This agreement was very much inspired by the already existing ILO convention on part-time work.[949] In the preamble of the Framework Agreement, it was explicitly stated that

938. Article 1(2) of the Written Statement Directive.
939. C. Barnard, *EU employment law*, pp. 426-427.
940. Points 7 and 8 of the Community Charter.
941. F. Hendrickx, *EU handbook on European labour law*, p. 141.
942. Directive 93/104/EC concerning certain aspects of the organization of Working Time.
943. The current version: OJ (2003) L299/9.
944. A. Davies, 'Regulating atypical work: beyond equality', p. 247.
945. Commission of the European Communities, *Proposal for a Council Directive concerning the Framework Agreement on Fixed-term Work*, 1999, p. 2.
946. European Commission, Background paper for first-stage consultations with social partners, 'Flexibility in working time and security for workers', 1995, p. 3.
947. *Ibid.*, p. 1.
948. *Ibid.*, p. 5.
949. C175 – Part-Time Work Convention, 1994. It allows exclusion of part-time work with working hours below a certain threshold in its Articles 3 and 8.

European social partners intended to conclude a similar *agreement for fixed-term work*. And indeed, such an agreement was concluded on 18 March 1999. Both agreements on part-time and fixed-term work concluded by the two sides of the industry at the EU level were given effect by means of two European directives.[950] These directives merely serve as 'implementing shells', whereas the main provisions for regulating part-time and fixed-term work can be found in the respective framework agreements, which are annexed to the directives.[951] Soon after the adoption of this directive, the European Parliament issued a report on atypical work in 2000, where it acknowledged that casual work is a crucial form of atypical work. The importance of this document lied especially in the fact that it introduced a working definition of casual work, which was understood as 'work which is irregular or intermittent with no expectation of continuous employment'.[952] Due to the position given to casual work in this report, this work typology started to gain more visibility at the EU level. What is more, this report also highlighted the often illegal position of casual workers, as it is not rare for casual work to be associated with the informal labour market.[953]

After the adoption of the Fixed-term Work directive, the European social partners could not reach a consensus anymore in regulating other specific forms of non-standard work.[954] It was the European Parliament and the Council which decided to adopt in 2008 a directive on temporary agency work.[955] Since the moment of the adoption of this directive and until the following decade, a period of stagnation underpinned not only non-standard work in general, but very flexible work more in particular.[956] Departing from this regulatory passivity, the following chapters focus, instead, on regulatory activism towards casual work. Important constituents of the casual work agenda, which date back some decades ago but are still in force, and can prove insightful in improving the legal situation of casual and platform workers, will be therefore scrutinized.

950. Council Directive 97/81/ EC of 15 December 1997 concerning the Framework Agreement on part-time work; Council Directive 1999/70/ EC of 28 June 1999 concerning the Framework Agreement on fixed-term work.
951. G. More, DG Employment, Presentation on Fixed-Term Work, Brussels, 2017.
952. European Parliament, *Atypical work in the EU*, p. 17.
953. *Ibid.*, pp. 41, 66 and 155.
954. L. Zappala, 'The Temporary Agency Workers' Directive: An Impossible Political Agreement?', *Industrial Law Journal*, Vol. 32, Issue 4, 2003, pp. 310-317.
955. Directive 2008/104/EC of the European Parliament and of the Council of 19 November 2008 on temporary agency work.
956. A. Piasna, 'Better Working Conditions, More Predictable Work – the New EU Directive', Social Europe, 2019 (blog), Available at: https://socialeurope.eu/better-working-conditions-more-predictable-work-the-new-eu-directive.

CHAPTER 9

The Importance of The Working Time Directive for the Working Time Security of Casual and Platform Workers

The Working Time Directive (WTD) has been considered as an important component of the regulatory setting on casual work. The rationale for its inclusion in this broad regulatory framework has to do with the weight that working time has in the case of casual and platform work arrangements. Against this backdrop, this chapter explores the relevance that the instrument in question has in regulating certain aspects of working time for casual and platform workers. In particular, the significant body of case law of the CJEU, which has broadly interpreted the working time concept, by including also certain stand-by time situations, will stand at the heart of this part of the dissertation. These EU judicial approaches will be examined in light of their potential extrapolation to certain time periods during which platform workers are available to undertake work, but are not effectively working.

9.1 SOME GENERAL CONSIDERATIONS ON THE WORKING TIME DIRECTIVE

The Working Time Directive was originally adopted in 1993.[957] Since then, many developments have occurred in the world of work, which have brought significant changes in the organization of working time.[958] As Supiot rightly puts it, 'gone is the time of formal and hierarchical systems of time'.[959] As a result of these developments, the directive on working time has constituted the subject of several regulatory attempts

957. OJ [1993] L307/18.
958. Interpretative Communication on Directive 2003/88/EC of the European Parliament and of the Council concerning certain aspects of the organization of working time (2017/C 165/01), p. 4.
959. A. Supiot, *Beyond Employment: Changes in Work and the Future of Labour Law in Europe*, Oxford University Press, 2001, p. 69.

to alter it. The current version of the WTD dates back to 2003,[960] and it has been observed that it is 'essentially identical' to the previous versions of 1993 and 2000.[961] A review of the instrument in question was carried out in 2013, which concluded that the directive was, in general, relevant in today's world of work.[962] As no revision has been carried out, the European Commission issued in 2017 an Interpretative Communication on the Working Time Directive, which sheds light onto its main provisions with consideration to the evolution of the CJEU case law on working time.[963]

The legal basis chosen for the adoption of this directive was Article 118a EEC, now Article 153(1) (a) TFEU, which provides for the improvement of the health and safety of workers. The choice of a health and safety legal basis determines the purpose of this legal instrument, which is concretely to lay down minimum health and safety provisions concerning the organization of certain aspects of the working time.[964] The CJEU has emphasized such an objective on several occasions, where it has pointed out that this rationale 'should not be subordinated to purely economic considerations'.[965] Furthermore, this directive does not engage with the issue of the remuneration of workers for working time, except for the provision of paid annual leave, and hence, it leaves such an issue in the hands of the Member States.[966] As laid down by Article 153(5) TFEU, pay is an area which is excluded from the EU's competences. In light of these considerations, it is evident that the WTD cannot be considered a legal instrument which is directly linked to the regulation of working conditions. As Barnard points out, this legal act stands in a 'grey area between traditional health and safety measures and the rights of employed persons'.[967]

As concerns the rights enshrined in this directive, they have been considered fundamental by the EU Charter on Fundamental Rights (EUCHFR).[968] The Court of Justice has made sure to extensively refer to Article 31(2) of the Charter and to interpret the WTD in light of it. In brief, these entitlements include minimum rest periods, such as daily rest, weekly rest, daily breaks, and paid annual leave; but also limitations, such as maximum weekly working time.[969] The directive provides details about each of these entitlements, by also establishing reference periods. For instance, a reference period of twenty-four hours has been set out for a minimum daily rest of eleven consecutive hours. Additionally, the directive makes these packages of rights subject to different derogations depending on the need of certain sectors, but also to individual

960. OJ [2003] L299/9.
961. Interpretative Communication, p. 8.
962. *Ibid.*, p. 6.
963. European Commission, 'Working Conditions: Working Time Directive: Interpretative Communication', Available at: https://ec.europa.eu/social/main.jsp?catId=706&intPageId=5115&langId=en.
964. Article 1(1) of the directive.
965. Recital 4 of the WTD; Case C-151/02, *Landeshauptstadt Kiel v. Norbert Jaeger*, 2003, paras 66-67.
966. Order of 11 January 2007, *Jan Vorel v. Nemocnice Český Krumlov*, C-437/05, paras 32-35; Case C-518/15, *Ville de Nivelles v. Rudy Matzak*, 2018, para. 49.
967. C. Barnard, *EU Employment Law*, Oxford University Press, 4th ed., 2012, p. 533.
968. Article 31(2) of the EU Charter on Fundamental Rights.
969. Article 1(2) (a) and Articles 3-7 of the WTD.

opt-outs,[970] where the latter applies, for example, to the maximum weekly working time. Importantly, the right to paid annual leave is the only provision of the directive, which cannot be subject to derogations.[971] By having regard to this set of exceptions, Supiot points out to the directive being 'positively schizophrenic', as it sets out rules, which later it allows to be avoided by way of derogations.[972] To be noted is that it is not the purpose of this chapter to delve into the detailed rules laid down by the WTD.

As important as it is to introduce the set of rights offered by the WTD, it is also essential to clarify the target group to whom these entitlements apply. In search for the personal scope of application of the directive, it can be noted that no specific provision has been dedicated to this matter, something which is in contrast with the already examined directives, e.g., those on part-time and fixed-term work. What the WTD does, instead, is that it acknowledges that the provisions of the Framework Directive on Health and Safety[973] fully apply to matters governed by it.[974] As a logical consequence, the 'worker' definition laid down in this Framework Directive will also be applicable to the matters regulated by the Working Time one. This extension of the 'worker' definition has been explicitly acknowledged by the accompanying document to the proposal for the 1993 Working Time Directive.[975]

The 'worker' definition, as set out by the Framework Directive, considers workers 'any person employed by an employer, including trainees and apprentices but excluding domestic servants'.[976] The way this definition has been formulated does not seem to reveal much about the workers covered by it. It was the CJEU, instead, which shed light on the 'worker's concept for the purpose of its application to the Working Time Directive.[977] The Court highlighted that this notion has an 'an autonomous EU law meaning',[978] as established by its case law on the free movement of workers. Pursuant to this jurisprudence, a worker is defined as a person who 'for a certain period of time [...] performs services for and under the direction of another person in return for which he receives remuneration'.[979] As a result, the 'worker' concept to which the

970. The opt-out presumes that the worker can determine by herself the working time, and hence, the worker needs to give her personal consent to a longer maximum weekly working time.
971. Case C-173/99, *The Queen v. Secretary of State for Trade and Industry, ex parte Broadcasting, Entertainment, Cinematographic and Theatre Union (BECTU)*, 2001, para. 43.
972. A. Supiot, 'On the Job: Time for Agreement', *International Journal of Comparative Labour Law and Industrial Relations*, Vol. 12 Issue 3, 1996, p. 195.
973. Council Directive 89/391/EEC of 12 June 1989 on the introduction of measures to encourage improvements in the safety and health of workers at work.
974. Article 1(4) of the WTD.
975. Explanatory memorandum concerning the proposal for a Council Directive concerning certain aspects of the organization of working time, 20 September 1990, COM(90) 317 final - SYN 295, p. 3.
976. Article 3(a) of Directive 89/391.
977. Case *Matzak*, para. 28; Case C-428/09, *Union syndicale Solidaires Isere v. Premier ministre and Others*, 2010, para. 28.
978. F. Hendrickx, S. De Groof, Being On-call at Home Is Working Time: The Matzak-Case, Regulation for Globalization blog, 2018, Available at: http://global-workplace-law-and-policy.kluwerlawonline.com/2018/02/27/call-home-working-time-matzak-case/.
979. Case C-66/85, *Lawrie-Blum v. Land Baden-Württemberg*, 1986, para. 17; Case C-256/01 *Allonby v. Accrington and Rossendale College*, 2004, para. 67; C-316/13, *Gérard Fenoll v. Centre d'aide par le travail 'La Jouvene' and Association de parents et d'amis de personnes handicapées mentales (APEI) d'Avignon*, 2015, para. 27.

WTD seems to refer displays as a quite broad one, and it can eventually encompass casual workers.[980] This interpretation seems to stand in stark contrast with the 'worker' definition set out by the directives on part-time, fixed-term, and temporary agency work, which accords to the 'worker' concept a national meaning.[981]

Providing a general understanding of the Working Time Directive was deemed necessary to move on to what constitutes the crux of this part: the examination of the concept of 'working time', with a special focus on on-call time situations. Digging into this aspect of the directive might provide some valuable outcomes to be extrapolated to certain working time situations faced by casual and platform workers. To this end, the most prominent jurisprudence of the Court of Justice with regard to on-call/ stand-by time will be first explored, and subsequently, the relevance of this judicial interpretation for casual and platform workers will be explained.

9.2 THE 'WORKING TIME' CONCEPT: AN EXPANSIVE INTERPRETATION OF THE CJEU

Defining the concept of 'working time' constitutes a first crucial step in the accordance with the entitlements provided by the WTD, save the paid annual leave.[982] Since the adoption of the directive, massive case law has accompanied it with the purpose of defining the boundaries of working time.[983] The Court's activity in this regard has been especially prominent on the qualification of on-call, or stand-by time, as either working time or rest period. This time period blurs the boundaries between working time and rest time, due to the fact that while being on-call or stand-by, workers are at the disposal of the employer, but without actually carrying out work.[984] While on-call time implies the physical presence of the worker at the place where work is usually performed, stand-by time presumes the worker's availability to undertake work in another place than the employers' premises. Supiot labels this time period as 'on-the-job inactivity', and acknowledges this problem, especially in the context of casual work, where these workers can be called in to respond to the employers' calls at any time.[985] Therefore, this interpretation by the judicial can be crucial for issues associated with modern working time, which are experienced especially by workers in casual and platform work arrangements.

980. Judgment in case C-428/09, *Union syndicale Solidaires Isere v. Premier ministre and Others*, 2010, paras 30-32.
981. N. Countouris, 'The Concept of "Worker" in European Labour Law: Fragmentation, Autonomy and Scope', *Industrial Law Journal*, Vol. 47 Issue 2, 2018, pp. 192-225, p. 201.
982. J. Kenner, 'Re-evaluating the Concept of Working Time: An Analysis of Recent Case Law', *Industrial Relations Journal*, Vol. 35 Issue 6, 2004, pp. 588-602, p. 588.
983. According to the Interpretative Communication 2017, p. 5, more than fifty judgments and orders have been issues on working time from 1993 to 2017.
984. A. Supiot, *Beyond Employment: Changes in Work and the Future of Labour Law in Europe*, Oxford University Press, 2001, p. 66.
985. *Ibid.*, p. 81.

As was the case with the 'worker' definition, concepts such as 'working time' and 'rest period' are concepts of EU law[986] and, as such, are given an autonomous EU meaning.[987] This means that Member States cannot unilaterally determine the working time,[988] which is corroborated by the fact that no derogations are permitted from this provision of the directive.[989] Instead, what the Court has held in several of its rulings, a uniform interpretation of working time should be maintained across Member States. In the course of interpreting the 'working time' notion, the Court was noticed to give consideration to objective characteristics and to the purpose of the Working Time Directive, which is to ensure the workers' health and safety.[990] As Kenner explains, this uniform application of the concept of 'working time' is necessary because 'the health and safety is the fulcrum that drives the operation of the Directive'.[991]

By having this in mind, the WTD defines 'working time' as 'any period during which (1) the worker is working, (2) at the employer's disposal, and (3) carrying out his activity or duties, in accordance with national law and/or practice'.[992] At the same time, this provision provides a negative definition of 'rest periods', concretely as periods that are not working time.[993] As the Working Time Directive stands, it seems to suggest a narrow interpretation of 'working time'.[994] The CJEU, nevertheless, has expanded the notion of 'working time', by extending it to some instances of time spent on-call or stand-by. While the second criteria of 'working time' set out by the WTD, i.e., being at the employer's disposal in order to respond immediately to calls of work,[995] is not disputable in the context of on-call work, the Court has focused on broadly interpreting the two other criteria of 'working time' with respect to on-call work. In order to determine the correct category to which a time period belongs, the Court conducts an overall assessment of the circumstances of each individual case.

The analysis of the Court's case law on the qualification of on-call time will start with the seminal case of *Simap*, which was decided by the Court in 2000.[996] In this case, the Court interpreted in a flexible way the third criterion of 'working time', which requires an actual performance of work, for a certain time period to be considered as working time. What the Court ruled was that the time that a doctor spent *at the health*

986. Frank, S. De Groof, Being On-call at Home Is Working Time: the *Matzak*-case, Regulating for Globalization, 2018
987. Judgment in *Matzak*, para. 45; Case C-344/19, *D.J. v. Radiotelevizija Slovenija*, 2021, para. 30.
988. J. Kenner, 'Re-evaluating the Concept of Working Time: An analysis of recent case law', *Industrial Relations Journal*, Vol. 35 Issue 6, 2004, p. 596.
989. Chapter 5 of the WTD, especially Article 17.
990. Judgment in *Matzak*, para. 62; Case C-14/04, *Abdelkader Dellas and Others v. Premier ministre and Ministre des Affaires sociales, du Travail et de la Solidarité*, 2005, para. 44; Case C-266/14, *Federación de Servicios Privados del sindicato Comisiones obreras (CC.OO.) v. Tyco Integrated Security SL and Tyco Integrated Fire & Security Corporation Servicios SA*, 2015, para. 27.
991. J. Kenner, 'Re-evaluating the Concept of Working Time: An Analysis of Recent Case Law', *Industrial Relations Journal*, Vol. 35 Issue 6, 2004, p. 598.
992. Article 2(1) of the WTD.
993. *Ibid.*, Article 2(2).
994. A. Supiot, *Beyond employment: Changes in work and the future of labour law in Europe*, pp. 65-66.
995. Interpretative Communication p. 17.
996. Case C-303/98, *Sindicato of Médicos of Asistencia Pública (SIMAP) v. Conselleria de Sanidad y Consumo de la Generalidad Valenciana*, 2000.

centre waiting for calls of work, even when *no actual work was carried out,* was considered in its entirety as *working time.* This decision was contrary to the general approach maintained by the Member States and the European Commission until then, which perceived inactivity while on-call as rest time.[997] Nevertheless, as Supiot rightly contends, if the element of the actual performance of work was to be stringently interpreted, it would 'leave the door open to classifying the time that an employee must be at the employer's disposal as free time'.[998] In Simap, the CJEU presumed that the third criterion is fulfilled,[999] due to the fact that the worker is bound to stay in one specific place established by the employer, by significantly restricting in this way the time to dedicate to his personal commitments.[1000] Additionally, in the *Simap* case, the Court also considered the situation when workers are *not required to be at the health centre,* but are 'contactable at all times'. In this last scenario, the judicial outcome was that *only periods of the actual performance of work should count as working time.*[1001] A paramount effect of the *Simap* case was that it made clear that 'working time' and 'rest time' constituted 'mutually exclusive' categories, and hence, time on stand-by periods should be classified as either 'working time' or 'rest period'. This outcome was essential in the face of the responses adopted by several Member States,[1002] but also the general interpretation of the European Commission, which had created intermediate categories between 'working time' and 'rest time' in order to fit the time spent on-call.[1003]

In *its Jaeger case* in 2003,[1004] the Court took one step further than Simap,[1005] by deciding that even the on-call time of a doctor, who was *resting or sleeping while at work,* while his services were not required, *counted as working time.* The fact that the doctor was resting while on-call did not change the fact that this worker was required to be physically present in order to provide his services immediately.[1006] Here, once again, the Court reaffirmed that 'working time' and 'rest time' are distinctive categories, and the creation of a third one is not permitted. In a nutshell, in these two cases, the Court concluded that the time spent on-call (at the employer's premises, or in a place where work is usually carried out) is working time in its entirety; while stand-by time (in a place other than the one where work is usually performed) can be working time only for the active period during which the worker is actually carrying out work. This approach, nevertheless, was altered some years later, when the Court showed that the inactive part of stand-by time should not be automatically precluded from being working time.

997. J. Kenner, 'Re-evaluating the concept of working time ...', p. 593.
998. A. Supiot, *Beyond employment ...*, p. 66.
999. Paragraph 48 of the judgment.
1000. J. Kenner, 'Re-evaluating the concept of working time ...', p. 594.
1001. Judgment in *Simap* case, paras 50 and 52.
1002. Commission Communication COM (2003) 843 on the re-examination of Directive 93/104/EC, p. 19.
1003. J. Kenner, 'Re-evaluating the concept of working time ...', p. 593.
1004. Case C-151/02, *Landeshauptstadt Kiel v. Norbert Jaeger*, 2003.
1005. *Ibid.*, J. Kenner, p. 596.
1006. Paragraphs 63-64 of the case.

The Court's answer concerning the *inactive part of the stand-by time* was given in 2018 in the pivotal case of *Matzak*. In *Matzak*, the worker was on stand-by at home, as agreed with the employer, under the duty to *answer work calls within 8 minutes*. The Court took into consideration the entire circumstances of this case, namely that the worker had to be physically present at a place determined by the employer, notwithstanding that this place was his home,[1007] together with the obligation to respond to calls of work within a few minutes. The Court found that the fact that the worker had to be at a place determined by the employer was enough to produce constraints in the organization of his free time. On top of this, the time limit imposed to respond to calls was very strict, as it was confined to only a few minutes. Due to these considerations, the Court reasoned that the worker was limited to the extent that he could not properly organize his personal life.[1008] As Hendrickx and De Groof contend, an innovation brought by *Matzak* case consisted in the fact that even stand-by time spent at home could be qualified as working time.[1009]

In the recent *Stadt Offenbach am Main* case,[1010] the CJEU construed the concept of the '*workplace*' broadly. This interpretation of the Court gave a broad meaning to the first criterion of the 'working time' definition as set out in the directive, namely that 'the worker is working'. Originally, this criterion was interpreted as a spatial one, i.e., it requires the worker to be physically present at the place where the work is usually performed, or at another workplace determined by the employer.[1011] With the Stadt Offenbach am Main ruling, the Court significantly broadened it, by clarifying that the 'workplace' included 'any place where the worker is required to exercise an activity on the employer's instruction, including where that place is not the place where he or she usually carries out his or her professional duties'.[1012] With regard to the facts of the case, as in *Matzak*, it also concerned a firefighter, however, with the difference that the employer did not determine the place from where the worker could be on stand-by. This freedom to choose the location was, nevertheless, restricted by the fact that in case of a call for work, the worker had to *reach the city within 20 minutes, by having with him his uniform and service vehicle*. The evaluation of the overall circumstances in the case at hand[1013] led the Court to determine that the imposed time limitation[1014] – twenty minutes to return to work – hampered the worker's freedom to organize his free time. Deriving from these considerations, the Court emphasized as a decisive element to determine whether the inactive part of stand-by time is 'working time', the significant restrictions the worker faces on organizing his free time.[1015] Within the same day, the Court took a different decision based on the circumstances of the case in *Radiotelevizija Slovenija*.[1016] In this case, the fact that the workers were on a stand-by

1007. Paragraph 61 of the judgment.
1008. *Ibid.*, para. 63.
1009. F. Hendrickx, S. De Groof, Being On-call at Home Is Working Time: the *Matzak*-case.
1010. Case C-580/19, *RJ v. Stadt Offenbach am Main*, 2021.
1011. Interpretative Communication p. 16; Case C-303/98 *Simap*, para. 48.
1012. Paragraph 35 of the judgment.
1013. Paragraph 61 of Stadt Offenbach am Main.
1014. *Ibid.*, para. 47.
1015. Paragraph 55.
1016. Case C-344/19, *D.J. v. Radiotelevizija Slovenija*, 2021.

system, according to which they were *contactable by phone* and *could return to the place of work within one hour,* was not considered a significant constraint to freely manage their personal lives. This was in contrast with the situation when the time limit to return to work was constrained to a few minutes, as in *Matzak and Stadt Offenbach am Main* case law.[1017]

In a more recent case of the CJEU, namely *MG v. Dublin City Council,*[1018] the Court had to consider whether a *stand-by period during which the worker* (a retained firefighter) *could carry out another job* as a taxi driver, however, with the *obligation in case of emergency to reach the fire station within 10 minutes,* constituted either 'working time' or 'rest period'.[1019] As the Court held in its previous case law, it is important to pay due attention to the restriction the worker faces with regard to the time to devote to his personal needs. In assessing this limitation in light of the *Irish* case, the Court considered that the ability of the worker to carry out another professional activity during his stand-by time means that no significant limitations were imposed on managing his own interests.[1020] In reaching this conclusion, the Court also took into consideration other specific elements, among others, that the worker is not bound to be in a specific place during his stand-by time.[1021] For these reasons, the Court held that stand-by time during the performance of another professional activity constituted a 'rest period'.[1022]

In addition to stand-by time being qualified as working time, the CJEU has also ruled that travel time can constitute working time under certain conditions. In its emblematic ruling in this regard – the *Tyco case* – the Court decided that, for mobile workers without fixed places of work, *travelling between their homes and their first and last customers' premises* constituted working time.[1023] According to the Court, these journeys undertaken by the workers formed a 'necessary means of providing those workers' technical services to those customers'.[1024] *Travelling in between assignments* was not scrutinized in the context of the *Tyco* case, as it was already agreed between the parties that it would amount to be working time. Nevertheless, in the Interpretative Communication of the WTD, the Commission explicitly clarified that these journeys should be qualified as working time if three conditions are met: the trips are necessary to provide services to customers, the worker is at the employer's disposal during that time frame, and the travelling time is integral to the work of the worker.[1025] Importantly, in the *Tyco* case, the Court emphasized that it is up to the Member States to determine the rate of remuneration for travel time and that this remuneration does not have to be uniform with the remuneration for other working time.[1026]

1017. Paragraphs 47-48 of the judgment.
1018. Case C-214/20, *MG v. Dublin City Council*, 2021.
1019. Paragraph 34 of the judgment.
1020. Paragraph 43 of the judgment.
1021. Paragraph 44 of the judgment.
1022. *Ibid.*, para. 46.
1023. Case C-266/14, *Federación de Servicios Privados del sindicato Comisiones obreras (CC.OO.) v. Tyco Integrated Security SL and Tyco Integrated Fire & Security Corporation Servicios SA*, 2015.
1024. *Tyco* case, para. 32.
1025. Interpretative Communication, p. 19.
1026. *Tyco* case, paras 47-49.

9.3 THE CONTRIBUTION OF THE WORKING TIME DIRECTIVE TOWARDS THE INSECURITIES EXPERIENCED BY PLATFORM WORKERS

9.3.1 The Relevance of the CJEU Case Law on Working Time for Platform Workers

Once some of the most prominent developments around the EU regulatory framework on working time have been pointed out, this part takes one step further and scrutinizes the potential extrapolation of these regulatory developments, especially the CJEU case law on stand-by time, to certain working time situations experienced by platform workers. As already observed, the WTD is based on what Supiot refers to as 'normal time',[1027] or 9 to 5 time. As a result, stand-by time constitutes an exception, which mainly concerns certain professions such as doctors and firefighters, whose nature of work requires them to be available and respond to calls of work if needed. On the other side, modern developments in working time, such as 'variable working hours, on-call hours and annual scheduling of working time'[1028] are showing that on-call time has now become the norm in several work arrangements, with the prominent examples of casual and platform work, whereas regular or fixed hours of work have been seen rather as an exception.[1029] To be noted is that, in the platform work context, the deployment of technology might create some peculiar situations in relation to the working time of platform workers. This section engages in identifying some of these situations when platform workers are not actually executing a task, however, they could be working based on the established case law of the CJEU on working time.

Prior to unfolding the just-mentioned time periods, something which Pulignano and others have referred to as 'time-based unpaid labour',[1030] it is worthwhile to recap the most relevant takeaways from the CJEU jurisprudence, which can prove insightful in a platform work setting. At the outset, it should be noted that these judicial practices have made clear that there is a dualistic approach between working time and rest periods, where the main characteristic of working time is the significant restriction imposed on the worker's ability to organize his/her personal and social life. Nevertheless, in order to reach a conclusion in this regard, the Court needs to carry out a fact-specific analysis of each case. For instance, the *Matzak* case provides an example of severe restrictions on the worker's ability to organize his own life, i.e., the strict time limit (a few minutes) imposed on the worker to return to the workplace if called by the employer. However, the CJEU held in the *Dublin City Council* case that being able to perform a second job showed that the worker was not restricted in deciding how to organize his free time. Concerning travel time, the Court has also ruled that it can

1027. A. Supiot, *Beyond employment ...*, p. 63.
1028. *Ibid.*, p. 83.
1029. *Ibid.*, p. 71.
1030. V. Pulignano, A. Piasna, M. Domecka, K. Muszynski, L. Vermeerbergen, 'Does It Pay to Work? Unpaid Labour in the Platform Economy', *ETUI Policy Brief*, 2021, p. 15.

constitute working time for those workers without fixed workplaces, who travel between their homes and the clients' premises. Finally, in its recent jurisprudence, the CJEU broadly defined the notion of the 'workplace', by extending it to any place where the worker carries out an activity under the instructions of the employers. As will be shown below, this corpus of case law from the CJEU can be indeed pertinent for instances of stand-by time of both crowdworkers and workers on demand via apps, but also the travel time of the latter.

Waiting Time to Be Assigned Orders/Shifts

Platform workers working via apps, e.g., Uber drivers or Deliveroo riders, frequently experience a lack of orders,[1031] and as a result, they spend time waiting for orders to be assigned to them.[1032] In other words, before receiving an order, platform workers log into the application and wait until an order is allocated. This time span has been considered, among other things, by the UK Supreme Court in its Uber decision.[1033] The Court concluded that this waiting time could meet the test of working time under the CJEU jurisprudence, upon completing three conditions. These conditions require the worker to log into the app, be within the area where they are licensed to operate, and finally, be 'ready and willing to accept trips'.[1034] Ewing compares this situation to that experienced by a supermarket worker, who clocks in the system, is at the supermarket (at work), and then waits to serve the customers. In this regard, Ewing suggests that the reach of working time should also be extended to 'out of territory work' situations. Furthermore, she points out the complications arising in case workers log into multiple apps simultaneously.[1035] Such a difficulty has also been mentioned by the UK Supreme Court in the Uber judgment, concretely that addressing the working time of those working on one platform is easier in comparison to those workers who are available and willing to accept trips from other operators.[1036] A parallel can be drawn in this regard with the circumstances of the *Dublin City Council* case ruled by the CJEU, where the fact that the applicant was able to perform a second job was considered as a rest period. Nevertheless, this situation might be different in practice for platform workers. As Prassl notes, those who work frequently for a certain platform might be actually hesitant to perform tasks for other operators, as they fear deactivation or other penalties from the main platform for which they operate.[1037] As a result, these consequences, which can deter the worker from accepting tasks from different

1031. *Ibid.*, p. 4.
1032. ILO, *World employment and social outlook 2021: the role of digital labour platforms in transforming the world of work*, 2021, p. 244.
1033. The Supreme Court 19 February 2021, Case No. [2021] UKSC 5, *Uber BV and others v. Aslam and others*.
1034. Paragraph 134 of the Uber decision; K. Ewing, 'Don't be fooled, Uber is still dodging the minimum wage', Institute of Employment Rights blog, March 2021, Available at: https://www.ier.org.uk/comments/dont-be-fooled-uber-is-still-dodging-the-minimum-wage/.
1035. *Ibid.*, K. Ewing.
1036. Paragraph 135 of the decision.
1037. J. Prassl, *Humans as a service* ..., p. 106.

platform operators, should be taken into account by courts when deciding on the working time of platform workers.

Just one month after the Uber decision in the UK, in its Mencap judgment, the UK Supreme Court altered its approach towards the stand-by hours of casual workers.[1038] As McCann argues, in this ruling, the Court 'departed from a sophisticated model of working time of the kind it had endorsed in Uber'.[1039] In this judgment, the Supreme Court rejected to consider the time during which the care workers were sleeping at their patients' premises, and were available to calls of work, as working time. This judicial outcome seems to also stand in contrast with the judgment delivered by the CJEU in the *Jaeger* case, according to which, the sleeping time of doctors on stand-by at healthcare centres was considered as working time. Furthermore, contrary to the dichotomy between 'working time' and 'rest period' highlighted by the CJEU on several occasions, the Supreme Court in the UK considered the stand-by time in Mencap to be merely 'availability',[1040] a concept which seems to be fluctuating in between 'working time' and 'rest periods', and suggesting, instead, an intermediate category between them.

Time Spent Looking for Tasks

The situation when workers on demand via apps log on to the app and wait for orders to be allocated to them can be compared to the situation of crowdworkers, who actively engage in searching for new tasks across different platforms. In the ILO report on 'Digital labour platforms and the future of work', underemployment has been emphasized as a serious concern for crowdworkers around the world.[1041] This implies that facing the unavailability of jobs, many crowdworkers spend a large amount of time in looking for work, and also, in doing research on their potential clients, in order to ensure that their work will be paid. For instance, a survey conducted by IG Metall showed that the amount of time crowdworkers spent looking for work was as high as the time of their actual work.[1042] In this regard, Prassl contends that the time spent looking for work should be considered as working time 'as long as sanctions for non-acceptance of work are in place'.[1043] These sanctions threaten workers to constantly become available and search for tasks, and together with the large amount of time spent searching, might significantly hamper workers' opportunities to organize this time for their personal needs.

1038. Judgment *Royal Mencap Society (Respondent) v. TomlinsonBlake (Appellant), Shannon (Appellant) v. Rampersad and another (T/A Clifton House Residential Home)(Respondents)*, 19 March 2021.

1039. D. McCann, 'Mencap and Uber in the Supreme Court: Working Time Regulation in an era of casualization', 2021, Oxford Human Rights Hub (blog), Available at: https://ohrh.law.ox.ac.uk/mencap-and-uber-in-the-supreme-court-working-time-regulation-in-an-era-of-casualisation/.

1040. K. Ewing, 'Don't be fooled, Uber is still dodging the minimum wage'.

1041. J. Berg, M. Furrer, E. Harmon, U. Rani, M.S. Silberman, *Digital Labour Platforms and the Future of Work, Towards Decent Work in the Online World*, International Labour Office-Geneva, 2018, p. 63.

1042. *Ibid.*, p. 53.

1043. J. Prassl, *Humans as a service …*, p. 106.

Waiting Time at Customers' Doors, or Restaurants (Delivery Sector)

Once an order was accepted, platform workers, especially in the delivery sector, were observed to encounter different delays that did not dependent on them. For instance, it is quite common for a delivery rider to wait for the restaurant to prepare the order, or for the client to come and pick up the order. This waiting time severely impacts the workers' ability to organize his/ her free time, and it cannot be used to search for new orders.[1044] Furthermore, considering the broad notion of a 'workplace' adopted by the CJEU, during these waiting periods, the worker is acting on the employer's instruction, and hence, should be considered at work.[1045] In this way, this waiting time can arguably check the boxes for being qualified as working time.

Travel Time to and Between Jobs

Travel time in the context of platform work is a concept relevant solely to workers on demand via apps. Insightful in this regard is the *Tyco* case of the CJEU, which considered the travel time of mobile workers between their homes and customers as working time. Against this background, it seems logical that also the travel time of platform workers, such as Deliveroo riders or Uber drivers, should be counted as working time. As concerns the time spent travelling between tasks, the Court has not given an explicit answer. However, the European Commission has indicated that this time span should as well be qualified as working time, upon the completion of certain conditions.

9.3.2 Some Final Words on the Importance of the Working Time Directive and Its Articulation with the dPWD

In a nutshell, the EU regulatory framework on working time, composed of *the Working Time Directive* and the CJEU jurisprudence on it, can be generally regarded as insightful in relation to certain working time situations experienced by platform workers. Nevertheless, the directive in itself views working time 'from the perspective of a standard worker who is expected to work excessively long hours'.[1046] This approach can indeed be beneficial for some platform workers who work long hours.[1047] On the other side, by focusing solely on governing maximum working hours, this legislative instrument seems to overlook an important problem of working time in the modern economy, namely the unpredictability of working hours, or constantly being on-call, which also poses challenges to the workers' health and safety.[1048] Addressing both

1044. Pulignano et al., *Does it pay to work? Unpaid labour in the platform economy*, p. 4.
1045. D. Mangan, 'The platform discount', Presentation at the Fourth Roger Blanpain lecture, Leuven, May 2022.
1046. A. Davies, 'Regulating Atypical Work: Beyond Equality', in *Resocialising Europe in a Time of Crisis*, eds N. Countouris and M. Freedland, Cambridge University Press, 2013, p. 247.
1047. *ILO World Employment and Social Outlook*, p. 234.
1048. K. Riesenhuber, *European employment law, Intersentia, 2012*; C. Barnard, *EU employment law*, Oxford University Press, 2012, p. 558.

sides of the coin becomes even more crucial in light of the categorization of health and safety as a fundamental right at work by the ILO.[1049]

As concerns *the CJEU case law* on interpreting the WTD, it has, indeed, looked into on-call time, but only in light of its qualification as either 'working time' or 'rest time'. Taking note of the above, on-call work seems to be an issue that is underpinning both EU traditional and new legal instruments. While traditional instruments, such as the Working Time Directive, deal with it to a limited extent, Chapter 11 explains that newer instruments, such as the TPWCD, seem to bring on-call work to the spotlight.

In searching whether the *dPWD* incorporates these working time considerations, it can be observed that its main provisions reflect a legal vacuum in this regard. The preamble of the directive simply enlists some legal instruments which govern working conditions, *inter alia*, the Working Time and the TPWCD Directives.[1050] In digging in further for a better correlation between the WTD and the dPWD, the explanatory memorandum to the directive points out the relevance of the CJEU jurisprudence with respect to working time, especially stand-by time, for platform workers.[1051] On the other hand, peculiar working time situations faced by platform workers, e.g., the waiting time for orders while logged into the app and willing to take tasks, are not acknowledged even in the explanatory documents of the draft directive. In the same vein, the CJEU has refused to provide some clarifications with regard to working time situations experienced by platform workers. For instance, prior to the issuance of the proposal for the Platform Work Directive by the European Commission, the CJEU was asked in the *Yodel* case to provide some guidance on the working time of some parcel delivery platform workers.[1052] The Court, nonetheless, did not provide any answer in this regard, but it simply ruled that the Working Time Directive precludes platform workers who are genuine self-employed workers from its personal scope of application.[1053]

As this EU initiative on platform work currently stands, it can be said that *the articulation between the directives on working time and platform work* amounts to be a poor one. In other words, the WTD and its extensive body of case law have a lot to offer for platform workers, however, the dPWD in itself does not acknowledge the main takeaways from this already available regulatory framework. Unpaid stand-by time still constitutes an unclear grey territory for platform workers.[1054] In light of improving the interaction between both legal initiatives, the dPWD should include certain important aspects of working time in its main text. For instance, the directive should provide examples of working time situations for platform workers, which might amount to be

1049. ILO Press Release, 'International Labour Conference adds safety and health to Fundamental Principles and Rights at Work', June 2022, Available at: https://www.ilo.org/global/about-the-ilo/newsroom/news/WCMS_848132/lang--en/index.htm.
1050. Paragraph 10 of the preamble.
1051. Explanatory Memorandum, Consistency with existing policy provisions in the policy area, p. 5.
1052. Order of the Court (Eighth Chamber) of 22 April 2020, *B v. Yodel Delivery Network Ltd*, Case C-692/19.
1053. Paragraph 46 of the judgment.
1054. M. Gruber-Risak, 'Platform work as a virtual form of precarious work', Presentation at the ETUI event 'Working conditions in the platform economy', February 2022.

working time. In this regard, the relevance of the CJEU case law on stand-by time for platform workers should be emphasized. The main takeaways from this jurisprudence, and especially the dichotomy of working time-rest period, should be definitely pronounced. On the contrary, if this draft directive is left without the just-mentioned legal interventions, the risk is that the working time issue for platform workers will be left exclusively in the hands of the national courts. And what courts can do in this regard, with the striking example of the UK Supreme Court in the *Mencap* case, is that they can create intermediate conceptions between working time and rest periods with regard to on-demand work. Therefore, if the legal gap identified in the Platform Work Directive remains unplugged, the working time of platform workers might risk having the same legal fate. These workers can end up being deprived of the full set of entitlements associated with the qualification of their on-call time as working time. And finally, to conclude with what Prassl has indicated in his book dedicated to the platform economy, 'on-demand workers aren't furthering a platform's economic interests only when they are actually at work; it's the very availability of a large workforce that underpins the business model'.[1055] Given the importance attached to the availability of platform workers, regulatory attempts to govern platform work, with the prominent example of the EU dPWD, should definitely provide a solution to the frequent availability of platform workers.

1055. J. Prassl, *Humans as a Service: The Promise and Perils of Work in the Gig Economy*, Oxford University Press, 2018, p. 106.

CHAPTER 10

The Relevance of the Fixed-Term Work Directive for the Job Security of Casual and Platform Workers

10.1 IMPORTANT LEGAL SAFEGUARDS CONTAINED IN THE PART-TIME WORK AND FIXED-TERM WORK DIRECTIVES

As already observed, the 'typical' part of non-standard work, i.e., part-time, fixed-term, and temporary agency work, has first constituted subject to national regulatory answers,[1056] which have been then followed by European responses.[1057] Furthermore, since the adoption of the EU directives, massive case law has been produced by the CJEU on the interpretation of the legal provisions of these instruments. In the quest for a European regulatory approach to casual work, two directives can be singled out as being particularly pertinent, namely the Part-Time Work (PTWD)[1058] and the FTWD. This relevance has to do with the fact that casual work shares important features with both part-time and fixed-term work. For instance, for many years, the risks of peaks and troughs, or discontinuity in running a business, were born by workers working in part-time, fixed-term, and casual work arrangements. These shared threads have also been confirmed in the ILO report on non-standard employment, where different forms of casual work have been included either within the broad concept of part-time work or that of fixed-term (or temporary) work.[1059] The common denominator between

1056. Background paper for first-stage consultations with the social partners on the flexibility in working time and security for workers, European Commission document, 1995, p. 5.
1057. N. Countouris, 'Regulating digital work: from laisser-faire to fairness', Social Europe (blog), 2021, Available at: https://socialeurope.eu/regulating-digital-work-from-laisser-faire-to-fairness.
1058. A. Davies in 'Regulating atypical work: beyond equality', p. 245 recognizes a strong link between part-time work and casual work.
1059. International Labour Office – Geneva, *Non-standard employment around the world: Understanding challenges, shaping prospects*, 2016, p. xxiii.

casual work (referred to in this report as on-call work) and part-time work was noted in the unpredictable nature of the working hours, or the working hours insecurity.[1060] As concerns the link between fixed-term and casual work,[1061] a shared risk of discontinuity and insecurity of employment was observed.[1062] As will be further demonstrated in this part, while the PTWD does not engage with the working hours insecurity aspect,[1063] the FTWD proposes solutions to address the job insecurity underpinning fixed-term work, but at the same time casual work.

As concerns the personal scope of application of these directives, a similar scope can be observed, in the sense that non-standard workers who fall under their protective realm are those who 'have an employment contract or employment relationship', as defined by the Member States in their national laws, collective agreements, or practices.[1064] Nevertheless, as Chapter 11 will demonstrate, this 'worker' definition can be interpreted more broadly in light of the practical effectiveness of these EU directives. With regard to casual workers, the CJEU established in the *Wippel* case,[1065] that even zero-hours workers could fall within the scope of the Part-time Work Directive, provided that they have an employment contract or relationship according to national law, collective agreement, or practice. On the other side, the Part-time Work directive allows Member States and/ or social partners, to exclude fully or partly part-time workers working on a casual basis (upon the provision of objective justification) from the scope of application of the directive.[1066] This exclusion of casual workers has been provided, however, without including a definition of casual work in the Framework Agreement. In this way, it leaves it up to the discretion of Member States to define the concept of casual work.[1067]

The triad of directives on non-standard work shares a key objective, namely to ensure equal treatment of non-standard workers with standard workers regarding working conditions.[1068] Equality is a topic which, as Davies rightly contends, is difficult to be objected by regulators.[1069] Accordingly, European lawmakers agreed on regulatory responses to atypical work, which centred around equality. The incorporation of an equality of treatment approach can, nevertheless, be accompanied by challenges,

1060. According to this ILO Report, p. 23, a considerable number of casual workers 'with unpredictable hours and very short hours work on a part-time basis'; The link between part-time and on-call work has been explained in p. 75.
1061. This link has been confirmed also in the European Parliament report on atypical work, pp. 65-66.
1062. ILO, *Non-standard employment around the world: Understanding challenges, shaping prospects*, pp. 7, 24 and 225.
1063. A. Davies, 'Regulating atypical work: beyond equality', p. 244.
1064. Clause 2, para. 1, of the Framework Agreement on Fixed-term Work and the Framework Agreement on Part-time Work.
1065. Case C-313/02, *Nicole Wippel v. Peek and Cloppenburg GmbH and Co. KG*, 2004.
1066. Clause 2 (2) of the Framework agreement on Part-time Work.
1067. European Parliament, *Atypical work in the EU*, p. 103.
1068. M. Szpejna, Z. Boudalaoui-Buresi, *The scope of EU labour law: Who is not covered by key directives?*, Publication for the committee on Employment and Social Affairs, Policy Department for Economic, Scientific and Quality of Life Policies, European Parliament, Luxembourg, 2020, p. 6; K. Riesenhuber, *European employment law*, p. 418.
1069. A. Davies, 'Regulating atypical work: beyond equality', p. 243.

such as finding a comparator for the non-standard worker.[1070] The latter has been considered 'the Achilles heel' of these directives.[1071] For instance, in the *Wippel* case, no comparator was found for a casual worker working under a zero-hours contract. A full-time worker working with fixed working hours was not considered to be in a comparable situation with a casual worker.[1072]

Furthermore, Part-time Work and FTWD also serve other purposes than ensuring equal treatment. For example, another goal of the PTWD consists in the promotion of this type of work arrangement, and in this regard, it demands that Member States and social partners eliminate all legal and administrative obstacles to part-time work.[1073] On the other side, the FTWD does not intend to promote fixed-term work arrangements.[1074] Instead, it aims to protect workers from potential abuses deriving from the use of successive fixed-term contracts.[1075] It is due to the provision of such a safeguard that the European Commission considers the FTWD as contributing to striking a balance between flexibility and security.[1076] This balance can be observed in the fact that the standard employment contract is viewed as the 'general form of employment relationship between employers and workers',[1077] while fixed-term contracts are mainly seen as exceptions, which can be used only in certain cases.[1078] This approach has also been confirmed by the CJEU in the *Adeneler* case.[1079] The most notable example that the FTWD is about workers' protection can be found in its anti-abuse clause (Clause 5). Due to the relevance of this clause for the jobs insecurity underpinning also casual and platform work arrangements, it will constitute the subject of a more in-depth analysis.

Finally, both the PTWD and the FTWD directives contain provisions about the so-called stepping stones effect, or in other words, provisions that aim to facilitate a change from atypical to typical employment, and *vice versa*.[1080] To this end, the PTWD requires employers to consider such requests and provide information to workers on the transfer opportunities to a more secure form of employment.[1081] What the FTWD provides under the title 'information and employment opportunities',[1082] is an obligation for employers to inform fixed-term workers about the vacancies on permanent jobs through an announcement published in a suitable place in the undertaking. Furthermore, it also lays

1070. The concept of the comparator is explained in Clause 3 (2) of the Framework Agreement on Fixed-term Work and the Framework Agreement on Part-time Work.
1071. C. Barnard, *EU employment law*, p. 434.
1072. *Wippel* Case C-313/02, para. 62.
1073. Clause 5(1) of the Framework Agreement on Part-time Work.
1074. A. Davies, 'Regulating atypical work: beyond equality', p. 236.
1075. C. Barnard, *EU employment law*, p. 438.
1076. Commission of the European Communities, *Proposal for a Council Directive concerning the Framework Agreement on Fixed-term Work*, p. 7; Framework Agreement on Fixed-term Work, Preamble para. 1.
1077. F. Hendrickx, *Handbook on European labour law*, p. 145.
1078. Recital 6 of Framework Agreement on Fixed-term Work.
1079. Case C-212/ 04, *Konstantinos Adeneler and Others v. Ellinikos Organismos Galaktos (ELOG)*, 2006, para. 62.
1080. K. Riesenhuber, *European employment law*, Intersentia, 2012, p. 419; A. Davies, 'Regulating atypical work: beyond equality', p. 239.
1081. Clause 5 (3) of the Framework Agreement on Part-time Work.
1082. Clause 6 of the Framework Agreement on Fixed-term Work.

down the responsibility for employers to facilitate access to training for fixed-term workers. Notwithstanding how important these provisions are for these non-standard workers, they seem to reflect a merely informative nature on the transition towards more secure employment.[1083] Furthermore, another prominent manifestation of the 'stepping stones' effect can be found in the anti-abuse clause of the FTWD, which also contributes to transfer workers from fixed-term contracts to permanent ones.

To sum up, the legal safeguards contained in these two instruments, namely the equality of treatment approach, the protection against abuses arising from the use of successive fixed-term contracts, and the 'stepping stones' provisions, can all be beneficial in governing the legal situation of casual workers. As Aloisi contends, the triad of directives on atypical work might have in place best practices for platform work 'in terms of both legislative techniques and substantive norms'. This has also been confirmed by Rosin, who acknowledges that notwithstanding the importance of the atypical work instruments for platform workers, this issue has been largely left unexplored.[1084] It is against this backdrop that the 1990s legal instruments on atypical work can be considered an important departure point for developing the regulatory matrix for casual work. Nevertheless, as will be shown in section 11.1, these legal channels through which casual work was created, as important as they were, were apparently insufficient to respond to casual workers' specific needs for protection.

10.2 THE PARTICULAR RELEVANCE OF THE FIXED-TERM WORK DIRECTIVE

As the title suggests, this part singles out the Fixed-Term Work Directive, as being particularly relevant for enhancing the labour protection of casual and platform workers. The rationale for excluding from the analysis the Part-Time Work Directive has to do with the focus of this instrument, which is namely to promote part-time work[1085] while overlooking solutions to address the insecurity of working hours that can be present in this work model.[1086] On the opposite side, the FTWD contains solutions against the job insecurity experienced by both casual and platform workers. An important legal safeguard in this respect is its anti-abuse clause (Clause 5) which constitutes the fulcrum of this section.

10.2.1 Platform Workers as Fixed-Term Workers

In assessing the application of the FTWD to platform workers, the first step is to evaluate whether platform workers can potentially fall within the personal scope of the FTWD. As the FTWD served mainly to implement the Framework Agreement (FA)

1083. A. Davies in 'Regulating atypical work: beyond equality', p. 241, gives some options on how to strengthen such provisions, such as through automatically shortlisting qualified part-time and fixed-term workers.
1084. A. Rosin, 'Platform Work and Fixed-Term Employment Regulation', *European Labour Law Journal*, Vol. 12 Issue 2, 2021, pp. 156-176, p. 158.
1085. Clause 1 (b) and 5 (1) of the Framework Agreement on part-time work.
1086. A. Davies, 'Regulating atypical work: beyond equality', p. 244.

concluded by the social partners, reference will be made to the main clauses of the FA, instead of the provisions of the directive. To start with, Clause 3 (1) defines a fixed-term worker by setting out three conditions. In order for platform workers to be considered fixed-term workers, they need to fulfil these conditions cumulatively. The *first condition* requires workers to have an employment contract or an employment relationship, which by referring to Clause 2 (1), needs to be defined 'in law, collective agreements or practice in each Member State'. The reference to the national definition of 'worker' might imply, at first sight, that it is difficult for platform workers to fall within the scope of this legal instrument. As already observed, the majority of them are qualified as self-employed workers by business service agreements. Nevertheless, this national definition of a 'worker' can be subjected to the requirement of the effectiveness of the EU directive, and end up being expanded. The CJEU has indeed, in certain instances,[1087] embraced a broader definition of the 'worker' notion than the one suggested by the wording of the directives on atypical work. For instance, in the *Del Cerro Alonso* case,[1088] which was about fixed-term work, the CJEU found that Member States cannot 'remove at will certain categories of persons from the protection offered by' the FTWD, otherwise this would jeopardize the effectiveness of this instrument.[1089] The same line of reasoning has been followed by the Court also in other cases about part-time, or temporary agency work. As already observed, all three directives on atypical work espouse the same 'worker' definition. Therefore, the CJEU's interpretation of the personal scope of application of one of them will, by analogy, also apply to the other two other directives. In the *O'Brien* case,[1090] which was about the personal scope of the PTWD, the CJEU accepted the Member States' discretion in defining who a worker is, however, it also acknowledged, that their powers are not unlimited in this regard. The rules applied by Member States cannot 'jeopardise the achievement of the objectives pursued by a Directive and, therefore, deprive it from it of its effectiveness'.[1091] The CJEU went even further in the *Betriebsrat der Ruhrlandklinik* case,[1092] which was about the scope *rationae personae* of the TAWD, where it made clear that defining the personal scope of application of EU labour law tools is a matter of EU law.[1093] With consideration to all these judicial outcomes, the chances for platform workers to be considered as workers falling under the personal ambit of the atypical work directives might not be as small as they seem.

1087. A. Rosin, 'Platform Work and Fixed-Term Employment Regulation', *European Labour Law Journal,* Vol. 12 Issue 2, 2021, pp. 160-161; A. Aloisi, ' Platform Work in Europe: Lessons Learned, Legal Developments and Challenges Ahead', *European Labour Law Journal,* Vol. 13 Issue 1, 2022, pp. 4–29, p. 24.
1088. Case C-307/05, *Yolanda Del Cerro Alonso v. Osakidetza-Servicio Vasco de Salud,* 2007.
1089. *Del Cerro Alonso* case para. 29. *See also* Order of the Court (Third Chamber) of 17 September 2014, *Maurizio Fiamingo, Leonardo Zappalà and Francesco Rotondo and Others v. Rete Ferroviaria Italiana SpA.,* Joined Cases C-362/13, C-363/13 and C-407/13, para. 31.
1090. Case C-393/10, *Dermond Patrick O'Brien v. Ministry of Justice,* 2012.
1091. *Ibid.,* paras 32-35.
1092. Case C-216/15, *Betriebsrat der Ruhrlandklinik gGmbH v. Ruhrlandklinik gGmbH,* 2016, paras 36-37.
1093. N. Countouris, 'The Concept of "Worker" in European Labour Law: Fragmentation, Autonomy, and Scope', *Industrial Law Journal,* Vol. 47 Issue 2, 2018, p. 207.

What is more, the *second element* laid down in Clause 3 (1) requires the existence of a direct employment contract or relationship between an employer and a worker. Therefore, the fixed-term work relationship, which includes an intermediary, such as temporary agency work, is excluded from the scope of application of the FTWD.[1094] As noted in this dissertation, platform work is quite heterogeneous, and as such, it might include a wide range of work relations. There can be cases where a direct, or a bilateral, relationship between the parties can be observed more easily than in others. For instance, in the food delivery and transport sector, it is the platform operator that mainly exercises control over the worker, by implying, thus, the existence of a bilateral relationship between the two parties.[1095] In these sectors, indeed, national courts are finding an employment relationship between the platform and the worker more and more. In contrast, in crowdwork, the client might also interfere in the relation between the worker and the platform, for example, by assigning duties to the worker. This situation can result in the formation of a tri-partite employment relationship, or even a bilateral one, either between the worker and the user of the services or the worker and the platform. In case a bilateral relation is detected, then the FTWD might apply.

The *third and final criteria* for a worker to be in a fixed-term contract or relationship has to do with the fact that the end of the relationship or contract is determined by objective reasons, such as completing a certain task, the occurrence of a specific event, or reaching a specific date. This constitutes the main distinguishing feature of a fixed-term contract, namely the job insecurity underpinning it, which leaves workers uncertain whether they will have work for the future, as the end of their contract is determined from the beginning. In platform work, work is performed on a task basis, and the completion of a certain task, as argued below, might amount to be a very short fixed-term contract. Considering the confusion that reigns in this domain, Risak has correctly pointed out that, in a platform work setting, it is not apparent 'whether there is an ongoing employment relationship or just a sequence of fixed-term contracts'.[1096]

To sum up, once the conditions foreseen by Clause 3 (1) of the FA are completed, platform workers can fall within the personal scope of the FTWD and, therefore, benefit from its specific legal protections. The most relevant one against the job insecurity experienced by platform workers has been enshrined in Clause 5 of the Framework Agreement.

10.2.2 The Anti-abuse Clause in the FTWD (Clause 5)

10.2.2.1 An Overview of the Protective Measures

Clause 5 constitutes one of the most important provisions of the FA, which has generated a large amount of case law from the CJEU in its interpretation. Through this

1094. Preamble of the Framework Agreement, para. 4; Case C-290/12, *Oreste Della Rocca v. Poste Italiane SpA*, 2013.
1095. A. Rosin, 'Platform Work and Fixed-Term Employment Regulation', *European Labour Law Journal*, Vol. 12 Issue 2, 2021, p. 168.
1096. M. Risak, *Fair Working Conditions for Platform Workers: Possible Regulatory Approaches at the EU Level*, Friedrich-Ebert Stiftung, 2017, p. 10.

provision, the intention of social partners was to implement one of the two objectives of the Framework Agreement, namely to limit the abuses arising from the recourse to successive fixed-term contracts. As it has been set out in the FA,[1097] but also repeated by the CJEU on several occasions,[1098] the FTWD aims to promote indefinite contracts and allow recourse to fixed-term contracts only in exceptional cases, when it is convenient for both workers and employers.

With a view to preventing the job insecurity inherent in fixed-term work,[1099] this anti-abuse clause calls on the Member States to combine, or choose one of three types of legal measures, in the event there are no equivalent measures in national law.[1100] In a nutshell, these measures include the stipulation of objective reasons justifying the renewal of fixed-term contracts, the establishment of a maximum duration for successive fixed-term contracts, and the limitation on the number of renewals of such contracts.[1101] A study undertaken by the European Commission in 2013 revealed that, generally, EU Member States set the maximum duration for successive fixed-term contracts between 2-5 years, while the number of renewals was noted to vary between 1-4 renewals.[1102] Furthermore, an evaluative study of both the FTWD and PTWD found that the most common measure adopted by the Member States was the provision of objective reasons for the renewal.[1103]

The CJEU's activity around Clause 5 has focused mainly on evaluating what Member States have accepted as objective justifications for the renewal of fixed-term contracts, but also what they have considered as successive contracts.[1104] As the Framework Agreement does not define what 'objective reasons' are, the Court has provided some clarifications in this regard. First of all, when evaluating what constitutes objective reasons, due regard should be given to the objective of the directive and the context of Clause 5 (1) (a).[1105] More specifically, the Court considers objective reasons as 'precise and concrete circumstances characterising a given activity, which are therefore capable in that particular context of justifying the use of successive fixed-term employment contracts'.[1106] These circumstances can result from the specific nature of the tasks, or the pursuit of a legitimate social-policy aim of a Member State. What has been, in general, accepted as an objective justification for the renewal of

1097. Recital 6 of the Framework Agreement.
1098. Order of the Court in Joined Cases C-362/13, C-363/13 and C-407/13, para. 55; Case C-212/04 *Adeneler*, para. 61.
1099. Order of the Court in Joined Cases C-362/13, C-363/13 and C-407/13, para. 54; *Adeneler* case, para. 63.
1100. Case C-268/06, *Impact v. Minister for Agriculture and Food and Others*, 2008, para. 71; Order of the Court in Joined Cases C-362/13, C-363/13 and C-407/13, paras 59-61.
1101. Clause 5 (1) of the FA.
1102. G. More, Presentation on fixed-term work, DG Employment, 2017, p. 15.
1103. Evaluative Study of Directive 1997/81/EC (supplemented by Directive 98/23/EC) on Part-Time Work and Directive 1999/70/ EC on Fixed-Term Work, Updated Final report submitted by ICF International in August 2016, p. 100, Table 4.12.
1104. A. Rosin, 'Platform Work and Fixed-Term Employment Regulation', *European Labour Law Journal*, Vol. 12 Issue 2, 2021, p. 169.
1105. *Adeneler* case, para. 60.
1106. Judgment of the Court (Third Chamber) of 23 April 2009, *Kiriaki Angelidaki and Others v. Organismos Nomarchiakis Autodioikisis Rethymnis (C-378/07), Charikleia Giannoudi v. Dimos Geropotamou (C-379/07) and Georgios Karabousanos and Sofoklis Michopoulos v.*

these contracts, is the temporary replacement of permanent staff.[1107] Notwithstanding that the temporary need for staff is 'not *per se* contrary' to the FTWD,[1108] in the Kücük judgment,[1109] the Court held that in order to prove whether this need is genuinely temporary, it must be considered together with the maximum total duration of the contracts, and the maximum number of renewals.[1110] It is evident that the Court has not accepted the employer's fixed and permanent needs to constitute objective reasons for using these contracts.[1111]

Regarding the consideration of fixed-term contracts as successive ones, the FA leaves, in principle, the margin of appreciation to the Member States in this regard.[1112] Nevertheless, even in this case, these prerogatives are not unlimited 'because it cannot in any event go so far as to compromise the objective or the practical effect of the Framework Agreement'.[1113] And indeed, the Court considered, in the *Adeneler* case, that a national provision that considered only fixed-term contracts interrupted by a period of time of up to twenty working days as successive, was capable of compromising the objective and practical effect of the FA.[1114] Furthermore, the FTWD does not oblige Member States to convert fixed-term contracts into permanent ones, and not even to determine the conditions under which these contracts can be used.[1115] Member States can decide whether they want to punish an abusive use of fixed-term contracts with an automatic conversion into an indefinite contract.[1116]

Finally, an important observation with regard to Clause 5 concerns its similarity with Article 11 of the TPWCD. The latter provision also envisages protective measures to be taken by Member States to prevent abusive recourse to on-demand contracts. In particular, the first type of measure enshrined thereof, which suggests a limitation on the use and duration of on-demand contracts,[1117] is in line with Clause 5 (1) of the FA.[1118] The second type of measure set out by Article 11 is the provision of a rebuttable presumption of an employment relationship,[1119] a measure which is designed to respond to the specific nature of on-demand contracts. An important difference between Clause 5 (1) of the FA and Article 11 of the TPWCD consists in the fact that the measures enshrined in the TPWCD can be applicable even to the first on-demand contract. On the contrary, the anti-abusive measures contained in Clause 5 apply only

Dimos Geropotamou (C-380/07), para. 96; *Adeneler* case, para. 69; Order of the Court (Third Chamber) of 12 June 2008, *Spyridon Vassilakis and Others v. Dimos Kerkyraion*, Case-364/07, paras 88-89.

1107. G. More, Presentation on fixed-term work, DG Employment.
1108. Case C-586/10, *Bianca Kücük v. Land Nordrhein-Westfalen*, 2012.
1109. *Ibid.*, para. 30.
1110. *Ibid.*, para. 43.
1111. Case C-16/15, *María Elena Pérez López v. Servicio Madrileño de Salud (Comunidad de Madrid)*, 2016.
1112. Clause 5 (2) of the FA.
1113. *Kücük* case, para. 82.
1114. *Adeneler* case, para. 84.
1115. *Kücük* case, para. 52.
1116. G. More, Presentation on fixed-term work, p. 14.
1117. Article 11(a) of the TPWCD.
1118. A. Aloisi, 'Platform work in Europe ...', p. 15.
1119. Article 11(b) of the TPWCD.

in the event of successive fixed-term contracts, i.e., the initial use of this type of contract is permitted.[1120]

10.2.2.2 The Importance of the Anti-abuse Clause for Platform Workers

Clause 5 of the FTWD might offer useful protections in terms of job security for platform workers. In order for it to be applicable to these workers, in addition to fulfilling the conditions set out in Clause 3 (1), they need to have completed successive tasks. The tasks performed by platform workers can have a short-term, or long-term nature, where both cases might signal the presence of fixed-term contracts.[1121] At the heart of the platform work's business model stand, nevertheless, short-term tasks or 'gigs', which display in a large number. As Novitz puts it, 'the nature of gig work [has a] tendency to "short-termism"'.[1122] Short-term tasks are prominent, especially in the delivery and transport of passengers' sectors. Deliveroo in the Netherlands provides the example of a platform company that offered fixed-term contracts to its workers in 2015-2018.[1123] As mentioned, the presence of long-term tasks, which are characterized by the lack of a promise for the continuation of work, cannot also be excluded in a platform work context.[1124] Nevertheless, long-term tasks risk being associated with long interruptions between assignments, something which might impede the consideration of these tasks as successive ones.[1125] On the other side, short-term tasks are usually completed one after the other, e.g., the completion of a ride, or a delivery. In this way, platform workers involved in these successive short-term tasks might be able to benefit from the protections afforded by Clause 5.

Once the tasks have been qualified as successive, an evaluation of the application of the legal measures contained in Clause 5 to platform workers can be carried out. The usefulness of extending these safeguards to platform workers has been recently confirmed by the TPWCD, which has re-introduced these protections in the specific context of on-demand contracts, which also include platform work.[1126] While the importance of Clause 5 for platform workers is undisputable, the legal measures contained thereof might need some update, considering that they were drafted to address traditional forms of flexibility, instead of the over flexibility characterizing platform work.

Starting with the *provision of objective grounds for the renewal*, the need for temporary staff, which constitutes the most common justification accepted by the CJEU, does not seem to represent a valid reason when it comes to platform work

1120. Case C-144/04, *Werner Mangold v. Rüdiger Helm*, 2005.
1121. According to Clause 3 (1) of the FA, the completion of a task can amount to a fixed-term contract.
1122. T. Novitz, 'Gig Work as a Manifestation of Short-Termism: Crafting a Sustainable Regulatory Agenda', *Industrial Law Journal*, Vol. 50 Issue 4, December 2021, pp. 636-661, p. 648.
1123. Rechtbaank Amsterdam 2019, Case No. ECLI:NL: RBAMS:2019:198.
1124. Rosin has provided the example of tasks performed in the TaskRabbit platform, which can even have two months of separation between them.
1125. A. Rosin, 'Platform Work and Fixed-Term Employment Regulation', *European Labour Law Journal*, Vol. 12 Issue 2, 2021, p. 171.
1126. Article 11 of the TPWCD.

arrangements. The business model of platform companies relies on an on-demand workforce – a group of workers who are called in whenever the business needs arise, something which implies that there is a permanent need for temporary staff. Nevertheless, other reasons can also be able to justify the renewal, but they need to be related to the specific nature of the tasks.[1127] In this regard, the temporary nature of the tasks might be able to justify the conclusion of fixed-term contracts.[1128] However, tasks performed in a platform work context cannot be viewed as temporary ones, as there is a constant demand from clients.[1129] Furthermore, as pointed out by Dermine, the nature of flexi-jobs *per se* cannot justify the renewal of these types of contracts.[1130] Having regard to these considerations, platform operators do not seem to have a valid reason to recourse to successive tasks, which may amount to be fixed-term contracts. Accordingly, they either need to stop using these work practices or accord some stability to platform workers, in compliance with the national rules of each Member State. Overall, the provision of objective grounds for using fixed-term contracts can effectively enhance the labour protection of platform workers.

Some update might, instead, become necessary when it comes to *limiting the maximum duration of fixed-term contracts* in a platform work context. As previously mentioned, Member States were observed to allow the overall duration of these contracts for a maximum period of 2 to 5 years. This overall duration appears to be excessively long considering the frequent short-term tasks performed by platform workers, where the overall duration of these tasks might end up being quite short. In this regard, the TPWCD considers working on-call for six months, as enough for on-demand workers to demand a more secure form of employment.[1131] Stemming from this consideration, an overall duration for the use of fixed-term contracts composed of several years, as currently set out by the Member States, does not seem conducive for enhancing the labour protection of platform workers. This is true, especially if this measure is the only one adopted by Member States. The United Kingdom, for example, allows fixed-term contracts for up to four years, and only after this period has elapsed, a justification needs to be provided for their use.[1132] As this legal provision stands, it practically has no protection to offer to platform workers.

On the contrary, the *limitation on the number of renewals* can arguably improve the legal situation of platform workers. It was noted that, in general, Member States allowed up to four renewals of fixed-term contracts. Within platform work, a significant number of tasks can be completed; hence, more than four renewals can occur per day. Therefore, as valuable as this legal protection can be for platform workers, it might

1127. Case *Adeneler* para. 69; *Angelidaki* para. 96; *Vassilakis* paras 88-89.
1128. Case *Maria Elena Perez Lopez*.
1129. A. Rosin, 'Platform Work and Fixed-Term Employment Regulation', *European Labour Law Journal*, Vol. 12 Issue 2, 2021, p. 173.
1130. E. Dermine, A. Mechelynck, 'Regulating Zero-Hour Contracts in Belgium: From a Defensive to a (too?) Supportive Approach?', *European Labour Law Journal*, Vol. 13 Issue 3, 2022, pp. 400-430, p. 425.
1131. Article 12 of the TPWCD.
1132. https://www.gov.uk/fixed-term-contracts/renewing-or-ending-a-fixedterm-contract.

warrant some adaptation, with consideration to the specifics of work performed through a platform.

To conclude with, a combination of at least two types of measures would certainly enhance the level of protection against abusive practices related to fixed-term contracts. In this regard, Rosin recommends that, in particular, a combination of the maximum number of renewals with the objective reason might be conducive for platform workers.[1133] In this regard, the limitation of the overall duration of fixed-term contracts needs to be definitely altered in order to respond more accurately to the needs of platform workers. The anti-abuse clause, but also the FTWD as a whole, have been very scarcely mentioned in the new legal initiative of the Commission on platform work. Actually, the articulation between the FTWD and the dPWD seems to be even weaker than the one identified between the dPWD and the WTD. To substantiate this, it is only in the preamble of the dPWD that the FTWD has been mentioned, however, merely as a legal instrument that provides minimum standards on working conditions and labour rights.[1134] No further explanation has been provided in this regard, not even in the Explanatory Memorandum to the dPWD. By having regard to this legal lacuna, as this section has demonstrated, Clause 5 of the FTWD might have in store useful protections to counteract the job insecurity inherent in platform work. In this regard, the 'stepping stones' provisions contained in the FTWD can also be conducive to enhancing the job security of platform workers. Taking note of the above, the draft PWD should certainly incorporate such considerations in its main body.

1133. A. Rosin, 'Platform Work and the Fixed-term Employment Regulation', *European Labour Law Journal*, Vol. 12 Issue 2, 2021, p. 176.
1134. Paragraph 10 of the preamble of the dPWD.

CHAPTER 11

The Present: The Transparent and Predictable Working Conditions Directive as an Endeavour to Counter the Insecure Working Conditions Experienced by Casual and Platform Workers

11.1 'BEYOND EQUALITY':[1135] INTRODUCING THE NEW REGULATORY APPROACH TO CASUAL WORK

In contrast to the hands-on approach of EU lawmakers and social partners to three specific forms of non-standard work,[1136] the particularly flexible part of it, which also includes casual work, was not given any particular attention.[1137] Nevertheless, active regulation of just one segment of non-standard work might bring as a result an increase in the unregulated part of it, especially in casual work arrangements.[1138] It was due to this proliferation, combined with the inactive and exclusionary approach[1139] of EU legislators towards casual work, that a need for a more targeted and comprehensive regulation was highlighted.[1140] This regulation would ideally encompass the overlooked and vulnerable part of non-standard work within its protective realm.

1135. A. Davies, 'Regulating Atypical Work: Beyond Equality', In *Resocialising Europe in a Time of Crisis*, eds N. Countouris and M. Freedland, Cambridge University Press, 2013.
1136. N. Countouris, 'Regulating digital work: from laisser-faire to fairness'.
1137. S. Garben, C. Kilpatrick & E. Muir, *Towards a European Pillar of Social Rights: Upgrading the EU Social Acquis*, College of Europe Policy Brief, January 2017, p. 2.
1138. A. Davies, 'Regulating atypical work: beyond equality', p. 246.
1139. V. De Stefano, 'Casual Work Beyond Casual Work in the EU: The Underground Casualization of the European Workforce – and What to Do About It', *European Labour Law Journal*, Vol. 7 Issue 3, 2016, p. 425.
1140. K. Riesenhuber, *European employment law*, p. 413.

The year 2017 constituted an important year to mark the turn of events. It was the year when EU leaders decided to take action to address challenges related to the new world of work, by paying special attention to workers standing at the edge of labour markets. The EPSR was the kick-off to important initiatives in this field, which culminated with the adoption in 2019 of a directive on TPWCD, and a proposal in 2021 for a directive on Improving Working Conditions in Platform Work (dPWD). These legal instruments, which will stand at the heart of the next chapters, reveal that the time of 'casual work (but also platform work)' exceptionalism' is now a thing of the past.[1141]

These EU directives represent a crucial leap from past legislative developments, as they finally brought to the fore work arrangements characterized by unpredictable working hours, such as casual work and platform work. The adoption of the TPWCD, in particular, introduced specific rights for the vulnerable category of workers who experience working hours' insecurity. In this way, the TPWCD contributes to plugging a prominent regulatory gap of the 1990s regulatory instruments, especially the Part-time Work and the Working Time directives. Neither of these legal instruments engaged with the insecurity of working hours' aspect. In more general terms, the adoption of these EU directives also made central the working conditions debate, whereas past regulatory instruments were predominantly focused on issues such as transparency, working time and rest time,[1142] and equal treatment.

Another important contribution of the TPWCD was that it showed that the equality of treatment approach, which stands at the heart of the directives on atypical work, could not do justice to casual work(ers). As Davies rightly contends, a focus on the equality of treatment alone does not solve, for instance, the issue of unpredictable working hours. In a similar vein, the ILO report on non-standard work stresses that 'ensuring equal treatment for workers in NSE is essential', however, certain workers, such as casual and part-time ones, need to be provided with some more specific safeguards, such as the establishment of minimum guaranteed hours.[1143] The TPWCD incorporates these considerations, by laying down specific rights to respond to a specific situation for casual workers, such as the unpredictability of their working hours. In this way, the TPWCD illustrates that the new European approach to casual work embraces a 'beyond equality' perspective, where the standard worker is no longer considered a benchmark for regulating atypical work. As will be widely elaborated in this chapter, the TPWCD takes on the issue of work with 'entirely or mostly unpredictable' patterns and proposes a set of solutions for countering the insecure nature of the work.

1141. V. De Stefano and A. Aloisi, 'The EU Commission takes the lead in regulating platform work', Social Europe (blog); 2021.
1142. C. Barnard, *EU employment law*, p. 533.
1143. ILO, *Non-standard employment around the world: Understanding challenges, shaping prospects*, p. xxiv.

11.2 THE TRANSPARENT AND PREDICTABLE WORKING CONDITIONS DIRECTIVE DID NOT COME OUT OF THE BLUE: A CHRONOLOGICAL ORDER OF EVENTS

11.2.1 The Predecessor of the TPWCD: The Written Statement Directive

In 1991, a legal instrument that aimed to provide employees with a written document on the essential aspects of their employment contract or employment relationship was adopted: the WSD.[1144] The directive enshrines the employer's obligation to provide employees with their working conditions in writing, within two months after starting employment. At the same time, it allows Member States to exclude a wide category of workers from its remit, namely those who work for up to or less than one month; workers who work up to or less than eight hours per week; and workers with a casual and/or specific nature of work.[1145]

After being in force unaltered for twenty-two years, it was only in 2013 that the need to evaluate the WSD was pointed out, in order to check whether it was still fit for purpose.[1146] The examination of whether EU law is still fit for purpose, and hence, contributes to 'a clear, stable and predictable regulatory framework supporting growth and jobs', is done through the Regulatory Fitness and Performance Programme (REFIT) of the European Commission.[1147] In this regard, the European Commission first assigned an external consultant to write a REFIT study on the WSD.[1148] Subsequently, and by referring extensively to this REFIT study, the Commission delivered its own views through a staff working document.[1149] This document pointed out a number of problematic aspects related to the WSD, which predominantly concerned its personal and material scope of application. At the outset, it was noted that the objective of the directive – a full coverage of all employees under its scope – was not accomplished.[1150] The reason for this can be found in the chosen concept of 'worker', as defined by the national laws of Member States, but also in the implementation of a vast number of exclusions by Member States. The directive, indeed, permitted Member States to 'exclude certain limited cases of employment relationship' from its remit, e.g., casual workers, however, several Member States excluded all casual workers, without being limited to a certain category of them, or a specific sector.[1151] In light of such broad exclusions, the WSD was considered unsuitable for responding to the legal uncertainty

1144. Council Directive of 14 October 1991 on an employer's obligation to inform employees of the conditions applicable to the contract or employment relationship (91/533/EEC).
1145. Article 1(2) of the directive.
1146. Communication on Regulatory Fitness and Performance (REFIT): Results and Next Steps', COM (2013) 685, annex p. 11. *See also* the Commission Work Programmes 2015 and 2016, respectively Annex 3 REFIT action No. 26 and Annex 2 REFIT initiative No. 23.
1147. *Ibid.*, p. 5.
1148. Refit Study to support the evaluation of the Written Statement Directive, Final report, 2016, Available at: https://op.europa.eu/en/publication-detail/-/publication/3e06d83f-b600-11e6-9e3c-01aa75ed71a1.
1149. Commission staff working document, REFIT evaluation of the Written Statement Directive, 2017.
1150. *Ibid.*, p. 35.
1151. *Ibid.*, p. 31.

surrounding new and non-standard forms of work.[1152] Additionally, the Commission's document highlighted problems related to the proper enforcement of the directive, together with an excessively long deadline of two months for providing written information to the employees.

11.2.2 The TPWCD as a Direct Follow-Up to the European Pillar of Social Rights

In April 2017, the EU leaders (the European Commission, Parliament, and Council) gathered in Gothenburg to proclaim a crucial initiative proposed by the European Commission in the direction of strengthening the EU social *acquis*:[1153] the EPSR (the EPSR, or simply the Pillar).[1154] The EPSR constitutes a short document, composed of twenty principles and rights around three main themes: equal opportunities and access to the labour market, fair working conditions, and social protection and inclusion. In this part of the dissertation, the fair working conditions' chapter will be singled out, considering its relevance for the TPWCD, which governs the issue of working conditions in the EU.

The Pillar opens up with some considerations on the changing labour markets[1155] and subsequently attempts to suggest answers to the challenges brought by them. Against this background, principle 5 on secure and adaptable employment highlights forms of work, which were not previously covered by the EU social *acquis*,[1156] such as very flexible work arrangements, innovative forms of work, and precarious ones.[1157] With a view to filling in this regulatory gap, principle 5 aims to ensure to all workers, notwithstanding their 'employment status, modality and duration',[1158] 'fair and equal treatment regarding working conditions [...]',[1159] by also encouraging conversion towards open-ended employment. Further on, the Pillar clarifies that it does not exclusively focus on the labour protection of workers, but aims to ensure a balance with the business needs of employers. Accordingly, it points out that the necessary flexibility for employers must be provided. Furthermore, the instrument encourages innovative work arrangements which provide for quality working conditions, while, at the same time, it calls for the prevention of precarious ones.

Another crucial aspect, which the Pillar has touched upon, concerns the transparency of working conditions. In this vein, principle 7 (a) on information about employment conditions and protection in case of dismissals sets out the workers' right

1152. *Ibid.*, p. 25; Preamble to the TPWCD, para. 5.
1153. S. Garben, C. Kilpatrick & E. Muir, *Towards a European Pillar of Social Rights: Upgrading the EU Social Acquis*, College of Europe Policy Brief, (2017).
1154. Commission, 'Communication from the Commission to the European Parliament, the Council, the European Economic and Social Committee and the Committee of the Regions Establishing a European Pillar of Social Rights' COM (2017) 250 final, 1.
1155. Preamble to the EPSR, para. 9.
1156. S. Garben et al., *Towards a European Pillar of Social Rights: Upgrading the EU Social Acquis*, College of Europe Policy Brief (2017), p. 2.
1157. Principle 5 of the EPSR.
1158. Preamble to the EPSR, para. 15.
1159. Principle 5 (a) EPSR.

to be informed about their working conditions in writing as soon as the employment relationship starts. In this way, this principle conflicts with the Written Statement Directive, which requires such information within two months. Moreover, paragraph (b) of this principle provides for protection against unjustified dismissal, in the form of a right: to be informed about the reasons for dismissal; to be granted an advance notice; to access effective and impartial dispute resolution; and to redress, 'including adequate compensation'.[1160] The inclusion of this right in the Pillar constitutes a step forward, as the EU social acquis has not dealt with individual dismissal law beforehand.[1161] The same holds true concerns the provision of the right to minimum wages in principle 6. Finally, principle 8 puts an emphasis on the role of social partners in creating and implementing social policies.

Overall, the fair working conditions' chapter of the Pillar provides an important blueprint for regulating working conditions in the context of new challenges faced by the labour market. The package of rights contained in it is very clearly formulated, however, it cannot be directly implemented. The rationale for this can be found in the legal nature of the Pillar, which resembles more to that of soft law instruments, which have a recommendatory nature, instead of legally binding ones. A confirmation of this legal nature can be found in the Pillar's preamble, where it has been pointed out that the Pillar serves as a 'guide towards efficient employment and social outcomes'.[1162] The accompanying Commission Working Staff document serves as a further affirmation, by stating that 'these principles and rights are not directly enforceable and will require a translation into dedicated action and/or separate pieces of legislation, at the appropriate level'.[1163] In light of these provisions, it can be argued that the Pillar might not be legally enforceable per se, however, it constitutes a basis or a broad framework for the creation of legally binding instruments. In the wording of some prominent EU law scholars, the Pillar's values are not limited to a mere (re-) statement of principles, as the instrument stimulates 'a courageous and ambitious agenda for the adoption of the concrete changes that are needed'.[1164] And indeed, the commitments laid down in the Pillar have turned into reality through the adoption of three legal instruments: the TPWCD (the first legal act stemming from it); the Work-Life Balance Directive;[1165] and the Council Recommendation on Access to Social Protection for Workers and the Self-employed.[1166] With regard to the TPWCD, the fair working conditions' principles of the EPSR have been a major inspiration for the rights established in the directive, as they have been referred to throughout its preamble and main provisions. On top of this,

1160. *Ibid.*, principle 7(b).
1161. F. Hendrickx, 'The European Social Pillar: A first evaluation', p. 5.
1162. Preamble to the EPSR, para. 12.
1163. Commission Staff Working document, Accompanying the document Communication from the Commission to the European Parliament, the Council, the European and Social Committee and the Committee of the Regions, Establishing a EPSR, 2017, p. 3.
1164. S. Garben et al., *Towards a European Pillar of Social Rights: Upgrading the EU Social Acquis*, College of Europe Policy Brief (2017), pp. 6-7.
1165. Directive (EU) 2019/1158 of the European Parliament and of the Council of 20 June 2019 on work-life balance for parents and carers and repealing Council Directive 2010/18/EU.
1166. Council Recommendation of 8 November 2019 on access to social protection for workers and the self-employed 2019/C 387/01.

the Pillar has the potential to be considered by the European Court of Justice in interpreting the TPWCD.[1167]

Subsequent to the proclamation of the EPSR, the 'legislative train' in the direction of fair working conditions, especially for the most vulnerable workers, went through the following route. In July 2017, the European Parliament adopted a resolution on working conditions and precarious employment.[1168] This resolution represented a call on the Commission and the Member States to tackle precarious employment. What is more, a revision of the WSD was also required, with a view to providing protection for new forms of employment. In the same vein, the Commission called for social partners' consultations, in order to decide on the direction of EU action in dealing with precarious working conditions and the new world of work. Following that, the Commission drafted an ambitious proposal for a TPWCD. The proposal went through an impact assessment, and afterwards, it was presented to the Parliament and the Council. After substantial changes were introduced to the original proposal, a political agreement was reached between the three EU institutions, as a result of which the TPWCD was adopted in June 2019. This directive repeals the old WSD with effect from August 2022.

11.3 THE TRANSPARENT AND PREDICTABLE WORKING CONDITIONS DIRECTIVE

11.3.1 A Meaningful Progress from the Written Statement Directive

The TPWCD constitutes an important step forward toward the improvement of working conditions for every worker in the EU. The purpose of this directive is to ensure more transparency and predictability of working conditions while maintaining labour market adaptability.[1169] The improvement of working conditions, hence, should be in respect of employers' needs for flexibility.[1170]

In comparing the TPWCD with its predecessor (the WSD), an enhanced 'written statement' on working conditions can be observed in the first place. According to the second chapter of the new directive, workers enjoy the right to be informed in writing about their working conditions at the start of the employment relationship. In addition to offering more transparency on working conditions, another added value of the TPWCD consists in introducing a new set of rights, which aims to equip workers with more predictability and security in the face of unpredictable business demands. These material rights are contained in the third chapter of the directive entitled minimum requirements relating to working conditions, and furthermore, they are reinforced by the fourth chapter of it. This chapter is dedicated to enforcement and redress, and in

1167. B. Bednarowicz, 'Delivering on the European Pillar of Social Rights: The New Directive on Transparent and Predictable Working Conditions in the European Union', *Industrial Law Journal*, Vol. 48 Issue 4, 2019, p. 608.
1168. European Parliament resolution of 4 July 2017 on working conditions and precarious employment (2016/2221(INI)).
1169. Article 1 of the TPWCD.
1170. Preamble to the directive, para. 6.

this way, it guarantees that the rights arising from the directive will be enforced by the Member States.

On top of these reasons, an important reason to consider the TPWCD as a breakthrough from the WSD is its enlarged personal scope of application. Due to the adoption of the TPWCD, decent employment does not constitute anymore an impossible prospect for a large share of workers who were previously deprived of it.[1171] In a nutshell, the TPWCD aimed at solving several problems, such as the working conditions of, in particular, vulnerable workers; the narrow 'worker' concept; and problems deriving from casuality and platform work.

11.3.2 The Personal Scope of Application: The Centrality of Casual (and Platform) Workers and the Adopted 'Worker' Concept

The TPWCD clearly indicates the intention to learn from past mistakes, as it puts on the spotlight an often-neglected category of workers, who are increasing in numbers and importance, namely vulnerable non-standard workers, in particular those experiencing working hours' insecurity. After years of being predominantly excluded from several legal acts at the national and supranational level, zero-hours workers, and other casual workers more in general, can finally become entitled to the long-awaited labour protection. From the very start, the directive makes it clear that these workers cannot be excluded from its personal scope of application.[1172] Unless they have a 'predetermined and actual working time', which amounts to or is less than an average of three hours per week, in a reference period of four consecutive weeks,[1173] Member States cannot exclude these marginal workers.

It is paramount, first of all, to make some observations on the terminology used throughout the directive to refer to casual work arrangements. As demonstrated in the first chapter of this dissertation, defining what is captured under the label of casual work represents a complex matter. There is no agreed definition in this regard,[1174] due to the chameleonic tendencies displayed by this work typology, which result in a wide range of definitions surrounding it. In the same vein with these considerations, the TPWCD does not provide a unified definition of casual work, and what is more, it does not even refer to the notion of casual work per se. Nevertheless, prior to the adoption of the directive, the analytical document of the European Commission, which accompanied the consultation document on a possible revision of the Written Statement Directive, made an explicit reference to the Eurofound's definition on casual work.[1175]

1171. B. Bednarowicz, 'Delivering on the European Pillar of Social Rights: The New Directive on Transparent and Predictable Working Conditions in the European Union', *Industrial Law Journal*, Vol. 48 Issue 4, 2019, p. 623.
1172. Article 1(4).
1173. Article 1(3).
1174. International Labour Office – Geneva, *Non-standard employment around the world, Understanding challenges, shaping prospects*, 2016, p. 23.
1175. Analytical document, Accompanying the consultation document, Second phase consultation of Social Partners under Article 154 TFEU on a possible revision of the Written Statement Directive (Directive 91/533/EEC) in the framework of the EPSR p. 23.

What has been noted, instead, throughout the whole text of the directive (preamble and main provisions), is a frequent reliance on terms such as '*work pattern [which] is entirely or mostly unpredictable*'[1176] and *work with no guaranteed working time*. These terms have been used interchangeably, as demonstrated in the wording of Article 3(2)(m), which enshrines the employer's obligation to inform workers, whose work schedule is variable, about guaranteed paid hours. Alongside this terminology, reference to 'on-demand or similar employment contracts' has been often encountered, where these forms of work have been pointed out as particularly unpredictable.[1177] More concretely, the directive provides several examples of work with no guaranteed or unpredictable working hours. For instance, in the recital, when affirming the inclusion of workers with no guaranteed working time within its remit,[1178] the examples of zero-hours workers and some on-demand workers, have been given. Furthermore, to ensure that other vulnerable workers are also covered, a non-exhaustive list of them has been indicated, which comprises 'domestic workers, on-demand workers, intermittent workers, voucher-based workers, platform workers ...'.[1179] Therefore, all forms of casual work, which constitute the subject of this dissertation, namely intermittent work, on-call work, and zero-hours work, are explicitly covered by the directive, provided they fulfil the criteria which will be elaborated below.

Therefore, casual work arrangements seem to have been finally brought to the attention of EU legislators. Indeed, attention has been paid to them through dedicated provisions, such as Article 4(2) (m), Articles 10 and 11, together with many paragraphs of the preamble, which demonstrate that casual work holds a special place at the heart of the TPWCD. Notwithstanding its broad scope of application-all workers in the Union – the TPWCD points out a centrality of casual workers. Taking note of these considerations, the TPWCD can be considered as the most pertinent, and at the same time, the most comprehensive legal instrument at the EU level to deal with the legal situation of casual workers. At the same time, the TPWCD does not intend to leave behind an important category of vulnerable workers, who experience an even higher degree of working hours insecurity, namely platform workers. This has been stated clearly in paragraph 8 of the preamble, where platform workers have been explicitly mentioned as potential beneficiaries of the directive. Such a reference, however, does not clarify who a platform worker is. As already mentioned for casual work, a definition of platform work can also be found in the analytical document of the European Commission, which refers to Eurofound' s concept of platform work.[1180] Furthermore, except for the preamble to the directive, an explicit reference to platform workers is lacking in the main text. Nevertheless, with consideration to the working hours' insecurity underpinning platform work arrangements, platform workers can fall within the broad category of workers with entirely or mostly unpredictable working

1176. Paragraphs 30-34 of the preamble, Article 4(2) (m), Article 10.
1177. Paragraph 35 of the preamble, Article 11.
1178. Paragraph 12 of the preamble and Article 1(4).
1179. Paragraph 8 of the preamble.
1180. Analytical document, Accompanying the social partners consultation on a possible revision of the Written Statement Directive, p. 30.

hours, and hence, benefit from the available protections offered by the directive in this regard.

Notwithstanding the just-mentioned achievements in terms of the comprehensive personal scope, the directive's provision, which delineates the personal scope, can be contentious at the same time. The rationale for this can be found in the definition agreed by the EU legislators of the 'worker's concept. In the wording of Article 1 (2), workers can be covered by the directive, provided that they fall within the concept of 'worker', as defined by each Member State in its laws, collective agreements, or practices, with consideration to the case law of the Court of Justice of the European Union (CJEU). Importantly, for the first time in EU labour law, the European Commission proposed a codified "worker" definition, which derived from the most prominent jurisprudence of the CJEU on the "worker" notion developed in the free movement of workers' context.[1181] This proposal was, nevertheless, rejected by the Member States, which are represented in the Council of the EU.[1182] The tri-partite negotiations agreed, instead, to insert a kind of a 'hybrid' legal definition,[1183] composed of a national definition of a 'worker', together with reference to the CJEU case law.[1184] This reference to the CJEU jurisprudence represents an important addition when compared to resorting exclusively to national definitions, as it expands the scope of application of the TPWCD with 'forms of employment not considered under national law'.[1185] For instance, the Court has already included some non-standard forms of work, such as intermittent[1186] and part-time work,[1187] within its own concept of work. In light of this, it can be said that the CJEU has produced not only a broad but also autonomous meaning of 'worker' specific to EU law. Such an EU 'worker' definition has to be considered by national legislators and judges when deciding on the categories of workers falling within the scope of the TPWCD.

This unified EU 'worker' concept originally emerged in a free movement of workers' context (Article 45 TFEU).[1188] 'The legal starting point' for defining the contours of who is an EU worker was the seminal case of *Lawrie-Blum*,[1189] where it was held that 'the essential feature of an employment relationship (...) is that who for a certain period of time a person performs services for and under the direction of another

1181. Case 66/85, *Deborah Lawrie-Blum v. Land Baden-Württemberg*, 1986; Case C-413/13, *FNV Kunsten Informatie en Media v. Staat der Nederlanden FNV Kunsten Informatie en Media v. Staat der Nederlanden*, 2014, etc.
1182. Council of the European Union, *Proposal for a Directive of the European Parliament and of the Council on transparent and predictable working conditions in the European Union – General approach*, Inter-institutional File: 2017/0355 (COD), 2018, 10054/18, pp. 4-5; Report Expert Group, *Transposition of Directive (EU) 2019/1152 on Transparent and Predictable Working Conditions in the European Union*, 2021, p. 9.
1183. Report Expert Group, *Transposition of the TPWCD*, p. 13.
1184. It is the first time that a 'hybrid' legal definition of worker has been set out in an EU act, as beforehand either a national or an EU definition has been provided.
1185. Study for the European Economic and Social Committee (EESC), *The definition of worker in the platform economy. Exploring workers' risks and regulatory solutions*, 2021, p. 61.
1186. Case C-197/86, *Steven Malcolm Brown v. The Secretary of State for Scotland*, 1988, paras 21-22.
1187. Case C-53/81, *D.M. Levin v. Staatssecretaris van Justitie*, 1982, para. 16.
1188. It was in the *Hoekstra* case of 19 March 1964 (Case C-75/63), where the Court acknowledged its own power to establish an EU worker definition.
1189. Study for the European Economic and Social Committee (EESC), p. 64.

person, in return for which he receives remuneration'.[1190] This free movement 'worker' concept was then extended by the Court to the equal pay area,[1191] and afterwards also to the EU labour law domain. It is worth noting that in an EU labour law context, the 'Lawrie-Blum formula' is mainly extrapolated to those legal instruments which do not explicitly defer to national definitions of 'workers'. Some examples in this regard are the Working Time Directive,[1192] the Pregnant Workers Directive,[1193] the Collective Redundancies Directive,[1194] etc. Three criteria need to be cumulatively accomplished for someone to be considered a worker at the EU level, namely subordination, remuneration, and the performance of effective and genuine economic activities. All these legal conditions have been subject to an expansive interpretation by the CJEU. To start with, the first criterion - subordination - has been interpreted beyond its traditional meaning, i.e., strict control exercised by the employer over all aspects of the work. Paramount in this regard is the *Danosa* case,[1195] which was about a pregnant woman who was part of the board of directors in a company, where the Court maintained that subordination could also be understood as 'direction or supervision', especially when workers are 'an integral part of' the company for which they provide services,[1196] or it can even amount to cooperation between the worker and the employer.[1197] Furthermore, more recently, the Court examined the assumption of commercial risks as an indicator of subordination. In case business risks were held by workers, the Court did not find the existence of subordination.[1198] As concerns the second requirement, that of remuneration, the Court has emphasized that neither the level nor the origin of the remuneration, matters for the purpose of establishing who is a worker under EU law.[1199] The payment of benefits in kind instead of a regular salary,[1200] and the payment of a 'share',[1201] were not circumstances to preclude a 'worker' qualification. Lastly, the third condition - the performance of effective and genuine economic activities - was interpreted as excluding activities 'on such a small

1190. Case *Lawrie-Blum*, para. 17.
1191. Case C-256/01, *Debra Allonby v. Accrington & Rossendale College, Education Lecturing Services, trading as Protocol Professional and Secretary of State for Education and Employment*, 2004, para. 67.
1192. Directive 2003/88/EC of the European Parliament and of the Council of 4 November 2003 concerning certain aspects of the organization of working time. *See* case *Union syndacale Solidaires Isere*, para. 28.
1193. Council Directive 92/85/EEC of 19 October 1992 on the introduction of measures to encourage improvements in the safety and health at work of pregnant workers and workers who have recently given birth or are breastfeeding, *See* case *Danosa*.
1194. Council Directive 98/59/EC of 20 July 1998 on the approximation of the laws of the Member States relating to collective redundancies, *See* Case *Balkaya v. Kiesel Abbruch – und Recycling Technik GmbH*, C-229/14.
1195. Case C-232/09, *Dita Danosa v. LKB Līzings SIA*, 2010.
1196. *Ibid.*, para. 56.
1197. *Ibid.*, para. 49.
1198. Case C-35/96, *Commission of the European Communities v. Italian Republic*, 1988, para. 37.
1199. Case C-139/ 85, *R. H. Kempf v. Staatssecretaris van Justitie*, 1986.
1200. Case C-196/87, *Udo Steymann v. Staatssecretaris van Justitie*, 1988, para. 12.
1201. Case C-3/87, *The Queen v. Ministry of Agriculture, Fisheries and Food, ex parte Agegate Ltd*, 1989, para. 36.

scale as to be regarded as purely marginal or ancillary'.[1202] The Court ruled that neither the duration of the employment relationship nor the fact that the income was lower than the minimum one should lead to considering economic activities as marginal.[1203] As Countouris contends, this criterion has been widely interpreted by the Court in order not to 'discourage persons engaging in low-intensity or low – productivity forms of employment from exercising their free movement rights'.[1204]

To be noted is that this free movement 'worker' concept has found its way also into those legal instruments which explicitly confer the margin of discretion to establish who is a 'worker' to the Member States. By acknowledging the Member States' prerogatives in this regard, this interference has been done in case national definitions compromise the effectiveness of the EU instruments.[1205] This issue will be explored more in detail in Chapter 12 of this dissertation, where the personal ambit of application of the Fixed-Term Work Directive will be analysed. Importantly, as concerns the national definitions of 'workers', notwithstanding their wide variety, as Countouris and De Stefano indicate, these national understandings have the tendency to converge when it comes to fundamental concepts, e.g., '(personal) subordination, control or the performance of work under the direction of the employer'.[1206]

In a nutshell, a 'fragmented approach'[1207] can be observed in the concept of 'worker' across different EU labour law instruments. In addition to a national and EU definition developed by the CJEU, it was only recently that a mixture between the two approaches was inserted into the TPWCD, but also in the Proposal for a Platform Work Directive. This lack of a unified concept is problematic in the sense that it threatens the 'consistent application of EU labour law', but it also weakens the protections to which workers are entitled.[1208] Different definitions of workers are especially confusing in the context of bogus self-employed workers, who formally appear as self-employed workers, but whose performance of services points out to an employee status.[1209] The 'hybrid' definition, in particular, can lead to ambiguity on the definition that prevails, in case of a clash between the national and the EU 'worker' definitions.[1210] A more complex legal situation can emerge in the case of countries that adopt a tri-partite system of employment, e.g., Italy and Germany, as they need to consider the EU

1202. Case *Levin*, C-53/ 81, para. 17; C-337/97, *C.P.M. Meeusen v. Hoofddirectie van de Informatie Beheer Groep*, 1999, para. 13.
1203. Joined cases C-22/08 and C-23/08, *Athanasios Vatsouras (C-22/08) and Josif Koupatantze (C-23/08) v. Arbeitsgemeinschaft (ARGE) Nürnberg 900*, 2009.
1204. N. Countouris, 'The Concept of "Worker" in European Labour Law: Fragmentation, Autonomy and Scope', *Industrial Law Journal*, Vol. 47 Issue 2, 2018, p. 199.
1205. *See* cases *O'Brien, Del Cerro Alonso, Ruhrlandklinik* (Chapter 10 of this dissertation).
1206. V. De Stefano and N. Countouris, 'New Trade Union Strategies for New Forms of Employment', *ETUC*, Brussels, 2019, p. 19.
1207. N. Countouris, 'The Concept of "Worker" in European Labour Law', *Industrial Law Journal*, Vol. 47 Issue 2, 2018, p. 208.
1208. EU Commission, *Green Paper Modernising Labour Law to Meet the Challenges of the 21st Century*, COM (2006) 708 FINAL, p. 14.
1209. F. Hendrickx, *Regulating Working Conditions Through EU Directives – EU Employment Law Outlook and Challenges*, Briefing requested by the EMPL Committee, 2019, p. 8.
1210. B. Bednarowicz, 'Delivering on the European Pillar of Social Rights: The New Directive on Transparent and Predictable Working Conditions in the European Union', *Industrial Law Journal*, Vol. 48 Issue 4, 2019, p. 613.

'worker' definition, which embraces a bi-partite system of employment.[1211] In several instances, the Court has repeated that, if a relationship of subordination cannot be detected, then, the activity must be classified as conducted in a self-employed capacity, instead.[1212] Therefore, some more guidance on the 'hybrid' definition is paramount to ensure its proper application by national authorities.

Finally, this 'hybrid' formulation might risk, in the end, excluding a large share of workers from its remit. A study forming part of the Impact Assessment of the TPWCD provides evidence that only 3 % of platform workers, and 53 % of casual workers, can be actually covered by the directive.[1213] Nevertheless, as Georgiou points out, these estimates risk shrinking in practice, if the Lawrie-Blum criteria apply to these workers.[1214] She singles out in this regard the criteria of 'control' and 'assumption of business risks', which notwithstanding the expansive interpretation of the CJEU in this respect, risk not being met by many casual (and platform) workers.

To conclude on a positive note, in its preamble, the TPWCD highlights the significance of the primacy of facts principle of the ILO Employment Relationship Recommendation,[1215] in serving as a guide in the context of abusive situations.[1216] According to this principle, in determining the existence of an employment relationship, the way work is performed should be decisive over the formal description of the relationship chosen by the parties. The reference made by the directive to the primacy of facts principle has resulted in being quite impactful, as some national courts, when dealing with cases involving platform workers, have derived the principle from the TPWCD.[1217]

11.3.3 A Set of Protections Against the Insecure Working Conditions Encountered in Casual and Platform Work

Provided that workers are classified as employees under national law, with consideration to the CJEU case law, they become entitled to a minimum floor of rights, contained in the third chapter of the TPWCD.[1218] As already said, these rights are reinforced in the fourth chapter, where according to Article 6, in case of non-compliance with these rights, workers can access 'effective and impartial dispute

1211. N. Countouris, *The changing law of the employment relationship. Comparative Analyses in the European Context*, Studies in Modern law and Policy, Aldershot Ashgate, 2007, Chapters 1 and 2.
1212. Joined cases, *Criminal proceedings against Claude Nadin, Nadin-Lux SA (C-151/04) and Jean-Pascal Durré (C-152/04)*, 2005, para. 31.
1213. Factsheet: Towards transparent and predictable working conditions (2019), p. 2, Available at: https://ec.europa.eu/social/main.jsp?langId = en&catId = 1313.
1214. D. Georgiou, 'The new EU Directive on Transparent and Predictable Working Conditions in the context of new forms of employment', *European Journal of Industrial Relations*, Vol. 28 Issue 2, 2022, pp. 193-210, p. 202.
1215. Paragraph 9 of the Employment Relationship Recommendation No. 198.
1216. Final sentence of para. 8 of the preamble to the directive.
1217. Tribunal Superior de Justicia núm. 1 de Madrid 27 de noviembre de 2019, Case No. ECLI: ES:TSJM:2019:11243; Tribunal Superior de Justícia de Catalunya 21 de febrer de 2020, Case No. 1034/2020.
1218. Paragraph 4 of the preamble; Articles 8-14.

resolution' mechanisms and enjoy the right to redress. By acknowledging that this set of rights is applicable to all workers, a part of these rights is dedicated exclusively to workers who experience unpredictable (entirely or mostly) working hours.[1219] With a view to guarantee the necessary predictability to these workers, Article 10 enlists their entitlements in a nutshell. These entitlements represent important protections against the working hours insecurity inherent in casual and platform work arrangements. To start with, the right to have *pre-established reference hours and days, and a reasonable*[1220] *advance notice prior to starting the job*, have been laid down. Both rights should be specified in writing by the employer at the start of the employment relationship.[1221] The establishment of the reference period by the employer, however, without specifying it, has constituted subject to criticism.[1222] As the provision stands, it gives leeway to the employers to set the reference period as they prefer, even seven days per week. The right to pre-established reference hours and days and the right to an advance notice constitute also obligations for employers, which must be fulfilled cumulatively when requesting work from the worker.[1223] In case work is required outside the reference hours or days, or without respecting the minimum advance notice, the worker has the right to reject it. This refusal should not be associated with adverse consequences for the worker, e.g., no future work assignments, or other restrictions.[1224] Additionally, the employer should bear the consequences of *late cancellation*. In case an assignment, which has been agreed upon, is cancelled 'after a specified reasonable deadline', financial compensation should be paid to the worker. This reasonable deadline needs to be enshrined in writing at the start of the employment relationship, while the level of compensation to which the worker is entitled, will be established by the Member States.[1225]

In addition to the provision of these specific rights, Article 11 suggests *some measures to be considered by Member States in order to prevent abusive practices*, which are often associated with on-demand contracts. Without prejudice to the right of Member States to ban these work arrangements, the TPWCD introduces two types of anti-abusive measures, which the Member States can choose. The first measure aims to limit the use (e.g., in specific sectors or situations) and duration of these types of contracts, while the second one focuses on a rebuttable presumption of an employment relationship, where some minimum working hours are guaranteed based on the hours worked on a certain period.[1226] Member States are not bound to adopt these two suggested measures, as other measures which provide the same level of protection against abusive practices can also be permitted. Against this background, Italy and the Netherlands provide examples of two Member States, which have embraced the two

1219. Articles 10 and 11.
1220. The establishment of a reasonable notice period depends on the sector and the nature of work, according to the report on the transposition of the directive, p. 52; Recital 32.
1221. Recital 31; Article 3(2) (m).
1222. A. Piasna, 'Better working conditions, more predictable work – the new EU directive'.
1223. Article 10(1).
1224. Report on the transposition of the directive, p. 52.
1225. *Ibid.*, p. 53.
1226. Article 11 of the TPWCD.

suggested measures, even prior to the adoption of the directive. The Italian scheme of on-call work focuses on the limitation in the use and duration of casual work. It limits the use of zero-hours work to needs pre-identified in collective agreements, with the exception of workers belonging to a certain age category. As concerns the limitation on the duration, casual work in Italy is permitted for up to four hundred days per three years, with the sectors of tourism, public service, and entertainment constituting an exemption from this restriction. On the other side, the Netherlands has opted for the legal presumption of an employment relationship, provided that a certain duration and frequency of work have occurred. After working for three consecutive months for the same person, on a weekly basis or for at least 20 hours per month, a worker can be presumed to be in an employment relationship.[1227] Furthermore, if the duration and frequency conditions are fulfilled, workers become also entitled to some minimum guaranteed hours, based on the hours worked in the previous three months.[1228] The provision of this second measure by the directive can arguably constitute an attempt to contribute to the employment status insecurity of casual and platform workers. Nevertheless, as the adoption of this measure is left to the discretion of the Member States, it does not seem to constitute a legal protection as strong as the ones provided to counter the uncertainty of working hours.

Going beyond the set of casual workers' specific rights, some more general rights have also been introduced, with some of them being highly pertinent for casual workers. To start with, *the right to request transition to another form of employment, which is more predictable and secure,* has been considered by some commentators as the most far-reaching provision of this directive.[1229] While this entitlement can be beneficial for non-standard workers in general, it is particularly valuable for workers with unpredictable working hours. Pursuant to it, workers have the right, after six months of working with the same employer, to request transition to a 'more predictable and secure' employment, if available. This ambitious right stems from a principle of the EPSR, which highlights the importance of 'transition towards open-ended forms of employment'.[1230] Along the same lines, the recital to the directive points out the encouragement of open-ended and full-time employment. Therefore, with consideration to the EPSR and the preamble to the directive, standard employment can arguably provide a benchmark for secure and predictable employment. The final word, nevertheless, is left to the Member States to clarify what secure employment means. As this right is translated into an obligation for the employer, a 'reasoned' reply to the worker's request should be provided within one month of this request. This deadline can be extended to three months, in case the employer is a natural person, or a small or medium size enterprise (SME).

The provision of such a right raises the question as to whether it constitutes a safeguard for enhancing the job security of casual and platform workers. While it certainly represents an attempt in that direction, employers have no obligation to

1227. Article 7:610a of the Dutch Civil Code (CC).
1228. *Ibid.*
1229. Article 12; Recital 36.
1230. Principle 5 (a) of the EPSR.

accept such requests from workers, but they merely have to provide an elaborate answer to their requests. This aspect has, indeed, led many critics to consider this right as a mere formality, as it simply serves to ask for something. In contrast, a stronger entitlement has been provided in the Netherlands for workers with unpredictable work schedules. After one year of working on-call, these workers become entitled to fixed working hours, i.e., to more predictable employment, instead of merely having the right to ask for it. In this way, the protection enshrined in the TPWCD against the job insecurity aspect can be considered as somehow weak.

Furthermore, a frequent issue experienced by casual workers is the prohibition to work for another employer, which has often been done by inserting exclusivity clauses in their contracts. In the UK, for instance, the only protection available to zero-hours workers is the prohibition of such exclusivity clauses. In the same vein, Article 9 of the TPWCD sets out the rule for *allowing another (or parallel) employment outside the working hours with one employer*. Exceptions to this rule are allowed based on objective grounds, such as 'health and safety, the protection of business confidentiality, the integrity of the public service or the avoidance of conflicts of interests'.

The just-mentioned legal safeguards at the EU level are in line with several good practices of regulation of casual work, as provided by some Member States. The comparative legal analysis of casual work conducted in the framework of this dissertation points out that, in particular, the Dutch casual work agenda intersects with the EU one. The Dutch national scheme has been positively appraised by many commentators for providing meaningful protections to casual workers. To sum up, both the national and supranational schemes highlight the importance of a minimum advance notice, not only prior to starting work but also prior to cancelling it. The payment of financial compensation follows in case of non-compliance with it by the employer. Furthermore, both legal frameworks seem to pay attention to secure employment for casual workers, however, some differences have been noticed in this regard. Differently from the EU legal framework, in the Dutch context, secure employment has been perceived as fixed working hours, instead of open-ended contracts, where reference is made to the hours worked in the previous twelve months. Casual workers in the Netherlands do not need to submit any request in this regard, as the employer must make an offer for fixed working hours after one year of on-call work. Furthermore, another layer of security is added through the so-called chain rule, which applies only to a specific type of casual work in the Netherlands: on-call work by agreement. Pursuant to on-call work by agreement, at the moment the worker accepts the call, a fixed-term contract will be concluded, where a maximum of three consecutive fixed-term contracts, or three years of fixed-term contracts with the same employer, paves the way to an open-ended contract. As has been already mentioned and in line with anti-abusive measures suggested by the directive, the Netherlands applies a presumption of employment after three months of work with the same employer, after which some working hours will also be guaranteed. Finally, an additional legal safeguard envisaged by the Dutch legislator consists of a minimum income of three working hours, for casual workers who have contracts with unspecified working hours, and whose actual working hours are less than three. By acknowledging that some Member States, such as the Netherlands, may already have in place some protection for casual workers, the directive lays down the non-regression rule, pursuant to which the existing level of protection offered by the Member States cannot be levelled-down.[1231] Additionally, it has been emphasized that the protection set out by the directive is a minimal one, and hence, more favourable provisions can be introduced in order to establish a higher level of protection.[1232] The Netherlands has already taken steps forward in ensuring compliance with the TPWCD and drafted a bill for this purpose.[1233]

While the bright side of the coin has been broadly elaborated, the other side of it should be equally watched. In this regard, some commentators have labelled the directive as a 'broken promise',[1234] or as a 'cold comfort',[1235] something which might indicate some gaps in it. These labels are primarily related to the 'worker' definition, which has been considered as being still narrow, as the final word is left to the discretion of Member States. In this way, a wide array of vulnerable workers who are subject to misclassification, especially platform and casual workers, risk being excluded from the protective scope of the directive. And while critics mainly surround the personal ambit of the directive, they are not limited to it, with the material scope being also targeted. As already mentioned, the right to request transition to more stable employment has been coined as a mere formality, as employers can easily refuse workers' requests, by simply writing down the reasons for such a refusal.

Another source of concern has been identified with regard to the adequate level of remuneration for on-demand workers.[1236] While directives on non-standard employment provide at least a comparative benchmark in this regard, by referring to the remuneration of a comparable worker within the same establishment,[1237] in the TPWCD, no benchmark for the remuneration of vulnerable workers has been indicated. In this way, the directive does not seem to lay down protective standards that are helpful in reducing the income insecurity inherent in casual work and platform work. Another observation concerns the right to be protected against unfair dismissal. When reading the TPWCD, it can be observed that it indeed provides for protection against dismissal, but this protection is limited only when workers exercise the rights accorded by the directive,[1238] such as the right to request transition to more stable employment, to reference hours and days, etc. Therefore, workers seem to not be protected if they get dismissed for reasons other than the enjoyment of the directive's entitlements. In

1231. Article 20(1) of the TPWCD.
1232. Article 20(2) of the TPWCD.
1233. Bill implementing the TPWCD, Available at: https://www.rijksoverheid.nl/documenten/kamerstukken/2021/11/12/wetsvoorstel-implementatie-richtlijn-transparante-en-voorspelbare-arbeidsvoorwaarden.
1234. L. Ratti, 'Crowdwork and Work On-demand in the European Legal Framework: Promises and Expectations', in *Platform Work in Europe: Towards Harmonization?*, eds M. T. Carinci and F. Dorssemont, Intersentia, 2021, p. 199.
1235. B. Bednarowicz, 'Delivering on the European Pillar of Social Rights: The New Directive on Transparent and Predictable Working Conditions in the European Union', *Industrial Law Journal*, Vol. 48 Issue 4, 2019, p. 610.
1236. V. De Stefano speech in the international seminar on zero-hours work event organized by the Université Libre de Bruxelles (ULB), 2021.
1237. Clause 4 of the Part-Time Work and FTWD, and Article 5 of the Temporary Agency Work Directive.
1238. Article 18 of the TPWCD.

contrast, the EPSR lays down the right to protection in case of dismissals, which consists of the right to be given reasons and an advance notice for the dismissal, together with the right to access dispute resolution mechanisms and to redress.[1239] Notwithstanding that the TPWCD constitutes a follow-up instrument to the Pillar, it does not mirror this level of protection for workers under its scope. In the specific context of casual and platform work, the application of the right to protection against dismissal can also be challenging in practice, as it usually requires a seniority period to be completed in order to trigger it. Finally, a potential inclusion of this entitlement within the TPWCD would have contributed to a forward-looking nature of this legal instrument, as this right has not been envisaged yet in the EU *social acquis*, with the exception of the Pillar of Social Rights. It also represents a missed opportunity to ensure better job security for workers engaged in casual and platform arrangements.

11.3.4 Some Final Remarks: The TPWCD as an Illustration of Regulating Platform Work in the Same Legal Framework as Casual Work

To sum up, the TPWCD represents the first and main legal instrument at the EU level to respond to the unpredictable work reality underpinning both casual and platform work arrangements. As indicated in the section about its personal scope, by framing both forms of work within the broad category of work with unpredictable working hours, the directive acknowledges that instead of being watertight categories, casual work and platform work intersect. A logical consequence of this intersection is their inclusion into an encompassing legal framework, which regulates both of them: the TPWCD. In this way, the TPWCD serves as an illustration that it is possible for platform work to be regulated within casual work's regulatory setting.

At the same time, this directive cannot be considered as 'an instrument which targets platform workers,'[1240] as only a very small share of them end up benefiting from its legal safeguards. The fact that the vast majority of platform workers remain excluded from the personal scope of the TPWCD clearly shows that the directive constitutes only the starting point when it comes to addressing concomitant challenges to platform work. For instance, this instrument does not really solve the most contentious issue surrounding platform work, which is the employment status of platform workers. Furthermore, peculiar issues, which arise from the use of technological tools, do not fall within the scope of the EU casual work agenda. Nevertheless, considering the high priority that platform work has in the EU agenda,[1241] some progressive steps have been taken in the pathway towards decent platform work at the EU level. After conducting a two-stage consultation with social partners, the European Commission proposed on 9 December 2021, a platform work-dedicated initiative, which constitutes the first legal framework at the transnational level to specifically and considerably protect platform workers.

1239. Principle 7(b) of the Pillar, p. 15.
1240. B. Bednarowicz, 'Delivering on the European Pillar of Social Rights ...', p. 621.
1241. Mission letter to Nicolas Schmit, 2019; Political guidelines 2019-2024 'A Union that strives for more – My agenda for Europe', Available at: https://ec.europa.eu/info/sites/default/files/political-guidelines-next-commission_en_0.pdf.

Chapter 12

The Future: The Proposal for an EU Directive on Improving Working Conditions in Platform Work and the Employment Security of Platform Workers

12.1 THE PANOPLY OF SCANT DOMESTIC RESPONSES TO PLATFORM WORK

In recent years, more and more institutional activism from national legislators and judges towards sustainable platform work has been noted. Around the world, and especially in the EU, a recent trend to, *inter alia*, contest the narrative of self-employment, standing at the heart of platform work's business model, has been spread.[1242] Against this background, national judges, especially of higher European courts, have ruled in favour of an employment relationship in the context of platform work.[1243] The courts' decisions have been taken by interpreting in a modern and flexible way certain indicators,[1244] which have traditionally pointed out to a self-employed status. For example, according to higher courts in Spain,[1245] France,[1246] and the United Kingdom,[1247] the flexibility of work schedules does not in itself rule out an employment relationship. In the same vein, it has been acknowledged that: the

1242. V. De Stefano et al., *The platform work and the employment relationship*, ILO Working Paper 27, 2021, p. 30.
1243. V. De Stefano et al., 'Exclusion by Default: Platform Workers' Quest for Labour Protections', in *A Research Agenda for the Gig Economy and Society*, eds I. Durri, C. Stylogiannis, M. Wouters, Edward Elgar Publishing, 2022, p. 6.
1244. These indicators are contained, among others, in the ILO Employment Relationship Recommendation, 2006 (No. 198).
1245. Tribunal Supremo 25 septiembre 2020, Case No. ECLI: ES: TS: 2020: 2924.
1246. Cour de Cassation d 4 mars 2020, Case No. ECLI: FR: CCAS: 2020: SO00374.
1247. The Supreme Court 19 February 2021, Case No. [2021] UKSC 5, *Uber BV and others v. Aslam and others*, para. 91.

existence of substitution clauses does not automatically preclude an employment relationship; control through technology can be as powerful as, or magnify, the traditional control of employers; the algorithmic infrastructure, which is owned by platforms, constitutes the essence of the business, and not the tools owned by the worker, such as the smartphone, the car, or the bicycle.[1248] Nevertheless, without denying the importance of judicial precedents,[1249] case law alone, whose outcomes are applicable, *inter partes*, cannot provide a comprehensive answer to platform work. A legislative intervention is, thus, paramount to dealing with platform work's challenges.

Accordingly, some Member States have attempted to regulate the phenomenon, by adopting different legal approaches.[1250] Spain, for instance, has recently passed a so-called Riders' law, which introduces a rebuttable presumption of an employment relationship for delivery riders and drivers in the food and parcel delivery sector.[1251] What is more, this law sets out the obligation to disclose algorithmic decision-making to all platform workers. On the opposite side, Belgium used to exclude platform workers from employment protections, through a 2018 Act,[1252] which the Constitutional Court later quashed.[1253] In France, an 'intermediate' approach has been, instead, followed, which strengthens the protections of self-employed workers, e.g., insurance against occupational accidents, the right to vocational training, the right to form and join trade unions.[1254] The same approach underpins the EU Regulation on more fairness and transparency for business users of online intermediation services.[1255] It extends certain protections, such as transparent conditions, fair treatment, and effective redress, to self-employed platform workers. Furthermore, the Italian legal perspective constitutes a sui generis one, as it extends all employment and labour protections to workers whose work is organized by a third party, including a platform unless a collective agreement says otherwise.[1256]

These legal strategies represent the first steps in governing a phenomenon, which is widely left unregulated. Nevertheless, these instruments can come with their imperfections, which are mainly related to a narrow scope of application, as they predominantly cover location-based platform workers, especially in the transport and delivery sectors. In this way, a large segment of platform workers, such as online and

1248. V. De Stefano et al., *The platform work and the employment relationship*, pp. 30-40.
1249. V. De Stefano and A. Aloisi, 'Who will be covered by an EU instrument on platform work', Social Europe (blog), 2021, Available at: https://socialeurope.eu/who-will-be-covered-by-an-eu-instrument-on-platform-work.
1250. I. Durri, Ch. Stylogiannis, Presentation 'Regulatory approaches to platform work' to the ILO Training Center (ITC), 2021.
1251. Real Decreto-ley 9/2021 de 11 de mayo, para garantizar los derechos laborales de las personas dedicadas al reparto en el ambito de las plataformas digitales, Articulo unico, Uno.
1252. La loi relative à la relance économique et au renforcement de la cohésion sociale du 18 juillet 2018.
1253. Cour constitutionnelle du 23 avril 2020, Case No. 53/2020.
1254. Act No. 2016-1088 of 8 August 2016, the so-called *El Khomri* Act.
1255. EU Regulation 2019/ 1150 on promoting fairness and transparency for business users of online intermediation services.
1256. Decreto-Legge 3 settembre 2019, n. 101 disposizioni urgenti per la tutela del lavoro e per la risoluzione di crisi aziendali.

domestic ones, end up being excluded.[1257] Another gap that has been usually observed, with the notable exception of the Spanish law, is the reluctance of Member States to stipulate platform-specific measures, which respond to issues associated with algorithmic management. On top of these legislative gaps, these regulatory solutions apply exclusively within the boundaries of one country, and cannot be simply transplanted to another legal system, due to the specific legal features of each of them.[1258] In the face of this normative disorder, caused by the lack of, or fragmented national regulatory answers, the proposed directive for improving working conditions in platform work, hereinafter the dPWD, attempts to create some order. This legislative intervention at the EU level is essential for Member States, which partially regulate platform work, but especially for those, which experience a legislative vacuum in this area. The dPWD has been welcomed as the first, most comprehensive, and far-reaching response to platform work so far.[1259]

12.2 THE SELF-EMPLOYMENT TALE IS FINALLY ON SHAKY GROUND: SOME CONSIDERATIONS ON THE EMPLOYMENT STATUS OF PLATFORM WORKERS

As already mentioned, the major problem underpinning platform work is the uncertain employment status of platform workers. They are qualified as self-employed workers by business service agreements, while their actual work performance can point out to an employee status. As the employment relationship still remains 'an essential gateway to labour protections',[1260] such as the right to minimum wage, collective bargaining, paid leave, working time, and social security protections, platform workers become deprived of basic labour protections associated with the employee status. For this reason, there has been an upsurge of cases before courts demanding a reclassification of platform workers. What the dPWD attempts to do is to go beyond these judicial outcomes, and provide a more comprehensive answer to this classification matter.

To start with a major achievement that this directive brings, and which makes it a frontrunner compared to other legal instruments, is that it embraces all platform workers within its ambit.[1261] Instead of covering exclusively those working in the most visible and popular segments of platform work, namely transport and delivery services, it also opens up to other less well-known forms, e.g., crowdwork and domestic work. In addition to being welcoming to the diversity of platform work, the directive further demonstrates to have a relatively broad personal scope of application. It covers, in the

1257. V. De Stefano et al., 'Exclusion by default: platform workers' quest for labour protections', p. 13.
1258. *Ibid.*, p. 10.
1259. V. De Stefano and A. Aloisi, 'The EU Commission takes the lead in regulating platform work' Social Europe (blog); 2021; J. Prassl and A. Kelly-Lyth, 'Improving working conditions in the gig economy: The EU's proposed Platform Work Directive', Oxford Human Rights Hub (blog), 2021; N. Countouris, 'Regulating digital work: From laisser-faire to fairness', Social Europe (blog), 2021.
1260. V. De Stefano et al., *Platform work and the employment relationship*, p. 41; N. Countouris, *Defining and regulating work relations for the future of work*, Geneva, ILO, 2019.
1261. Article 2(1) (1) C of the dPWD.

first place, those platform workers, who are already classified as employees by Member States, with reference to the CJEU case law. Until here, the dPWD' scope of application overlaps with that of the TPWCD, and hence, the enjoyment of the rights provided for by the dPWD becomes conditional upon an already acquired employee status. Nevertheless, the instrument's protective scope goes even further, by also extending to those platform workers who 'may be deemed to have an employment contract or employment relationship', based on an assessment of the facts of the case.[1262] This provision constitutes a notable achievement for two main reasons. First, it acknowledges the misclassification issue standing at the heart of platform work,[1263] and enables platform workers who are not genuinely self-employed, to claim the rights accorded by the directive. Second, this provision highlights the importance of 'an assessment of facts', or the principle of primacy of facts, in the correct determination of the employment status. According to this principle which has been recognized internationally,[1264] 'the actual performance of work' should prevail over the classification of the relationship by the parties. From being internationally stipulated at the ILO level, the primacy of facts principle has made it also to the European level, as it can be found in the preamble of the TPWCD, as well as in the main provisions of the dPWD.[1265] Within the dPWD, this principle has been placed in the specific context of platform work, as pursuant to Article 3(2), when assessing the facts of a case involving platform work, due regard should also be given to the use of algorithms in organizing platform work. The insertion of this clause is in line with the outcomes of some judicial cases discussed above, which acknowledge the powerful control exerted by 'algorithmic bosses'.

In addition to expanding its protective scope to platform workers with an ambiguous status, the directive also suggests a solution to tackle this ambiguity, concretely through a rebuttable legal presumption of an employment relationship.[1266] A reference to this presumption can be traced back to the ILO Employment Relationship Recommendation No. 198,[1267] but also in the TPWCD, where the presumption has been suggested as one of the measures to be selected by Member States in tackling abuses related to on-demand contracts. Instead of making optional the application of this presumption, the dPWD mandates Member States to apply this legal presumption, whenever platform workers introduce reclassification demands to courts. Nevertheless, it remains to be seen whether the Commission's proposal for a legal presumption of an employment relationship will be accepted at the Council level, considering how sensitive the employment status matter is for the Member States.

The nature of legal presumptions favouring an employment status can also vary. For example, presumptions can have a general nature, with a broad application to all workers, including platform workers. The Netherlands, for instance, has opted for this type of presumption. On the other side, countries can also opt for more specific

1262. *Ibid.*, Article 1(2).
1263. V. De Stefano and A. Aloisi, 'The EU Commission Takes the Lead in regulating platform work', Social Europe (2021).
1264. Paragraph 9 of the Employment Relationship Recommendation No. 198, 2006.
1265. Articles 1(2) and 3(2) of the dPWD.
1266. *Ibid.*, Article 4.
1267. Paragraph 11 (b) of the Employment Relationship Recommendation No. 198, 2006.

presumptions, which target a certain category of workers. The presumption laid down in the dPWD is created specifically for platform workers, and hence, it falls within this typology. Furthermore, legal presumptions can be implemented in two main ways.[1268] The first option, which is more favourable for the worker, is an absolute presumption, according to which, workers are automatically presumed as employees unless the hiring entity demonstrates the non-applicability of the presumption before a court. Pursuant to the ex-Assembly Bill 5 (AB5 law) in California, the hiring entity had to prove that the conditions of an ABC test were accomplished,[1269] as proof of an independent contractor status. Alternatively, in the proposed directive, the European Commission has opted for a presumption with a more moderate nature, in the form of an alleviation of the burden of proof for the platform worker.[1270] Instead of benefiting automatically from the presumption, the worker has to prove in front of a court the fulfilment of two out of five criteria, which demonstrate that the digital labour platform has exercised control. In a nutshell, these criteria include: remuneration-setting; imposition of behavioural standards; limitation of freedom to work for another party, or to create 'a client base'; assessment of workers' performance, also by electronic means; and constraint of freedom to perform work, e.g., in the choice of working hours, or the right to be substituted.[1271] These criteria mirror the outcomes of several litigations worldwide, especially those of higher European courts, which have ruled in favour of an employment relationship. Therefore, the directive on platform work materialized an already available blueprint provided by national judges. And last but not least, the legal presumption can be rebuttable by the parties who, in this case, have to prove that the relationship in question is not an employment one.[1272]

The enshrinement of an EU-wide legal presumption constitutes an undeniable step forward in combating false self-employment within platform work.[1273] This is certainly true, especially if compared with the enshrinement of the same protection in the TPWCD. While the presumption favours, indeed, an employee status for vulnerable platform workers, it also considers the business needs of platform operators, and those of genuine self-employed platform workers, due to its moderate and rebuttable nature. Furthermore, the criteria selected to prove the existence of an employment relationship are already familiar to many national judges in Europe, something which will hopefully make it easier for workers to activate the presumption, and will arguably

1268. A. Aloisi, 'Platform Work in Europe: Lessons Learned, Legal Developments and Challenges Ahead', *European Labour Law Journal*, Vol. 13 Issue 1, 2022, pp. 4-29, p. 27.
1269. These conditions have been laid down in subdivision (a) of section 2750.3 of the Labor Code of California and they are: '(a) the person is free from the control and direction of the hiring entity in connection with the performance of the work, both under the contract for the performance of the work and in fact, (b) the person performs work that is outside the usual course of the hiring entity's business, (c) the person is customarily engaged in an independently established trade, occupation, or business of the same nature as that involved in the work performed'.
1270. Analytical document, Accompanying the consultation document of social partners under Article 154 TFEU on a possible action addressing the challenges related to working conditions in platform work, 2021, p. 82.
1271. Article 4(2) of the dPWD.
1272. *Ibid.*, Article 5.
1273. V. De Stefano and A. Aloisi, 'The EU Commission takes the lead in regulating platform work'.

inform future decisions when applying this presumption. Nevertheless, the enshrinement of this legal presumption is no panacea to the classification issue of platform workers.[1274] First of all, the worker's initiative is required to invoke the presumption before a court. Notwithstanding that the chances to be successful are higher than before the stipulation of the EU legal presumption, a judicial process is associated with inherent costs and risks,[1275] where the last word remains to the judiciary. Recent case law in Belgium, indeed, upholds this, as a Brussels court disregarded a presumption of employment applicable in the transport industry, and hence, refused to grant an employee status to Deliveroo couriers.[1276] What is more, the formulation of the directive's criteria to activate the presumption has been criticized as a rigid one, as the directive enshrines some fixed criteria, which in combination with the prerequisite for the worker to complete at least two of them,[1277] can reduce the chances to benefit from the presumption.[1278] All these things considered, the enshrinement of a legal presumption of an employment relationship for platform workers can, indeed, be paramount in the direction of more employment security for this category of workers. Nonetheless, the way it has been formulated might suggest that this protection can be less effective in reducing employment status precariousness in practice.

12.3 THE DIRECTIVE'S RESPONSE TO THE DISTINCT CHALLENGES ARISING FROM PLATFORM WORK

12.3.1 Algorithmic Management Measures

After paying extensive attention to the contractual status of platform workers, the third chapter of the directive turns its focus to the most idiosyncratic feature characterizing platform work: the algorithmic management. In an attempt to respond to its distinct challenges, the directive aims to ensure more 'transparency (a), fairness (b), and accountability (c)' in algorithmic management.[1279] Importantly, the applicability of the algorithmic-specific measures is not conditional upon the platform worker having an employment relationship or employment contract,[1280] as the impact of automated systems on the working conditions of platform workers, does not depend on their

1274. M. Kullman, 'Platformisation of Work: An EU Perspective on Introducing a Legal Presumption', *European Labour Law Journal*, Vol. 13 Issue 1, 2021, pp. 66-80, pp. 68 and 72.
1275. *Ibid.*, p. 10.
1276. Tribunal du travail francophone de Bruxelles 25e chambre, Judgment 2021/014148, *L'auditeur du travail contre la SPRL Deliveroo Belgium*, 8 décembre 2021, https://www.tribunaux-rechtbanken.be/sites/default/files/tt_bruxelles/news_files/20211208-ttfb-deliveroo.pdf.
1277. A. Aloisi, D. Georgiou, Two steps forward, one step back: The EU's plans for improving gig working conditions (blog), 2022, Available at: https://www.adalovelaceinstitute.org/blog/eu-gig-economy/.
1278. V. De Stefano et al., 'Exclusion by Default: Platform Workers's Quests for Labour Protection', In V. De Stefano, I. Durri, C. Stylogiannis, M. Wouters (ed.), *A Research Agenda for the Gig-Economy and Society*, 2022, p. 15.
1279. Article 1(1) dPWD.
1280. *Ibid.*, Article 10(1).

employment status.[1281] With the exception of health and safety provisions contained in Article 7(2), the algorithmic management chapter of the dPWD extends its protective scope also to self-employed platform workers.

Moreover, the directive clarifies that in case of a conflict between this chapter and the EU Regulation 2019/1150 on more fairness and transparency for business users of online intermediation services (P2B), the Regulation's provisions will prevail.[1282] By acknowledging that also other EU legal initiatives can contribute to tackling algorithmic management challenges, e.g., the GDPR, or the proposed Artificial Intelligence Act (AI),[1283] the below sections will elaborate on the protection offered by the dPWD in the direction of a better deployment of algorithms by platforms.

More Transparency in Algorithmic Management: Important Information Displayed to Platform Workers

The need for more transparency in algorithmic decision-making has already been laid down at the domestic level, concretely by the Riders' law in Spain.[1284] At this point, both the Spanish and this EU legal instrument intersect, as they put an obligation on platforms to display to all platform workers important decisions, which impact their working conditions, varying from hiring to firing, denial of remuneration, or a change in their contractual terms. More specifically, the dPWD provides that platforms should share information with platform workers on 'automated monitoring and decision-making systems'.[1285] Subsequently, it explains the type of information which should be made available to platform workers, such as: the deployment of such systems; the type of actions 'monitored, supervised or evaluated', together with clients' evaluation;[1286] and the categories of decisions taken, together with the parameters considered in decision-making, including the rationale for decisions with a particular detriment effect, e.g., termination of the relationship with the platform, refusal of payment by the platforms, or the contractual status of platform workers.[1287] This information package should be made available in the form of a document, also in electronic format, upon the request of platform workers or their representatives, and no later than the first working today.[1288]

More Fairness in Algorithmic Management: Human Control Over Automated Decisions

The dPWD goes one step further than merely tackling the opacity of automated monitoring and decision-making systems. Given the potential detrimental effects of

1281. Preamble to the directive, para. 40.
1282. Article 10(2) dPWD.
1283. Analytical document, Accompanying the consultation document of social partners on a possible action addressing the challenges related to working conditions in platform work, p. 83.
1284. Real Decreto-ley 9/2021 de 11 de mayo, para garantizar los derechos laborales de las personas dedicadas al reparto en el ambito de las plataformas digitales, Articulo unico, Uno.
1285. Article 6 dPWD.
1286. Article 6, para. (2) (a) (ii).
1287. Article 6, para. (2) (b).
1288. Article 6(3) and (4).

automated systems, which have limited human involvement, the control of humans over them becomes essential. To this end, the directive espouses a human-in-the-loop approach,[1289] according to which, platforms have to monitor the impact of individual decisions taken by automated systems.[1290] For this purpose, platforms should put in place human resources, which need to be competent and well-trained for exercising this monitoring function.[1291] As automated decisions taken by algorithms may impact the health and safety of platform workers, human resources have the important task of not only assessing these risks but also checking whether there is suitable protection in place to counter them, and, finally, provide for 'preventive and protective measures'.[1292]

More Accountability in Algorithmic Management: Platform Workers can Challenge Important Decisions

For important decisions influencing their working conditions, platform workers are, first, accorded the right to have an explanation.[1293] Article 6(1) (b) of the directive provides with examples of what are considered as important decisions made by automated systems. With a view to giving platform workers an explanation of the decisions taken, platforms should designate a contact person, who must clarify the facts and reasons leading to the decision. In case the explanations provided are unsatisfactory, or the platform worker insists that the decision infringes her rights, platform workers can exercise the right to review the decision. In this case, platforms have to provide a reasoned reply to the worker's request, within one week of introducing such a request. In the event of a favourable reply for the platform worker, the platform needs to revise the decision, or where this is unfeasible, it should accord an adequate compensation to the worker. For a number of self-employed platform workers, with the exception of those who work for platforms, which are not merely online intermediation services, such as Uber and Deliveroo, a redress solution is guaranteed by the so-called P2B Regulation. The Regulation obliges the providers of online intermediation services to set an 'internal complaint-handling system'[1294] for dealing swiftly and cost-free with workers' complaints.

12.3.2 Dealing with the Cross-Border Aspect of Platform Work: More Transparency Obligations for Platform Operators

The use of technology grants platform work a truly global nature, as platforms, workers, and clients, can all be located in different countries, with crowdwork best illustrating this situation. This cross-border dimension of platform work can bring further complexity to the table. Against this background, the dPWD lays down a

1289. V. De Stefano & A. Aloisi, 'The EU Commission takes the lead in regulating platform work'.
1290. Article 7(1) dPWD.
1291. Article 7(3).
1292. Article 7(2).
1293. Article 8(1).
1294. Article 11 of the P2B (Platform to Business Regulation).

transparency obligation for 'platforms which are employers', to declare platform work to the competent authorities of the Member States where work is carried out.[1295] In particular, platform companies should make available not only to national authorities but also to platform workers' representatives, data on the number of platform workers working on a regular basis, their contractual status, together with the terms and conditions applicable to them, provided that they are determined unilaterally by the platforms, and they apply widely to a large share of platform workers.[1296] In addition to supplying such information, platforms also have the duty to provide substantiated replies, in case further explanation is demanded on the above-mentioned data.[1297]

As concerns this transnational nature of platform work, the analytical document of the European Commission, which accompanies the document on the consultation of social partners, rightly points out the need for some guidance in case of disputes between parties involved in a cross-border situation.[1298] Such disputes are characterized by a lack of clarity on the applicable law and jurisdiction, a matter on which the directive on platform work remains silent, by merely engaging to enhance transparency on platform work as such.

12.3.3 Platform Work-Related Challenges Can Be Better Counteracted When Platform Workers Have a Collective Voice

The directive on platform work, furthermore, contributes to a certain extent to strengthening the collective voice of platform workers. This is done, first, through the enshrinement of the right of platform workers' representatives to take legal actions to protect the rights arising from the directive.[1299] Further on, the directive attempts to address another problematic aspect underlying platform work, which is the dispersal of workers in the crowd.[1300] The isolation of platform workers adversely impacts communication with their counterparts and representatives. To this end, the solution proposed by the directive consists of the creation of communication channels, which must be enabled by platforms, e.g., within their digital infrastructure.[1301] Platforms, furthermore, bear a negative obligation to not interfere in any way in such communications. These legal safeguards can somehow contribute to the improvement of platform workers' collective voice, as a result of which, workers will be in a stronger position when facing challenges arising from platform work.[1302]

Furthermore, the European Commission is preparing to launch an initiative – the Draft Guidelines on collective bargaining of self-employed workers – with the aim to

1295. Article 11 of the dPWD.
1296. Article 12(1) of the dPWD.
1297. Article 12(3) of the dPWD.
1298. Analytical document, Accompanying the consultation document of social partners on a possible action addressing the challenges related to working conditions in platform work, p. 84.
1299. Article 14 of the dPWD.
1300. V. De Stefano, 'The rise of the just-in-time workforce: on-demand work, crowd work and labour protection in the "gig economy"', p. 8.
1301. Article 15 of the dPWD.
1302. Analytical document, p. 84.

ensure that EU competition law does not constitute an obstacle for the enjoyment of the right to bargain collectively by platform workers.[1303] The dPWD, on the other side, does not engage with this issue at all, by remaining silent not only regarding the right to collective bargaining but also regarding fundamental collective labour rights more in general.

12.4 THE ARTICULATION BETWEEN THE TRANSPARENT AND PREDICTABLE WORKING CONDITIONS DIRECTIVE AND THE DRAFT PLATFORM WORK DIRECTIVE

Platform workers can now explicitly fall within the protective realm of two different legal instruments, namely the TPWCD and the dPWD. In this regard, the dPWD mentions, both in its explanatory memorandum[1304] and preamble,[1305] that the TPWCD is a legal instrument which can be relevant for platform workers. This mere recognition, nonetheless, makes it clear that the articulation between these instruments is far from optimal. The dPWD does not explicitly set out that the TPWCD offers platform workers an additional set of protections against a number of insecurities inherent to their work arrangement, with working hours insecurity constituting a prominent example in this regard. In other words, it does not acknowledge in a straightforward way that platform workers can enhance their labour protection by referring to this legal instrument.

As the situation stands, two issues can be pointed out. The first one is that the dispersal of legal protections can give rise to confusion, and make the protections weaker in practice,[1306] as platform workers are left in the dark concerning the additional layer of protections to which they are entitled. The second issue detected has to do with an inconsistency in platform workers' coverage by these two EU directives. For instance, the dPWD shows to have a more encompassing scope of application for platform workers, as it also covers those with an ambiguous employment status. In contrast, the TPWCD extends only to those platform workers who already have an 'employee' status. As this formulation stands, platform workers with an ambiguous legal status, who want to benefit from the insecurity-related protections contained in the TPWCD, must first refer to the dPWD and activate the legal presumption contained therein. In light of this, a better alignment between both instruments should take place, focusing on making more clear to platform workers that, legal safeguards contained in the TPWCD, e.g., the right to reference hours and days, and the right to request more predictable employment, are fully applicable to them.

1303. Draft Guidelines on collective bargaining of self-employed, https://ec.europa.eu/competition-policy/public-consultations/2021-collective-bargaining-2_en.
1304. Explanatory Memorandum of the Platform Work Directive, p. 4.
1305. Paragraph 10 of the Preamble.
1306. D. Mangan, 'The platform discount', Presentation at the Fourth Roger Blanpain lecture, Leuven, May 2022.

Conclusions

For quite some time, platform work was considered a new work reality. As such, tailor-made regulatory solutions, which incorporate this understanding, have often been perceived as appropriate to deal with the legal complexities stemming from such work arrangements. Contrary to this line of reasoning, this doctoral dissertation argues that the very nature of platform work suggests that, instead of being novel, platform work is part of broader trends toward the casualization of employment. By following this logic, it was assessed whether rules aimed at improving the legal protection of casual workers can also be applicable to platform workers. In light of these considerations, the central question of this research was formulated: can the casual work agenda contribute to enhancing the labour protection of platform workers?

It is the intention of this final part to provide a precise answer to this research question. This will be done by first introducing the main findings, deriving from the three constitutive parts of this dissertation, followed by the specific responses to the research question(s). Finally, some recommendations will be formulated for redefining the platform work agenda, with a special focus on the dPWD.

1 MAIN FINDINGS

1.1 Understanding Casual (and Platform) Work

Part I centred around *casual work arrangements*, a form of work that has been among us for many centuries now, but it still entails difficulties to understand it. Therefore, it was the intention of this part to shed some light on the 'chameleonic tendencies' of casual work and advance a working definition for the purpose of this dissertation. Casual work, in the context of this research, was considered as a label for capturing those work arrangements, which have a very short duration and can be called in by the employer on a regular or irregular basis, such as daily work, seasonal work, etc.; but also work arrangements, which can be long-lasting or continuous, but are characterized by some or severe working hours insecurity, such as min-max and zero-hour work arrangements. Subsequent to this understanding of casual work, the aim was to scrutinize its main legal features. This was done through a *comparative legal analysis of casual work in four industrialized countries*. This comparative exercise was essential given a prominent research gap in the existing analysis of an extensive comparative study on casual work in industrialized countries. The comparative study conducted in the framework of this doctoral project affirmed that casual work is not only under-researched in developed countries but is also frequently facing a legal vacuum. The latter aspect has been especially confirmed by the study of zero-hours work in the United Kingdom, where scarce legal protection for casual workers has been observed. Nevertheless, in order to make the comparison more prominent, contrasting regulatory models on casual work have been considered, such as the ones adopted by Italy, the Netherlands, and Belgium.

The main findings of this comparative legal analysis reveal that the Italian scheme regulates casual work in detail, however, by limiting its use simultaneously, e.g., by limiting its duration, or use in different sectors. In a similar vein, Belgium was noted to apply even a more stringent approach to casual work. On the other side, the Dutch regulatory approach was observed to display a more protective nature, as it has not only enshrined a rebuttable legal presumption of an employment relationship but has also provided specific legal safeguards suited to the needs of casual workers. Both the restrictive and protective regulatory models, implemented respectively by Italy and the Netherlands, have been considered effective measures to deal with casual work at the EU level, concretely by the TPWCD. In the academic discourse, the Dutch model has been particularly praised for offering not only a comprehensive set of protections to casual workers but also for considering the flexibility needs of both employers and workers.

Another important contribution of Part I consists in highlighting *the interrelation between casual work and platform work*. This interrelation has been identified by looking at the legal situation of both casual and platform workers in the national context of the four selected countries. Both forms of work were observed to display a similar work reality, characterized by an unpredictable nature of the working hours, something which goes hand in hand with the insecurity of jobs for the future, and income insecurity, which is also often associated with a low level of income. Furthermore, a reliance on an 'on-demand' workforce, a pool of workers who can be called upon at the employers' discretion, and a frequent exclusion from labour protection, has also been noted for both work arrangements. All these features can be traced back to the late nineteenth century when they characterized the daily work of mainly dock and construction workers. In the digital age, these previous challenges seem to have incurred an exacerbation by platform work arrangements. It was in light of all these considerations that the assumption underlying this doctoral dissertation was formulated: casual work and platform work largely overlap, and hence, platform work is a significant part of the casualization of work arrangements' trend. This overlap between casual work and platform work has also been widely acknowledged in the academic discourse and at the institutional level, e.g., in the authoritative studies of the International Labour Office and Eurofound.

By having in mind that the work reality underlying platform work is not new, Part II has put in the spotlight *platform work per se*, in an attempt to look for what is truly novel in this form of work. In this regard, the deployment of algorithmic management to 'match' both the demand and supply sides of labour has been identified as a cutting-edge feature of platform work, which distinguishes it from other work forms. Furthermore, this 'matching' realized by means of an algorithm happens with a speed, which has been compared to the lightning one, as a result of which, a 'just-in-time-workforce' can be supplied. Nevertheless, the deployment of technology in a platform work context was found to be associated with several issues. Some of them have been identified, and they include, in a nutshell: the lack of transparency in the way algorithms operate; the treatment of ratings as exclusive properties by platform companies; the perception of platform workers as extensions of IT devices; the asymmetry of the rating system; and the obstruction of the right to challenge unfair decisions taken by platforms. To be noted is that, it was not the intention of this dissertation to look for legal solutions to the above-mentioned issues. The final aim, which will be delineated below, is to analyse whether existing regulatory strategies on casual work can be valuable to enhance the labour protection of platform workers.

1.2 The Contribution of the Casual Work Agenda for the Labour Protection of Platform Workers

Prior to assessing the contribution that the casual work agenda can make to the labour protection of platform workers, a clarification of two chief concepts, such as the casual work agenda, and the labour protection of platform workers, was deemed essential.

1.2.1 The Casual Work Agenda

For the purpose of this dissertation, the notion 'casual work agenda' refers to a broad regulatory framework, which is pertinent for the regulation of casual work arrangements at the EU level. That said, this doctoral research opens up the big picture of regulating casual work, and hence, it is not limited only to targeted legal instruments that govern it. In this regard, a set of EU directives have been singled out as important constituents of the casual work agenda. More specifically, these are the Working Time Directive (WTD), the Fixed-Term Work Directive (FTWD), and the TPWCD.

The selection of these legal instruments was made based on their particular relevance for casual and platform workers. For instance, given the importance that working time has for these work arrangements, the Working Time Directive was selected as a pertinent instrument. Furthermore, a common denominator between casual work arrangements and fixed-term work was observed to be the insecurity of jobs. What is more, casual work also resembles with part-time work, as both work typologies can be underpinned by short and insecure working hours. Nevertheless, as the Part-Time Work Directive does not include any considerations to address the insecurity of working hours, this directive has been elaborated only briefly in this thesis. Importantly, both these EU directives on atypical work, i.e., the FTWD and the PTWD, centre around an equality of treatment approach. Nevertheless, this approach was considered insufficient to respond to the special needs for protection of casual workers, e.g., against the unpredictable nature of their work schedules.

Against this backdrop, the TPWCD incorporates a 'beyond equality' approach, according to which, the standard worker has no longer been considered a benchmark for regulating atypical work. Instead, some tailor-made protections to respond to the needs of workers with 'entirely or mostly unpredictable' work patterns have been enshrined, which makes this EU directive extremely relevant for casual and platform workers. For this reason, the TPWCD was considered to stand at the heart of the EU casual work agenda, as the most pertinent and comprehensive legal instrument to deal with casual work. This directive marks a crucial leap from past legislative developments, not only for bringing to the spotlight the problem of casuality but also for making the working conditions debate central, and for giving a broader meaning to the 'worker' concept in comparison to the national meaning accorded by previous EU legal instruments.

1.2.2 The Labour Protection of Platform Workers

It should be made clear that, since this doctoral project kicked off in October 2018, the issue of the labour protection of platform workers has undergone important changes. Platform work used to constitute a phenomenon, that was widely left unregulated, and accordingly, platform workers were faced with a protection gap. On top of this, the majority of business service agreements qualified these workers as self-employed ones. While this classification by platform companies still remains predominant in 2022, a boom of legal developments has surrounded platform work. Several judicial decisions from different courts, especially higher European ones, together with national regulatory strategies, have attempted to unplug the labour protection gap of platform workers. These attempts culminated with a proposal at the supranational level to adopt an EU directive on the working conditions of platform workers. With consideration to this landmark legal initiative, it can be said that once adopted, it will mark the end of 'platform work' exceptionalism', and hence, platform workers in the EU will no longer face a severe labour protection gap. They might actually benefit from a platform work agenda. As Prassl rightly contends, it was about time 'to disrupt the disruptors', or in other words, to bring platform work explicitly within the scope of labour law, especially at a supranational level.

This recent legal development altered the original research question of this dissertation, in the sense that, now, an evaluation of the applicability of the casual work agenda will be done in light of enhancing the labour protection of platform workers, instead of merely filling in a protection gap. In particular, evaluating how the casual work agenda contributes to reducing the insecurities standing at the heart of the labour protection problem is essential.

1.2.3 'Connecting the Dots' Between the Casual Work Agenda and the Labour Protection of Platform Workers

This research departs from a normative framework, which has been explained as referring to casuality understood in terms of insecurities and precariousness in different dimensions, i.e., employment status, work, income, working hours. This section takes a more systematic approach by looking at how these four components have been addressed in different legal instruments. This will be discussed in a 'connecting the dots' approach. More specifically, it will be scrutinized how existing more traditional, and newer legislative answers are being connected in terms of these different components, in order to see what they deliver.

To start with, the issue of the employment status insecurity of casual and platform workers does not seem to constitute a main preoccupation in the TPWCD. Instead, the set of protections introduced by this legal instrument seems to focus mainly on the other labour-related insecurities, as will be outlined below. Nevertheless, an attempt to reduce the insecurity of these workers' employment status has been noted. The TPWCD suggests to the Member States to adopt, *inter alia*, a rebuttable legal presumption of an employment relationship, as a measure to fight abuses related to on-demand contracts. The way this presumption has been formulated indicates that Member States can choose whether to incorporate it or not into their legal systems, but also how to formulate it. On the opposite side, the dPWD grants a mandatory nature to this legal presumption, by mandating Member States to apply it every time a platform worker introduces a reclassification demand to the court. In this way, the dPWD makes a more prominent contribution to reducing the vulnerability that platform workers experience in relation to their employment status, in comparison with the TPWCD. Nonetheless, as explained in this dissertation, the activation of the presumption contained in the PWCD might be difficult in practice. This is mainly due to the way it has been formulated, but also because of the different costs and risks which can be associated with legal proceedings.

As concerns the national agendas on casual work, two of them can be singled out for attempting to respond to this insecurity. In line with the EU agenda, the Dutch agenda also provides for the legal presumption of an employment relationship as a legal solution in this regard. According to it, in order to be granted the employee status, workers need to have completed a certain duration and frequency of work. Differently from the just-mentioned regulatory solutions, Italy has recently introduced a peculiar one to bring platform workers within the protective scope of labour law, which does not interfere with their employment classification. According to the Italian legislation, workers should be accorded all labour protections, in case their work is organized by a third party, including a platform. Again here, workers have to initiate litigations in order to be accorded these entitlements.

The Working Time Insecurity

Combatting the working hours insecurity inherent in casual and platform work models constitutes the crux of the TPWCD and the Dutch legislation, which lay down several legal safeguards for this purpose. For instance, the TPWCD sets out the right to reference hours and days, and the right to have a reasonable advance notice, which should be cumulatively respected by employers. In the same vein, the right to an advance notice before starting work or cancelling it has also been enshrined in the Dutch legal framework. This national regulatory strategy seems more concerned with ensuring more predictability of work schedules than its EU counterpart. This has been done by providing for a right to minimum guaranteed hours after three months of work with a certain frequency, but also the right to fixed working hours after working one-year on-call. Such entitlements arguably illustrate the blurring boundaries between the security of working hours and jobs, as minimum and fixed working hours can be translated respectively into a minimum and fixed volume of work.

On the other hand, the Working Time Directive does not seem to engage with the issue of unpredictable work schedules. Nevertheless, this directive can be insightful as it concerns other working time insecurities faced by many casual and platform workers. Importantly, the EU regulatory framework on working time has a lot to offer with regard to the unpaid stand-by time of casual and platform workers. A corpus of case law from the CJEU on the WTD can be inspirational in qualifying as working time those time periods during which these workers are available to work, but they are not actually carrying out any work. Finally, the WTD also represents a valuable instrument in ensuring maximum working time, which is important for many platform workers who experience long working hours.

The Jobs (Work) Insecurity

As seen in the above section on working time insecurity, the Dutch agenda grants the right to more predictable employment, in the form of fixed working hours, after working one-year on-call. In this regard, the EU legislators have opted for a more cautious approach in the TPWCD. As a solution to reduce the work insecurity of casual and platform workers, a right to request transition to a more predictable and secure form of employment after six months of work with the same employer was introduced. Nonetheless, by simply requesting this transition, no guarantee has been provided towards more work security. This is the reason why some commentators tackle this right as being a mere formality, or simply a right to ask for something.

On the contrary, the Fixed-Term Work Directive, through its anti-abuse clause (Clause 5), can make a greater contribution to the work insecurity issue. Nevertheless, in light of the short-termism underpinning casual work and platform work, this legal provision should be updated in order to effectively better the work insecurity of these workers. The update should touch upon the legal measures contained in the anti-abuse clause, e.g., the maximum duration and the maximum number of renewals, and the consequences in case an abuse with consecutive contracts/tasks has been identified. In line with the Dutch model, which provides for some fixed working hours after one year of work, a sufficient volume of work should be at least ensured in case an abuse is detected.

The Income Insecurity

Finally, income insecurity deriving from the insecurity of jobs represents an issue that seems to be overlooked by the EU legislators. All EU instruments examined in this dissertation reflect a legal vacuum in this regard. Some national agendas, nonetheless, seem to include some considerations in light of reducing it. Italy, e.g., has introduced monthly payment as a compensation for the availability of casual workers, who have promised to accept offers of work. This so-called availability indemnity can be regarded as a form of compensation for the lack of a steady income in the context of casual work arrangements. Furthermore, income security also takes the form of the payment of three working hours, in case of work with no guaranteed hours, or with less than three guaranteed hours. This legal solution has been adopted by the Netherlands.

2 RESPONSES TO THE RESEARCH QUESTION(S)

(a) What is Casual Work and What Are the Main Legal Features of Casual Work in Selected Industrialized Countries? (Part I)

There is no crystal clear answer to the question of what casual work is. As explained, its 'chameleonic tendencies' have hampered its understanding as a unitary phenomenon. Notwithstanding these difficulties, a working definition of casual work was construed in the framework of this dissertation. According to it, casual work was understood as a label for capturing those work arrangements, which have a very short duration and can be called in by the employer on a regular or irregular basis, such as daily work, seasonal work, etc.; but also work arrangements, which can be long-lasting or continuous, but are characterized by some or severe working hours insecurity, such as min-max and zero-hour work arrangements.

As varied as these work arrangements are, so are the legal responses to them, ranging from scarce to comprehensive ones. This has been substantiated by the comparative analysis of casual work in the United Kingdom, Italy, Belgium, and the Netherlands. Countries, such as the United Kingdom, with almost no regulatory responses to this work model, make more evident that there is a labour protection problem for these workers. On the extreme side of the spectrum, countries such as Italy and the Netherlands, have provided important regulatory answers for reducing the insecurities inherent in these work arrangements. The Italian scheme, indeed, offers legal safeguards, such as the availability indemnity, or the advance notice; at the same time, it limits the duration of casual work, or its use in different sectors. In a similar vein, Belgium also applies limitations to the use of casual work, however, without laying down specific protections against the inherent labour-related insecurities. On the other side, the Dutch regulatory approach offers valuable legal insights in light of labour protection, which consider, at the same time, the flexibility needs of both employers and workers. This regulatory approach attempts to address the employment status insecurity of, *inter alia*, casual workers, through the enshrinement of a rebuttable legal presumption of an employment relationship. Furthermore, it provides some tailor-made protections for casual workers in addressing the other identified insecurities, i.e., working hours, income, and work insecurity.

The identification of the set of insecurities surrounding casual work has been paramount in setting it off against the phenomenon of platform work. A similar work reality, characterized by an unpredictable nature of working hours, insecure work for the future, and income insecurity, pointed out a major overlap between both forms of work. Framing platform work within the broad trend of casual work arrangements was also confirmed at the academic discourse and the institutional level. Finally, the precariousness underpinning these work arrangements was observed to become extreme in the extraordinary situation brought about by the COVID-19 pandemic.

(b) What Is so Peculiar About Platform Work? (Part II)

Going back in time, concretely in the late nineteenth century, a proliferation of daily labour practices, especially among dock and construction male workers, was prominent. A middleman was appointed to deal with the work organization of dock workers, where the hiring process was mainly based on the workers' reputation, such as regular attendance, obedience, and hard work. Such work arrangements have long been features of labour markets, also in industrialized societies. A similar work reality can also be found in platform work if looking under the technological vest. What is more, platform work was observed to exacerbate previous challenges, which led to it being considered as a 'bad' successor of the casualization of work originating in the nineteenth century.

The way platform operators exercise control over the workforce resembles the managerial prerogatives of employers. Indicators of such a control exerted by platforms are: the selection of workers; the provision of explicit instructions; the limitation on workers' freedom to choose working hours, as workers might have to log in during certain working hours, especially peak hours; the control over the work tools; unilateral price-setting; the evaluation of the work performance; and the termination of the work relation. All these indicators point out to an employee status, rather than a self-employed one, as contended by platform operators. This work reality, coupled with the fact that platform workers experience unstable work patterns inherent to casual work arrangements, undermines the novelty tale surrounding platform work.

Deriving from these considerations, platform work might be distinctive from other forms of work, only in terms of 'matching', by means of an algorithm, both the demand and supply sides of labour. This matching happens, indeed, with a speed not encountered in the past, which supplies with an immediately available workforce. The deployment of algorithmic management can, nonetheless, be associated with some issues, which are not novel to the world of work. They comprise problems such as discriminatory algorithms; the treatment of ratings as exclusive properties of platform companies; overlooking the human aspect of platform work; the asymmetry of the rating system; and the obstruction of the right to challenge perceived unfair situations. The dPWD has attempted to solve some of these identified issues.

(c) What Are the Chief Legal Safeguards Available for Casual and Platform Workers in the EU? (Part III)

This dissertation has looked into EU instruments, which are pertinent for enhancing the labour protection of casual and platform workers. Under scrutiny have been not only targeted regulatory strategies for these forms of work but also broader regulatory frameworks, which could be insightful for the labour protection needs of these workers. These regulatory strategies were coined for the purpose of this dissertation as the casual work agenda. Efforts to develop such an agenda were traced back to the EU's response to what was considered 'the first wave of flexibility', which consisted mainly of a set of directives adopted in the 1990s. In this regard, the directives singled out for the purpose of this dissertation were the Part-Time Work, the Fixed-Term Work, and the Working Time directives. The Part-Time Work Directive, nevertheless, did not constitute the subject of an in-depth analysis like the other directives, as it did not enshrine any protection against the insecurity of working hours. On the contrary, the Fixed-Term Work Directive and the Working Time Directive set out crucial protections, respectively the anti-abuse clause against abuses arising from the use of successive contracts, and the provision of paid stand-by time, in case workers are available to undertake work but are not actively working.

At the heart of the EU casual work agenda was placed a more recent legal instrument – the TPWCD – which focuses on the needs of workers with 'entirely or mostly unpredictable' work schedules. In addition to being the first EU legal instrument which brings to the fore the issue of casuality, it also makes central the working conditions debate and introduces a broader definition of the 'worker' concept. The main protections contained in the TPWCD include the right to advance notice, to reference hours and days, to request a transition to more predictable and stable employment, etc. Moreover, a set of tailor-made protections for platform workers was recently proposed by the European Commission in the form of a Platform Work Directive. This draft instrument lays down an important safeguard against the employment status insecurity of platform workers, namely the rebuttable legal presumption of an employment relationship. In addition, it also presents some measures targeting algorithmic decision-making.

(d) Can the Legal Safeguards on Casual Work Advance the Labour Protection of Platform Workers? (Part III)

The wide set of protective standards contained in the casual work agenda is certainly helpful in advancing the labour protection of platform workers. In particular, this agenda offers important legal avenues to reduce *working time insecurity*, which is inherent in casual work arrangements. At the EU level, the TPWCD is particularly insightful in reducing this insecurity, through protective standards such as the provision of an advance notice and pre-established reference hours and days. The Dutch agenda on casual work further contributes in this regard through the enshrinement of some minimum guaranteed or fixed working hours, after a certain duration of time. The Working Time Directive then points out the importance of paying stand-by time, something highlighted extensively in its jurisprudence.

Furthermore, the casual work agenda also offers solutions to reduce the work and income insecurity of casual and platform workers. Inspiring in terms of reducing *work insecurity* is the anti-abuse clause contained in the FTWD. An update of this legal provision is necessary in light of the short-termism underpinning platform work. More specifically, an update is needed in relation to the legal measures contained therein, and the consequences in case an abuse in the use of successive contracts/tasks is detected. The work security of platform workers would be enhanced if a sufficient volume of work is ensured after an abuse has been identified. This happens in the Netherlands, where some minimum guaranteed and fixed working hours are provided in case a maximum duration of the work has been reached. Concerning the *income insecurity* problem, some domestic regulatory responses to casual work can be valuable. The Italian and Dutch schemes, respectively provide a monthly payment in case the worker accepts to be available for offers of work, and three hours paid work for work which lasts less than three hours. On the other side, it should be acknowledged that, the casual work agenda only scarcely contributes to the issue of the *employment status insecurity*. This issue can arguably find a better response in the EU dPWD.

To sum up, these protective standards, in their totality, highlight the relevance of the casual work agenda in advancing the labour protection of platform workers. Nevertheless, it is also paramount to improve the casual work agenda *per se*, especially the TPWCD, which should enhance the protections against work insecurity, and find ways to deal with income insecurity. Finally, it is important, for this set of protections contained in the casual work agenda, to be materialized in regulatory efforts which govern platform work, such as the dPWD.

Can the Casual Work Agenda Contribute to Enhancing the Labour Protection of Platform Workers?

Having regard to the above-mentioned responses to the sub-research questions, the answer to the principal research question is affirmative: the casual work agenda offers valuable contributions to improve the labour protection of platform workers. While the identification of loopholes in the casual work agenda should certainly not be overlooked, it does not undermine the importance of these regulatory strategies in the pathway to better labour protection for platform workers. In order to effectively contribute to this goal, lessons learned from the casual work agenda should be incorporated into the regulatory strategies on platform work, with the prominent example of the draft Directive on Platform Work.

3 RECOMMENDATIONS FOR REDEFINING THE AGENDA ON PLATFORM WORK

The casual work agenda is self-evidently crucial to understanding and regulating platform work. In this crucial concept of casual work, the research shows that some key elements are not yet subject to regulation in many national or EU legal systems. In this regard, the three elements that have come to the fore are insecurity, stand-by time, and work insecurity. It is in light of these three elements that recommendations to redefine the agenda on platform work have been formulated. Until now, this agenda has been mainly represented by the draft EU directive on platform work. Hence, these recommendations are primarily addressed to this legal initiative.

3.1 The dPWD Should Explicitly Acknowledge the Insecure Nature Inherent in Platform Work and the Solutions Available in the TPWCD

First of all, it is obvious that the dPWD does not understand platform work as part of broader trends of casual work arrangements. This legal instrument does not explicitly recognize the insecure nature inherent in platform work, composed of insecurities such as that of working hours, jobs, and income. Instead, the dPWD only points out the employment status insecurity and proposes a rebuttable legal presumption of an employment relationship as a solution to it. As the situation stands, platform workers are currently facing a dispersal of their legal protections in two EU legal instruments, namely the dPWD (basic labour protections) and TPWCD (targeted labour protections to their specific needs). This dispersal creates confusion and makes these protections weaker in practice.

This approach needs to be drastically modified. Adding a legal provision in the dPWD, which explicitly recognizes the insecure nature of platform work and the protections contained for this purpose in the TPWCD, is essential. Platform workers need to be aware that rights, such as the right to reference hours and days, to a reasonable advance notice, and to request transition to more predictable and secure employment, are fully applicable to them. This does not, in any way, mean that these protections do not need to be broadened. As pointed out before, there might also be some room for improvement regarding the TPWCD. This legal instrument seems to, in particular, offer weak protection against jobs insecurity, and no protection at all against the income insecurity' issues identified in this dissertation. Strengthening such protections represents an important step in the pathway towards better labour protection for casual and platform workers.

3.2 The dPWD Should Provide for the Recognition and Payment of Stand-by Time of Platform Workers

The dPWD does not incorporate any considerations on the working time of platform workers at all, let alone on the stand-by time of platform workers. Therefore, the latter issue still constitutes an unclear grey area for these workers. It is paramount, therefore, for EU legislators to react to this problem. This can be done by including a legal measure in the dPWD, which provides for the recognition and payment of stand-by time. Payment should not be limited only to the actual work, e.g., a delivery performed, but it should also extend to the availability and preparation time needed for that delivery. The details of this legal measure need to be worked out by the legislator.

3.3 The dPWD Should Consider the Anti-abuse Clause as a Building Block for Addressing the Work Insecurity of Platform Workers

As highlighted on several occasions in this dissertation, platform and casual workers face a serious problem of work insecurity. Some inspiration for addressing this issue can be found in the anti-abuse clause contained in the FTWD. Nevertheless, EU legislators should certainly consider updating this rule in the specific context of platform work, where the 'short-termism' pattern is predominant. For instance, the current legal measures enshrined in the anti-abuse clause of the FTWD need an update, as they were designed to address traditional forms of flexibility, instead of the overflexibility characterizing the platform work model. In particular, the measures providing for a maximum number of renewals of contracts/tasks, and a maximum duration of them, need to be suitable for the short-term contracts encountered in a platform work setting. Furthermore, in case an abuse arising from the completion of successive tasks which transfer the risk from the employer to the worker has been detected, then some work security should be ensured for the worker. Inspirational in this regard can be the Dutch regulatory model, according to which, after a maximum duration of the on-call work relation, a sufficient volume of work, in the form of minimum guaranteed or fixed working hours, should be ensured to the workers. In light of these considerations, the dPWD should consider delivering work security to platform workers, at least in the form of security about the volume of work.

4 FINAL OBSERVATIONS

This research has shown that the casual work agenda is helpful in advancing the labour protection of platform workers. This casual work agenda does not only provide guidance for the regulatory strategies, and to identify and understand the legal challenges related to platform work, but it also gives better insight into the approaches of the dPWD. This draft legislation is clearly not a full response to the challenges of platform work. This research has made an attempt to address a series of key challenges, taking into account the lack of security related to work and working conditions in the platform world. There are self-evidently many other legal challenges related to a platform work agenda, including – for example – the role of minimum wages, work-life balance, privacy protection, or collective rights.

Taking into account the limits of this research, at least a number of recommendations can be made to improve the regulation of platform work in light of the casual work agenda. To this end, a platform work-related legal initiative should provide a response to the following key legal issues and challenges:

- The insecure nature of platform work: the dPWD should explicitly acknowledge this dimension and the full applicability of the protections contained for this purpose in the TPWCD.
- The unpaid stand-by time of platform workers: the dPWD should provide for the recognition and payment of stand-by time of platform workers.
- The work insecurity experienced by platform workers: the dPWD should consider the anti-abuse clause as a way to address the work insecurity of platform workers and ensure them with at least some security about the volume of the work.

In case no action on these issues is taken, the available protection for platform workers will remain incomplete, scattered, give rise to confusion and make the legal protection of platform work weaker in practice. The contribution that this set of regulatory strategies can make will lead toward an enriched legal landscape for platform workers and lay a better foundation for a sustainable and responsible platform economy.

Bibliography

Books

Barnard, C., *EU Employment Law*, Oxford University Press, 4th ed., 2012, p. 426.
Bell, M., Ales, E., Deinert, O., Robin-Olivier, S., *International and European Labour Law, Article-by-Article Commentary*, Bloomsbury Publishing, 2018.
Casale, G., *The Employment Relationship: A Comparative Overview*, Oxford Hart Publishing, ILO, Geneva, 2011.
Collins, H., Ewing, K., Mccolgan, A., *Labour Law*, Cambridge University Press, 2012.
Countouris, N., *The Changing Law of the Employment Relationship. Comparative Analyses in the European Context*, Studies in Modern Law and Policy, Aldershot Ashgate, 2007.
De Stefano, V., and Aloisi, A., *Il lavoro che vogliamo, governare le technologie per reinventare il futuro*, Laterza, 2020.
Deakin, S., Morris, G., *Labour Law*, Hart Publishing, 6th ed., 2012.
Esping-Anderson, 'The Three Worlds of Welfare State Capitalism', Princeton University Press, 1990.
Freedland, M., & Countouris, N., *The Legal Construction of Personal Work Relations*, Oxford University Press, 2012.
Hendrickx, F., *Handbook on European Labour Law*, (2011).
Hyman, L., *How American Work, American Business and the American Dream Became Temporary*, Penguin Random House, (2018).
Hendrickx, F. (ed.), *International Encyclopedia for Labour Law and Industrial Relations*, Wolters Kluwer.
Jensen, V., 'Hiring of Dock Workers and Employment Practices in the Ports of New York, Liverpool, London, Rotterdam, and Marseilles', *Harvard University Press*, 1964.
Kestemont, L., *Handbook on Legal Methodology. From objective to Method*, Intersentia, 2018.
Mayhew, H., 'The Morning Chronicle Survey of Labour and the Poor', *The Metropolitan Districts*, Vol. 6, 2016, Routledge.

O'Sullivan, M., Lavelle, J., Mcmahon, J., Ryan, L., Murphy, C., Turner, T., Gunnigle, P., eds, *Zero Hours and On-call Work in Anglo-saxon Countries*, 2019, Springer.

Riesenhuber, K., *European Employment Law*, Intersentia, 2012.

Standing, G., *The Precariat: The New Dangerous Class*, Bloomsbury Publishing, 2011.

Stone, K.V.W. & Arthurs, H., eds, *Rethinking Workplace Regulation: Beyond the Standard Contract of Employment*, New York: Russell Sage Foundation, 2013.

Supiot, A., *Beyond Employment: Changes in Work and the Future of Labour Law in Europe*, Oxford University Press, 2001.

Prassl, J., *Humans as a Service. The Promise and Perils of Work in the Gig Economy*, Oxford University Press, 2018.

Wouters, M., 'International Labour Standards and Platform Work. An Analysis of Digital Labour Platforms Based on the Instruments on Private Employment Agencies, Home Work and Domestic Work', *Bulletin of Comparative Labour Relations*, Vol. 110, 2021.

Book Chapters

Adams, A., Adams, Z. & Prassl, J., 'Legitimizing Precarity: Zero-Hours Contracts in the United Kingdom', in *Zero Hours and on Call Work In Anglo-Saxon Countries*, eds O'Sullivan, M., Lavelle, J., Mcmahon, J., Ryan, L., Murphy, C., Turner, T., and Gunnigle, P., Springer, 2019, pp. 41-65.

Blanpain, R., 'Belgium', in *International Encyclopedia for Labour Law and Industrial Relations*, ed. Hendrickx, F., Kluwer Law Online, 2012.

Bogg, A., Buendia Esteban, R., 'The Law and Worker Voice in the Platform Economy', in *A Research Agenda for the Gig-economy and Society*, eds V. De Stefano, I. Durri, C. Stylogiannis, M., Wouters, 2022.

Campbell, I., Zero-Hours Work Arrangements in New Zealand: Union Action, Public Controversy and Two Regulatory initiatives, In *Zero-hours and On-call Work in Anglo – Saxon countries*, eds M. O'Sullivan et al., Springer, 2019.

Cefaliello, A., Inversi, C., 'The Impact of the Gig-economy on Occupational Health & Safety: Just an Occupation Hazard?', In *A Research Agenda for the Gig-economy and Society*, eds V. De Stefano, I. Durri, C. Stylogiannis, M. Wouters, Edward Elgar Publishing, 2022.

Davies, A., 'Regulating Atypical Work: Beyond Equality', In *Resocialising Europe in a Time of Crisis*, eds Countouris, N., and Freedland, M., Cambridge University Press, 2013.

De Stefano, V., Durri, I., Stylogiannis, C., Wouters, M., 'Exclusion by Default: Platform Workers' Quest for Labour Protections', In *A Research agenda for the gig economy and society*, eds V. De Stefano, I. Durri, C. Stylogiannis, M. Wouters, Edward Elgar Publishing, 2022.

Dukes, R., 'On Demand Work as a Legal Framework to Understand the Gig Economy', In *A Research Agenda for the Gig Economy and Society*, eds V. De Stefano, I. Durri, C. Stylogiannis, M. Wouters, Edward Elgar Publishing, 2022.

Hendrickx, F., 'Regulating Flexicurity and Responsive Labour Law', In *Flexicurity and the Lisbon Agenda, A Cross-disciplinary Reflection*, ed. F. Hendrickx, Intersentia, Social Europe Series, No. 17, 2008, pp. 123-161.

Kenner, J., 'Inverting the Flexicurity Paradigm: The United Kingdom and Zero Hours Contracts', In *Core and Contingent Work in the European Union: A Comparative Analysis*, eds Ales, E., Deinert, O., and Kenner, J., Oxford: Hart Publishing, Bloomsbury Collections, 2017, pp. 153-184.

O'Sullivan, M., 'Introduction to Zero Hours and On-call Work in Anglo-Saxon Countries', In *Zero Hours and on Call Work in Anglo-Saxon Countries*, eds O'Sullivan, M., et al., Springer, 2019.

Ratti, L., 'Crowdwork and Work On-demand in the European Legal Framework: Promises and Expectations', In *Platform Work in Europe: Towards Harmonization?*, eds Carinci, M. T., and Dorssemont, F., Intersentia, 2021.

Stevens, Y., Put, J., 'Het laatste heilige huisje: professionele apartheid in de sociale zekerheid', In *De taal is gans het recht*, eds R. De Corte, M. De Vos, P. Humblet, F. Kéfer and E. Van Hoorde, Liber Amicorum Willy van Eeckhoutte, Mechelen, Kluwer, 2018.

Travieso, M.M., 'Regulating Technology at Work', In *Regulating the Platform Economy: International Perspectives on New Forms of Work*, eds Mella Mendez, L., Routledge, 2020.

Van Voss, G.H, Atypical Employment Relationships: The Position in the Netherlands, In *Restatement of Labour Law in Europe: Atypical Employment Relationships*, eds Waas, B., and Van Vosshendric Stolzenberg, G.H., Assisted by. Oxford: Hart Publishing, 2019, pp. 591-622.

Journal Articles

Adams, A., Freedland, M., and Prassl, J., 'The "Zero-hours Contract": Regulating Casual Work, or Legitimating Precarity?', *Oxford Legal Studies*, Research Paper No. 11/2015, 2015.

Adams-Prassl, A., Boneva, T., Golin, M., and Rauh, C., 'Inequality in the Impact of the Coronavirus Shock: New Survey Evidence for the UK', *IZA Discussion Paper* No. 13183, 2020.

Albin, E., and Prassl, J., 'Fragmenting Work, Fragmented Regulation: The Contract of Employment as a Driver of Social Exclusion', *Hebrew University of Jerusalem Legal Studies* Research Paper Series No. 17-39, 2015.

Aloisi, A., 'Platform Work in Europe: Lessons Learned, Legal Developments and Challenges Ahead', *European Labour Law Journal*, Vol. 13 Issue 1, 2022, pp. 4-29.

Bano, F., 'Contratti flessibili: Lavoro a tempo parziale e lavoro intermittente', *Lavoro e diritto*, 2-3/2006, 2006.

Barnard, C., 'New Forms of Employment in the United Kingdom', *Bulletin of Comparative Labour Relations*, New Forms of Employment in Europe, 2016.

Basselier, R., Langenus, G., and Walravens, L., 'The Rise of the Sharing Economy', *Economic Review*, Vol. 3, 2018.

Bednarowicz, B., 'Delivering on the European Pillar of Social Rights: The New Directive on Transparent and Predictable Working Conditions in the European Union', *Industrial Law Journal*, Vol. 48 Issue 4, 2019, pp. 604-623.

Bennaars, H., 'COVID-19 and Labour Law in the Netherlands, *European Labour Law Journal*, Vol. 11 Issue 3, 2020, pp. 324-331.

Bosch, G., 'Towards a New Standard Employment Relationship in Western Europe', *British Journal of Industrial Relations*, Vol. 42 Issue 4, 2004, pp. 617-636.

Campbell, I., 'Casualised Work Arrangements in Developed Societies: Historical Parallels and New Regulatory Challenges', Forthcoming.

Countouris, N., 'The Concept of 'Worker' in European Labour Law: Fragmentation, Autonomy and Scope', *Industrial Law Journal*, Vol. 47 Issue 2, 2018, pp. 192-225.

Countouris, N., 'The Legal Determinants of Precariousness in Personal Work Relations: A European Perspective', *Comparative Labor Law & Policy Journal*, Vol. 34 Issue 1, 2012, pp. 21-46.

De Stefano, V. 'Casual Work Beyond Casual Work in the EU: The Underground Casualization of The European Workforce – and What to do about it', *European Labour Law Journal*, Vol. 7, Issue 3, 2016, pp. 421-441.

De Stefano, V., and Aloisi, A., 'Fundamental Labour Rights, Platform Work and Human-rights Protection of Non-standard Workers', *Bocconi Legal Studies Research Paper No. 3125866*, 2018.

De Stefano, V., 'Introduction: Crowdsourcing, the Gig Economy and the Law', *Comparative Labor Law and Policy Journal*, Vol. 37 Issue 3, 2016, pp. 461-471.

De Stefano, V., 'Labour is not a Technology: Reasserting the Declaration of Philadelphia in Times of Platform-work and Gig-economy', *IUSLabor 2*, 2017, pp. 1-17.

De Stefano, V., 'Smuggling Flexibility: Temporary Working Contracts and the 'Implicit Threat' Mechanism', *Bocconi Legal Studies Research Paper Series*, No. 1433350, 2009.

De Stefano, V., 'The Rise of the "Just-in-time Workforce": On-demand Work, Crowdwork and Labour Protection in the Gig-economy', *International Labour Office, Inclusive Labour Markets, Labour Relations and Working Conditions Branch-Geneva: ILO, Conditions of Work and Employment Series*; Issue 71, 2016.

Deakin, S., 'New Forms of Employment: Implications for EU Law – The Law as it Stands', *Bulletin of Comparative Labour Relations*, New Forms of Employment in Europe, 2016.

Dermine, E., and Mechelynck, A., 'Regulating Zero-hour Contracts in Belgium: From a Defensive to a (too?) Supportive Approach?', *European Labour Law Journal*, Vol. 13 Issue 3, 2022, pp. 400-430.

Dukes, R., 'Regulating Gigs', *Modern Law Review*, Vol. 83 Issue 1, 2019, pp. 217-228.

Fabrellas, A., 'The Zero-hour Contract in Platform Work. Should We Ban it or Embrace it?', *IDP*: Revista de Internet, Derecho e Politica 28, 2019.

Fredman, S., 'Labour Law in Flux: The Changing Composition of the Workforce', *Industrial Law Journal*, Vol. 26 Issue 4, 1997, pp. 337-353.

Freedland, M. and Prassl, J., 'Employees, Workers and the Sharing Economy, Changing Practices and Changing Concepts in the UK', *Spanish Labour Law and Employment Relations Journal*, Vol. 6, Issue 1-2, 2017.

Freedland, M., 'New Trade Union Strategies for New Forms of Employment: A Brief Analytical and Normative Framework', *European Labour Law Journal*, Vol. 10 Issue 3), 2019, pp. 179-182.

Freedland, M., 'Rethinking the Personal Work Contract', Current Legal Problems, *Oxford University Press*, Vol. 58 Issue 1, 2005, pp. 517-542.

Freedland, M., 'The Contract of Employment and the Paradoxes of Precarity', *University of Oxford, Legal Research Paper Series*, Paper No. 37/2016, (2016).

Georiou, D., 'The New EU Directive on Transparent and Predictable Working Conditions in the Context of New Forms of Employment, *European Journal of Industrial Relations*, Vol. 28 Issue 2, 2022, pp. 193-210.

Goldfays, M., 'Travailleurs à la demande – zero-hours contracts', *Kluwer-Orientations* 2014/8, 2014.

Hendrickx, F., 'Foundations and Functions of Contemporary Labour Law', *European Labour Law Journal*, Vol. 3 Issue 2, 2012, pp. 108-127.

Hendrickx, F., Taes, S., and Wouters, M., 'Covid-19 and Labour Law in Belgium', *European Labour Law Journal*, Vol. 11 Issue 3, 2020, pp. 276-285.

Hendrickx, F., 'The European Social Pillar: A First Evaluation', *European Labour Law Journal*, Vol. 9 Issue I), 2018, pp. 3-6.

Kamanabrou, S., 'Successful Rules on Successive Fixed-term Contracts?', *International Journal of Comparative Labour Law and Industrial Relations*, Vol. 33, Issue 2, 2017, 2017, pp. 221-240.

Kenner, J., 'Re-evaluating the Concept of Working Time: An Analysis of Recent Case Law', *Industrial Relations Journal*, Vol. 35 Issue 6, 2004, pp. 588-602.

Kullman, M., 'Platformisation of Work: An EU Perspective on Introducing a Legal Presumption', *European Labour Law Journal*, Vol. 13 Issue 1, 2021, pp. 66-80.

Novitz, T., 'Gig Work as a Manifestation of Short-Termism: Crafting a Sustainable Regulatory Agenda', *Industrial Law Journal*, Vol. 50 Issue 4, 2021, pp. 636-661.

Novitz, T., 'The Potential for International Regulation of Gig Economy Issues', *King's Law Journal*, Vol. 31, Issue 2, 2020, pp. 275-286.

Prassl, J., 'Pimlico Plumbers, Uber Drivers, Cycle Couriers, and Court Translators: Who Is a Worker?', *Oxford Legal Studies Research Paper* No. 25/2017, (2017).

Prassl, J., 'What If Your Boss Is an Algorithm: Economic Incentives, Legal Challenges and the Rise of Artificial Intelligence at Work', *Comparative Labor Law and Policy Journal* Vol. 41 Issue 1, 2019, pp. 123-146.

Rauws, W., 'New Forms of Employment in Belgium', *Bulletin of Comparative Labour Relations*, New forms of employment in Europe, eds Blanpain, R., and Hendrickx, F., 2016.

Rosin, A., 'Platform Work and Fixed-term Employment Regulation', *European Labour Law Journal*, Vol. 12 Issue 2, 2021, pp. 156-176.

Rymkevich, O., 'The Impact of Atypical Work in Italy and Russia', *European Labour Law Journal*, Vol. 7 Issue 1, 2016, pp. 81-108.

Schoukens, P. and Arrio, A., 'The Changing Concept of Work: When Does Typical Work Become Atypical?, *European Labour Law Journal*, Vol. 8 Issue 4, 2017, pp. 306-332.

Siberman, S., Irani, L., 'Operating an Employer Reputation System: Lessons from Turkopticon', 2008-2015, *Comparative Labour Law and Policy*, Vol. 37, Issue 3, 2016, pp. 505-542.

Stanford, J., 'The Resurgence of Gig Work: Historical and Theoretical Perspectives', *The Economic and Labour Relations Review*, Vol. 28 Issue 3, 2017.

Supiot, A., 'On the Job: Time for Agreement', *International Journal of Comparative Labour Law and Industrial Relations*, Vol. 12, Issue 3, 1996.

TassinariI, A., Maccarone, V., 'The Mobilisation of Gig Economy Couriers in Italy: Some Lessons for the Trade Union Movement', *Transfer: European Review of Labour and Research*, 3/2017, (2017).

Ter Haar, B., 'Covid-19 and Labour Law: The Netherlands', *Italian Labour Law e-Journal*, Vol. 13, Special Issue 1, 2020.

Wouters, M., and Pecinovsky, P., 'Marginal Part-time in Europe: 2018's Expansion of Flexi-jobs in Belgium', *Comparative Labor Law and Policy Journal*, iss. Dispatch No. 9, (2018).

Zappala, L., 'The Temporary Agency Workers' Directive: An Impossible Political Agreement?, *Industrial Law Journal*, Vol. 32 Issue 4, pp. 310-317.

Reports and Papers

Adams, A., and Prassl, J., *Zero-Hours Work in the United Kingdom*, ILO, (2018).

Berg, J., Furrer, M., Harmon, E., Rani, U. and Silberman, M.S., *Digital Labour Platforms and the Future of Work, Towards Decent Work in the Online World*, ILO, (2018).

Berg, J., *Income Security in the On-demand Economy: Findings and Policy Lessons from a Survey of Crowdworkers*, International Labour Office, (2016).

Brinkley, I., *Flexibility or Insecurity? Exploring the Rise in Zero Hours Contracts*, The Work Foundation, (2013).

Buffel, V., and Nicaise, I., *In-work Poverty in Belgium*, European Social Policy Network, (2019).

Burri, S., Heeger-Hertter, S., and Rossetti, S., *On-call Work in the Netherlands: Trends, Impacts and Policy Solutions*, ILO Working Paper, (2018).

Campbell, I., *On-call and Related Forms of Casual Work in New Zealand and Australia*, International Labour Organization, (2018).

Choudar, S. P., *The Architecture of Digital Labour Platforms: Policy Recommendations on Platform Design for Worker Wellbeing*, ILO Future of Work Research Paper Series, (2018).

Ceneri, G., Rausei, P., *Il lavoro intermittente e la forza della contrattazione aziendale*, ADAPT, (2018).

CIPD, *To Gig or Not to Gig? Stories from the Modern Economy*, Survey Report, (2017).

CIPD, *Zero-hours Contracts: Myth and Reality*, Research Report, (2013).

Codagnone, C., Abadie, F., and Biagi, F., *The Future of Work in the Sharing Economy. Market Efficiency and Equitable Opportunities or Unfair Precarisation*, JRC, (2016).

Conseil National du Travail, Conseil Central de l' Economie, Rapport No. 107, *Diagnostic des partenaires sociaux concernant la digitalisation et l'économie collaborative: Execution de l'accord interprofessionnel 2017-2018*, (2017).

Countouris, N., *Defining and Regulating Work Relations for the Future of Work*, ILO, Geneva, (2019).

Cutean, A., Herron, C., and Quan, T., *Loading: The Future of Work: Worldwide Remote Work Experimentation and the Evolution of the Platform Economy*, Information and Communications Technology Council (ICTC), Ottawa, Canada, (2020).

De Becker, A., De Coninck, M., *New Employment Forms and Challenges to Industrial Relations, Country Report Belgium*, NEWEFIN Project, (2020).

De Stefano, V., Aloisi, A., *Employment and Working Conditions of Selected Types of Platform Work, National context analysis Italy*, Eurofound Working Paper, (2018).

De Stefano, V., and Aloisi, A., *European Legal framework for digital labour platforms*, European Commission, Luxembourg, (2018).

De Stefano, V., and Countouris, N., 'New Trade Union Strategies for New Forms of Employment', *ETUC*, Brussels, 2019.

De Stefano, V., Durri, I., Stylogiannis, C., Wouters, M., *Platform Work and the Employment Relationship*, ILO Working Paper 27, (2021).

Haipeter, T., Owczarek, D., Faioli, M., and Iudicone, F. (eds), *Don't Gig Up! Project*, Final Report, (2020).

Drahokoupil, J., Piasna, A., *Work in the Platform Economy: Deliveroo Riders in Belgium and the Smart Arrangement*, ETUI Working Paper 2019.01, (2019).

Eurofound, *Aspects of Non-standard Employment in Europe*, Publications Office of the European Union, Luxembourg, (2017).

Eurofound, *Back to the Future: Policy Pointers from Platform Work Scenarios*, New forms of employment series, Publications Office of the European Union, Luxembourg, (2020).

Eurofound, *Employment and Working Conditions of Selected Types of Platform Work*, Publications Office of the European Union, Luxembourg, (2018).

Eurofound, *Flexible Forms of Work: 'Very Atypical' Contractual Arrangements*, (2010).

Eurofound, *Italy: New voucher-based Scheme Provokes Debate*, (2017).

Eurofound, *New Forms of Employment*, Publications Office of the European Union, Luxembourg, (2015).

Eurofound, *Non-standard Forms of Employment: Recent Trends and Future Prospects*, (2018).

Eurofound, *Platform Economy: Developments in the Covid-19 Crisis*, (2020).

Eurofound, *Platform Work: Maximizing the Potential While Safeguarding Standards?*, (2019).

Eurofound, *Work on Demand: Recurrence, Effects and Challenges*, Publication Office of the European Union, Luxembourg, (2018).

Eurofound, *Casual Work: Characteristics and Implications*, New forms of employments series, Publications Office of the European Union, Luxembourg, (2019).

Eurofound, *Living and Working in the Netherlands*, (2020).

European Parliament, Directorate General for Research, *Atypical Work in the EU*, Working Paper, (2000).

European Parliament, Directorate General for Internal Policies, *The Social Protection of Workers in the Platform Economy*, (2017).

European Parliament, *Precarious Employment in Europe: Patterns, Trends and Policy Strategies*, Study for EMPL Committee, (2016).

European Parliament, *Temporary Contracts, Precarious Employment, Employees' Fundamental Rights and EU Employment Law*, Study for the PETI Committee, (2017).

European Social Policy Network, *New Dutch Draft Law to Reduce the Gap Between Permanent and Flexible Contracts*, ESPN Flash Report 2018/67, (2018).

Field, F., and Forsey, A., *Sweated Labour: Uber and the 'Gig economy'*, Business and Human Rights Resource Centre, (2016).

Global Commission on the Future of Work, *Work for a Bright Future*, International Labour Office - Geneva: ILO, (2019).

Government of the UK, *Good work: a response to the Taylor Review of modern working practices*, (2018).

Hauben, H., Lenaerts, K., Wayert, W., *The Platform Economy and Precarious Work*, Study for the EMPL Committee, (2020).

Huws, U., Spencer, N.H., Syrdal, S.D., Holts, K., *Work in the European Gig Economy*, FEPS, UNI-Europa and University of Hertfordshire, (2017).

ILC 109/iii(b) - *Promoting Employment and Decent Work in a Changing Landscape*, 2020.

INPS (Istituto nazionale della previdenza sociale), XVII Rapporto Annuale, *L'INPS al servizio del Paese*, (2018).

International Labour Office, Governance and Tripartism Department, *Regulating the Employment Relationship in Europe: A Guide to Recommendation No. 198*, Geneva, ILO, (2013).

International Labour Office - Geneva: ILO, *World Employment and Social Outlook 2021: The Role of Digital Labour Platforms in Transforming the World of Work*, (2021).

International Labour Office-Geneva, *Non-standard Employment Around the World: Understanding Challenges, Shaping Prospects*, (2016).

Istat, *Rapporto Il mercato del lavoro 2018. Verso una lettura integrate*, (2019).

Kilhoffer, Z., De Groen, W., Lenaerts, K., Smits, I., Hauben, H., Waeyaert, W., Giacumacatos, E., Lhernould, J.-P., and Robin-Olivier, S., *Study to Gather Evidence on the Working Conditions of Platform Workers*, Luxembourg, Publications Office of the European Union, (2020).

Kilhoffer, Z., and Lenaerts, K., *What Is Happening with Platform Workers' Rights?, Lessons from Belgium*, CEPS Publications, (2017).

Kremer, M., Went, R., Knottnerus, A., *For the Sake of Security, the Future of Flexible Workers and the Modern Organization of Labour*, The Netherlands Scientific Council for Government Policy (WRR), The Hague, (2017).

Marmot, M., Goldblatt, P., and Allen, J., *Fair Society, Healthy Lives: (The Marmot Review)*, Strategic Review of Health Inequalities in England post-2010, (2010).

Marx, I., and Vandelannoote, D., *Matthew Runs Amok: The Belgian Service Voucher Scheme*, IZA Working Paper, (2014).

Messenger, J., and Wallot, P., *The Diversity of Marginal Part-time*, INWORK Policy Brief No. 7, ILO, (2015).

Nautet, M., and Piton, C., *An Analysis of Non-standard Forms of Employment in Belgium*, NBB Economic Review, (2019).

OECD, *Employment Outlook 2019: The Future of Work*, (2019).

OECD, *Input to the Netherlands Independent Commission on the Regulation of Work*, (2019).

OECD, *Policy Responses to New Forms of Work*, OECD Publishing, Paris, (2019).

ONS, *Contracts that Do Not Guarantee a Minimum Number of Hours*, (2018).

ONS, *EMP17: People in Employment on Zero-Hours Contracts*, (2019).

Pesole A., Urzi Brancati, M.C., Fernandez Macias, E., Biagi, F., and Gonzalez Vazquez, I., *Platform Workers in Europe, Evidence from the COLLEEM Survey*, Publications Office of the European Union, Luxembourg, (2018).

Pickavance, N., *Zeroed Out: The Place of Zero Hours Contracts in a Fair and Productive Economy*, (2014).

Rasche, M., *Coronavirus Highlights Sick Pay Void for Platform Workers*, Eurofound publications, (2020).

Risak, M., *Fair Working Conditions for Platform Workers: Possible Regulatory Approaches at the EU Level*, Friedrich-Ebert Stiftung, (2017).

Rodgers, G., *Precarious Jobs in Labour Market Regulation: The Growth of Atypical Employment in Western Europe*, Brussels, International Institute for Labour Studies, Free University of Brussels, ILO (1989).

Seo economisch onderzoek, *De opkomst en groei van kluseconomie in Nederland, in opdracht van Ministerie van Sociale Zaken en Werkgelegenheid*, Amsterdam, (2018).

Six Silberman, M., and Johnston, H., *Using GDPR to Improve Legal Clarity and Working Conditions on Digital Labour Platforms*, ETUI Working Paper, No. 5, (2020).

Study for the European Economic and Social Committee (EESC), *The Definition of Worker in the Platform Economy. Exploring Workers' Risks and Regulatory Solutions*, (2021).

Szpejna, M., and Boualaoui-Buresi, Z., *The Scope of EU Labour Law: Who Is Not Covered by Key Directives?*, Publication for the committee on Employment and Social Affairs, Policy Department for Economic, Scientific and Quality of Life Policies, European Parliament, Luxembourg, (2020).

Taylor, M., *Good Work: The Taylor Review of Modern Working Practices*, (2017).

Fairwork, *The Gig-economy and Covid 19: Looking Ahead*, Oxford, United Kingdom, (2020).

Van Guys, G., *Belgium: Flexible Forms of Work: Very 'Atypical' Contractual Arrangements*, Eurofound Report, (2010).

Vaughan, R. and, Daveio, R., *Assessing the Size and Presence of the Collaborative Economy in Europe*, PwC UK, Impulse Paper for the European Commission, (2016).

Wood, A., and Burchell, B., *Zero Hours Contracts as a Source of Job Insecurity Amongst Low Paid Hourly Workers*, University of Cambridge, Individual in the Labour Market Research Group, (2014).

EU Policy Documents

Analytical document, Accompanying the consultation document of social partners under Article 154 TFEU on a possible action addressing the challenges related to working conditions in platform work, 2021.

Commission Communication COM (2003) 843 on the re-examination of Directive 93/104/EC.

Commission of the European Communities, *Proposal for a Council Directive concerning the Framework Agreement on Fixed-term Work*, 1999.

Commission Staff Working Document, Analytical Document, Accompanying the Consultation Document on a possible revision of the WSD in the framework of the EPSR, (2017).

Commission staff working document, REFIT evaluation of the Written Statement Directive, (2017).

Commission, 'Communication from the Commission to the European Parliament, the Council, the European Economic and Social Committee and the Committee of the Regions, Establishing a European Pillar of Social Rights' COM (2017) 250 final.

Communication on Regulatory Fitness and Performance (REFIT): Results and Next Steps', COM (2013) 685.

Council of the European Union, *Proposal for a Directive of the European Parliament and of the Council on transparent and predictable working conditions in the European Union – General approach*, Inter-institutional File: 2017/0355 (COD), 2018, 10054/18.

EC Flash Eurobarometer 438 (2016) and 467 (2018) – The use of collaborative platforms.

EU Commission, *Green Paper Modernising Labour Law to Meet the Challenges of the 21st Century*, COM (2006) 708 FINAL.

European Commission, *Background paper for first-stage consultations with social partners, Flexibility in working time and security for workers*, 1995.

European Commission, *Flash reports on labour law*, (2017).

European Parliament resolution of 15 June 2017 on a European Agenda for the collaborative economy (2017/2003(INI)).

European Parliament resolution of 4 July 2017 on working conditions and precarious employment (2016/2221(INI)).

Evaluative Study of Directive 1997/81/EC (supplemented by Directive 98/23/EC) on Part-Time Work and Directive 1999/70/ EC on Fixed-Term Work, Updated Final report submitted by ICF International, 2016.

Explanatory memorandum concerning the proposal for a Council Directive concerning certain aspects of the organization of working time, 20 September 1990, COM(90) 317 final – SYN 295.

Explanatory Memorandum of the Platform Work Directive.

Factsheet: Towards transparent and predictable working conditions (2019).

Interpretative Communication on Directive 2003/88/EC of the European Parliament and of the Council concerning certain aspects of the organization of working time, C/2017/2601.

Mission letter to the Commissioner for Jobs, (2019).

Political guidelines 2019-2024 'A Union that strives for more – My agenda for Europe'.

Opinion of Advocate General *Szpunar* on Case C-434/15, *Asociación Profesional Elite Taxi v. Uber Systems Spain SL*, 2017.

Refit Study to support the evaluation of the Written Statement Directive, Final report, (2016).

Report Expert Group, *Transposition of Directive (EU) 2019/1152 on Transparent and Predictable Working Conditions in the European Union*, 2021.

Online Sources

Adams, Z., and Deakin, S., Work is intermittent but capital is not: what to do about zero hours contracts, Institute of Employment Rights, Available at: https://www.ier.org.uk/comments/work-intermittent-capital-not-what-do-about-zero-hours-contracts/ (2014).

Aloisi, A., and De Stefano, V., Delivering employment rights to platform workers, Il Mulino, Available at: https://www.rivistailmulino.it/news/newsitem/index/Item/News:NEWS_ITEM:5018, (2020).

Aloisi, A., and Georgiou, D., Two steps forward, one step back: The EU's plans for improving gig working conditions, Ada Lovelace Institute, Available at: https://www.adalovelaceinstitute.org/blog/eu-gig-economy/, (2022).

Aloisi, A., De Stefano, V., Silberman, S., A manifesto to reform the gig economy, Regulating for Globalization, Available at: http://regulatingforglobalization.com/2019/05/01/a-manifesto-to-reform-the-gig-economy/ (2019).

Arteaga, A., Platform economy in the Netherlands: Deliveroo rider is self-employed, Terralex, Available at: https://www.terralex.org/tlglobal/publications/platform-economy-in-the-netherlands-deliveroo-rider-is-self-employed, (2018).

Balmer, C., Italy scraps employment voucher system to avoid referendum showdown, Reuters, Available at: https://www.reuters.com/article/uk-italy-employment-reform-idUKKBN16O1UV, (2017).

Barbieri, F., Lavoro a chiamata dal turismo alla sanita, Il sole 24 ore, Available at: https://www.ilsole24ore.com/art/-lavoro-chiamata-turismo-sanita-AEcBqTKH, (2019).

Berg, J., and De Stefano, V., La gig-economy e il 'nuovo' lavoro occasionale, Eticaeconomia, Available at: https://archivio.eticaeconomia.it/la-gig-economy-e-il-nuovo-lavoro-occasionale/, (2017).

Centre for Longitudinal Studies, UCL, Being on a zero hours contract is bad for your health, new study reveals, Available at: https://cls.ucl.ac.uk/being-on-a-zero-hours-contract-is-bad-for-your-health-new-study-reveals/, (2017).

Cliclavoro, Lavoro intermittente o a chiamata, Cliclavoro, Available at: https://www.cliclavoro.gov.it/NormeContratti/Contratti/Pagine/Contratto-di-lavoro-intermittente-o-a-chiamata.aspx.

Countouris, N., Regulating digital work: from laisser-faire to fairness, Social Europe, Available at: https://socialeurope.eu/regulating-digital-work-from-laisser-faire-to-fairness, (2021).

Countouris, N., De Stefano, V., Ewing, K., and Freedland, M., Covid-19 crisis makes clear a new concept of 'worker' is long overdue, Social Europe, (2020).

De Stefano, V., and Aloisi, A. The EU Commission takes the lead in regulating platform work, Social Europe, Available at: https://socialeurope.eu/european-commission-takes-the-lead-in-regulating-platform-work, (2021).

De Stefano, V., and Aloisi, A., Who will be covered by an EU instrument on platform work, Social Europe, Available at: https://socialeurope.eu/who-will-be-covered-by-an-eu-instrument-on-platform-work, (2021).

De Stefano, V., Platform work and labour protection. Flexibility is not enough, Regulating for Globalization, Available at: http://regulatingforglobalization.com/2018/05/23/platform-work-labour-protection-flexibility-not-enough/?doing_wp_cron=1583405629.7317709922790527343750, (2018).

De Stefano, V., Labour and social protection in times of Covid-19, Available at: https://www.youtube.com/watch?v=UQPzbdP0kEY&feature=youtu.be, (2020).

De Ree, M., CBS mapping online platforms, Available at: https://www.cbs.nl/en-gb/corporate/2019/12/cbs-mapping-online-platforms, (2019).

DOP, J., On call employees, Russell Advocaten, Available at: https://www.russell.nl/publication/on-call-employees-netherlands-rights-obligations, (2019).

Doug, H. Fired from Uber: why drivers get deactivated, and how to get reactivated, Ride sharing driver, Ridesharing Driver, Available at: https://www.ridesharingdriver.com/fired-uber-drivers-get-deactivated-and-reactivated/, (2016).

Economics Online, Zero hours contracts, Available at: https://www.economicsonline.co.uk/Labour_markets/Zero-hours-contracts.html, (2020).

European Parliament News, Better working conditions for all: Balancing flexibility and security, Available at: http://www.europarl.europa.eu/news/en/headlines/society/20181018STO16583/better-working-conditions-for-all-balancing-flexibility-and-security, (2018).

European Public Service Forum, Zero hours and the spread of precarious employment, Available at: https://www.epsu.org/article/zero-hours-and-spread-precarious-employment.

Ewing, K., Don't be fooled, Uber is still dodging the minimum wage, Institute of Employment Rights, Available at: https://www.ier.org.uk/comments/dont-be-fooled-uber-is-still-dodging-the-minimum-wage/, (2021).

Feeding Britain, When Work Doesn't Pay, Working Paper on zero hours contracts, Available at: https://heidiallen.co.uk/newsite/wp-content/uploads/2019/07/Work-doesnt-pay_-002.pdf, (2019).

Financial Times, Zero hours take huge physical and mental toll, Available at: https://www.ft.com/content/d8d82ebe-9cbc-11e8-88de-49c908b1f264, (2019).

Gilfillan, S., Zero-hours contracts: what you need to know and why they should be banned, TUC, Available at: https://www.tuc.org.uk/blogs/zero-hours-contracts-what-you-need-know-and-why-they-should-be-banned#skipTo, (2019).

Government information for entrepreneurs, Corona crisis: Temporary Emergency Bridging Measure for Sustained Employment NOW, Available at: https://business.gov.nl/subsidy/corona-crisis-temporary-emergency-measure-now/, (2020).

Government information for entrepreneurs, Temporary Bridging Measure for Self-Employed Professionals TOZO, Available at: https://business.gov.nl/subsidy/temporary-bridging-measure-self-employed-professionals-tozo/, (2020).

Government of the Netherlands, Coronavirus: Dutch government adopts package of new measures designed to save jobs and the economy, Available at: https://www.government.nl/latest/news/2020/03/19/coronavirus-dutch-government-adopts-package-of-new-measures-designed-to-save-jobs-and-the-economy, (2020).

Heerekop, A., Zelfstandingen over TOZO: Gemeente die snel uitkeert, wordt het meest gewaardeerd, Available at: https://www.fnv.nl/nieuwsbericht/algemeen-nieuws/2020/05/zelfstandigen-over-tozo-gemeente-die-snel-uitkeert, (2020).

Hendrickx, F., and De Groof, S., Being on-call at home is working time: the Matzak-case, Regulating for Globalization, Available at: http://global-workplace-law-and-policy.kluwerlawonline.com/2018/02/27/call-home-working-time-matzak-case/, (2018).

Hendrickx, F., The coronavirus and the new world of work: renewed labour law questions, Regulating for Globalization, Available at: http://regulatingforglobalization.com/2020/04/01/the-coronavirus-and-the-world-of-work-renewed-labour-law-questions/, (2020).

Human in Progress Netherlands, WAB: Approved bill on Balanced Labour Market Act, Several changes to varying employment laws, Available at: https://hrmnetherlands.com/bill-balanced-labour-market-act/, (2020).

Hunter, R., and Prassl, J., Worker status for app-driver: Uber-rated?, Oxford Human Rights Hub, Available at: http://ohrh.law.ox.ac.uk/worker-status-for-app-drivers-uber-rated/, (2016).

ILO Press Release, International Labour Conference adds safety and health to Fundamental Principles and Rights at Work, Available at: https://www.ilo.org/global/about-the-ilo/newsroom/news/WCMS_848132/lang--en/index.htm (2022).

Ilsole 24 ore, Lavoro a chiamata: nessun limite d'impiego per alberghi, bar e ristoranti, Available at: https://www.ilsole24ore.com/art/lavoro-chiamata-nessun-limite-d-impiego-alberghi-bar-e-ristoranti--AE3bwaFH, (2019).

Kalman, F., Yes, the gig economy is great – but it isn't the future of work, Talent Economy, Available at: https://www.linkedin.com/pulse/yes-gig-economy-great-isnt-future-work-frank-kalman/, (2016).

Langlois, S., Don't tip your Uber driver? It could cost you a 5-star rating, Market Watch, Available at: https://www.marketwatch.com/story/dont-tip-your-uber-driver-it-could-cost-you-a-5-star-rating-2015-08-12, (2015).

Littler Mendelson PC, New rules regarding on-call workers in the Netherlands are in effect, Lexology, Available at: https://www.lexology.com/library/detail.aspx?g=37826b2c-4abb-4b91-9b5e-5691de55246e, (2020).

Marshall, A., Covid-19 opens the door for gig workers to win sick pay, Wired, Available at: https://www.wired.com/story/covid-opens-door-gig-workers-sick-pay/, (2021).

Mccann, D., Mencap and Uber in the Supreme Court: Working Time Regulation in an era of casualization, Oxford Huma Rights Hub, Available at: https://ohrh.law.ox.ac.uk/mencap-and-uber-in-the-supreme-court-working-time-regulation-in-an-era-of-casualisation/, (2021).

Mccann, K., Contracts could soon change for Deliveroo couriers, Brussels Express, Available at: https://brussels-express.eu/contracts-could-soon-change-for-deliveroo-couriers/, (2018).

Michalopoulos, S., Proper voucher use will move people into labour market, EU official says, Euractiv, Available at: https://www.euractiv.com/section/economy-jobs/news/commission-proper-voucher-use-will-move-more-people-into-labour-market/1141564/, (2017).

Morris, N., Most workers on zero-hours contracts are paid less than the national average wage, Independent, Available at: https://www.independent.co.uk/news/uk/politics/most-workers-on-zero-hours-contracts-are-paid-less-than-the-national-average-wage-9246957.html, (2014).

Piasna, A., Better working conditions, more predictable work – the new EU directive, Social Europe, Social Europe, Available at: https://socialeurope.eu/better-working-conditions-more-predictable-work-the-new-eu-directive, (2019).

Pieters, J., Temps and flexible staff facing lost wages, unemployment: Union, NL Times, Available at: https://nltimes.nl/2020/07/15/temps-flexible-staff-facing-lost-wages-unemployment-union, (2020).

Prassl, J., and Kelly-Lyth, A., Improving working conditions in the gig economy: The EU's proposed Platform Work Directive, Oxford Human Rights Hub, Available at: https://ohrh.law.ox.ac.uk/improving-working-conditions-in-the-gig-economy-the-eus-proposed-platform-work-directive/, (2021).

PwC, Gig economy employment status, Available at: https://www.pwclegal.be/en/news/gig-economy-employment-status-belgium.html, (2019).

Resolution Foundation, A matter of time: the rise of zero hours contracts, Available at: https://www.resolutionfoundation.org/publications/matter-time-rise-zero-hours-contracts/, (2013).

Schneider, O., Nearly 50.000 flexi-jobs filled in 2018, The Brussels Times, Available at: https://www.brusselstimes.com/news/belgium-all-news/52949/nearly-50-000-flexi-jobs-filled-in-2018/, (2019).

Rtbf, Coronavirus en Belgique: prolongation jusqu'au 30 juin des mesures de soutien aux indépendants, Available at: https://www.rtbf.be/info/belgique/detail_coronavirus-en-belgique-prolongation-jusqu-au-30-juin-des-mesures-de-soutien-aux-independants?id=10706915, (2021).

Public Sector Executive, Vital role for zero hours contracts-CBI, Available at: https://www.publicsectorexecutive.com/Public-Sector-News/vital-role-for-zero-hours-contracts-cbi-, (2013).

The Brussels Times, Effects of the pandemic will be felt for decades, says WHO, Available at: https://www.brusselstimes.com/news/124505/coronavirus-pandemics-effects-will-be-felt-for-decades-says-who/, (2020).

The Brussels Times, Support measures for the self-employed extended until 30 June, Available at: https://www.brusselstimes.com/news/belgium-all-news/157288/support-measures-for-the-self-employed-extended-until-june-30/, (2021).

The Guardian, Gig economy in Britain doubles, accounting for 4.7 million workers, Available at: https://www.theguardian.com/business/2019/jun/28/gig-economy-in-britain-doubles-accounting-for-47-million-workers, (2019).

The Guardian, Uber to ban riders with low ratings: will you pass the test?, Available at: https://www.theguardian.com/technology/2019/may/31/uber-to-ban-riders-with-low-ratings, (2019).

The Guardian, Rail worker killed by train in South London was on a zero hours contract, Available at: https://www.theguardian.com/business/2019/jul/12/rail-worker-killed-by-train-in-south-london-was-covering-for-brother, (2019).

The Guardian, The sharing economy is not as open as you might think, Available at: https://www.theguardian.com/sustainable-business/2014/nov/12/algorithms-race-discrimination-uber-lyft-airbnb-peer, (2014).

The Guardian, Uber loses right to classify UK drivers as self-employed, Available at: https://www.theguardian.com/technology/2016/oct/28/uber-uk-tribunal-self-employed-status?CMP=share_btn_tw, (2016).

The Guardian, Thumbs down to the fake reviewers ruining the internet for all of us, Available at: https://www.theguardian.com/commentisfree/2019/aug/07/fake-reviews-internet-ratings (2019).

The Italian Times, Contratto a chiamata 2020, cos'e e comme funziona, requisiti, durata, Available at: https://www.theitaliantimes.it/economia/contratto-a-chiamata-cos-e-come-funziona-requisiti-durata-retribuzione_291119/, (2020).

TUC, A ban on zero-hours contracts – a victory for Irish trade unions, Available at: https://www.tuc.org.uk/blogs/ban-zero-hours-contracts-victory-irish-unions, https://www.tuc.org.uk/take-action-unions-are-fighting-stamp-out-zero-hours-contracts, (2019).

TUC, Zero-hours contracts, what you need to know and why they should be banned, Available at: https://www.tuc.org.uk/blogs/zero-hours-contracts-what-you-need-know-and-why-they-should-be-banned, (2019).

TUC, Great jobs with guaranteed hours. What do workers really think about 'flexible' zero-hours contracts?, Available at: https://www.tuc.org.uk/sites/default/files/great-jobs-with-guaranteed-hours_0.pdf, (2017).

Other Sources

Chaibi, L., Will the EU end the free ride? The state of the art of the Directive on improving working conditions in platform work, Presentation at the ETUI event Working conditions in the platform economy – New evidence from the 2021 ETUI Internet and Platform Work Survey, (2022).

De Stefano, V., Casual work, Speech at the International seminar on zero-hours work organized by the Université Libre de Bruxelles (ULB), (2021).

Department for Business Innovation and Skills, Consultation Zero hours employment contracts, (2013).

Department for Business, Energy and Industrial Strategy, Good Work Plan, Consultation on measures to address one-sided flexibility, (2019).

Durri, I., *Asociación Profesional Élite Taxi v. Uber Systems Spain SL*, Cambridge University Press, (2019).

Durri, I., review of the book Regulating the platform economy: international perspectives on new forms of work, Comparative Labor Law and Policy Journal, (2021).

Durri, I., Stylogiannis, C., Regulatory approaches to platform work, Presentation at the ILO Training Center (ITC), (2021).

Garben, S., Kilpatrick, C., and MUIR, E., Towards a European Pillar of Social Rights: Upgrading the EU social acquis, College of Europe Policy Brief, (2017).

Gruber-Risak, M., Platform work as a virtual form of precarious work, Presentation at the ETUI event 'Working conditions in the platform economy', (2022).

Government information for entrepreneurs, Hiring on-call employees with a zero-hours contract, (2020).

Hendrickx, F., Regulating working conditions through EU directives – EU employment law outlook and challenges, Briefing requested by the EMPL Committee, (2019).

HM Government, The Queen's Speech 2014 – Lobby Briefing (2014).

Instructions administratives ONSS – 2019/1/ Les cotisations de securite sociale, Le travail occasionnel dans le secteur de l'horeca, (2019).

Mangan, D., The platform discount, Presentation at the Fourth Roger Blanpain lecture, (2022).

More, G., The Fixed-Term Work Directive, Presentation at DG Employment, European Commission, (2017).

Pulignano, V., Piasna, A., Domecka, M., Muszynski, K., and Vermeerbergen, L., Does it pay to work? Unpaid labour in the platform economy, ETUI Policy Brief, (2021).

Pieters, D., Comparative research methods, Presentation at the Young Researchers School, Research Design and Methodology in Comparative Social Security, Spetses, Greece, (2021).

Survey conducted by FNV (Federatie Nederlandse Vakbeweging), Onzeker werk [Insecure work], FNV Press, Amsterdam, (2011).

Surveys commissioned by KU Leuven and prepared by IPSOS, High level summary of key findings, (2020).

The Institute of Employment Rights, Rolling Out the Manifesto for Labour Law, eds Ewing, K.D., Hendy, J., and Jones, C., (2018).

Table of Cases

Court of Justice of the EU

Case C-143/16, *Abercrombie & Fitch Italia Srl v. Antonino Bordonaro*, 2017, 60, 61
Case C-313/02, *Nicole Wippel v. Peek and Cloppenburg GmbH and Co. KG*, 2004, 168, 169
Case C-434/15, *Asociación Profesional Élite Taxi v. Uber Systems Spain SL*, 2017, 70, 130
Case C-66/85, *Deborah Lawrie-Blum v. Land Baden-Württemberg*, 1986, 187
Case C-413/13, *FNV Kunsten Informatie en Media v. Staat der Nederlanden FNV Kunsten Informatie en Media v. Staat der Nederlanden*, 2014, 187
Case C-197/86, *Steven Malcolm Brown v. The Secretary of State for Scotland*, 1988, 187
Case C-53/81, *D.M. Levin v. Staatssecretaris van Justitie*, 1982, 187, 189
Case C-75/63, *Hoekstra v. Bestuur der Bedrijfsvereniging voor Detailhandel en Ambachten (Administration of the Industrial Board for Retail Trades and Businesses)*, 1964, 187
Case C-256/01, *Debra Allonby v. Accrington & Rossendale College, Education Lecturing Services, trading as Protocol Professional and Secretary of State for Education and Employment*, 2004, 188
Case C-229/14, *Ender Balkaya v. Kiesel Abbruch – und Recycling Technik GmbH*, 2015, 188
Case C-232/09, *Dita Danosa v. LKB Līzings SIA*, 2010, 188
Case C-35/96, *Commission of the European Communities v. Italian Republic*, 1998, 188
Case C-139/ 85, *R. H. Kempf v. Staatssecretaris van Justitie*, 1986, 188
Case C-196/87, *Udo Steymann v. Staatssecretaris van Justitie*, 1988, 188
Case C-3/87, *The Queen v. Ministry of Agriculture, Fisheries and Food, ex parte Agegate Ltd*, 1989, 188
Case C-337/97, *C.P.M. Meeusen v. Hoofddirectie van de Informatie Beheer Groep*, 1999, 189
Joined cases C-22/08 and C-23/08, *Athanasios Vatsouras and Josif Koupatantze v. Arbeitsgemeinschaft (ARGE) Nürnberg 900*, 2009, 189

Table of Legislations

EU and International Legislation

National Legislation

Legislative Decree No. 50/2017 on urgent financial provisions, initiatives in favour of territorial authorities, further interventions for areas affected by seismic events and development measures (Italy), 66, 67

Decreto – Legge 12 Luglio 2018, n.87 Disposizioni urgenti per la dignita' dei lavoratori e delle imprese (Italy), 66, 67

Legislative Decree of 3 September 2019, n.101 disposizioni urgenti per la tutela del lavoro e per la risoluzione di crisi aziendali (Italy), 69, 198

Law of 29 May 2019 amending Book 7 of the Dutch Civil Code, the Allocation of Workforce by Intermediaries Act, the Social Insurance Financing Act and any other laws to improve the balance between permanent and flexible employment contracts (Balanced Labor Market Act) (the Netherlands), 77

Dutch Civil Code, Book 7, Title 10, Article 628a (the Netherlands), 78

Act of 14 May 1998, amending the Civil Code, the Extraordinary Decree on Labor Relations 1945 and other laws (Flexibility and security) (the Netherlands).

Act of 14 June 2014 amending various laws relating to the reform of the dismissal law, changing the legal position of flex workers and amending various laws relating to the amendment of the Unemployment Insurance Act, broadening the opening of the Income Support Act for the Older Unemployed and the restriction of access to the Income Provision of Older and Partially Disabled Unemployed Employees Act (Work and Security Act) (the Netherlands), 79, 80, 87

Coalition Agreement 'Trust in the future', (2017) (the Netherlands), 79, 80

Loi du 16 March 1971 sur le travail (Belgium), 95, 96, 99

Arrêté royal relatif à l'occupation des travailleurs occasionnels dans le secteur de l'horeca du 12 Novembre 2013 (Belgium), 97

The Belgian Civil Code.

Loi portant des dispositions diverses en matière sociale du 16 November 2015 (Belgium), 99

Loi portant des dispositions fiscales diverses IV du 25 December 2017 (Belgium), 100

Loi visant à favoriser le développement de services et d'emplois de proximité du 20.07.2001 (Belgium), 101

Arrêté royal concernant les titres-services du 12.12. 2001 (Belgium), 101

Loi-programme du 1 Juillet 2016, the so-called De Croo Act (Belgium), 105, 106, 114

Loi relative à la relance économique et au renforcement de la cohésion sociale du 18 Juillet 2018 (Belgium), 105, 198

Arrêté royal du 30 mars 2020 visant à adapter les procédures dans le cadre du chômage temporaire du au virus Covid-19 et à modifier l'article 10 de l'arrêté royal du 6 mai 2019 modifiant les articles 27, 51, 52bis, 58, 58/3 et 63 de l'arrêté royal du 25 novembre 1991 portant réglementation du chômage et insérant les articles 36sexies, 63bis et 124bis dans le même arrêté, publié le 2 mars 2020 (Belgium), 111

Loi modifiant la loi du 22 décembre 2016 instaurant un droit passerelle en faveur des travailleurs indépendants et introduisant les mesures temporaires dans le cadre du COVID-19 en faveur des travailleurs indépendants (Belgium), 112

BCLR - BULLETIN OF COMPARATIVE LABOUR RELATIONS

Vol. Author/Title/Year/ISBN

1. Roger Blanpain, *Individual Employment Contracts: Collective Agreements,* 1970.
2. Roger Blanpain, *Social Planning,* 1971 (ISBN 90-312-0018-2).
3. Roger Blanpain, *Guaranteed Income Funds,* 1972 (ISBN 90-312-0019-0).
4. Roger Blanpain, *Employee Participation at the Level of the Enterprise,* 1973 (ISBN 90-312-0020-4).
5. Roger Blanpain, *Vastheid van Betrekking: Staking en Bezetting,* 1974.
6. Roger Blanpain, *Labour Law and Industrial Relations (International Bibliography),* 1975 (ISBN 90-312-0023-9).
7. Roger Blanpain, *Multinational Enterprises,* 1976 (ISBN 90-312-0024-7).
8. Roger Blanpain, *Worker's Participation in the European Company,* 1977 (ISBN 90-312-0044-1).
9. Roger Blanpain, *Women and Labour,* 1978 (ISBN 90-312-0077-8).
10. Roger Blanpain, *European Conference on Labour Law and Industrial Relations: Multinational Enterprises,* 1979 (ISBN 90-312-0091-3).
11. Roger Blanpain, *Job Security and Industrial Relations,* 1980 (ISBN 90-312-0147-2).
12. Roger Blanpain, Greg Bamber & Russell Lansbury, *Technological Change and Industrial Relations: An International Symposium,* 1983 (ISBN 90-312-0205-3).
13. Roger Blanpain, James Janssen van Raay & A. Moulty, *Worker's Participation in the European Community: The Fifth Directive,* 1984 (ISBN 90-654-4187-5).
14. Roger Blanpain, *Equality and Prohibition of Discrimination in Employment,* 1985 (ISBN 90-654-4215-4).
15. Roger Blanpain, *Restructuring Labour in the Enterprise: Law and Practice in France, F.R. of Germany, Italy, Sweden and the United Kingdom,* 1986 (ISBN 90-654-4283-9).
16. Roger Blanpain & E. Kassalow, *Unions and Industrial Relations: Recent Trends and Prospect: A Comparative Treatment,* 1987 (ISBN 90-654-4294-4).
17. Roger Blanpain & Marco Biagi, *Trade Union Democracy and Industrial Relations,* 1988 (ISBN 90-654-4394-0).
18. Roger Blanpain & Jelle Visser, *In Search of Inclusive Unionism,* 1990 (ISBN 90-654-4439-4).
19. Roger Blanpain, *Flexibility and Wages: A Comparative Treatment,* 1990 (ISBN 90-654-4461-0).

20. Roger Blanpain, Stephen Frenkel & Oliver Clarke, *Economic Restructuring and Industrial Relations in Industrialised Countries,* 1990 (ISBN 90-654-4488-2).
21. Roger Blanpain & Friedrich Fürstenberg, *Structure and Strategy in Industrial Relations,* 1991 (ISBN 90-654-4559-5).
22. Roger Blanpain, Amira Galin & Ozer Carmi, *Flexible Work Patterns and Their Impact on Industrial Relations,* 1991 (ISBN 90-654-4572-2).
23. Roger Blanpain, *Workers' Participation: Influence on Management Decision-Making by Labour in the Private Sector,* 1992 (ISBN 90-654-4600-1).
24. Roger Blanpain, Brian Brooks & Chris Engels, *Employed or Self-Employed,* 1992 (ISBN 90-654-4613-3).
25. Roger Blanpain & Tiziano Treu, *Industrial Relations Developments in the Telecommunications Industry,* 1993 (ISBN 90-654-4642-7).
26. Roger Blanpain & Marco Biagi, *Industrial Relations in Small and Medium Sized Enterprises,* 1993 (ISBN 90-654-4696-6).
27. Roger Blanpain & Marco Biagi, *Participative Management and Industrial Relations in a Worldwide Perspective,* 1993 (ISBN 90-654-4769-5).
28. Roger Blanpain, Jacques Rojot & Hoyt N. Wheeler, *Employee Rights and Industrial Justice,* 1994 (ISBN 90-654-4804-7).
29. Roger Blanpain & Ruth Ben-Israel, *Strikes and Lock-Outs in Industrialized Market Economies,* 1994 (ISBN 90-654-4841-1).
30. Roger Blanpain, Kazuo Sugeno & Yasuo Suwa, *The Harmonization of Working Life and Family Life,* 1995 (ISBN 90-411-0064-4).
31. Roger Blanpain & Laszio Nagy, *Labour Law and Industrial Relations in Central and Eastern Europe,* 1996 (ISBN 90-411-0298-1).
32. Roger Blanpain, *Labour Law and Industrial Relations in the European Union,* 1997 (ISBN 90-411-0527-1).
33. Taco Van Peijpe, *Employment Protection under Strain,* 1998 (ISBN 90-411-0528-8).
34. Roger Blanpain, Takashi Araki & Ryuichi Yamakawa, *The Process of Industrialization and the Role of Labour Law in Asia,* 1999 (ISBN 9-041-1104-7-X).
35. Roger Blanpain & Marco Biagi, *Non-standard Work and Industrial Relations,* 1999 (ISBN 90-411-1117-4).
36. Roger Blanpain, *Private Employment Agencies: The Impact of ILO Convention 181 (1997) and the Judgment of the European Court of Justice of 11 December 1997,* 1999 (ISBN 90-411-1118-2).
37. Roger Blanpain, *Multinational Enterprises and the Social Challenges of the XXIst Century: The ILO Declaration on Fundamental* Principles *at Work, Public and Private Corporate Codes of Conduct,* 2000 (ISBN 90-411-1280-4).
38. Roger Blanpain, Ryuichi Yamakawa & Takashi Araki, *Deregulation and Labour Law: In Search of a Labour Concept for the 21st Century,* 2000 (ISBN 90-411-1370-3).
39. Roger Blanpain, *The Council of Europe and the Social Challenges of the XXIst Century,* 2001 (ISBN 90-411-1543-9).

40. Roger Blanpain, *On-Line Rights for Employees in the Information Society, Use & Monitoring of E-Mail & Internet at Work*, 2002 (ISBN 90-411-1626-5).
41. Roger Blanpain, *The Evolving Employment Relationship and the New Economy: The Role of Labour Law & Industrial Relations*, 2001 (ISBN 90-411-1691-5).
42. Roger Blanpain, *Involvement of Employees in the European Union, Works Councils, Company Statute, Information and Consultation Rights*, 2002 (ISBN 90-411-1760-1).
43. Michele Colucci, *The Impact of the Internet and New Technologies on the Workplace: A Legal Analysis from a Comparative Point of View*, 2002 (ISBN 90-411-1824-1).
44. Roger Blanpain, *White Paper on the Labour Market in Italy: The Quality of European Industrial Relations and Changing Industrial Relations*, 2002 (ISBN 90-411-1841-1).
45. Roger Blanpain, Russell D. Lansbury & Young-Bum Park, *Impact of Globalisation on Employment Relations: A Comparison of the Automobile and Banking Industries in Australia and Korea*, 2002 (ISBN 90-411-1850-0).
46. Roger Blanpain & Antoine Jacobs, *Employee Rights in Bankruptcy: A Comparative-Law Assessment*, 2002 (ISBN 90-411-1942-6).
47. Roger Blanpain, Takashi Araki & Shinya Ouchi, *Corporate Restructuring and the Role of Labour Law*, 2003 (ISBN 90-411-1949-3).
48. Roger Blanpain, *Collective Bargaining, Discrimination, Social Security and European Integration*, 2003 (ISBN 90-411-2010-6).
49. Roger Blanpain & Luis Aparicio-Valdez, *Labour Relations in the Asia- Pacific Countries*, 2004 (ISBN 90-411-2239-7).
50. Roger Blanpain & Ronnie Graham, *Temporary Agency Work and the Information Society*, 2004 (ISBN 90-411-2252-4).
51. Roger Blanpain, *The Actors of Collective Bargaining: A World Report*, 2004 (ISBN 90-411-2253-2).
52. Roger Blanpain & Michele Colucci, *The Globalisation of Labour Standards: The Soft Law Track*, 2004 (ISBN 90-411-2303-2).
53. Roger Blanpain, Takashi Araki & Shinya Ouchi, *Labour Law in Motion: Diversification of the Labour Force & Terms and Conditions of Employment*, 2005 (ISBN 90-411-2315-6).
54. Roger Blanpain, *Smoking and the Workplace*, 2005 (ISBN 90-411-2325-3).
55. Roger Blanpain, *Confronting Globalization: The Quest for a Social Agenda*, 2005 (ISBN 90-411-2381-4).
56. Roger Blanpain, Thomas Blanke & Edgar Rose, *Collective Bargaining Wages in Comparative Perspective: Germany, France, the Netherlands, Sweden and the United Kingdom*, 2005 (ISBN 90-411-2388-1).
57. Roger Blanpain & Anne Numhauser-Henning, *Women in Academia & Equality Law: Aiming High - Falling Short?*, 2006 (ISBN 978-90-411-2427-6).
58. Roger Blanpain, *Freedom of Services in the European Union: Labour and Social Security Law: The Bolkestein Initiative*, 2006 (ISBN 978-90-411-2453-5).
59. Roger Blanpain, Frans Pennings & Nurhan Sural, *Flexibilisation and Modernisation of the Turkish Labour Market*, 2006 (ISBN 978-90-411-2490-X).

60. Roger Blanpain & Boel Flodgren, *Corporate and Employment Perspectives in a Global Business Environment*, 2006 (ISBN 978-90-411-2537-X).
61. Roger Blanpain, Shinya Ouchi & Takashi Araki, *Decentralizing Industrial Relations and The Role of Labor Unions and Employee Representatives*, 2007 (ISBN 978-90-411-2583-3).
62. Roger Blanpain, *European Framework Agreements and Telework: Law and Practice: A European and Comparative Study*, 2007 (ISBN 978-90-411-2560-4).
63. Roger Blanpain, Jim Kitay, Leanne Cutcher & Nick Wailes, *Globalization and Employment Relations in Retail Banking*, 2007 (ISBN 978-90-411-2620-1).
64. Roger Blanpain, Russell Lansbury, Jim Kitay, Nick Wailes & Anja Kirsch, *Globalization and Employment Relations in the Auto Assembly Industry:* A *Study of Seven Countries*, 2008 (ISBN 978-90-411-2698-6).
65. Roger Blanpain & Michele Tiraboschi, *The Global Labour Market: From Globalization to Flexicurity*, 2008 (ISBN 978-90-411-2722-8).
66. Roger Blanpain, Michele Colucci & Frank Hendrickx, *The Future of Sport in the European Union: Beyond the EU Reform Treaty and the White Paper*, 2008 (ISBN 978-90-411-2761-7).
67. Roger Blanpain, Linda Dickens, *Challenges in European Employment Relations: Employment Regulation, Trade Union Organization, Equality, Flexicurity, Training and New Approaches to Pay*, 2008 (ISBN 978-90-411-2771-6).
68. Roger Blanpain, Hiroya Nakakubo & Takashi Araki, *New Developments in Employment Discrimination Law, 2008* (ISBN 978-90-411-2782-2).
69. Roger Blanpain, Andrzej Marian wiątkowski, *The Laval and Viking Cases: Freedom of Services and Establishment v. Industrial Conflict in the European Economic Area and Russia*, 2009 (ISBN 978-90-411-2850-8).
70. Roger Blanpain, William Bromwich, Olga Rymkevich, Silvia Spattini, *The Modernization of Labour Law and Industrial Relations in a Comparative Perspective*, 2009 (ISBN 978-90-411-2865-2).
71. Roger Blanpain, Juan Pablo Landa & Brian Langille, *Employment Policies and Multilevel Governance*, 2009 (ISBN 978-90-411-2866-9).
72. Roger Blanpain, European Works Councils; *The European Directive 2009/ 38/EC of 6 May 2009, 2009* (ISBN 978-90-411-3208-6).
73. Roger Blanpain, William Bromwich, Olga Rymkevich & Silvia Spattini, *Labour Productivity, Investment in Human Capital and Youth Employment: Comparative Developments and Global Responses*, 2010 (ISBN 978-90-411-3249-9).
74. Greg J. Bamber & Philippe Pochet, *Regulating Employment Relations, Work and Labour Laws: International Comparisons between Key Countries*, 2010 (ISBN 978-90-411-3199-7). General Editor: Roger Blanpain.
75. Roger Blanpain, Desislava Nikolaeva Dimitrova, *Seafarers' Rights in the Globalized Maritime Industry*, 2010 (ISBN 978-90-411-3349-6).
76. Roger Blanpain, Hiroya Nakakubo & Takashi Araki, *Regulation of Fixed- Term Employment Contracts*, 2010 (ISBN 978-90-411-3356-4).

77. Roger Blanpain, William Bromwich, Olga Rymkevich & Iacopo Senatori, *Rethinking Corporate Governance*, 2011 (ISBN 978-90-411-3450-9).
78. Roger Blanpain & Frank Hendrickx, *Labour Law between Change and Tradition: Liber Amicorum Antoine Jacobs*, 2011 (ISBN 978-90-411-3424-0).
79. Roger Blanpain, Thomas Klebe, Marlene Schmidt & Bernd Waas, *Trade Union Rights at the Workplace*, 2012 (ISBN 978-90-411-3460-8).
80. Roger Blanpain, William Bromwich, Olga Rymkevich & Iacopo Senatori, *Labour Markets, Industrial Relations and Human Resources Management: From Recession to Recovery*, 2012 (ISBN 978-90-411-4004-3).
81. Roger Blanpain, Hiroya Nakakubo & Takashi Araki, *Systems of Employee Representation at the Enterprise: A Comparative Study*, 2012 (ISBN 978-90-411-4080-7).
82. Roger Blanpain & Frank Hendrickx, *Temporary Agency Work in the European Union and the United States*, 2013 (ISBN 978-90-411-4769-1).
83. Roger Blanpain, Toker Dereli, Y. Pınar Soykut-Sarıca & Aslı en-Tabaı, *Emerging Patterns of Work and Turkish Labour Market Challenges under Globalization: Readings on Labour and Employment Relations*, 2014 (ISBN 978-90-411-4983-1).
84. Roger Blanpain, Pablo Arellano Ortiz, Marius Olivier & Gijsbert Vonk, *Social Security and Migrant Workers: Selected Studies of Cross-border Social Security Mechanisms*, 2014 (ISBN 978-90-411-4770-7).
85. Roger Blanpain & Nikita Lyutov, *Workers' Representation in Central and Eastern Europe: Challenges and Opportunities for the Works Councils' System*, 2014 (ISBN 978-90-411-4746-2).
86. Roger Blanpain, Ulla Liukkunen & Chen Yifeng, *China and ILO Fundamental Principles and Rights at Works*, 2014 (ISBN 978-90-411-4984-8).
87. Roger Blanpain, *The Use of Languages and Employment Relations*, 2014 (ISBN 978-90-411-5606-8).
88. Roger Blanpain, Hiroya Nakakubo & Takashi Araki, *Protection of Employees' Personal Information and Privacy*, 2014 (ISBN 978-90-411-5608-2).
89. Roger Blanpain, Jan Wouters, Glenn Rayp, Laura Beke & Axel Marx, *Protecting Labour Rights in a Multi-polar Supply Chain and Mobile Global Economy*, 2015 (ISBN 978-90-411-5662-4).
90. Roger Blanpain & Stefania Marassi, *Globalization and Transnational Collective Labour Relations: International and European Framework Agreements at Company Level*, 2015 (ISBN 978-90-411-4748-6).
91. Roger Blanpain, Frank Hendrickx & Petra Herzfeld Olsson, *National Effects of the Implementation of EU Directives on Labour Migration from Third Countries*, 2016 (ISBN 978-90-411-6257-1).
92. Roger Blanpain, Frank Hendrickx & D'Arcy du Toit, *Labour Law and Social Progress: Holding the Line or Shifting the Boundaries?* 2016 (ISBN 978-90-411-6747-7).

93. Roger Blanpain & Frank Hendrickx, *Reasonable Accommodation in the Modern Workplace: Potential and Limits of the Integrative Logics of Labour Law*, 2016 (ISBN 978-90-411-6258-8).
94. Roger Blanpain, Frank Hendrickx & Bernd Waas, *New Forms of Employment in Europe*, 2016 (ISBN 978-90-411-6239-7).
95. Roger Blanpain, Frank Hendrickx, Hiroya Nakakubo & Takashi Araki, *The Notion of Employer in the Era of the Fissured Workplace: Should Labour Law Responsibilities Exceed the Boundary of the Legal Entity?*, 2017 (ISBN 978-90-411-8470-2).
96. Elena Sychenko, *Individual Labour Rights as Human Rights: The Contributions of the European Court of Human Rights to Worker's Rights Protection*, 2017 (ISBN 978-90-411-8629-4).
97. William Bromwich & Olga Rymkevich, *Improving Workplace Quality: New Perspectives and Challenges for Worker Well-Being*, 2017 (ISBN 978-90-411-8628-7).
98. Sarah De Groof, *Work-Life Balance in the Modern Workplace: Interdisciplinary Perspectives from Work-Family Research, Law and Policy*, 2017 (ISBN 978-90-411-8630-0).
99. Sylvaine Laulom, *Collective Bargaining Developments in Times of Crisis*, 2018 (ISBN 978-90-411-8999-8).
100. Frank Hendrickx & Valerio De Stefano, *Game Changers in Labour Law: Shaping the Future of Work*, 2018 (ISBN 978-90-411-9953-9).
101. Ivana Palinkaš, *The Legal and Institutional Framing of Collective Bargaining in CEE Countries: Between Europeanisation and Decentralisation*, 2018 (ISBN 978-90-411-9199-1).
102. Jeremy Waddington, *European Board-Level Employee Representation: National Variations in Influence and Power*, 2018 (ISBN 978-90-411-9202-8).
103. Jan Pichrt & Kristina Koldinská, *Labour Law and Social Protection in a Globalized World: Changing Realities in Selected Areas of Law and Policy*, 2018 (ISBN 978-94-035-0093-5).
104. Matthew W. Finkin, *American Labor and the Law: Dormant, Resurgent, and Emergent Problems*, 2019 (ISBN 978-94-035-0654-8).
105. Giuseppe Casale & Tiziano Treu, *Transformations of Work: Challenges for the Institutions and Social Actors*, 2019 (ISBN 978-94-035-0891-7).
106. Miguel De la Corte-Rodríguez, *EU Law on Maternity and Other Child-Related Leaves: Impact on Gender Equality*, 2019 (ISBN 978-94-035-1452-9).
107. Valeria Pulignano & Frank Hendrickx, *Employment Relations in the 21st Century: Challenges for Theory and Research in a Changing World of Work*, 2020 (ISBN 978-94-035-1764-3).
108. Matteo Bottero, *Posting of Workers in EU Law: Challenges of Equality, Solidarity and Fair Competition*, 2021 (ISBN 978-94-035-2860-1).
109. Bernd Waas & Christina Hießl, *Collective Bargaining for Self-Employed Workers in Europe: Approaches to Reconcile Competition Law and Labour Rights*, 2021 (ISBN 978-94-035-2373-6).

110. Mathias Wouters, *International Labour Standards and Platform Work: An Analysis of Digital Labour Platforms Based on the Instruments on Private Employment Agencies, Home Work and Domestic Work*, 2022 (ISBN 978-94-035-4024-5).
111. Luca Ratti, *In-Work Poverty in Europe: Vulnerable and Under-Represented Persons in a Comparative Perspective*, 2022 (ISBN 978-94-035-4996-5).
112. Silvia Rainone, *The Role of the Court of Justice in EU Labour Law: A Case Study on the Transfer of Undertakings Directive*, 2023 (ISBN 978-94-035-2896-0).
113. Frank Hendrickx, Elena Gramano & David Mangan, *Privacy@work: A European and Comparative Perspective*, 2023 (ISBN 978-94-035-3106-9).
114. Elena Sychenko & Adalberto Perulli, *Employment Law and the European Convention on Human Rights: The Research of the Recent Jurisprudence of the ECtHR Related to Employment Law (2017-2021)*, 2023 (ISBN 978-94-035-3556-2).
115. Ilda Durri, *Casual Work Arrangements and Platform-Based Work: The Casual Work Agenda as a Way to Enhance the Labour Protection of Platform Workers*, 2023 (ISBN 978-94-035-3107-6)

Made in United States
Orlando, FL
04 November 2026

90200449R00151